Sven Hedin

THROUGH ASIA

By SVEN HEDIN. *With
Nearly Three Hundred Illus-
trations from Sketches and
Photographs by the Author*

In Two Volumes

Vol. I.

HARPER & BROTHERS PUBLISHERS
NEW YORK AND LONDON
1899

PREFACE

This work does not claim to be anything more than a plain account of my journeys through Asia during the years 1893 to 1897. It has been written for the general public, and presents nothing more than a description of my travels and the more memorable of my experiences—not by any means the whole of my experiences. To have recorded everything that I set down in my note-books would have swelled out the book to twice its existing length. Nevertheless those portions of my journey which I have merely touched upon, or have passed over altogether in silence, will not, I trust, be altogether lost. If this book is received with the indulgence which I venture to hope for it, I propose to issue a supplementary volume, to contain a multitude of matters of varied interest and of not less importance than those contained in these pages.

For these reasons the great bulk of the scientific observations I made find no place in the present volumes. All the same, I believe the geographer will be able to discover in them something or other that will be of interest to him.

In this place I will content myself with a bare mention of the scientific labors, upon which the chief part of my time, energy, and attention was constantly expended—the drawing of geological sections of the meridional border ranges on the east side of the Pamirs and of the mountain-chains of the Kwen-lun system; the collecting of anthropometrical measurements from a number of Kirghiz; an inquiry into the periodical migrations of the nomads; a study of the etymology of the geographical nomenclatures; measurement of the volume of every river I crossed; bathymetrical soundings in the lakes; and the collection of botanical specimens, more especially of algæ from the lofty alpine regions of the Pamirs and Tibet. Moreover, I devoted special attention to the taking of meteorological observations regularly three times a day. These Dr. Nils Ekholm has kindly undertaken to work out for me. Another important task was the collection of voluminous materials dealing with the geographical character and extent of the Desert of Gobi, as also with the complicated river-system of the Tarim, which I was enabled to study at many different points all the way from the Pamirs and the highland regions of Tibet down to the termination of the stream in the far-distant lake of Lop-nor. Further, I noted the periodical fluctuations in the volumes of the Central Asiatic rivers; how during the summer they swell to flood-like dimensions, and then during the winter dwindle away to, in many cases, paltry rivulets, or even dry up altogether; and how these fluctuations occur with unvarying regularity—the ebb and flow, as it were, that accompany the heart-beats of the mighty continent.

The astronomical observations, which I made for the purpose of checking and controlling my instrumental calculations, consisted of determinations of latitude and time in seventeen several places. The instrument I employed was a prismatic circle, and the object I observed the sun or, failing that, the moon. Mr. Rosén, who has kindly calculated my results, is satisfied that the errors in the latitudinal observations are in every instance less than fifteen seconds, and in the temporal determinations in all cases under one second. The longitudes of certain of the stations were already known with scientific exactitude; these data I employed as bases for the determination of the longitudes of the remaining places. By this means, too, I was enabled to check more effectually the accuracy of my chronometers, a circumstance the more needful seeing that these latter were frequently subjected to the rough vicissitudes of travel through difficult regions. I brought home latitudinal observations for seven fresh places, and longitudinal observations for six.

As soon as I passed beyond the fairly well-known regions of the Russian Pamirs, I took up, in the summer of 1894, the strictly topographical division of my labors, and with diopter, plane-table, and calculation of paces measured the environs of the lake Little Kara-kul; next I mapped the glaciers of that king of the Central Asiatic mountain-giants, Mus-tagh-ata. After that I surveyed every route I travelled over during the years 1894, 1895, 1896, and the early part of 1897. These important labors were never for a single day remitted. Throughout the whole of the long red line, which marks my travels through Asia, there is not a single break right away to the day (March 2d, 1897) when I rode in at the gate of Peking, and recorded my last entry on the five hundred and fifty-second sheet of my field-book or surveying journal.

In making these measurements I used only a compass and a base-line. The latter varied from 200 (656 feet) to 400 (1312½ feet) meters, and was in every case accurately measured with the meter-measure. After measuring my base-line, I carefully noted the time it took the caravan, properly laden and travelling at its ordinary average pace, to traverse it from the one end to the other; at the same time I was scrupulous to make all due allowance for the inclination of the ground and other inequalities of the surface.

As a rule, I laid down my maps on the scale 1 : 95,000. Across the level expanses of the deserts, however, I worked to the scale 1 : 200,000; and in mountainous regions, where the road wound through defiles, where numerous side-valleys

joined the main valley, and where the morphological character
of the surface underwent frequent and varying changes, I used
the scale of 1 : 50,000. The aggregate distance of the route
I mapped in this way amounts to 1049 Swedish miles, or 6520
English miles—that is to say, nearly four and a half times the
distance from London to Constantinople, two and a half times
the distance from New York to San Francisco, and one and
a half times the distance from Cairo to Cape Town; in other
words, more than one-quarter of the earth's circumference.
If to this be added more than 8000 miles which I travelled
by carriage or rail in the better known portions of the continent, we get for the entire extent of my travels a grand total
of 14,600 miles, or more than the distance from the North
Pole to the South Pole. The rate of travel of my caravans,
calculated from the results of the whole of the journey, aver-
ages a little over two and three-quarter miles an hour.

Out of the above-mentioned 6520 miles no less than 2020
were through regions which no European had ever before
visited. Over certain portions of the remaining 4500 miles
one traveller had preceded me, over other portions two travellers, but in no case more than three. Despite that, my observations along even those stretches may claim to possess a
certain degree of originality; for being able to speak Jagatai
Turki with fluency, I was independent of the errors and will-
ful deceits of interpreters, and, consequently, was in a position to gather a good deal of information of a more or less
important character which will be new to most readers. For
one thing, I was able to record a vast number of geographical
names, none of which had hitherto appeared on any map,
European or Asiatic.

As a curiosity, I may mention that the 552 sheets upon
which my route is laid down measure 121 yards in length;
and this does not include the maps I made of the glaciers of
Mus-tagh-ata. For the present these sheets and such other

cartographical materials as I brought home with me are
lodged at the famous geographical institute of Justus Perthes
in Gotha, where they are all being worked out in detail,
and the results will be eventually published in *Petermann's
Mitteilungen*.

Although fully conscious of the mistakes of my journey,
and of the shortcomings of this, my book, and while aware
that a more experienced traveller would have reaped a richer
and a more valuable harvest from the fields upon which I
labored, I nevertheless comfort myself with the reflection
that I believe I really did my best as far as lay in my power.

A word or two as to the accessories of the book. The two
principal maps have been prepared at the Lithographical Institute of the (Swedish) General Staff, under the superintend-
ence of Lieut. H. Byström; my original place-determinations being embodied upon Curzon's map of the Pamirs, and
Pievtsoff's map of Central Asia, as foundations for the two
maps respectively. Their primary purpose is to illustrate
and make clear the routes I followed. Hence they do not
claim to be accurate in matters of minute detail; indeed,
they could not be so, seeing that my cartographical data have
not yet been completely worked out.

In consequence of the generosity of my publishers, I am
fortunately enabled to impart a fuller measure of life and
reality to certain exciting and characteristic incidents of my
story by means of pictures drawn by Swedish artists. The
illustrations to which I allude must not, however, be regarded
as mere products of the artistic imagination. For each of
them I supplied sufficient material in the nature of sketches
and photographs, and where such were wanting I furnished
precise and detailed descriptions. In a word, each individual
picture has come to life as it were under my own eye and
under my own controlling hand; and I cannot help express-

ing my admiration of the quickness of apprehension and the lively interest which the several artists have manifested in their work.

For the original calculation of the altitudes, which occur throughout these pages, I am indebted to the kindness and skill of Dr. Nils Ekholm. For the conversion of the metric heights and other measurements into feet, miles, etc., and for the conversion of the Celsius scale into the Fahrenheit scale, as well as for the transliteration of the place-names, the translator is responsible.

Finally, it gives me pleasure to acknowledge a special debt of thanks to Mr. J. T. Bealby, B.A., sometime of the editorial staffs of the *Encyclopædia Britannica, Chambers's Encyclopædia*, etc., for the ability and experienced and conscientious care with which he has rendered my original Swedish into English. In the translation of a portion of the book, Mr. Bealby was assisted by Miss E. H. Hearn.

SVEN HEDIN.

STOCKHOLM, *May 1st*, 1898.

CONTENTS

INTRODUCTION

A WINTER JOURNEY OVER THE PAMIRS

CONTENTS

THE MUS-TAGH-ATA AND ITS GLACIERS

CONTENTS

ACROSS THE TAKLA-MAKAN DESERT

CONTENTS

ILLUSTRATIONS

CHAPTER I

RÉSUMÉ OF CENTRAL ASIAN EXPLORATION

A NEW era is approaching in the historical development of geographical discovery. The pioneers will soon have played their part; the "white patches" on the maps of the continents are gradually decreasing; our knowledge of the physical conditions of the ocean is every year becoming more complete. The pioneers of the past, who cleared the way through increasing danger and difficulty, have been followed by the explorers of the present day, examining in detail the surface of the earth and its restless life, always finding new gaps to fill, new problems to solve.

Although many regions have already been the object of detailed investigation, there are several still remaining in which the pioneer has not yet finished his work. This is particularly the case with the interior of Asia, which has long been neglected. Immense areas of the almost inaccessible Desert of Gobi, and endless wastes in the highlands of Tibet, are to this day as little known as the Polar Regions.

It was with the view of contributing my little to the knowledge of the geography of Central Asia that I set out on the journey which this book describes. I had prepared myself for it by years of work in my study; and in 1890-91 I made a reconnaissance into Russian Turkestan and Kashgar, in order to examine the suitability of those territories as a base of operations for exploring unknown country.

After my return from Kashgar, my chief concern was to procure the necessary means for carrying out my undertaking. To His Majesty King Oscar of Sweden and Norway I accordingly addressed the following particulars of my plan, which I give here, as they will best show how far and in what manner I succeeded in fulfilling the task I set myself. Somewhat abbreviated, my memorandum ran as follows:

In the heart of Asia, between the two highest chains of mountains on the earth, the Kwen-lun and the Himalayas, is the most stupendous upheaval to be found on the face of our planet—the Tibetan Highlands. Its average height is 13,000 feet, and in the north it attains as much as 15,000 feet. Its area, therefore, of 770,000 square miles (two and a half times that of the Scandinavian peninsula), is on a level with the highest peaks of the Alps. According to the Chinese maps, its northern parts, which constitute one of the least known tracts of Asia, appear to consist of a system of uninhabited lake-basins possessing no outflow. Farther south the Tibetan and Mongol nomads lead a wandering shepherd life; and it is only in the extreme south of the region that there is any population.

Tibet lies aside from the great highways used by travellers of the nineteenth century. Only a few of the more adventurous Europeans have done their share towards collecting the scanty material upon which our present knowledge of the country is based. Its desolate scenery, its lofty, inaccessible mountains, and its extreme remoteness, situated, as it is, in the heart of a vast continent, have deterred travellers, and driven them to find scope for their activity in other parts of the world—in the Polar Regions, among the oceanic islands, or where the coast has provided a certain point of departure to unknown regions lying within comparatively easy reach. And yet there is scarcely any part of the world in which the explorer is so richly rewarded for his pains, or finds such an inexhaustible field for observation of every kind, as in Tibet—the country whence the light of holiness streams forth upon the world of Lamaism, just as its waters, in the form of mighty rivers, stream forth to give life and nourishment to the countries which surround it. Many important problems in physical geography still await their solution in Tibet and in the Desert of Gobi, each of which would be a distinct gain to science. In a strictly geographical sense, Tibet is one of the least known regions

n the world. Even the maps of Africa cannot now show
a white patch of such vast extent as occurs under the name
of Tibet on our maps of Central Asia. In this respect
the Polar Regions alone are comparable with Tibet. The
itineraries furnished by the Roman Catholic missionaries,
at a period when the country was more easily accessible
than it is at the present time, cannot be followed on the
map with absolute certainty, and from a geographical stand-
point are often of little value.

But even this country, jealously closed as it is by fanaticism, has been compelled to open its doors to the per-
sistency of European inquiry. The western and eastern
parts, in particular, have been traversed by English, Russian, and French travellers. In modern times the only explorers who have gained entrance to Lhasa (Lassa) have
been a few Indian pundits, trained by British officers. The
jealous apprehensions of the Chinese Government, the religious fanaticism of the Tibetans, and the wild nature
of their country—these are the factors which have kept
Tibet in isolation longer than any other country in Asia.
At a time when the influence of neither Russia nor England was so great as it is now, more than one European
succeeded in crossing the country, and even in reaching
the capital. The first European to enter Lhasa was a
monk, Odorico di Pordenone, who travelled from China to
Tibet in the first half of the fourteenth century. In 1624
the Spanish Jesuit Antonius de Andrade went from India
to Tibet; and in 1661 the two Jesuit missionaries, Grueber
and D'Orville, made their remarkable journey from Peking
to Lhasa by way of Koko-nor (Koko-nur), Tsaidam, and the
country of the Tanguts. They remained in the capital
for two months, and then returned by way of Nepal to
Agra, and thence to Europe. In the eighteenth century
the mysterious city was visited by several missionaries.
Desideri lived in Lhasa from 1716 to 1729, and Della
Penna from 1719 to 1735, and again from 1740 to 1746;
they, however, have left no writings, except a few letters.
Between the years 1729 and 1737 the bold Dutchman Van

der Putte travelled from India, by way of Lhasa and Koko-
nor, to Peking, whence he returned through Farther India
to Lhasa. On his return home he burned all his papers,
under the impression that nobody would believe his wonderful narrative. In 1811 Manning reached Lhasa; and in
1845 the two French missionaries, Huc and Gabet, made
their celebrated journey from Peking by way of Koko-nor,
Burkhan-buddha, and Tan-la to the capital of Tibet, a
journey which Father Huc described in an interesting book.
Since then no European has succeeded in penetrating to
Lhasa. Every subsequent expedition which started with
that city as its goal has been compelled to turn back, its
mission unaccomplished.

As I mentioned before, the outlying parts of the country
have been visited by several European travellers, not all of
whom, however, have done scientific work or brought home
valuable information. The extreme west of Tibet was explored in 1856 and 1857 by the brothers Schlagintweit, in
1865 by Johnson, in 1868–70 by Shaw, in 1868–70 by Hay-
ward, and in 1870 and 1873–74 by Forsyth and his many
associates, in 1885–87 by Carey and Dalgleish, in 1888–90
by Grombtchevsky. Kishen Singh, an Indian pundit, who
was a member of Forsyth's expedition, succeeded in penetrating somewhat farther into the country than the others.
One of the most remarkable journeys ever made in Tibet
was that of the pundit Nain Singh, who had taken part in
Schlagintweit's and Forsyth's expeditions, and was sent by
Captain Trotter, in July, 1874, from Leh in Ladak to Lhasa.
His caravan consisted of twenty-six sheep, carrying light
loads. Only four of them survived the journey, which extended to a thousand miles and lasted four months. The
animals subsisted on such herbage as they were able to find
on the way. At the town of Niagzu, on the boundary between Ladak and Tibet, they met with both forest and
pasture. The tract east of Lake Panggong was uninhabited, except by a few shepherds and their flocks. The natives
called themselves Changpas or Northmen; but to the inhabitants of Turkestan they were known as Taghliks or Moun-

taineers. The Tibetan plateau stretched away east for 800 miles, to the sources of the Chinese rivers and the Burkhan-buddha Mountains.   As far as eye could reach, it appeared to consist of a grass-grown plateau region diversified by hills and valleys, with snow-clad mountains in the distance. Occasionally a shepherd's tent was seen; and antelopes, wild asses, and wild sheep abounded. The results of the journey were 276 determinations of latitude, the mapping of 1200 miles of unknown country, 497 observations for altitude with the boiling-point thermometer, and a series of meteorological observations.

Among those who have travelled in Eastern Tibet the Russian General Przhevalsky (Prjevalsky) ranks first. The 17th (29th) November, 1870, he started from Kiakhta with three Russian followers, and passed through the Desert of Gobi by way of Urga and Kalgan to Peking. After a trip to Dalai-nor, he left Kalgan, in May, 1871, and travelled west, through the mountain-chains of In-shan and Muni-ula, then up the Yellow River (Hwang-ho) until he reached the country of Ala-shan, and its capital Dyn-yuan-in. He afterwards returned to Kalgan. Then, after a good rest, he went back to Dyn-yuan-in, where we find him in June, 1872. Here began the most remarkable part of his travels, the country which he next traversed being little known. He first explored the highlands of Kan-su, a well-wooded mountain region lying northeast of Koko-nor; then, having made the circuit of the lake, and crossed the Southern Range of Koko-nor, the expedition reached the great swamps of Tsaidam, whence it ascended into the higher regions of Tibet, the home of the wild yak. Several of the mountain-chains of the Tibetan highlands were crossed on the way to the Yang-tse-kiang, which was reached on January 10th (22d), 1873. Although it was Przhevalsky's intention to penetrate as far as Lhasa, which he approached within twenty-seven days' journey, he was constrained to abandon the plan, owing to his caravan animals becoming exhausted and his provisions running short. Przhevalsky's first journey terminated at Irkutsk in Siberia, at which place he arrived on October 8th, 1873.

For three years the expedition had struggled against difficulties which seemed almost insurmountable; had defied the
summer heat of the Mongol desert, the winter cold of the
Tibetan highlands; had spent months in a small, frail tent,   .
often at a temperature of forty degrees below zero (Fahr. and
C.), living on game killed by members of the expedition.
The energy and endurance which Przhevalsky showed are
worthy of every admiration.   It is evident he was swayed by
a clear understanding of the great importance of his undertaking.   Although surrounded by a hostile population, and
exposed to every kind of danger, he disregarded both, and,
amid the pestilential smoke from the argal (dry dung) fire in
his tent, went on working out his memoranda and sorting his
collections.   It was a geographical achievement which has
rightly placed Przhevalsky's name in the forefront of Asiatic
exploration.   The most wonderful thing is that this journey,
which amounted to 7350 miles, cost very little more than
6000 roubles (say £600), a proof that it is possible to travel
inexpensively in Asia, if you only know how to set about it.

Przhevalsky's second journey lasted from August, 1876, to
July, 1877.   Although it extended to less than 2650 miles,
the cost was more than 19,000 roubles (or about £1900); but
this time his equipment was more complete and his escort
more numerous.   The results of this journey also were of extreme importance.   The region which he added to the domain of geographical knowledge was one of the least known
in Central Asia.   Previously our sole conceptions of its nature were derived from hearsay, from Chinese maps, and from
tradition.

From Kulja his route led through the Ili valley to Yul-
duz, afterwards south by way of Korla, and, along the lower
Tarim, to Lop-nor (Lob-nor) and the Altyn-tagh.   When
Przhevalsky saw that it was impossible to reach Tibet, and
particularly Lhasa, the object of his desire, by way of Lop-
nor and the desolate region south of the Altyn-tagh, he determined to try what he could do by way of Gutshen and
Khami; but he was taken ill on the road, and was constrained to return to Russia.

The crowning feature of this expedition was the discovery of the new Lop-nor, and of the great chain of mountains Altyn-tagh, which has so greatly altered the appearance of our maps of Central Asia. He also discovered the existence of the wild camel, a discovery afterwards confirmed by other travellers—viz., Carey, Younghusband, and others.

Przhevalsky's third expedition lasted from March, 1879, to November, 1880, and covered some 4750 miles. On this occasion he was accompanied by twelve natives, and had a sum of 23,500 roubles (£2350) at his disposal. He chose Saisansk on the Russian frontier as a point of departure, and travelled, by way of Bulun-tokhoi and the Urungu River, through Dzungaria to Barkul, and thence over the Tian-shan Mountains to Khami. After that he crossed the Desert of Gobi, touching his former route at a couple of points. This time he penetrated much farther to the south—namely, across the Yang-tse-kiang and the Tan-la Mountains as far as 32° N. lat.

Przhevalsky's fourth and last journey began in October, 1883, and ended in the same month two years later. With twenty followers, most of them Cossacks, he accomplished a distance of 4850 miles; the cost of the expedition being 42,-250 roubles (£4225).

From Kiakhta he crossed the Gobi by the same route he had taken on a previous occasion, and went on farther through the highlands of Kan-su as far as the two lakes of Tsaringnor and Oring-nor, the twin sources of the Hwang-ho. This was the culminating-point of the fourth journey. After a deviation to the Yang-tse-kiang, he continued on through Tsaidam, thence over the Altyn-tagh to Lop-nor and Khotan, at the northern foot of the Kwen-lun Mountains, and finally down the Khotan-daria and over the Tian-shan Mountains.

The extensive journeys in 1878–82 of the intrepid Indian pundit Krishna, commonly called A—K, were of the greatest importance for the geography of Northern Tibet. In the spring of 1878 he was ordered by the Indian Government to explore the territory bordered on the north by Przhevalsky's journeys, on the east by the routes of the

French missionaries Desgodins and Durand and of the Eng
lishman Gill, on the south by the Sang-po (Brahmaputra
River) and the Himalayas, and on the west by the meridian
which runs through Lhasa and Lop-nor.   In more recen
years this region has only been crossed by Huc and Gabet
and by Bonvalot and Prince Henry of Orleans.

Disguised as a merchant, and provided with plenty o
money and instruments, A—K went, by way of Sikkim, tc
Lhasa, reaching that city in September, 1878.   There he
stopped for a whole year, waiting to find a large and well
armed caravan with which he might travel northward, as the
Tangut robbers make the roads in that direction very unsafe
On September 17th, 1879, a Mongol caravan arrived.   A hun
dred of its members, Mongols, with a few Tibetans, were go
ing back at once.   All were mounted and all armed with
spears, swords, and fire-arms.   A—K seized the opportunity
Great caution was observed during the march ; patrols were
sent on ahead, and a watch kept at night.   The route which
was followed at first coincided with that of Nain Singh in
1875, when he journeyed from Tengri-nor to Lhasa.   South
of Tan-la, A—K touched the route taken by Przhevalsky or
his third journey.   The highest pass in the Tan-la, 16,400
feet, marked the water-shed between the upper Mekong and
the Yang-tse-kiang.   After five months on the plateau he
reached the Anghirtakshia Mountains over a pass 15,750 feet
in altitude.   A halt was made at Tenghelik in Tsaidam ; but
just as the caravan was on the point of starting again it was
attacked by two hundred robbers, who relieved A—K of all
his goods and baggage animals.   He managed, however, to
retain his notes and instruments, and in spite of his reverses
determined to persevere with the solution of the prob
lems which had been set him.   He wintered on the western
shore of the Kurlyk-nor until March, 1880.   Thence he in
tended to steer his course towards Lop-nor ; but his Indian
servant deserted him, carrying off most of his possessions
He himself was obliged to take service with a Mongol, who
was going to Sa-chow.   There he was well treated by a lama
but was compelled by the Chinese governor to turn back

This turning-point is of importance. It was from that region Przhevalsky made his journey towards Tsaidam and Tan-la in 1879–80; and in the same quarter Count Széchenyi's expedition through China came to an end. With one faithful follower, A—K started on his return journey, but was again compelled to take service with " Chinese Tatars." Finally, however, he reached Darchendo (Tatsien-lu) in safety, and at the mission-station there received every help from the bishop; and thence returned by way of Batang and Darjiling to India.

In 1888–89 the American Rockhill made a journey into Eastern Tibet. Starting from Peking with only one follower and a few horses, he proceeded to the Koko-nor and Alaknor, crossed the Yang-tse-kiang, and eventually got back to Shanghai. He could speak Chinese and Tibetan, and travelled in disguise. He did some first-rate mapping, measured heights, made notes, and says that previous European maps are incorrect and unreliable in respect of both orography and hydrography.

Several other travellers, induced by the desire for research or by ambition, have of late undertaken journeys into inner Tibet and towards Lhasa. Many have failed, while others can show good results. The most successful expedition was that of Bonvalot and Prince Henry of Orleans, which crossed Asia from northwest to southeast. The expedition followed Przhevalsky's route along the Tarim as far as the Lop-nor and the Altyn-tagh. On November 17th, 1889, they set out from the Lop-nor, and on the 23d crossed the Altyn-tagh, leaving Przhevalsky's and Carey's routes behind them. They then struck a direct course to the south, across unknown country and without guides. This march lasted till February 17th, 1890, and extended to two days' journey south of the Tengri-nor. The Tibetan plateau, on which they were travelling for three months, nowhere falls below the altitude of thirteen thousand feet. Some of the mountain-chains of the Kwen-lun system were crossed by passes at more than 18,000 feet in altitude, and numerous lakes were discovered. The country was barren in the extreme, totally devoid of trees or bushes; it did not even provide sufficient provender

for the camels and horses of the caravan, which, in conse
quence of the fatigue, the privations, and the severe cold
gradually died off until very few were left. From Decembe
4th to January 30th not a human being was encountered
Two days' journey south of the Tengri-nor the expeditior
was stopped by the Tibetans, and in spite of negotiations
lasting nearly seven weeks it failed to obtain permission to
continue its march to Lhasa. The travellers were therefore
obliged to make a considerable circuit, and reached Tong
king in September.

In May, 1890, the Russian Captain Grombtchevsky en
deavored to penetrate into Western Tibet from Polu, but, be
ing unsuccessful, he turned aside to Khotan, and spent July
and August in exploring the Tisnab valley, the upper Yar
kand-daria, and the water-shed between these two rivers. Af
ter a visit to the Pamirs, he proceeded, by way of Kashgar
to Tashkend (Tashkent), where I met him at the end of the
same year. He had covered a distance of more than 4700
miles, and his researches form a connecting link betweer
those of Kuropatkin (1877), Forsyth (1873–74), Przhevalsky
(1885), and Pievtsoff (1889–90). He met the last-named in
Niya, where the two travellers were able to compare note
and place-determinations.

In 1889 and 1890 General Pievtsoff, accompanied by Przhe
valsky's companions, Roborovsky and Kozloff, and by the
geologist Bogdanovitch, made a journey into East Turkestan
crossing the Tian-shan Mountains, proceeding up the Yar
kand-daria to Yarkand, thence to Khotan, and wintered a
Niya. From the northern foot of the Kwen-lun Mountain:
they made several expeditions on to the Tibetan plateau, and
explored, in particular, that part of it which lies to the north
of the Arka-tagh. The return journey was by way of the
Lop-nor, Karashahr, and Dzungaria. Pievtsoff's journey i
one of the most important that has been undertaken in these
parts, and no traveller has made such reliable place-determi
nations as he.

In the Altyn-tagh and the tracts south of them Przheval
sky's route in his fourth journey was crossed at several point

by that of the Englishman Carey. Accompanied by Dalgleish, who was afterwards murdered, Carey crossed the Altyn-tagh, the Chamen-tagh, and the uninhabited plateau between these two ranges of mountains, before he was able to reach the Kwen-lun proper and the Tibetan highlands. He passed over these chains at a point rather more to the west than that chosen by Przhevalsky, and afterwards intersected Przhevalsky's route on the plateau between the Chamen-tagh and the Kwen-lun Mountains. Carey afterwards proceeded to the east along the foot of the Kwen-lun, went a short distance between this range and the Koko-shili, and crossed the pilgrim road from Mongolia to Lhasa immediately south of the point where it climbs over a pass in the Kwen-lun Mountains. At the river Ma-chu he turned northward and traversed a portion of A—K's route. This journey took place in 1885–87.

Captain Younghusband, whose name is well known for his travels in the Pamirs, travelled in 1888 from Peking, *via* Barkul, Ak-su, and Kashgar, to India; and Captain Bower, between June, 1891, and March, 1892, crossed Tibet and China from Leh to Shanghai.

The expeditions which I have here summarized are the most important within the regions which I propose to visit.

It would lead me too far were I to endeavor to render an account of the great problems that still await solution in the interior of Asia. The discovery of new chains of mountains, lakes, and rivers, of the traces of an ancient civilization, of antiquities which might possibly throw light on the great migrations of the races through Asia, the identification of old, disused caravan roads, and, finally, the mapping of an entirely unknown region—all this possesses an irresistible attraction for the explorer; but I can only touch upon one or two questions of peculiar interest.

In the Asiatic highlands the geologist has unique opportunities of studying phenomena of the greatest possible interest, interesting not only on account of the processes of evolution which the mountain-chains are actually undergoing there, but also for the reason that those mountain-chains

themselves are so little known. The table-land of Tibet rises
like an enormous platform up to a mean height of thirteen
thousand feet above the lowlands of Hindustan on the one
side and the desert of the Tarim basin on the other, the
latter being one of the lowest depressions in the interior of
any continent. Lake Lop-nor has an absolute altitude of
not more than two thousand five hundred feet, and at Luk-
tchin, south of Turfan, a depression has been found which
actually lies a considerable distance below the level of the
sea. On the side next the Tarim basin the Tibetan highlands are bounded by the Himalayas and the Kwen-lun,
whose western extremities meet in the Pamirs and the regions south of it. While the older geographers and discov-
erers bestowed their attention upon little else save the topographical appearance, or at most the surface elevations, of a
country, modern geographical discovery claims from its sur-
veyors reliable knowledge of the original causes of the present condition of the surface of the earth, and the genetic
connection, origin, age, and relation of the mountain-chains
to each other. There are important questions still to be
solved in High Asia on these points, and a long period of
time must necessarily elapse before these problems can be
brought within measurable distance of solution. During the
last twenty-five years only four geologists of standing have
devoted any attention to the region of the Kwen-lun system—
namely, Stoliczka, Von Richthofen, Loczy, and Bogdanovitch.

But vast gaps still divide the regions which they have
severally investigated. It is my intention during this projected journey to contribute as far as lies in my power to the
filling in of these gaps, where every observation, every con-
tour-line, is of the utmost value.

Another problem of intense interest is the Lop-nor question, which was raised by Baron von Richthofen. I will
mention here some of the points set forth in his article en-
titled " Bemerkungen zu den Ergebnissen von Oberst-lieu-
tenant Prjewalski's Reise nach dem Lop-noor und Altyn-
tagh" (*Verhandlungen der Ges. für Erdkunde*, V., 1878, pp.
121 *et seqq.*).

Marco Polo was the first to make the Lop desert known to Europeans, and on D'Anville's map of Asia Lop-nor with its rivers is found for the first time, though in latitude 42° 20' N. Shortly before Przhevalsky's journey the lake was supposed to be situated in an enormous basin, and at a greater distance to the south than to the north of the mountains which bounded it. Przhevalsky, however, found that the lake lay much farther south than was supposed from the maps and Chinese accounts, and the result of this and his other expeditions was that the maps of the interior of Asia came to present quite a different appearance from what they had heretofore. The territory between Korla and Altyn-tagh was quite unknown; as was also the fact that the lower Tarim ran for such a long distance in a southeasterly direction. The discovery of the Altyn-tagh possessed equal importance as a contribution to the knowledge of the physical geography of Asia as for the comprehension of the position and direction of the ancient trading-routes. It now became clear why the ancient silk caravans from China to the West kept so near the south of Lop-nor, necessitating their passing through the much-dreaded desert between Sa-chow and the lake.

Basing his deductions partly on certain geological laws, and partly on a large map of China and Central Asia published in Wu-chang-fu in 1862, Von Richthofen says:

"The most remarkable thing about Przhevalsky's Lop-nor is that he discovered a fresh-water lake where we are constrained to assume the presence of salt water. It is an absolute impossibility that a *lake-basin*, which for a series of geological periods has acted as a reservoir for the deposition of salt from a great river, should contain fresh water and be the resort of fish. This would be inconceivable even though the whole course of the Tarim lay through regions which in the general estimation were quite free from salt. But as a matter of fact, all the regions whence the lake gathers its drainage are so saline that fresh-water springs are quite an exception, and occur only close to the foot of the mountains. Now the water of the Tarim must contain a greater quantity of salt than almost any other large river in the world. The concentration of these saline ingredients by evaporation must take place to a very great extent in the last reservoir of the Tarim, and the continuation of the process from time immemorial must therefore have caused an unusually large deposit of every kind of steppe salt. From the remotest ages the Chinese have called Lop-nor 'the Salt Lake.' . . . Contrary to all theoretical conclusions and historical accounts, we now have from the first European eye-witness, who is furthermore gifted with uncommon powers of observation, the distinct assurance that the last basin of the Tarim is a fresh-water lake. There must therefore exist peculiar circumstances to account for this apparent contradiction."

It might perhaps be supposed that during the winter, when the evaporation is slight, the fresh water rises and spreads above the salt water; but the inconsiderable depth of the lake sufficiently nullifies this supposition. Another explanation is that the Tarim, which often changes its channel, has abandoned its former reservoir in favor of another, the present one, which is supposed to be of comparatively recent formation.

The most probable explanation is that, besides the two reservoirs visited by Przhevalsky (the Kara-buran and Kara-kurchin—*i.e.*, Kara-koshun), there is yet a third, into which an arm of the Tarim debouches. No Chinese map shows a southern branch of the Tarim, but a large lake is indicated in latitude 41° N.—*i.e.*, in the direct line of any continuation of the Tarim—and is called on the maps Lop-nor. The circumstance, among other things, that Przhevalsky did not find the name of Lop-nor in use also points to the same conclusion. On the other hand, he did hear the name in use for that part of the Tarim which lies east of where the real Lop-nor should be.

Another important argument is implicit in the fact that the Tarim, at its confluence with the Ughen-daria, has a breadth of three hundred to three hundred and sixty feet and a strong current; but below the junction of all its various tributaries a breadth of only one hundred and eighty to two hundred and ten feet, and a slow current. It is possible that when Przhevalsky journeyed among these tributaries, or rather anastomosing arms, the most easterly branch discharged a part of its water eastward through another and separate channel into the inaccessible salt desert, and that the traveller overlooked this channel. Von Richthofen concludes his investigation with the words, "However highly we may value what Przhevalsky has done towards the exploration of the Lop-nor, we cannot consider that the problem, for the sake of which he underwent such great hardships, is as yet definitively solved."

The three expeditions of Carey and Dalgleish, Bonvalot and Prince Henry of Orleans, and Pievtsoff, each of which has visited Lop-nor since Przhevalsky, have not added to our knowledge of this remarkable lake, for the reason that they all followed the same route that he took.

The solution of the Lop-nor question is still a desideratum for all who are interested in the geography of Asia. The future traveller to Lop-nor must not content himself with proving the existence of the basins discovered by Przhevalsky; he must make a systematic and accurate investigation of the districts north of them in order to try and find the lake into which the Tarim, according to Von Richthofen, empties a portion of its waters. This lake, too, is marked on the Chinese maps, which as a rule are remarkable for their great topographical-accuracy.

2

CHAPTER II

THE PLAN AND OBJECTS OF MY JOURNEY

FOR several years I have been occupied in studying the
geography of Central Asia, partly at home and partly at the
University of Berlin, under Baron von Richthofen, the celebrated authority on Chinese geography. I have also prepared myself by two journeys to Persia and Central Asia, in
the years 1885–86 and 1890–91 respectively, the latter after
the conclusion of Your Majesty's mission to Shah Nasr-eddin
of Persia. During these journeys I had the opportunity of
becoming accustomed to Asiatic travel, to association with
the natives, and of learning one or two of the most important
languages. In the hope of being able to make these prepar-
atory studies of use in the cause of science, I have ventured
to seek Your Majesty's protection and support for the execu-
tion of a scheme which, if all goes well, will reflect honor on
our country and contribute to disperse the clouds which still
rest over a great part of Central Asia. An expedition into
that part of the world which was the cradle of the Aryan race,
and from whose dim interior the Mongols streamed out over
the whole of Asia and part of Europe, and where there is
such a host of geographical questions still awaiting solution,
is one of the most important undertakings within the domain
of geographical discovery. The object of my prospective
journey is to traverse Asia from west to east, from the Caspian Sea to Peking, and in particular to explore the intermediate regions which are least known.

The Swedish expedition should, if possible, leave Stockholm in the month of May of the present year (1893). Its
equipment should be completed in Turkestan and Ladak,
and nothing need be taken from Stockholm except instru-

ments and fire-arms. Accompanied by one assistant, whose
duty it would be to take astronomical observations, I propose to travel through Russia to Baku, across the Caspian
Sea to Usun-ada, and thence by rail to Samarkand. It is
my intention to drive through West Turkestan in a tarantass by way of Tashkend, Kokand, Margelan, and Osh, and
thence over the pass of Terek-davan—all places well known
to me—to Kashgar in East Turkestan, the termination of
my former journey in 1890–91. In Kashgar I shall hire a
horse caravan to take us, by way of Yarkand and the Kara-
korum pass, to Leh, where there are an English agent and
English merchants. The journey to Kashgar will take two
months to accomplish, thence to Leh one month, so that, if
all goes well, the beginning of August should see us in Leh.

It was also my intention originally, from the region around
Lop-nor, to try and penetrate over the Kwen-lun Mountains
into Northern Tibet. But in December of last year, while
on a visit to St. Petersburg, I met General Pievtsoff, who in
1889–90 made the expedition previously mentioned into East
Turkestan. General Pievtsoff advised me against attempting to carry out my plan along the lines which I then unfolded to him. He had had unfortunate experience of the
difficulties which travellers encounter in those regions, having endeavored unsuccessfully to penetrate into the country
with horses and camels. Train animals perish in great numbers, owing to the difficulties of the country, the inclement
weather, the rarefied air, and the almost entire absence of pasturage. General Pievtsoff advised me to make Leh, in Ladak,
the starting-point for my proposed expedition into Tibet.
There one can procure not only the necessary provisions and
articles essential to an adequate equipment—such as tents,
saddles, furs, felt carpets, household utensils, boxes for collections, etc.—but also reliable men, natives of the adjacent
provinces of Tibet. Above all, he told me that tame yaks
were also procurable at Leh, animals to which the rarefied
atmosphere is natural, and which find their way with inconceivable sureness of foot in places which seem quite impassable. In regions which to all appearance are absolutely barren,

they are further able to find mosses and lichens, which th
lick from the rocks.   The expedition will require a carav
of fifteen yaks, and an escort of six well-armed natives.

According to Pievtsoff, the autumn is the best time of ye
for travelling in Northern Tibet.   The expedition oug
therefore to leave Leh in the middle of August, and str
an east-southeasterly line towards the lake Tengri-nor, abc
the same direction as that taken by the pundit Nain Sin
in 1874.   Somewhere north of Tengri-nor, in an uninhabit
tract, I propose to encamp, and, disguised and accompan
by one or two followers, endeavor to penetrate to Lha
returning thence to the chief encampment at Tengri-n
This somewhat adventurous method of trying to enter t
capital of Tibet I shall naturally not resort to unless circu
stances are favorable and the reaching of Lhasa seems lik
to prove of undoubted value in the interests of geograp
From Tengri-nor we shall strike through Tibet and endea
to reach East Turkestan over the Kwen-lun Mountains; t
town of Cherchen would then be our nearest goal.   A
there we ought to arrive in February of next year.

After exchanging the yaks for camels, we shall proce
northward through an entirely unknown part of the Des
of Gobi, until we reach the course of the river Tarim.
the desert there are no roads and no springs, nothing l
barren, moving sand-hills.   The inhabitants of the N
oasis on its southern confines, however, told Przhevals
that in the winter it is possible to traverse the desert,
there are in that season occasional falls of snow, which r
der it possible to procure water.   It is my intention to stu
the aspect of this desert and the movements of its sand hi

We shall then follow the east bank of the Tarim in or
to discover whether the river does or does not send of
branch to the east, so as to form a lake in 41° N. lat., to
north of Przhevalsky's Lop-nor.   The investigation of
Lop-nor problem should be completed by June, 1894, a
our expedition will then have accomplished its most imp
tant as well as its most difficult objects.

From Lop-nor we shall steer a direct course to the e

and proceed through the unknown portion of the desert known as Kum-tagh; then go on by way of Su-chow (Su-chau) to Ala-shan, where we ought to discover inscriptions and memorials of the earliest times of the Uigurs; then across the Yellow River, through Ordos, where we shall keep north of the Great Wall, and finally through the two northern provinces of China, Shan - si and Pe - chi - li, to Pe-king, where we ought to arrive in November, 1894.

It is easier to devise a scheme of this character at one's writing-table than it is to carry it out. My programme must therefore be regarded as the ideal which I shall endeavor to attain. If the whole plan cannot be realized, still I will hope that at least I may have strength and energy to execute a considerable portion of it. It is evident, especially in a land so little known as Tibet, that it is impossible to determine on a particular route beforehand, as unforeseen circumstances must inevitably arise, and perhaps necessitate a radical change in any predetermined scheme.

In Peking the expedition may be regarded as at an end. From that city I shall send my Swedish companion home with the collections, notes, and general results. Should my funds hold out, I shall probably seize the opportunity to make acquaintance with southern Mongolia and the Desert of Gobi proper. I propose, therefore, to return home by way of Khami and Turfan, as in any case I should be responsible for the safe return of my followers to their own country.

The expedition, starting from Osh, in Fergana, where Russian means of communication cease and caravans have to be resorted to, will, I reckon. cover a distance of about 5300 miles. The cost of the whole expedition I estimate at about 30.000 kronor (£1670).

The scientific work which should be done may be comprised under the following heads :

1. The construction of a topographical map of the entire route traversed. The determination of geographical latitudes and longitudes wherever possible. The determination of fixed altitudes with the hypsometer or boiling-point thermometer and three aneroids, and the indication of them on the map.

2. Geological investigations, the sketching of profiles and contours, and the collection of petrological specimens.

3. Anthropological researches and measurements among the peoples we come in contact with. The photographing of various racial types. Study of the religious beliefs of the semi-savage tribes, and their mode of living, etc. Linguistic studies.

4. Archæological researches. The description, measurement, and sketching of the ruins of noteworthy towns, burial-places, etc.

5. The photographing of towns, places of geological interest, etc.

6. Meteorological observations. Periodical determinations of the temperature of the atmosphere of the earth, and of river and lake water; ascertaining the amount of moisture in the atmosphere, the direction of the winds, etc.

7. Hydrographical investigations. The depth of lakes, the volume of water in the rivers, together with their variations at the different seasons of the year, the velocity of currents, their direction, etc.

8. The collection of plants, particularly algæ.

9. The keeping of a diary during the entire period of the expedition.

This was the scheme which I laid before the King, and which was stamped with his approval. Now that my work is at an end, and I am able to compare the journey I planned with the real journey I carried through, I congratulate myself that on the whole the two routes coincided fairly well across East Turkestan, Tibet, and Mongolia, although there were noteworthy deviations, caused by the course of events. In the first place, the route I actually followed was much longer than the one projected, and included regions which I at first considered altogether inaccessible. Furthermore, I altered my plans at the very outset, and instead of crossing over the Caspian Sea, which I already knew well, I went from Orenburg through the Kirghiz steppe. The Pamirs, which were not included in my original programme, became the object of three extended excursions, during which the eastern, or Chinese Pamirs, in particular, were explored in many directions. The Takla-makan, the great western extension of the Desert of Gobi, was crossed in two directions; and there I had the great satisfaction of making important archæological discoveries. Finally, I made several expeditions into the country between Kashgar, Ak-su, and Khotan.

After the expedition through the desert to the Tarim and Lop-nor, and back again to Khotan, there only remained one of the chief objects of the programme—namely, Tibet—unaccomplished. Then I heard of Dutreuil de Rhins's and Littledale's expeditions to pretty nearly the same parts as those I intended to visit, and that both had tried to reach Lhasa and failed. I therefore thought it would be better to work those parts of Northern Tibet which were still a complete *terra incognita*. Everywhere there, with the exception of the point where I should intersect Bonvalot and Prince Henry of Orleans's route, I should be the first European pioneer, and every step would be an accession of geographical territory, every mountain, lake, and river a discovery.

After I had successfully accomplished this undertaking, although not without great difficulty, instead of following the route I had mapped through Mongolia to Urga, I preferred to strike a more southerly line—namely, through Tsaidam, the country of the Tanguts, the territory of Koko-nor, and the province of Kan-su, where, on several occasions, I could not help following or crossing the routes of other travellers. In Ala-shan I chose a route which had not hitherto been travelled over, and it was not until I reached Ordos, Shan-si, and Pe-chi-li that I entered regions which have long been well known. Between Peking and Kiakhta I travelled through Mongolia proper, and afterwards hastened homeward through Siberia.

Of other discrepancies between my original plan and my journey as actually carried out, I will only mention that at the last moment I decided to go alone. This was partly for the sake of economy, and partly because I did not like the idea of being involved in dangers and hardships, which I

could endure myself, but in which a companion might n
have cared to risk his life.

Moreover, instead of making one continuous journey, as
had originally intended, I found it advisable to break it ι
into several expeditions. This was rendered possible throug
the boundless hospitality shown me by the Russian Consu
General in Kashgar, Mr. Petrovsky. He has since bee
specially honored by the King of Sweden and Norway fc
his invaluable services to my undertaking.

After crossing the Pamirs in the winter and spring c
1894, I employed the summer and autumn for a new expe
dition into the east and middle Pamirs, Kashgar being m
point of departure. In the spring and summer of 1895
traversed the Takla-makan Desert and the north of Eas
Turkestan; and finally, in the summer and autumn of th
same year, I made a third excursion into the southern Pamir
In the same way I subsequently made Khotan a new bas
of operations, leaving there in the beginning of 1896 fc
my long journey round East Turkestan to Lop-nor. It wa
only when I left Khotan in the end of June, 1896, that
really burned my boats behind me, cutting off every cor
nection with the West until I reached the extreme East–
Peking. This arrangement made the journey longer bot
as regards distance and time; but, on the other hand, the re
sults were much greater, and after each expedition, thanks t
the Russian post, I was able to send home my collection
I do not think I am wanting in modesty if I say that I no
look back with satisfaction on the many important gec
graphical discoveries made during this journey, and on th
solution of problems which had long been the subject ι
controversy among geographers.

The breaking-up of my journey into several shorter e:
peditions was a happy thought. After each such expeditio
I was able to rest, and recover strength necessary for a ne
campaign. I also worked out the results of my journe
provisionally, and prepared for the work awaiting me durin
my next expedition; and each time I started off with ne
interests and new points of view.

In this account of my travels I have aimed to depict the reminiscences and impressions which I gathered during my long and lonely wanderings in the heart of Asia. It is clear that the results of a journey which occupied three and a half years are too voluminous to be comprised in a single book; and I have thought it wiser to separate the scientific data from matter which is of more general interest. I propose, therefore, to give a description of the journey, the countries I passed through, the peoples with which I came into contact, and the adventures I and my men experienced in unknown and uninhabited regions. The scientific results, which require a longer time for their working-out, and which are of more special interest, will be published separately at some future date.

Thanks to King Oscar's protection and generous aid, I had no difficulty in raising the 30,000 kronor, or £1670, I required. More than half the sum was given by the King, the Nobel family, and friends of geography in Gothenburg through Mr. Westin. The other half was contributed by Baron Åkerhielm, a former minister of state, and Messrs. E. Cederlund, Treschow, Andersson, J. Bäckström, C. von Platen, Carl Lamm, Sager, and Davidsson, and Mrs. Emma Benedicks and Mrs. Clara Scharp.

Five of these are no longer living; but to the others I desire to take this opportunity of expressing my sincerest thanks.

On my arrival at Peking I was, however, obliged to borrow 4000 kronor, or about £220; so that the cost of the entire journey, instruments and equipment included, amounted to 34,000 kronor, or rather less than £1900.

Among other contributions I must mention a Husqvarna double-barrelled rifle from Mr. W. Tamm, an express carbine from Consul-General J. W. Smitt, an aluminium craniometer from Professor G. Retzius, and an artificial horizon from Baron Nordenskiöld.

My luggage from Stockholm was not very great, as the bulkier part of my outfit was to be obtained in Asia. I had the following instruments: a prismatic circle (Wegener) with two horizons, two chronometers (one Frodsham from the Royal Academy of Science in Stockholm, and one Wirén from the observatory in Tashkend), three French aneroids, a number of thermometers and other meteorological instruments from Fuess in Berlin, among them black-bulb insulation thermometers, psychrometers, spring thermometers, maximum and minimum thermometers. I also took with me a plane-table with stand, together with compasses, a camera by Watson, and a kodak by Eastman, with a complete supply of films and plates, chemicals, and other necessaries. Furthermore, I took two ordinary watches, a field-glass, and a small aluminium telescope; about forty pairs of glasses and snow-spectacles; finally, geologists' hammers, metre measures, a water-color box, drawing materials, and a number of sketch-books and note-books, etc.

My weapons consisted throughout the entire journey of the two above-mentioned rifles, a Russian Berdan rifle, a Swedish officer's revolver, and half a dozen other revolvers, and two cases of ammunition.

The library was naturally reduced to the smallest possible compass, and consisted only of a few important scientific books and the Bible. On the other hand, I took with me a very complete collection of itineraries laid down during the last ten years in the interior of Asia; and also Russian and English survey maps of the Pamirs, maps of the Desert of Gobi and of Tibet.

Thus equipped, and provided with a Chinese passport, I left my dear old home in Stockholm on October 16th, 1893; and on board the *Von Döbeln* steamed eastward towards my unknown fate.

It was a cold, dark, autumn evening, such as I shall never forget; heavy rain-clouds hung over the city of Stockholm, and her lights soon vanished from sight. More than a thousand and one nights of loneliness and longing were before me; everything I held dear was behind me. Yet that first night was the bitterest of all; I never suffered so much from homesickness again.

Only those who have left their country for a lengthened

period, and with the clouds of uncertainty before them, can conceive the feelings which such a break occasions. But, on the other hand, the whole wide world was before me, and I determined to do all that lay in my power to solve the problems which I had set myself.

CHAPTER III

ACROSS RUSSIA TO ORENBURG

AN unbroken railway journey of 1400 miles, the distance which separates Orenburg from St. Petersburg, is hardly an unmixed pleasure. Still less is it so at a period of the year when rain, snow, and wind take away all desire on the part of the traveller to while away the time of waiting by promenading the platform; while smoky or overheated stoves make it unpleasant to remain in the carriage.

The four days and nights which it takes to cross European Russia in this manner are, however, neither long nor dull. After leaving Moscow there is always plenty of room in the train. You can arrange your corner of the carriage as comfortably as circumstances will allow, and let your gaze wander away over the endless fields and steppes of Russia. You may smoke your pipe in perfect peace, drink a glass of hot tea now and then, trace the progress of your journey on a map, watch how one government succeeds another, and while away the time generally in conversation. In the dominions of the Tsar it is considered the most natural thing in the world for every one to address his fellow-passengers. If no other pretext presents itself, you may always begin a conversation by asking your neighbor's destination. My fellow-travellers, in most cases, were going to places in the governments of Ryazan, Penza, and Samara. When they asked me, in return, where I was going, and were told in answer "Peking," they were not a little surprised, and often were not quite clear where the place was.

Endless steppes, arable land, bearded peasants with fur caps and long coats, white churches with green onion-shaped domes and surrounded by rustic houses, wind-mills, which

. now, at any rate, had no need to complain of want of wind—
these were the chief objects to be seen from the carriage windows. Hour after hour, day after day, the same picture was
unrolled before our eyes. The only tract of forest we passed
through was in the east of Tamboff, but the trees were all low,
except an occasional pine, which lifted its head above the rest.

On we hastened eastward through the governments of
Ryazan, Tamboff, Penza, Saratoff, and Simbirsk, until at last
we reached the greatest river in Europe. We crossed it at
Syzran by one of the longest bridges in the world, 1625
yards in length. The Volga resembled a large lake rather
than a river. The opposite bank was lost in the mist; the
muddy, brownish-gray masses of water rolled sluggishly on
under the vast span of the railway bridge, every whit as lifeless as the landscape through which they flowed. Two or
three rowing-boats and a paddle-steamer moored to the bank
were the only signs of life we saw. Then on again we were
whirled across the never-ending steppe. On the boundary
between the governments of Samara and Orenburg we began
to detect signs of the proximity of the southwestern extension of the Urals. The country became more broken, and
the railway often curved in and out between the hills. For
considerable distances the line was bordered by wooden pal-
ings intended to protect it from the snow. The farther east
we travelled the more desolate became the landscape. We
never saw human beings except at the stations. The steppe
was occasionally dotted with herds of cattle, sheep, and goats.
The sky was gray and dull; and the fields had the yellow
tint of faded grass. Such were the border-lands between
Europe and Asia.

At the end of four days of railway travelling I arrived,
considerably shaken and jolted, at the important town of
Orenburg, situated near the point where the Sakmar joins
the river Ural. The town was not very interesting. Its low
stone houses are arranged in broad streets, unpaved and full
of choking dust, and overtopped by neat churches, of which
the still unfinished Kazansky *sobor* (Kazan cathedral) is the
largest.

The outskirts of the town, however, were not destitute of artistic sights; for there the Tatars and Kirghiz held their mart, partly in the open air, partly in low wooden sheds. In one place were sold all kinds of carts and conveyances, telegas and tarantasses, brought the most part from Ufa; in another, vast quantities of hay, piled up on carts, drawn by teams of four Bactrian camels; in another, horses, cattle,

A STREET IN ORENBURG

sheep, fowl, geese, turkeys, and various other live-stock. Of the 56,000 inhabitants of Orenburg, 8000 were Mohammedans, the greater number being Tatars, the rest Bashkirs and Kirghiz. The principal *mesjid* (mosque) of the Tatars was particularly beautiful, having been built at the expense of a rich merchant. Among the Mohammedans there were a number of merchants from Khiva and Bokhara, who sold cotton imported from Central Asia.

In time of war Orenburg furnishes eighteen, and in time of peace six, Cossack regiments of a thousand men each. The regiments take it in turn to serve, so that in time of peace each six regiments serve for three years. Sometimes the men of the other twelve till the land which the Crown grants them in exchange for their services. As a rule, the government provides them with nothing more than a rifle; horse and uniform they have to furnish themselves. The six regiments on service are usually quartered at Tashkend, Margelan, Petro-Alexandrovsk, Kieff, Warsaw, and Kharkoff. The Cossacks of Orenburg always amount to a considerable force, and are only exceeded in numbers by the Cossacks of the Don, and by the Kuban Cossacks. The Ural Cossacks, at the time of my visit, had only three regiments on duty, one in Samarkand and two on the Austrian frontier. The men are well-to-do, as they own the exclusive right of fishing in the lower Ural River, while above their chief town, Uralsk, they have built dams to prevent the sturgeon from going up to Orenburg. The Cossacks' chief bears the title of " Ataman." The Ataman of the Orenburg Cossacks was at that time General Yershoff, the governor of Orenburg.

In conclusion, if I add that Orenburg is situated on the threshold of Asia, at the extreme east of Russia; that it can boast of barracks, a hospital, a poor-house, schools, and hotels, of which the best was significantly called " Europe ": that it has a theatre, in which the plays of Turgenieff and Ibsen have the best " runs "; that it is the seat of the governor and vice-governor of the government of Orenburg, and that the military governor of the province of Turgai (between the Ural River and Lake Aral) also resides there, I think I have mentioned all that is of importance with regard to this town.

Its climate is essentially continental. In summer the heat is dry, close, and oppressive, and the atmosphere is filled with dust. In winter the thermometer often falls forty degrees, Fahr., below zero; the cold, however, is not particularly noticeable, as the atmosphere is usually still. From time to time snow-storms choke the streets, and as the snow, which falls in vast quantities, is not cleared away with any great expedition, it is often impossible to go out for a whole day at a time. But, the bulk of the snow removed, the sledging is perfect; the handsome black horses trot briskly along the streets, their bells jingling, and the sledge gliding easily over

the surface.   During spring and autumn the climate is ve ɪ
variable, and when the thaw sets in the streets become veri **t**
ble swamps.

The distance between St. Petersburg and Orenburg i:
1400 miles, and between Orenburg and Tashkend 1300 miles,
so that I now had before me a drive nearly as long as the
four days' railway journey.   Thirteen hundred miles in a
tarantass, in the month of November, across steppes and
wastes, over roads probably as hard as paving-stones, or else
a slough of mud, or impassable from snow!

I did not look forward to the prospect of driving a distance
farther than from Stockholm to Rome, or than from Berlin to
Algiers; but I had already (1890–91) made the railway journey to Samarcand, and wished to take this opportunity of
seeing the boundless Kirghiz steppes and the Kirghiz Kara-
kum Desert (the Black Sand) in order to compare it with
the desert of the same name in the Transcaspian region.

It is possible for those who prefer it to travel by the post.
But this means a change of conveyance at every station; and
as there are ninety-six stations, the inconvenience and waste
of time caused by the repeated unstrapping and rearranging
of one's luggage may easily be imagined.   It is better to buy
your own tarantass at the beginning of the journey, stow
away your baggage once for all, stuff the bottom of the conveyance with hay, and make it as comfortable and soft as
possible with cushions and furs — a tarantass has neither
springs nor seats—and only change horses at the stations.

Before starting, a stock of necessary articles, notably provisions, has to be laid in, for as a rule nothing eatable is to
be obtained at the stations.   On payment of fifteen kopeks
(kopek = ¼d.) the traveller may demand the use of a samovar,
and sometimes a piece of black bread may be bought.   In
addition to provisions, you should always be provided with
rope, twine, nails, screws, etc., so that you may be able to repair any damage that may happen to the equipage, and, last
but not least, cart grease, for at every third station the process of greasing the wheels has to be gone through.   Upon
quitting Orenburg you leave behind every trace of civiliza-

tion; you plunge into tracts of absolute desolation, and are entirely dependent upon yourself.

For the first 180 miles we were still on European soil, through the government of Orenburg; the next 330 lay through the province of Turgai, and the remainder of the distance through the province of Syr-daria, alongside Lake Aral and the Jaxartes or Syr-daria (river). The road passed through six small towns—namely, Orsk, Irghiz, Kazalinsk, Perovsk, Turkestan, and Chimkent—and many villages; but as a rule the white-painted station-houses, with their square court-yards for horses and vehicles, stood quite isolated in the desert, their nearest neighbor being probably a Kirghiz winter *aul* (tent-village). In the heart of the steppe some of the stations were primitive in the extreme, the station-house being merely a Kirghiz *yurt* (tent), surrounded by a hedge of rushes laced through branches of trees. But even these, like the rooms in the better stations, were embellished by a portrait of the Tsar, as well as provided with a leather sofa, chairs, and a table. In one corner hung an *ikon* (sacred image), with its censer, and there was a Testament on the table for the edification of the traveller. Every station between Orenburg and Orsk possessed a copy of the Bible, presented by the great traveller Przhevalsky.

The master of the posting-station, *staresta* or *starshina*, also called *piser*, or clerk, is always a Russian, and spends his life with his family in a state of terrible loneliness and isolation. The only break in their solitary existence is the advent of the post-courier, or when some traveller comes rolling along in his tarantass. But this touch with the outer world is short-lived. The traveller's one thought is to get away from the lonely house as quickly as possible. He orders fresh horses, drinks his glass of tea while they are being put to, and hastens away as fast as he can drive. The staresta receives from one hundred and fifty (£15) to two hundred and eighty (£28) roubles a year in salary, and has under him four *yamshtchiks*, or drivers, nearly always Tatars or Kirghiz. Neither is their lot to be envied; for they have to be ready to climb into their seats in all weathers and at all times, and

3

drive their *troika* (team of three horses) over the same road
which in rain or darkness, in scorching heat or wind, in cold
and snow, they have traversed a thousand times before.
They undoubtedly have a habit of dropping asleep as soon as
they get well started ; but in so doing they only follow the
example of their passengers, and it is easy to forgive them.
Each yamshtchik receives from sixty (£6) to sixty - five
roubles (£6 10*s*.) a year, and a monthly allowance of fifty-four
pounds avoirdupois of bread, and half a sheep.   Provisions,
and everything else that may be wanted at the station, are
brought at intervals by a special messenger, whose chief occupation it is to travel up and down the whole long line of
posting-stations.

The whole of the posting - road between Orenburg and
Tashkend is private property.   No *gosudarstvenny sbor*, or
"fee to the Crown," is paid at any of the stations between
Orenburg and Orsk, for the station-masters own their own
horses and vehicles.   For a part of the road between Tokan
and Terekli, which is owned by a merchant of Orenburg,
Miakinoff by name, a fee to the Crown of ten kopeks (2½*d*.)
per horse is demanded for each stage.   Payment of the entire distance to Terekli is made in Tokan.   From Terekli to
Tashkend a merchant named Ivanoff, belonging to the latter
place, is the owner of the post-road.   He pays the station-
masters and yamshtchiks, and provides horses and vehicles,
receiving payment for the entire distance at either of the terminal stations.

Everywhere I went people talked of the good old times
when this road was the only road leading to Russian Turkestan ; when numbers of travellers were continually going backward and forward ; and when every station had its nine or
ten troikas (some thirty horses).   General Skobeleff's campaign against the Turkomans, and Annenkoff's railway to
Samarcand, introduced a new order of things.   The mail-post
to Tashkend, and the large majority of travellers prefer the
new route, because it is shorter, cheaper, and more convenient, and the days of the old posting-road through the Kirghiz
steppe are numbered.   Travellers are now a rarity.   The

towns have lost both in importance and size. The once
flourishing vehicular traffic between Turkestan and Russia
has been diverted to other routes.   The caravans which carried cotton and wool to Orenburg have grown fewer and
fewer. The local post, combined with political and strategi-
cal interests, alone prevents this road from becoming entirely
disused.

During my short stay in Orenburg the vice-governor,
General Lomachevsky, placed at my disposal an honest old
chinovnik, Solovioff by name, who had seen forty-five years'
service in the town. With his help I was able to procure
everything I required both well and cheaply. I bought a
perfectly new tarantass, roomy and strong, and provided with
thick iron rims round the wheels, for seventy-five roubles
(£7 10s.); I subsequently sold it in Margelan for fifty (£5).
It was an easy matter to stow myself and my luggage (about
six cwt.) away in it; and for nineteen days and nights without a break it was my only habitation.

CHAPTER IV

ACROSS THE KIRGHIZ STEPPES

On November 14th a *buran* (snow-storm), the first of the winter, raged in Orenburg, and the thermometer at mid-day sank to 21.2° Fahr. (−6° C.). As everything was ready, however, I did not postpone my departure. My trunks and ammunition-cases were all sewn up in matting, and lashed with strong rope on the back of the tarantass and in front of the driver's seat. Bags which were likely to be in constant use, cameras, and boxes of provisions, together with carpets, cushions, and furs were all crammed inside. The wheels were well greased, and the first troika of horses harnessed. It was, however, evening before everything was quite ready for a start. General Lomachevsky and the inmates of the hotel kindly bade me God-speed. The heavy carriage rolled through the gates of the court-yard, and its jingling bells began to echo merrily through the streets of Orenburg. Before dark we reached the edge of the barren steppe. The wind howled and whistled round the hood of the carriage, and drove clouds of powdery snow in our faces. By degrees, however, the wind went down, and the stars came out and lighted up the thin mantle of snow with which the whole country was covered.

In Nexhinka I was overtaken by the post, which goes to Tashkend twice a week. As it only conveys the local mails, there were but two troikas; the mail-bags, however, weighed in the aggregate between 16 and 17 cwt. The first postilion only goes as far as Orsk. From that place another courier conveys the post to Irghiz, a third takes it to Kazalinsk, a fourth to Perovsk, a fifth to Turkestan, and the last to Tashkend. We joined company as far as Orsk, and shortly afterwards our three heavily laden troikas set off from the station-house. The road to Kamenaya Osernaya was hilly and heavy, but later on the country became leveller, the snow-storm abated, and the road was often bare. On the way to Gherial we met the first wayfarers we had fallen in with—namely, a caravan of a hundred camels or so, conveying bales of cotton from Orsk to Orenburg. The train with its Kirghiz attendants made a very picturesque appearance in the desolate landscape. About this time the axle of one of the post-telegas came to grief, and the vehicle had to be left behind. My luggage, too, owing to the incessant chafing and shaking, got loose, and had to be refastened. The sky was cloudy; it was blowing, but not snowing. The temperature was 27.5° Fahr. (−2.5° C.). The river Ural was not yet visible, but we crossed several of its tributaries by means of small wooden bridges. There were numerous small stanitsas (forts) in the neighborhood, garrisoned by Orenburg Cossacks.

At Krasnogornaya, which we reached at daybreak, we stopped for breakfast. The postilion, a stalwart, shaggy old Russian, bemoaned that it was a fast day, when all flesh, with the exception of fish, is forbidden. Great, therefore, was his surprise and delight when I offered him a tin of preserved sturgeon. He made alarmingly short work of it, and consumed eleven glasses of tea in a quarter of an hour. He told me that during the past twenty years he had made the journey to and fro between Orenburg and Orsk (175 miles) thirty-five times a year—that is to say, a distance which exceeds the space between the earth and the moon by more than six thousand miles.

In Verkhne Osernaya, a large village, with a church in the middle, prettily situated near a ravine, the women were offering for sale shawls woven of goats' wool. They resembled Kashmir shawls, and could be pulled through a ring.

Steppes! Nothing but steppes, though there were mountains in the distance. The road follows the frozen, snow-sheeted river Ural. Except for an occasional Kirghiz yurt (tent), the landscape was desolate in the extreme, and the distances between the stations long. But the incessant jolting

over the hard-frozen ground and the monotonous jingling
the horses' bells had a somnolent effect, and time after tir
I dropped off to sleep.

At Podgornaya the country became more broken. O
next stopping-place was in the Guberla Mountains. The

MY TARANTASS WITH A TROIKA (TEAM OF THREE HORSES)

I took a four-in-hand (*chetvorka*) and drove up hill and dov
dale, twice crossing the broad river Guberla. Along th
stage an accident once happened to a Russian officer, h
driver being killed, since then railings have been put up
all the more dangerous places.

At some of the better stations we met great droves
cattle, chiefly oxen, being driven to Orenburg, and then
farther on into Russia. After forty-eight hours' travellii
we eventually reached Orsk, a place of 20,000 inhabitan
situated on the left bank of the river Ural and on the rig
bank of the Or. It stands therefore on Asiatic ground, a

is entered by a narrow wooden bridge thrown across the majestic stream of the river Ural. The houses cluster round an isolated and commanding hill, crowned by a clock-tower, from which a watch is kept at night in case of fire. The view is very extensive. Low mountains are visible in the vicinity. The country is only flat towards the southwest, where runs the road towards Tashkend. The *sobor* (governor's house), institutions and schools, post, telegraph, and bazaars are situated between the river Ural and the hill; there, too, the merchants and burghers have their houses. On the south side of the hill dwell the poorer classes, the peasantry, Tatars, and Kirghiz.

It was intended to erect the chief church of the town on the top of the hill, and the foundations are even partially laid; but the necessary funds were not forthcoming, and the work was discontinued. The church would have been visible for many a mile in both Europe and Asia.

During the spring the Ural rises to a great height, and sometimes inundates the lower parts of Orsk, as well as forms vast lakes in the vicinity. The inhabitants then climb their hill to admire the transformation of the steppe into a sea. When the ice begins to melt in the spring it destroys the bridge, which is simply built on poles, so that it has to be rebuilt every year. At such times the post is carried across the river in boats.

Between the river Ural, the Caspian Sea, Lake Aral, the Syr-daria, and the Irtysh stretches the vast level of the Kirghiz steppe. Thinly inhabited by Kirghiz nomads, the steppe is also the home of a few species of animals, such as wolves, foxes, antelopes, hares, etc., and there, too, certain prickly steppe plants struggle against the inclement conditions of the region. Where there is sufficient moisture, *kamish*, or reeds, grow in great quantities; and even the driest sandy wastes are diversified by the tufted bushes of the saksaul (*Anabasis ammodendron*), often attaining six or seven feet in height. The roots, which are excessively hard, provide the chief fuel of the Kirghiz, and are collected during the autumn for winter use. At nearly every aul (tent-

... big stacks of them, and we frequently met
... conveying nothing else.

... then the steppe was traversed by water-
... at this season of the year they were gener-
... into small salt lakes, on whose shores in-
... of passage congregate in spring and autumn.
... these streams that the Kirghiz pitch their
... black tents (uy) and sheds made of kamish.
... the other hand, are huts built of clay or
... they move northward, with their herds
... the oppressive heat, and to find pasturage
... up by the sun. Many Kirghiz own as
... of sheep and 500 horses, and are then
... very good circumstances. The winters
... bitterly cold. During the months of
... snow-storms rage with unmitigated
... then seek their old winter settlements,
... in pens hedged round with reeds. In
... typically continental.

... half-savage people, but capable, healthy.
... they love to call themselves Kaisak—i.e.,
... content with their lonely life on the
... recognize no authority, and despise
... or labor at agriculture. In the
... their lot is a hard one. Their herds
... of subsistence, providing them with
... scanty vegetation and the soil itself
... their dwellings. The long, glowing
... protect them against the cold of winter.
... very rich; when they talk together
... comprehension by very vivacious gest-
... devoted love for their desolate steppe.
... lived the life of freedom, and find it
... although the stranger seeks in vain for
... rest his eye. It is true that, like the
... and impressive; but it is utterly
... melancholy. I drove across it, day in, day
... but the landscape always remained the

same. The tarantass was always the centre of a vast expanse without boundary or horizon, so vast indeed that it seemed almost possible to discern the globular shape of the earth. Spring is the only season in which it can afford the stranger any pleasure to visit these regions. The air is then perfumed with the delicious scent of flowers; for vegetation develops with incredible rapidity, in order to make the most of the short space of time before the burning sun of summer comes to scorch everything up.

As might be supposed from the physical conditions of the region in which they live, the sense of locality and power of

KIRGHIZ CAMEL-RIDER ON THE STEPPES

vision displayed by the Kirghiz are developed to a high degree of keenness and exactitude. In a country across which the stranger may travel for days and days without, so far as he can perceive, anything to vary its uniform flatness, and across which there is not the slightest indication of a road, the Kirghiz finds his way, even at night, with unerring certainty. Nor do the heavenly bodies serve him as a guide. He recognizes every plant, every stone; he notices the places

... grass grow more thinly or more closely
... he observes irregularities in the surfa
... could not discover without an instrume
... the color of a horse on the horizon lo
... with the best will in the world, is ev
... presence; and he can tell whether a ca
... through a field-glass appears to be a me
... advancing or receding.

... was well greased, the baggage
... crept into my moving domicile. T
... horses; the troika set off with lig
... and — farewell to Europe! At t
... paid forty-four roubles (£4 8s.) to
... entire journey of 320 miles to Juli
... show the receipt. Between Ore
... miles; thirty-four roubles, or £3 8
... separately.

... posting-road followed the right bank of t
... almost imperceptibly diversified count
... Buguti-sai, near which there was a Kirgl
... inhabitants did not seem to be particula
... as I had my two cameras with r
... if the bigger one was a gun; a
... them to group themselves in front
... succeed in getting some of them to sit

... at Buguti-sai, we finally left the valley
... threw a silvery glamour over the lon
... here and there with snow, but there w
... our settlements to be seen. The silence
... by the sound of the horses' bells, the sho
... the crunching of the snow as the wheels
... pounded over it.

... were all exactly alike—plain wood
... painted red, with a flight of steps in
... wall, leading up to the principal do
... steps was a pole for a lantern, and on
... giving the distances to the two near

stations. From the entrance-passage you passed into the station-master's room on the right, and on the left into the parlor for travellers. The latter was furnished with two sofas, two tables, a mirror, a good many chairs, and a large stove, in which the dried roots of the steppe plants were always burning. The fuel was kept piled up by the side of enormous hay-stacks, a short distance from the house. In the large square yard at the back were a number of carts and sledges; and there also were the stables and a room for the drivers.

At the station of Tamdi I rested for some hours during the night, and in the morning saw on the ice of the Tamdi stream the tracks of a number of wolves, which had been bold enough to enter the yard and steal three of the staresta's geese. The thermometer showed 4.1° Fahr. (- 15.5° C.), and the thin snow crackled under the wheels of the tarantass when we drove off in the early morning. Every blade of grass was feathered with hoar-frost, and it was bitterly cold.

The first Russian " town " we passed on Asiatic soil was Kara-butak, which, like Rome, is built on seven hills, though

THE " TOWN " OF KARA-BUTAK

it is somewhat smaller than the latter, as it only consists
thirty-three houses, inhabited by thirty odd Russians, about
hundred Tatars, and a few Kirghiz.   The only claim whi
Kara-butak possesses to notice lies in the fact that it is
small fort, erected twenty-five years ago by General Obr
tcheff, to keep in check the Kirghiz, who were then harryii
the Russian frontier.   The *vayenny natyalnik*, or commandai
in command of eighty-four men, told me that his life the
was no better than transportation, and that he could not e
dure it for longer than one year.   His only distractions we
reading, shooting-matches with the soldiers, and sport.
had been very different in the days when there was a dai
post.   There were several large Kirghiz settlements in t
vicinity, and several others all the way to Irghiz, but sou
of that place they became rarer and rarer, until they ceas
altogether on the border of the Desert of Kara-kum.

The road to Irghiz ran for the most part close beside ti
Irghiz River, at that time of the year almost dried up.   V
crossed it between the stations of Kum-sai and Kara-s
On we went day and night across the monotonous stepp
drawn by the swift post-horses.   By this time I had becor
so used to travelling in a tarantass that I found no difficul
in sleeping at night, rolled up in my rugs and furs at t
bottom of the vehicle, and only awoke when we sudden
pulled up before a new station-house.   Having shown n
receipt to the staresta, and put to fresh horses, we we
soon on the road again.   An awakening of this kind in t
middle of the night, with the thermometer only 5° Fal
above zero (−15° C.), is anything but exhilarating; you a
stiff and bruised and sleepy, and long for a glass of tea.   /
last the sun rises above the horizon, floods the steppe wi
its golden rays, melting the rime-frost which during the nig
has decked the grass with its delicate white down, and drivii
the wolves from the posting-road.

A few more stations and we reached Irghiz, standing on ;
eminence overlooking the river of the same name, west of t
point where it runs into the salt lake Chalkartenis.   Irghiz
a *ukreplenye* (fort), and its commandant a *uyäsdny natyaln*

or chief administrative officer of the district. The place has a small church, and about a thousand inhabitants, including the garrison of a hundred and fifty men, of whom seventy were Orenburg Cossacks. The greater number of the inhabitants were Sart merchants, who come there periodically

HARNESSING A TROIKA

to barter with the Kirghiz. They bring their wares from Orenburg, Moscow, and Nizhni - Novgorod. Irghiz was founded in 1848 by the Russians, and, like Kara-butak and Turgai, is entirely Russian. It was one of the forts erected immediately after the occupation of the steppe, in 1845, for the pacification of the Kirghiz. At first the whole of the steppe region was subject to the governor-general of Orenburg, but afterwards was divided between the provinces of Turgai and Syr-daria, at the same time that Ordenburg was made a "government." Before the Russian occupation Irghiz was called Yar-mollah (the Holy Grave on the Terrace), and was merely an unimportant Kirghiz burial-place and resort for pilgrims. After the Russian conquest of Turkestan, this place, like others in the same region, increased in importance, and the larger caravans began to make it a halting-place. Fewer caravans visit it now; still there were some lying outside the village. The reason why we never met with them on the posting-road was that they take shorter and quicker routes. The traffic with the Kirghiz flourishes more particularly at Troitsk and Uralsk, for it is in the neighborhood of these towns that the richest nomad auls exist.

Off we went again with our four-in-hand. The sun set about five o'clock; and as he lingered for a moment, like a fiery cannon-ball, on the distant horizon, a subdued purple radiance was diffused across the steppe. At that hour the light produced very extraordinary effects. Having nothing with which to make comparisons, you are liable to fall into the strangest blunders with regard to size and distance. A couple of inoffensive crows hobnobbing together a short distance from the road appeared as large as camels, and a tuft of steppe grass, not more than a foot in height, looked as big as a vigorous tree. After the sun disappeared, the purple tints changed to violet and light blue; and in a few minutes these gave place to still darker shades, which finally merged into the darkness of the night. The night, however, did not get very black, for the air was pure and clear; the stars shone out like electric lamps, and the moon poured her silver glamour over the scene.

At Ak-sai, at 1 A.M. on November 21st, I noted the lowest temperature, − 3.1° Fahr. (− 19.5° C.), we had during the journey. The countless facets of the hoar-frost shimmered in the moonlight, and the windows of the station-house were transfigured with the lacelike trees and flowers of frost.

The stage to Terekli was the longest of the whole journey, amounting to 22½ miles; in the course of it we crossed the boundary between the provinces of Turgai and Syr-daria. At Juluz, the first station belonging to the merchant Ivanoff, which had a comfortable room for travellers, I paid twenty-five roubles (£2 10s.) for the 150 miles to Kazalinsk.

CHAPTER V

FROM LAKE ARAL TO TASHKEND

Four miles north of Terekli we plunged into the Desert of Kara-kum (the Black Sand). Vegetation grew scantier and scantier, and in a short time we were immersed in an ocean of sand. This region was at one time covered by the waters of the Aralo-Caspian Sea, a fact evidenced by the prevalence of shells of *Cardium* and *Mytilus*, which are said to have been found far in the desert.

It was a moonlight night when I arrived at the little station of Konstantinovskaya, where the travellers' "room" was merely a Kirghiz *kibitka* (tent), not very inviting at that period of the year. From this place to Kamishli-bash, a distance of eighty miles, Bactrian camels are generally used, as horses are not strong enough to drag the conveyances through the *barkhans*, or sand-hills, which occur along that portion of the route.

I had not been waiting many minutes at Konstantinovskaya when I heard a well-known gurgling sound, and the fantastic silhouettes of three majestic camels became visible in the moonlight. They were harnessed all three abreast to the tarantass, and, when the driver whistled, set off at a steady trot. Their pace was swift and even, and they often broke into a gallop.

Ere long I noticed that the surface gradually sloped towards the southwest. A thick bank of vapor hung over Lake Aral in the same direction; while in the north and east the sky was clear. Between the stations of Alti-kuduk and Ak-julpas the road ran close by the side of the lake, often not more than half a dozen paces from it. The fine yellow sand was so hard and compact that the camels' hoofs left scarcely a perceptible trace; but farther up it rose into sand-hills, and there the tarantass sank in up to the axles.

Lake Aral lies 157 feet above the level of the sea; and its area is 27,000 square miles, ten times the size of Lake Wener, or nearly the same size as Scotland. The shores of the lake are barren and desolate, its depth inconsiderable, and the water so salt that it cannot be used for drinking purposes except at the mouths of the rivers; but far out in the lake there are said to exist certain fresh-water belts. Close to the shore

THE STATION OF KONSTANTINOVSKAYA

at the northeast end is the station of Ak-julpaz, and near it a low ridge of sand, on the top of which the Kirghiz have made a burying-place, with square tombs built of slabs of stone. Eight years ago the station stood on the actual shore. But at certain seasons it was threatened by inundation and became entirely cut off from the posting-road; it was therefore moved about half a mile farther inland. When there is a high wind from the southwest the water is driven up the bay towards the desert, and overflows the shore for great distances, filling up all the hollows and depressions of the ground. In these pools sturgeon and other fish may be caught with the hand. At the time of which I write, the bay was frozen over, and at a distance of some miles from the shore I saw a caravan crossing the glassy ice. The

ame passage is also used in summer, for the water is then
extremely shallow, not more than seven feet at its deepest,
and in most places only two or three feet. During the
warm season of the year, when the sand is dry, it is blown
by the wind in the direction of the lake, continually changing the coast - line, filling up the creeks, and forming sand-
spits, islets, and sand - banks. The coast is bordered by

MY TARANTASS DRAWN BY THREE CAMELS

a number of salt lagoons, called by the Russians *solonets*,
which, however, are generally dry in summer. They are
former creeks or bays which have been cut off from the
great lake by the drift-sand. The fishing in these lagoons
is first-rate; the Ural Cossacks, who engage in it, lay their
nets at a distance of ten or a dozen miles from the shore.
When the water is frozen they use sledges or camels to
reach their fishing-holes in the ice; at other times they row
out in boats of a moderate size.

The climate in these tracts is good. The summer heat is
tempered by the proximity to Lake Aral, while in the winter

I—I

the cold is seldom severe; but, on the other hand, rain and thick mists are common phenomena. At the time of my visit it rained continuously, so that in many places the road was covered with broad pools. The water splashed and spouted up as the camels tramped through it; the convey-ance threatened every moment to stick fast in the moist, tenacious sand; and the rain pattered ceaselessly on the tilt.

THE KIRGHIZ STEPPE, NEAR LAKE ARAL.

When, at nine o'clock on the evening of November 23d, the temperature rose to 31.1° Fahr. (—0.5° C.), the air seemed to be quite warm.

As a rule, the camels were obedient and docile, and the driver was able to keep on his seat; but one or two of the teams became cantankerous, and insisted on going their own way, so that the postilion was obliged to ride the mid-dle animal. The reins are fastened to a piece of wood in-serted through the nostrils, and in this cruel manner the beasts are compelled to obey.

Strange as it had been to drive with camels, it was with a feeling of relief that I again saw three black horses being

harnessed to the tarantass. My joy was short-lived, however;
for before we got half-way to the next station the vehicle
stuck fast in a salt marsh, and, in spite of our utmost exertions, could neither be dragged backward nor forward.
The driver shouted and lashed with his whip, the horses
flung out, and stumbled, and broke their traces. But it
was all no use. The driver had to unharness one of them
and ride back to the station for help.

After a couple of hours' waiting in the rain, wind, and
darkness, wondering whether the wolves would come and
pay me a visit, I was joined by a couple of Kirghiz, who
harnessed two fresh horses in front of the troika, thus making a *patyorka*, or team of five. Their united exertions at
length succeeded in extricating the vehicle from its sandy
bed, into which it had sunk deeper and deeper. When at last
we got under way again and rolled off across the steppe,
large cakes of wet sand and clay hung dripping from the wheels.

At Yunyskaya, the last station before we reached the Syr-
daria, I stopped awhile during the night of the 24th; but
as I was drinking my tea a violent buran (snow-storm) came
on, smothering everything in fine, driving snow. The tarantass was covered over with tarpaulins, and there was no
alternative but to wait till daybreak. The road was so bad
the last two stages before reaching Kazalinsk that I was
obliged to drive after the patyorka and engage an extra man
to ride on the near leader.

Kazalinsk stands on the right bank of the Syr-daria, 110
miles by river and 50 miles by road, from Lake Aral. It
consisted of 600 houses, of which 200 were inhabited by
Russians, and had 3500 inhabitants, of whom 1000 (their
families included) were Ural Cossacks. The rest of the
population was made up of Sarts, Bokharans, Tatars, Kirghiz, and a few Jews. The richest merchants were natives of
Bokhara; the Kirghiz, on the other hand, being poor. Their
more wealthy kinsmen live on the steppe, and derive their
riches from their herds. In the month of May, when the
pasturage is good, countless sheep are driven to Orenburg
to be sold.

At the time of the Russian advance upon Khiva, Kazalinsk had a certain claim to importance as a depot and fortified place. The Lake Aral fleet of five small steamers made
this place their station, and the garrison consisted of a whole
battalion. The town has now a garrison of only twenty-four
men and two launches, the other vessels having been moved
to Charjui on the Amu-daria. There is no longer any life

MY TARANTASS DRAWN BY A PATVORKA (TEAM OF FIVE HORSES)

or movement in the place. The whirring sails of the wind-
mills and the numerous fishing-boats on the lake were the
only objects which gave relief or color to the monotony of
the scene. The streets of the town were at that season of
the year impassable, even to the wearer of water-proof boots
reaching to the knee. The Russian houses were built of
bricks, and were low and white; those of the Sarts, Bokharans, and Kirghiz of dried clay, and were gray and dilapidated, and often surrounded by long and dreary-looking
walls. There were two schools, a church, and some public
buildings, the residence of the chief of the district (*uyásdny*

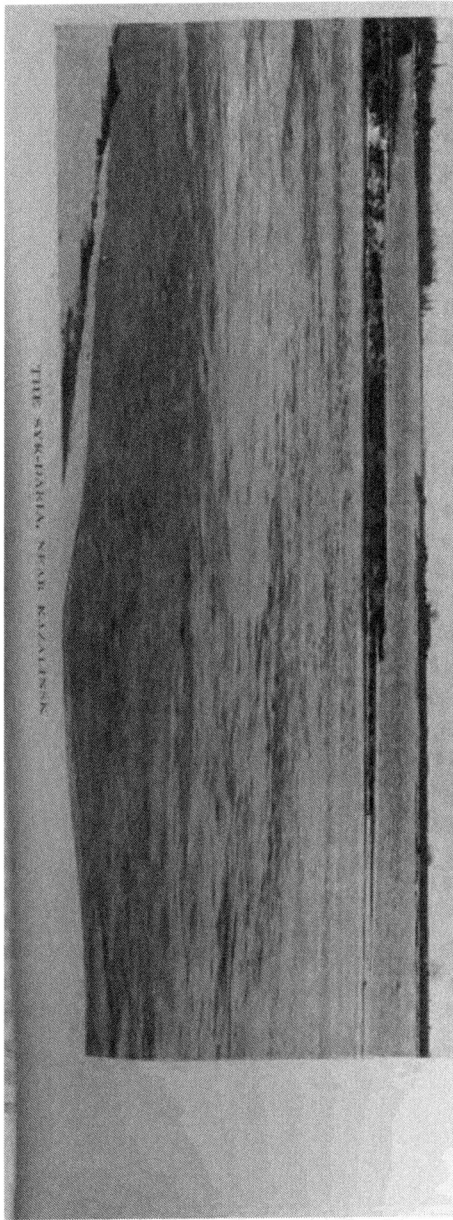

THE SYR-DARIA, NEAR KAZALINSK

natyalnik) being the most important.   Each was surrounded by a grove of fine silver poplars, in the tops of which a host of crows kept up an incessant chatter.

The Ural Cossacks have the exclusive right of fishing in the river.   They confine themselves principally to its estuary; the previous year (1892) they had taken 14,000 sturgeon.   At the time of my visit the river was expected to freeze every day; and as it often becomes frost-bound in a single night, the fishermen had already beached their boats.   Higher up, the adjacent land does not rise much above the level of the current, so that a hard, frosty night often inundates extensive tracts of country.   The water, flowing over the ice, freezes again thicker than before, and so compels the stream to find another course.   Sometimes this puts a stop to traffic, for the inundated tracts can be crossed neither on horseback nor with *arba* (cart), and the post-troikas are compelled to make long détours into the steppe.

Accompanied by seven Cossacks, I made a short excursion for the purpose of examining the current, etc., of the river.   Near the fort, on the right bank, we found a depth of not less than forty-nine feet.   The volume of water was just now the lowest that had been observed for fifteen years. In the months of July and August the stream is highest, and it gradually sinks during the autumn.   The water was a yellowish-gray color, but good to drink.

The climate of Kazalinsk is also influenced by the proximity of Lake Aral, although in the winter the thermometer sinks as low as from $-22°$ to $-31°$ Fahr. ($-30°$ to $-35°$ C.). The snowfall is inconsiderable, and the snow disappears quickly; for this reason sledging is not common.   At the time of my visit there was a good deal of mist and fine rain.   I paid forty-nine roubles (£4 18s.) there for the 240 miles, and for four horses, to Perovsk; and in the latter town, for the 385 miles and for three horses to Tashkend, sixtyone roubles (£6 2s.).

As I had nothing further to do in Kazalinsk, I continued my journey up beside the stream with the patyorka.   The alluvial soil of yellow clay was as flat as the top of a table, and at short distances clay mounds, with a bunch of kamish (reeds) on the top have been built to guide the yamshtchiks (post-drivers) in the winter, when everything is buried under the snow, and it is impossible to discern any trace of the road. These mounds are the beacons and sea-marks of the desert ocean. The scene was as desolate as ever, neither

ANOTHER VIEW OF THE SYR-DARIA NEAR KAZALINSK

people nor habitations being met with during the whole day's journey, except a couple of Kirghiz on horseback, driving a hundred camels or so into the steppe. The noble Syr-daria was the only other object which arrested the attention.

The road followed the bank of the Jaxartes (Syr-daria) as far as the unimportant garrison town of Karmakchi, generally called by the Russians Fort No. 2. It consisted of seventy Mohammedan (native) and nine Russian houses. At this place we again turned into the steppe, to make the détour round the extensive marshes of Bokali-kopa, which are annually inundated by the Syr-daria. In this region we passed the two poorest stations of the whole journey—namely, Alexandrovskaya and Semionnovskaya — each consisting of not more than three Kirghiz yurts—one for the staresta, one for

travellers, and one for the post-drivers and their families.
The former place contained also four-legged inhabitants—a
number of big rats running unconcernedly backward and
forward across the felt carpets. The station was surrounded
by a reed wall, outside which tarantasses and telegas stood in
a row.

For several stages the road had run through a barren
waste, where nothing grew except a few thinly scattered sak-
sauls. We now entered a region which bore traces of recent
inundation, and where the kamish (reeds) grew high and
thick.

All the way from Fort Perovsk—which is situated on the
bank of the Jaxartes, and in every way resembles Kazalinsk,
except in being cleaner—to the station of Chumen-arik, vegetation was very abundant. It consisted of kamish, saksaul,
and prickly shrubs, which grew in thickets, forming a veritable jungle, and through which the road often wound in a sort
of narrow tunnel. This was a favorite haunt of tigers, wild
boar, and gazelles; and there were geese, wild ducks, and,
above all, immense numbers of pheasants. These last were
so bold that they sat by the side of the road and calmly
contemplated the passer-by; but the moment we stopped to
fire they rose with whirring wings. Their delicate white flesh
was indeed a welcome addition to my bill of fare, the more
so as my provisions, so far as delicacies were concerned, had
very nearly come to an end. The Kirghiz shoot the pheasants with wretched muzzle-loaders, and sell them generally
for six (1½d.) or seven kopeks (1¾d.) apiece. They charged
me, however, ten or twelve (3d.) kopeks. In Orenburg a
pheasant costs as much as a rouble and a half (3s.); in St.
Petersburg, two or three. Officers and lovers of sport from
Tashkend often visit this sportsman's El Dorado, and always
return with a good bag.

The station-house at Julsk was built only ten yards or so
from the river-bank, and is annually threatened with inundation. Between that place and Mesheh-uli the country was
rather broken. We crossed some narrow sand-belts, then
some canals and dried-up watercourses by means of wooden

bridges. All this part of the road was strewn with dried reeds, to prevent vehicles from sinking into the mud during the rainy season. At the time of my journey the ground was hard and lumpy, owing to the frost. Here the Kirghiz again became numerous. We frequently passed their auls, and saw their herds grazing among the thickets.

A MISERABLE STATION NEAR THE SYR-DARIA

On November 29th the sunset was very beautiful. The heavens in the west glowed as from the reflection of a prairie fire, and against it the gnarled and tufted branches of the saksaul stood out in inky blackness. The whole steppe was lit up by a magic, fiery glow, while in the east the sombre desert vegetation was bathed in gold.

A railway journey is certainly a very much more convenient mode of locomotion than driving in a tarantass. In the former you have no need to trouble yourself about the friction of the wheels or the safety of the axles; in a tarantass, on the contrary, you must always be prepared for contingencies of the kind, and be continually inspecting the vehicle. My astonishment may easily be imagined when, on examining the carriage at Mesheh-uli, I found that the front axle was snapped right across, and only held by four screws,

The staresta gave me the comforting consolation that I should find a blacksmith at the town of Turkestan, about 120 miles farther on, and he thought that the evil moment might be postponed if the driver went very slowly downhill.

Yani-kurgan, a Kirghiz village, with a caravanserai and the ruins of an old Kokand fortress, was situated immediately on the bank of the Syr-daria. The road in places was miserable, and I sat on thorns, expecting the axle to give way every minute, which would have been anything but pleasant in the middle of the steppe. The endless monotony of the landscape was at this stage somewhat relieved by the Kara-tau Mountains, which became visible on the left, looking like a low wall.

At Tash-suat, where the Syr-daria flowed in a broad, stately stream, visible to a great distance, we left the river on the right hand, and directed our course for the old city of Turkestan. The vegetation once more became extremely scanty; but along the hard, level road, which not even the continuous fall of rain had succeeded in spoiling, we met a number of caravans travelling at a steady pace.

At last we came within sight of the gardens of Turkestan, with its tall poplars, long, gray, clay walls, in part new, though mostly old and ruinous, and its magnificent saint's tomb dating from the time of Tamerlane (fourteenth century). We were soon driving through the empty bazaar—it was a Friday (December 1st), the Mohammedan Sabbath—to the station-house, where a Kirghiz smith at once set to work to mend the broken axle of the tarantass.

Turkestan, which was conquered in 1864 by General Chernyayeff, is at all times a ruinous and uninteresting town, but in the rain and mist it became actually disagreeable. The only object that could at all justify a delay of a few hours is the colossal burial mosque, erected in 1397 by Tamerlane in memory of a Kirghiz saint, Hazrett Sultan Khoja Ahmed Yasovi. Its *pishtak*, or arched façade, is unusually high, and is flanked by two picturesque towers. The mosque is further embellished by several melon-shaped domes. All the tiles have fallen off the façade, but on the longer wall and the back wall of the rectangular building, they are still intact. Their iridescent shades of blue and green resemble the tiles one sees at Samarkand. The mosque abuts upon the quadrangular clay fortress wall, which Khodiar Khan caused to be built; and within this also the Russian barracks are situated. Guided by some Sart boys, I threaded my way through a labyrinth of narrow lanes, and up the dark, chilly staircase leading to the summit of one of the towers, whence there was a splendid view over Turkestan and the neighboring country. In my case, however, it was considerably veiled and restricted by the heavy rain that was falling. The usual melancholy impression of the East made itself felt even here. The monuments of ancient architecture fettered me by their beauty and impressed me by reason of their age; but the modern houses were nothing better than miserable mud huts, with flat roofs, divided from each other by narrow, crooked lanes.

As I said before, it was the Mohammedan Sabbath, and I went to see the mosque just as service (*namaz*) was about to begin. Numbers of Sarts in gay-colored coats and white turbans gathered outside; then, removing their hard, clattering, heavy boots at the entrance, they solemnly filed into the huge mosque. The middle of the floor was occupied by a large copper bowl, flanked by a number of *tughs—i.e.*, tufts of black horse-hair on long sticks. The walls were plastered white, and inscribed with proverbs. I was politely motioned out by an old *akhun* (attendant) when the summons to prayer was called at the entrance; but I went up into one of the galleries, whence, unseen and unsuspected, I could observe the long rows of kneeling and bowing Sarts—a striking picture, which put me in mind of the nights of Ramadan in Constantinople.

The first two stages from Turkestan were extremely dirty and rugged; it was without comparison the stiffest piece of road on the whole journey. Between Ikan and Nagai-kura we literally stuck fast in the mud. I am not superstitious, but it was the thirteenth stage from Tashkend, and we had still thirteen versts (8½ miles) to Nagai-kura. It was impos-

sible to move the horses. The shaft-horse reared and became unmanageable; while the other two had apparently
made up their minds to kick the tarantass to pieces. It was
midnight, and pitch dark. There was nothing for it but to
send the yamshtchik back to Ikan for a couple of extra
horses. Meanwhile I went to sleep and slept for three hours,
only awaking when the "five-in-hand" were hard at work
hauling us out of the mud. It had taken us 6½ hours to do
a paltry fourteen miles.

The country from Aris to Buru-jar was very much broken,
and it was considered advisable to keep on the team of five.
The pace downhill was terrific; the horses fairly laid themselves flat with the ground, so that the air whistled past our
ears. Now and again we sped past a village, a horseman, or
a caravan, or a big lumbering arba (high-wheeled Turkestan
cart) with its wheels literally fast embedded in the mud.

At intervals along the road there were small pyramids of
sun-dried clay, intended to serve as sign-posts in the winter.
You would suppose that the telegraph-posts would be sufficient for that purpose; but the road wound now to the right,
now to the left of them, and after a heavy fall of snow they are
altogether buried from sight. The post-couriers, therefore,
who are not under any circumstances allowed to stop or
wait, often have an adventurous time of it when crossing the
steppe in a snow-storm. From one telegraph-post it is often
impossible to discern the next, and they may easily lose their
way while going from one to the other. It not infrequently
happens that the post-troikas, when overtaken by a snow-
storm, are forced to spend the night in the snow-drifts and
wait till the storm abates or day breaks.

The Aris is quite a respectable river. It was formerly
crossed on high-wheeled arbas; but a few weeks before my
arrival a ferry had been started. The equipage with its
patyorka was placed on long boats lashed together, and was
hauled across the river by the ferry-men pulling at a thick
rope stretched from bank to bank.

Beyond Buru-jar numerous ravines and steep slopes were
encountered. Going downhill the yamshtchik held in the

middle or shaft horse as hard as he could, for on that animal rested the entire weight of the carriage; but as soon as it became too much for him he let him go, and the momentum carried down the tarantass at a terrific pace, so that it was as

CROSSING THE RIVER ARIS

much as ever the horses could do to keep their feet. The other two horses, which were harnessed in front of the troika with loose traces, had to keep a sharp lookout so as not to be run into by the shafts; if the near horse, with its rider, had gone down, he would almost certainly have been run over by the heavy tarantass.

All went well, however, although our lives often seemed to be in jeopardy; the horses were sure-footed and the men reliable and careful. At one of the stations one of the side horses of the troika became unmanageable, kicked and reared, and would on no account let himself be harnessed. It took six men to hold him—two on each side, one at his head, and one at his tail; and when at last he was harnessed and let go, he started off at a furious pace, so that his eyes blazed and sparks flew from his hoofs. Just as darkness was coming on we reached the town of Chimkent, the first place that was familiar to me from my former journey. The streets were silent and deserted; everything was quiet, although lamps and candles were shining through the windows.

GENERAL VIEW OF TASHKEND

We were now nearing Tashkend (Tashkent), where the governor-general of the province resides. Two more long stages, through mud a foot deep, and there was only a short piece of the road left. The way seemed to be endless, although the road was now very good. I had had enough of tarantass driving, and it was with a feeling of real pleasure that I turned into the streets of Tashkend, shortly after midnight on December 4th, and secured a couple of comfortable rooms at the Ilkin Hotel.

Thus ended my nineteen days' drive, in the course of which I had covered 1300 miles and passed over 11½ degrees of latitude. I had watched the days growing longer, although midwinter was approaching, and had left behind me a region that was swept by snow-storms, and where winter was in full career. At the beginning of the journey the thermometer was three to four degrees below zero Fahr. (− 19.5° C.), and I had now reached a land where spring seemed to be approaching, for the soft, balmy air made it a pleasure to be out-of-doors, and the thermometer showed 50° to 55° Fahr. (10° to 12° C.).

I.—5

CHAPTER VI

FROM TASHKEND TO MARGELAN

I SPENT nearly seven weeks in Tashkend; but as I have already described the town in my former book, I will only record here one or two special reminiscences. The governor-general, Baron Vrevsky, received me with boundless hospitality; I was his daily guest, and enjoyed the opportunity of making acquaintances who were of great assistance to me in my journey across the Pamirs.

During Christmas and New-year I was a guest at many festivities. Christmas Eve, the first and pleasantest during my travels in Asia, I spent at the residence of Baron Vrevsky in almost the same manner as at home in the North. Many of the Christmas presents laid out awaiting their future owners were accompanied with French verses; and in the middle of one of the rooms of the palace stood a gigantic Christmas tree, made of cypress branches, and decorated with a hundred tiny wax candles. We spent the evening in the customary way—in conversation, by a smoking samovar in the drawing-room, which was tastefully furnished with all the luxury of the East. Portraits of King Oscar, the Tsar, and the Emir of Bokhara, each signed with the autograph of the original, adorned the walls. The fair sex could not have been represented more worthily than by the Princess Khavansky, the governor-general's charming daughter, who did the honors at all entertainments, private as well as official, with grace and dignity.

Christmas Eve was kept *en famille*; but for New-year's Eve Baron Vrevsky invited some thirty guests to his house. As midnight approached, champagne was served round, and silent and with uplifted glasses we awaited the striking

A VIEW OF A VILLAGE.

of the clock. As the New-year came in, the words "*S'*
novom godom !" ("A Happy New-year to you!") were spoken
to right and to left by each person.

On January 2d the usual official dinner was given in the
banqueting-hall of the palace. The guests were all civil
and military officials of high rank, the emissary of the Emir
of Bokhara, the three chief kadis or judges of the Sarts in
Tashkend, and so forth. Every year the Emir of Bokhara
sends a special emissary to convey to the governor-general
the compliments of the season. This year it was the handsome, black-bearded Tajik, Shadi Beg Karaol Begi Shigaol,
whom the Emir sent to welcome me when I crossed the
frontier between Samarkand and Bokhara two years previously.

According to custom, Shadi Beg brought with him presents amounting in value to over eleven hundred pounds.
In this case they consisted of eight horses, with handsome
saddle-cloths of red and blue satin embroidered in gold and
silver, carpets, cloths, ornaments, and several hundred costumes, chiefly from Bokhara, but some also from Kashmir
and China.

Among the guests was a man who had played a prominent part in the modern history of Central Asia—namely,
Jura Beg. When a young man he was in the service of
Emir Nasrullah of Bokhara, and on his death had seized
the native province of Shahr-i-Sebs, the ancient Kesh, where
Tamerlane was born. There he ruled as beg for some years,
but was ousted by a rival and thrown into prison. The
people, who were not satisfied with the rule of the new
beg, liberated Jura Beg and reconstituted him their prince.
When the Russians, under General Kaufmann, took Samarkand in 1868, Jura Beg hastened with a considerable force
to the relief of the famous city, and besieged it obstinately,
reducing the Russians to great distress, from which they
were only saved at the last moment by a relief expedition.
General Kaufmann thereupon made a compromise with
Jura Beg, by which the latter was to retain his position as
beg of Shahr-i-Sebs, upon his pledging himself not to

molest the Russians. When, however, a few years later, some Cossacks were killed on his territory, he was treated so harshly by General Kaufmann that he was constrained to flee from Shahr-i-Sebs, where he had ruled for ten years. He then wandered about in the mountains, with his friend Baba Beg, and finally went to Kokand, to seek aid and

VIEW FROM THE MOHAMMEDAN PORTION OF TASHKEND

hospitality from the last khan, Khan Khodiar. The latter however, took him prisoner, threw him in chains, and sent him to his enemy, General Kaufmann.

Kaufmann received him with kindness, but kept him under military surveillance. The Russians in Tashkend treated him in a manner befitting his dignity, and he enjoyed comparatively a large measure of freedom. When General Skobeleff initiated his campaign against the Khanate of Kokand, Jura Beg, who knew the country and hated Khodiar Khan, offered his services. During this campaign, which proved the death-blow of Kokand, Jura Beg greatly distinguished himself, and was made a Russian colonel, and given the order of the Cross of St. George. He is now,

in manner and speech and dress, completely Russianized, lives in a well-appointed house in Tashkend, receives a yearly pension of £300 from the Russian government and £500 from the Emir of Bokhara, who, however, is his sworn enemy. He leads a life of ease and leisure, studies learned Oriental works, and is content with the great change which has taken place in his existence. But the story of his adventurous and exciting life, which he told me during the evenings I spent at his house, is indeed pathetic—a powerful Asiatic prince to become a Russian colonel!

To return to the dinner. It was truly sumptuous, with glittering candelabra and resplendent, star-decorated uniforms. The only thing that served to remind the stranger that he was in Central Asia was the presence of the Oriental guests in their costly gay-colored khalats (coats) and turbans. When the champagne was served, the governor-general rose and read aloud a telegram from the Tsar, and proposed his health. Standing, and with their faces turned towards the Tsar's portrait, all the guests listened to the Russian national anthem. Baron Vrevsky then proposed the health of the Turkestan army and the Emir of Bokhara, and was himself the subject of a speech by the governor of the province of Syr-daria.

It was not, however, social enjoyments which kept me so long in Tashkend. I was busily engaged the whole time with preparations for the continuation of my journey eastward. I worked off large arrears of correspondence, took a number of photographs in the Sart quarter of the town, adjusted my instruments at the observatory, and collected a good deal of information, both written and oral, regarding the Pamirs. All my instruments were in good preservation, except the quicksilver barometer, which had come to grief on the journey from Orenburg, and had to be thoroughly repaired by the German mechanic at the observatory. The only other thing which was the worse for the continual jolting of the tarantass was the ammunition. When I opened the two cases in which it was packed, a sorry sight met my eyes. The paper cases of two or three hundred cartridges

were ground to powder, and the tin boxes in which they had
been packed were crumpled together like paper. That none
of the many sharp corners had struck a cap and caused a
serious explosion was little short of a miracle; my journey
would then have had a speedier conclusion and a different
termination. Having put the ammunition in order again,
and made it up to the original amount, I had it all repacked.

Lastly, I had a great deal of shopping to do. I laid in a
stock of tinned provisions, tea, cocoa, cheese, tobacco, etc.,
sufficient to last several months; I also bought sundry small
articles, such as revolvers, and the ammunition for them,

KIRGHIZ YURTS (TENTS) IN TASHKEND

clocks, compasses, musical boxes, field-glasses, kaleidoscopes,
microscopes, silver cups, ornaments, cloth, etc., all intended
as presents for the Kirghiz, Chinese, and Mongols. In the
interior of Asia textiles almost take the place of current coin;
for a few yards of ordinary cotton material you may buy a
horse, or provisions to last a whole caravan several days may
be bought. Finally, on the special recommendation of the
governor-general, I was enabled to purchase the latest and
best ten-verst maps of the Pamirs, a chronometer (Wirén), and
a Berdan rifle, with cartridges and twenty pounds of shot.

When at length my preparations were all completed, I bade farewell to my friends in Tashkend, and started again on January 25th, 1894, at three o'clock in the morning.

I had not got farther than Chirchick—where I had to pay 37 roubles (£3 14s.) for the ninety odd miles to Khojent and for eight horses (for two carriages were now necessary)—when I was delayed for want of horses. There was so much traffic that, although the stations keep as many as ten troikas, they are often short of horses; and when a traveller is unfortunate enough to clash with the post, for which the station-masters are responsible, there is nothing for it except to possess one's soul in patience.

It had turned considerably colder again, and at nine in the morning the thermometer registered only 12.2° Fahr.(–11° C.). The face of the country was hidden under snow; but the road was hard and lumpy, and made the tarantass shake to such an extent that it was more like an instrument of torture than a means of locomotion. The quicksilver barometer was again in the utmost danger, and to protect it I was obliged to lay it on a cushion on my knees and nurse it like a baby. Through the thick, chilly mist, in which everything was enveloped, I caught occasional glimpses of the camel-caravans we met or overtook.

The town of Biskent possesses a certain interest in the recent history of Central Asia, as being the birthplace, about the year 1825, of Yakub Beg, who in 1865 conquered the whole of Kashgar. He was one of the most remarkable rulers that have ever lived; and his memory in the interior of Asia, where he is usually called "Bedawlet," or "The Happy," will long remain green. Ever since he was murdered in Korla, in the year 1877, the country has been in a state of great confusion. His son Hak Kuli Beg marched with his father's army, which was fighting against the Chinese, to Kashgar, where he too was murdered, according to report by his brother, Beg Kuli Beg. The latter still lives in Biskent, where he owns several houses and farms, and draws a Russian pension. He is a strong, shapely man, fifty years of age or so, with a jet black beard and hard features. Surrounded by

his eight sons, he is awaiting with impatience the first sign of
dissension in Kashgar, when he will hasten thither to take
possession, if possible, of his father's throne. At least, that
is what he told me himself. Poor fellow! long may he live

A VIEW FROM TASHKEND

on in that hope, for he does not know what great political
changes have taken place in East Turkestan since the days
of Yakub Beg!

After several delays, caused by want of horses, I at last, on
the 27th, reached Khojent, where my sole errand was to take
measurements of the Syr-daria.

I shall say a few words about these further on; of
the town itself I have already given a description in my
former book. Suffice it, therefore, to say a word or
two only about the large bridge which spans the Syr-daria.
It is divided into two parallel roadways for the convenience of traffic, is provided with a black railing, and is
built on piles resting on three wooden caissons filled with
stones.

The owner, who is a private person, made a profitable contract with the government for thirty years.   During the first
twenty he was to be allowed free possession of his bridge;
but for the following ten he was to pay 3000 silver roubles
(£300) a year to the government.   Of these ten years six
have still to run.   The cost of building the bridge was put
down at £5000; but it has had to be rebuilt twice.   When
the ten years have run out, the bridge is to be handed over
to the government in good condition.

Of Kokand, which I reached on January 29th, I am now
able to add a few details, for the completion of my former
description.   There are thirty-five *madrasas*, or Mohammedan
theological colleges, in the town.   I mention in particular the
madrasa Hak Kuli, which was founded in the year 1221 of
the Hejira (1806).   The madrasa Khan has eighty-six rooms
and three hundred pupils.   The madrasa Jami, with its large
quadrangle shaded by poplars, willows, and mulberry-trees,
its minaret, its beautiful cloisters, with varicolored paintings
on the checkered ceiling, and its carved wooden pillars, between which a number of young mollahs (theological students) were sitting reading, likewise has eighty-six rooms,
but only two hundred pupils.

I also went to see the Hakim Ayim, which was built
twenty-three years ago by Khodiar Khan's mother; it has a
library with a picturesque balcony or *kitab-khaneh* within the
quadrangle.   She gave land and gardens at the same time,
the income from which amounts to 1500 tillahs (about £560)
yearly, and is devoted to the maintenance of the college and
the students.   The madrasa Sultan Murad Beg was built by
Khodiar Khan's younger brother, and has ninety-nine rooms
and a hundred and fifty pupils.   The Madrasa-i-Mir is the
oldest college in Kokand, having been founded by Narbuta
Khan and restored in the year 1212 of the Hejira (1797); it
has fifty-seven rooms and one hundred and forty pupils.

At the time of my visit there were five thousand students
at the different madrasas in Kokand maintained by dona-
tions, while three hundred were living at their own expense.
Besides the institutions which I have just mentioned, there

were, connected with Mohammedan instruction, forty-eight *mekteb-khaneh*, or schools, for six hundred boys and two hundred girls, and thirty *kharik-haneh*, or schools founded with money left for the purpose and situated near the testators' graves.   In these some three hundred and fifty pupils are educated.   Finally, there were three Jewish schools, with sixty pupils.   The population of Kokand was about 60,000, of whom 35,000 were Sarts, 2000 Kashgarians and Taranchis, 575 Jews, 500 Gypsies (Lulis), 400 Dungans, 100 Tatars, 100 Afghans, 12 Hindus—as usual, money-lenders—and 2 Chinese.   To this add 350 Russians and a garrison of 1400 men.   The rest were Tajiks.   A dozen or so of Chinese are in the habit of visiting the place every spring with carpets from Kashgar.   The town consisted of 11,600 houses, and possessed nine cotton factories.   During the last few years Kokand has shown a tendency to prosperity; the Russian quarter in particular has increased steadily.   In addition to the Russian administration, there is also a native administration for the maintenance of order.   The burgomaster is called *kur-bashi*, and under him are four *aksakals*, each of whom has the supervision of a "large" quarter (*katta-mähälläh*); under them again there are ninety-six *allik-bashis*, each presiding over a *kishkintai-mähälläh*, or "little" quarter.

In Kokand I visited a couple of *hammam* (hot baths), naturally without making use of them; for they offered the opposite of what we understand by a bath, and were rather hot-beds for the propagation of skin diseases.   They were entered through a large hall, with carpet-covered benches and wooden columns; this was the room for undressing in. From that you passed through a number of narrow, labyrinthine passages to dark, steamy, vaulted rooms of different temperatures.   In the middle of each there was a platform on which the bather is rubbed and washed by a naked shampooer.   A mystic twilight prevailed in these cellarlike crypts, and naked figures with black or gray beards flitted about through the steam-laden atmosphere.   The Mohammedans often spend half their day in the bath, smoking, drinking tea, and sometimes even taking dinner.   The moral condition of

THE MAIN ENTRANCE TO A BAZAAR

the town is terribly degraded; the female dancers, who perform at weddings and other ceremonies, contribute to this in no small degree.

Instead of driving direct by the post-road to Margelan, I chose the détour of two hundred versts (130 miles) by way of Chust and Namangan, so as to obtain further opportunities of completing my soundings of the river Syr-daria.

After sending my baggage direct to Margelan in a couple of arbas (carts), I left Kokand on January 30th, in my old tarantass, and directed my course northward to Urganchi, a largish *kishlak* (winter village), where the fair was in full swing and the streets full of people. The road led through an unbroken succession of villages, and on either side of it were *ariks*, or channels, tributaries of the irrigation system which waters the oasis of Kokand. At the village of Gurum-serai wayfarers are ferried across the Syr-daria in a large boat. Thence a miserable road leads by way of Pap to the little town of Chust, whose only claim to importance lies in its cultivation of cotton, rice, and grain. After that the road passed over small hills composed of yellow loess and conglomerates. The going was now first-rate everywhere, and we made good progress. At Tura-kurgan we crossed the stream of Kazan-sai, which in summer brings down great quantities of water from the Chotkal Mountains; though it never attains the volume of the Syr-daria, as the water is distributed through a number of ariks which irrigate the rice-fields.

Namangan is surrounded by villages and gardens, and is the residence of a *uyäsdny natyalnik* (chief of a district). The Seid Kuli Beg, Khoja Ishan, and Serdabi madrasas were the only buildings in the town of even passing interest to the traveller. The square market-place, Ispar-khan, which extended in front of the madrasa last named, was the rendez-vous for the smiths and venders of hardware.

It was no easy matter to get out of Namangan. Through the frozen mud of the streets the wheels of a thousand arbas had cut two deep ruts, which we had no choice but to follow. We had to drive slowly all the way to the Naryn, the source proper of the Syr-daria, jolting and shaking the whole time.

I.—6

The Naryn was crossed close to the confluence of its principal tributary, the Kara-daria, by a simple wooden bridge, which is destroyed every summer by the rising of the waters, and has to be rebuilt annually. From the village of Balikchi, on its left bank, the driver took me to Min-bulak on the Syr-daria. Somewhat higher up, this river sends out a curious bifurcating arm, the Musulman-kul, and this again forms a reed-grown marsh, Sari-su, which was entirely frozen over, the ice being covered with snow. The landscape was still desolate, but somewhat diversified in places. Occasionally I saw a flock of grazing sheep, but what it was they were eating I could never quite make out. On February 4th, *via* Yaz-auan, I reached Margelan, the chief town of Fergana, where the governor, General Pavalo-Shveikovsky, received me with great courtesy. During the twenty days I spent in his house, occupied in completing the last preparations for my journey across the Pamirs, he showed me the greatest kindness and gave me much valuable advice.

CHAPTER VII

THE SYR-DARIA

But before I leave Fergana and set forth on the adventurous winter journey across the Pamirs, I will give a short summary of my survey of the Syr-daria River.

The first series of soundings, which I made on November 25th, 1893, at Kazalinsk, gave a volume of 20,000 cubic feet in the second; the depth of the river varied between 6½ feet and 10 feet; the average depth being 8 feet, and the average velocity 2 feet 6 inches in the second. The temperature of the water was 31.3° Fahr. (0.4° C.). The air was quite still, and the observations were made from a boat at six points in a direct line across the river, the boat being anchored for each sounding and measurement.

Two months later, on January 27th, 1894, I make a similar series of observations at Khojent. The temperature of the air at 1.30 p.m. was 26.8° Fahr. (−2.9° C.). A slight wind was blowing from the east, and in the water the thermometer showed 32.9° Fahr. (0.5° C.). Along the right bank there was a thin sheet of ice 9 or 10 yards wide; under the left a belt 18 yards in width; both had formed in the shelter of the bridge. Above and below this there was no ice to be seen, except a few small flakes drifting on the water, which was much clearer here than at Kazalinsk. Thanks to the bridge, which was 574 feet in length, of which 114 feet were over dry land, it was easy to get the width of the river—namely, 430 feet. The observations were made, like those at Kazalinsk, at six points, from a boat which was kept in position 65 yards below the bridge by a rope. The depth was measured with a pole 20 feet long, and the velocity, as usual, with a stationary and a free float.

As might be expected from the rugged character of the Fergana valley, the greatest depth, and consequently the greatest velocity, of the river were not far from the right bank, where there is a steep, detached mountain ridge; whereas the left or south bank is comparatively low. All the same, it is sufficiently high above the current to make it difficult for the inhabitants of Khojent to get their water-supply from the river when the little stream Ak-su, which flows through the town, fails.

The mean depth was 12 feet 8 inches (maximum, 18 feet 11 inches); the area of a vertical section, 1720 square feet; the mean velocity of the current, 2 feet 6 inches (maximum, 3 feet 1 inch) in the second; and the volume, 12,900 cubic feet in the second. The space between the bridge and the surface of the water was 20 feet 3 inches; but on the piers there were marks which showed the water to have been nearly 14 feet 9 inches higher the previous summer.

It may seem remarkable that I found upward of 7000 cubic feet less water at Khojent than at Kazalinsk; but this fact admits of a natural explanation. In the first place, the river Chirchick, near Tashkend, had at its lowest level a volume of 3500 cubic feet; then, farther down, the Syr-daria receives several tributaries from the mountains Kara-tau and Talas-tau, one of which, the river Aris, being, as I have said before, of very considerable size. Finally, it must be borne in mind that the river is deprived of very little water for the irrigation canals during the winter, that the evaporation during the cold season is inconsiderable, that at its lowest level little or no water is absorbed by the marshes at the sides of the river, and that, finally, the observations at Khojent were made two months later than those at Kazalinsk.

The Syr-daria has never been sounded during the summer; but we may fairly conclude that at that season of the year the conditions are reversed; that is to say, that the volume of water at Chinaz (near Tashkend) is considerably greater than at Kazalinsk.

In January, 1891, on my return journey from Kashgar to Issyk-kul, I had an opportunity of observing what enormous masses of snow accumulate during the winter on the mountains south of Issyk-kul. When these masses melt in the spring and summer, the Naryn becomes a large river, foaming torrentially along its rocky bed down to the valley of Fergana. The Kara-daria also becomes a river of considerable dimensions, although the snowfall in the part of the Tian-shan Mountains where its sources are situated is not so great as in the tracts south of Issyk-kul. Like the Chirchick, the Kara-daria also contributes a large volume of water to the Syr-daria, so that at Chinaz the latter is a noble river during the spring and autumn months, though it does not outrival its sister river, the Amu-daria. It rolls swiftly through the heated steppe, and empties its waters into Lake Aral. The whole of its water does not, however, reach the destination which the formation of the country would naturally seem to prescribe for it. Chinaz lies 610 feet above the level of Lake Aral; but from that point the river flows a distance of 882 miles, and the fall is, therefore, only $8\frac{1}{3}$ inches in every mile. The water has plenty of time to evaporate, a process which takes place the more rapidly as during the summer the air is excessively hot and dry. But other factors are at work to despoil the river. Part of the water is absorbed by the soil; another part is used for irrigation; a third, and very considerable portion, leaves its bed and forms, particularly on the right bank, extensive swamps and lakes. The largest swamps extend between Kazalinsk and the mouth of the river. Others occur east of Perovsk; more particularly between Perovsk and Karmakchi, where the reed-grown Bokali-kopa is nearly 2000 square miles in area. In this way, then, the river loses much of its flood; hence it may easily be conceived that in summer the volume of water is much greater at Chinaz than at the mouth of the river.

Between Min-bulak and Khojent the Syr-daria was crossed by fifteen ferries, the traffic being conveyed across by twenty-seven barges hired from a Russian. The greatest amount of traffic crosses at the Shakhand ferry; there the earnings in summer amount to 1200 roubles (£120) a month; but in winter to only 300 or 400 roubles (£30 to £40). An arba (cart) laden with goods pays twenty-five kopeks (6¼d.), a loaded camel fifteen (3¾d.), a horse five (1¼d.), and a foot-passenger two (½d.).

At Gurum-serai, one of the most important of the ferries, I made another series of observations. The sky being clear and the atmosphere still, the temperature of the air at 4.30 P.M. was 23.2° Fahr. (−4.9° C.), and the mean temperature of the water 35.4° Fahr. (−1.9° C.). The width of the river, which was measured trigonometrically, was 640 feet. The right bank was low and flat; the left very steep, 10 feet high, and much excavated by the current. The greatest depth— viz., 9 feet 5 inches—occurred at a distance of only 33 feet from the left bank; but, remarkably enough, the greatest velocity (4 feet 1 inch in the second) occurred at a distance of only 16 feet from the right bank. In the middle of the river there was a sand-bank, over which the velocity was inconsiderable. But on both sides of it—that is, between the sand-bank and the river-banks, where the deeper places were —the velocity was much greater.

The mean depth was 5 feet 3 inches; area of vertical section, 3070 square feet; mean velocity, 2 feet 7 inches in the second; and volume, 7850 cubic feet in the second. The great difference of 5050 cubic feet between Khojent and Gurum-serai is striking, particularly as the river just at this part does not take up any tributary worth mentioning; but, as I shall point out shortly, this is explicable from modifying conditions of temperature and rainfall.

On the way from Namangan to Margelan I crossed the lower Naryn at the kishlak (winter village) of Jidda-köpö, and the lower Kara-daria between the two villages of Chuja and Balikchi. Respecting the two tributaries of the Syr-daria, it is generally stated that the Naryn is the more voluminous and the Kara-daria the swifter. In point of fact, the Kara-daria is always the swifter, for within a distance of ninety-one miles from Usghen (3220 feet) to Chuja (1310 feet) it falls 1910 feet, or 21 feet in every mile. The Naryn, on the other hand, in a distance of eighty-seven miles—that is to say, from a point near the ruins of the fortress of Ketmentube (2800 feet) to Jidda-köpö (1310 feet)—falls only 1490 feet, or 17 feet in every mile. Although these differences in altitude are not very great, they are so far appreciable that the Kara-daria, even in its lower reaches, is somewhat swifter than the Naryn. The other assertion, on the contrary, is not always right, for during the winter the Kara-daria is always much larger than the Naryn, sometimes even twice as large. This is due to the fact that the Naryn flows through a more northern and colder tract, and because it is on all sides surrounded by chains of high mountains, in which severe cold obtains; while the Kara-daria has a more southerly course, through the eastern extension of the Fergana valley, where the winter temperature is considerably milder, and high mountains protect it from the cold north winds.

The volume of the Naryn diminishes also owing to a large quantity of its drainage supply being locked up in the form of ice. This is particularly the case with regard to the small streams and tributaries which flow through the high side valleys. In the tract through which the Kara-daria flows, the winter temperature, on the contrary, is not so low, and the river, therefore, receives during the cold period of the year a comparatively large quantity of water, although here again the snowfall is less. The Kara-daria is thus deprived of a smaller quantity of its water through the formation of ice than the Naryn. In the spring, as soon as the ice and snow on the mountains surrounding the Naryn begin to melt, the river rises, and in a short time becomes much larger than its sister stream, which has not been able to collect any great provision of ice and snow within its bounds during the winter

The pile-bridges that the Sarts have built across the Naryn and the Kara-daria greatly simplified the task of sounding those two rivers. On February 2d, at two in the afternoon, the weather being favorable and the temperature 21.9° Fahr. (—5.6° C.), I made the following observations in the Naryn:

The mean depth was 5 feet 10 inches (maximum, 8 feet 7 inches); the area of the vertical section, 840 square feet;

mean velocity, 3 feet 8 inches (maximum, 4 feet 6 inches); and the volume of water, 3070 cubic feet. The greatest depth and the greatest velocity occurred on the right side of the river; and there, too, the stream was loaded with large quantities of packed ice. The greatest quantity of drift-ice I found in a current only 12 yards from the right bank; thus it did not follow, as might be expected, the swiftest current, which was 25 yards out from the same bank.

About one mile to the south I crossed the Kara-daria, about a couple of hours later, and I then made the following observations in that river: mean depth, 5 feet, 3 inches; maximum depth, 10 feet 11 inches; area of vertical section, 1220 square feet; mean velocity, 3 feet 10 inches (maximum, 4 feet 6 inches); volume of water, 4700 cubic feet.

Together, therefore, the Naryn and the Kara-daria carried 7770 cubic feet of water, or almost precisely the quantity I found in the Syr-daria at Gurum-serai.

Comparing the two streams, it will be found that the Kara-daria is 9 feet broader than the Naryn, but as a rule is shallower, while the maximum depth is greater. In both rivers the maximum depth is near the right bank, and in both the greatest velocity of the current occurs to the left of the greatest depth. In both the right bank is much more eroded than the left. It is also higher and steeper; the left bank sloping up gently and gradually from the water's edge. The same thing is true of the Syr-daria at Khojent.

These conditions seem to be dependent upon the tendency which the river shows to shift its channel to the right. In 1892 there was unmistakable proof that the Naryn in its lower reaches also exhibited the same tendency. Nearly seven miles above Utch-kurgan the Naryn quits its transverse valley and flows through the level valley of Fergana. As soon as the river leaves its deep, sharply defined, rocky bed, it becomes broad and shallow, and is filled with shoals and islets of sand, and only confines itself to one bed for short distances, and that when the water is lowest.

About a mile below Utch-kurgan the Yanghi-arik, the largest irrigation canal that carries water to the rice-fields of

the district of Namangan, branches off from the right bank
of the river. At the same time the Naryn itself shows a
tendency to break through and join the Yanghi-arik, which,
if accomplished, would naturally prove very disastrous to the
agriculturists in that fruitful region. To prevent this, the·
Russian government in 1893 built four dams in the river, at
right angles to the right bank, so as to force the water back
to its proper channel. The highest dam up the stream was
141 feet long, the lowest 942 feet; the first three were 33
feet broad, the fourth and lowest 20 feet. They were all
constructed of piles, stones, and fascines. The work was
done in two months by a Russian officer with 200 to 400
Sart workmen, and cost about 18,000 roubles (£1800). In
the dead water below each dam large quantities of sand and
mud quickly accumulated, in places to such a degree that it
was possible to plant trees, with the view of imparting a
greater power of resistance to the structure. This fact plainly shows that at this point the river manifests a strong tendency to trend to the right.

On the way from Min-bulak to Margelan I observed in
several places traces of former river-beds. The largest was
the Sari-su, which flowed into the reed-grown marsh of the
same name. At the time of my visit it was entirely frozen,
a sheet of glittering ice. It is very probable that the continuation of the Musulman-kul arik, farther east, is an old
bed of the Syr-daria.

South of the Syr-daria, between the meridians of Kokand
and Margelan, there is an unbroken string of marshy lakes
—Atchi-kul, Dam-kul, and Sari-su. In the spring these are
fed with water from the river through the old discarded
river-beds; the surplus water from the ariks (irrigation canals)
of Andijan also flows into them. South of these marshy
tracts stretches the desert. North of the Syr-daria, on the
other hand, there are no swamps or ancient river-beds;
though in the lower course of the river there are marshes
and lagoons, for the greater part situated on the right bank.
Here again we find plain indications that the river is trending to the right or northeast. For a distance of close upon

400 miles, from Kazalinsk to Tash-suat, the post-road runs close beside the right bank. Several station-houses, which were originally built at a certain distance from the river, have now been reached by it, and some of them have had to be abandoned and new ones built at a greater distance from the bank.

On further comparison between the Naryn and the Kara-daria, I found that the Naryn carries a large quantity of drift-ice; while in the Kara-daria, on the contrary, there is not a trace of it. The water of the Naryn was almost clear and transparent; that of the Kara-daria turbid and impure. The water of the Naryn had a mean temperature of 32.2° Fahr. (0.1° C.); in the sister river the thermometer showed 37.9° Fahr. (3.3° C.). The quantity of sedimentary matter is, naturally, partly dependent on the varying nature of the country through which the rivers flow, partly on the volume of the streams and their rate of fall, possibly also on the temperatures of their waters.

Finally, I must add a few words as to the influence which the volume of water in the Naryn and the Kara-daria had on the Syr-daria at Min-bulak, Gurum-serai, and Khojent. I wished to take another series of soundings at Min-bulak; but unfortunately the ferry was so arranged that it was impossible to keep the boat still on the river. The width was 590 feet. Eleven yards from the left shore the depth was 4 feet 11 inches, and the velocity of the current not less than 4 feet 10 inches in the second; 22 yards from the right bank the depth was 4 feet 9 inches, and the velocity only 1 foot 10 inches. In about the middle of the river the depth was 8 feet 2 inches.

The differences of temperature and color of the water in different places furnished materials for some interesting conclusions. On the right bank of the Syr-daria the thermometer showed 34° Fahr. (1.1° C.); sixty-five yards out, 34.7° Fahr. (1.5° C); sixty-five yards from the left bank, 35.8° Fahr. (2.1° C.); while close under the same bank it was 36.1° Fahr. (2.3° C.). Here the river was steaming at 11 A.M., the temperature of the air being 14.5° Fahr. (−9.7° C.). That is to say, thick columns of vapor rose into the air; and the ferry-man told me that early in the morning the mist is so dense that the ferry-boat vanishes from sight a few yards from the shore. The phenomenon appeared to be very common at this time of the year. On the right bank, where the cold water flowed, the river did not steam at all. There, on the contrary, a strip of water 16 yards in breadth was of the same clear, light-green color as the water of the Naryn; but outside this belt the water suddenly became muddy, and continued so right across to the left bank—exactly as in the Kara-daria. This proves that at the distance of 4½ miles below their confluence the two currents have not commingled, or rather that the warm muddy water of the Kara-daria spreads over the cold clear water of the Naryn, except for a narrow belt near the right bank. The fact that lower down the latter increases a whole degree in warmth in such a short distance is naturally due to its close contact with the warmer water of the Kara-daria.

At Gurum-serai the temperature of the water, as I mentioned before, was everywhere 35.4° Fahr. (1.9° C.), and the same muddy color prevailed across its entire breadth; moreover, the river was quite free from ice. Even without the aid of calorimetry these phenomena prove that the current of the Kara-daria is more powerful than the current of the Naryn, and that in the intervening 55 miles all the drift-ice has time to melt. That the conditions were the same on January 30th and February 2d is proved by the volume of water being the same in both cases. At Khojent, on the contrary, the conditions were very different. In the first place, the volume of the water was 5050 cubic feet greater than at Gurum-serai. The temperature of the water was only 32.9° Fahr. (0.5° C.); that is to say, more than two degrees and a half colder than at Gurum-serai, which is 110 miles distant from Khojent. Finally, the water was much clearer than at Gurum-serai, and carried a not inconsiderable quantity of drift-ice. For this reason the bulk of the current flowing through the bed of the Syr-daria at Khojent on January 27th consisted of Naryn water; for it possessed

generally the same characteristics as the latter—it was cold,
clear, and charged with drift-ice.

Shortly afterwards the temperature of the air sank. On
January 30th, at nine in the morning, at Chust, I read 11.7°
Fahr. (−11.2° C.). At Namangan, on February 1st, at eight
in the morning, 14.9° Fahr. (−9.5° C.); and the following day,
at the same place and time. 12.9° Fahr. (−10.6° C.).

The temperature had, without doubt, fallen in the mountains, and to a very great extent. The tributaries of the
Naryn, and even the Naryn itself in part, began to freeze;
the river was thus much reduced and became less than the
Kara-daria. The Syr-daria dropped rapidly, and at Gurum-
serai its volume was 5000 cubic feet less than on any previous day.

It is no doubt astonishing that the volume of a river can
decrease to so great an extent in such a short space of time;
but it is a common phenomenon, and admits of easy explanation. The chief of the district of Namangan told me that
the Naryn often rose there ten feet during the course of five
days, and fell again afterwards just as rapidly. This phenomenon always takes place after violent and continuous rain in
the neighboring mountains. As I have mentioned previously, it cannot be affirmed positively that the Naryn is always
the larger of the two rivers, for their respective volumes
change with the seasons—i.e., with the changes of temperature and the rainfall in the country through which they respectively flow.

The Syr-daria does not freeze at any point of its course
through Fergana; but at Chinaz it often forms ice so thick
that it will bear the post-troikas.

CHAPTER VIII

UP THE ISFAÏRAN VALLEY

ON the borderlands between East and West Turkestan the earth's crust is thrust upward into a lofty plateau or mountain-knot of gigantic dimensions. From it radiate some of the most stupendous mountain-ranges in the world, eastward the Kwen-lun, southeastward the Himalayas, and between these two the Kara-korum Mountains, stretching into Tibet. From the same elevated region the Tian - shan highlands branch off towards the northeast, and in the opposite direction, towards the southwest, the Hindu-kush Mountains. It is here that several authorities place the home of the first parents of our race. The traditions of a dim and distant antiquity declare that the four sacred rivers of Paradise, mentioned in the Bible, had their origin in these sublime altitudes. The people of High Asia still revere the Pamirs, calling them the Roof of the World, and regarding them as the coign of vantage from which the towering mountain-giants look abroad over the whole world.

Until quite recently the Pamirs were, politically, subject to the Khans of Kokand. But when Khodiar Khan, the last ruler of the country, was deprived of both kingdom and crown by his powerful neighbor on the north, Russia, she also laid claim to the sovereignty of the Pamirs. For some time, however, as they were both difficult of access and almost uninhabited. she bestowed but little attention upon them. This indifference on the part of the Russians gave encouragement to the adjacent states to annex one portion after another of the former territories of the Khans. The Afghans occupied Badakshan and Shugnan, overran Roshan and Wakhan, and in the last-mentioned district built strong posts of observation all along the river Pänj. The Chinese took possession of the frontier districts on the east, and the British established themselves in Chitral and Kanjut. But the Russians were not unobservant of what was going on. In the year 1891 Colonel Yonnoff, with a force of something like 1000 Cossacks, and a long train of pack-animals, carrying commissariat and ammunition stores, and even machine-guns, started from Margelan, and marched right over the Pamirs to the Hindu-kush, as far as the Baroghil pass, where he came into collision with a small Afghan outpost. A short time afterwards he built, on the river Murghab, the fort Shah Jan, a name which was subsequently changed to Fort Pamir. There he left behind a permanent garrison of two or three hundred Cossacks to watch over the interests of his country.

This was the origin of the Pamir Question, the subject of so much animated discussion in the immediately succeeding year. And thus the region of the Pamirs, hitherto shrouded and almost forgotten among the arctic-like severities of the heart of Asia, became the object of the liveliest interest, the focus of political and strategic movements of a momentous character.

Certain portions of the Pamirs were, however, left unclaimed, abandoned to the few Kirghiz who were content to stay there and struggle for existence against the bitter cold. These nomads acknowledged no man's sovereignty and paid no tribute; although each of their neighbors around them laid claim to it, and possessed frontier garrisons strong enough to enforce their claim. But they were all fully conscious of the fact that a movement in that direction by any one of them would be the signal for hostilities; and though all the three powers were ready to fight, none wished to incur the grave responsibility of taking the first decisive step.

During the course of my stay with Baron Vrevsky, governor-general of Russian Turkestan, we had many conversations together about the Pamirs, the outcome of which was that I conceived the idea of crossing that region on my way to Kashgar. But no sooner did I mention my purpose than, almost with one accord, wellnigh every voice was raised to dissuade me from it. The officers who had taken part in Colonel Yonnoff's reconnaissance across the Pamirs prophesied that I should have a dangerous journey, and advised me to wait two or three months longer. One of these gentlemen, a captain, who had spent the previous winter on the Murghab, earnestly represented that I should be exposing myself to the greatest possible dangers, and running a grave risk from the severities of the winter climate. Nobody, he said, not even a native of the Far North, could form any conception of the intensity of the cold and the fury of the snowstorms which rage on the Pamirs in the depth of winter. Even in the middle of summer, during a snow-buran (hurricane), the thermometer frequently drops to 14° Fahr. (−20° C.). In the winter of 1892–93 the temperature fell to −45.4° Fahr. (−43° C.) in the end of January, and snow-storms were an every-day occurrence. These burans or snow-hurricanes come on with startling suddenness. One minute the sky will be perfectly clear; scarcely one minute later, and down swoops the storm. In an instant the path is obliterated. The atmosphere grows dark with whirling snow-flakes. It is impossible to see a yard before you. All you can do is to stand perfectly still, wrap your furs about you, and thank God if you escape with your life.

One piece of advice the captain insisted upon above all else—that I should never on any account separate myself from my caravan during the march. If at such a moment a buran were to sweep down upon me, I should be hopelessly lost. It would be impossible to get back to my followers, even though they were no more than a dozen paces away. The air becomes thick and black with blinding flakes. Nothing can be seen—nothing; you have hard work to see even the horse you ride. To shout is useless. Not a sound can be heard, not even the report of a rifle. All echoes are completely drowned in the roar of the hurricane. The unhappy traveller who has the ill-fortune to be thus caught alone, without tent or provisions, furs or felts, may resign himself to the inevitable—his fate sealed. Neither Colonel

I.—7

Yonnoff nor Captain Vannofsky envied me my journey in
the smallest degree; and yet both were experienced travellers, well acquainted with the fascinating perils of travel on
the Pamirs. Both were of one mind in warning me to prepare for a hard campaign.

And yet there were two men who did not see my project
in such dark colors—namely, General Vrevsky and Major-
General Pavalo-Shveikovsky, the governor of Fergana. Instead of throwing cold water on my plan, they encouraged
me in it, and promised to do all that lay in their power to
render it as practicable and as easy as possible. Both kept
their promise in a most gratifying way.

A week before the day I had fixed for starting from Margelan, the governor of Fergana, at the suggestion of Baron
Vrevsky, sent *jighits* (Sart couriers) to the Kirghiz who
were wintering in the valleys of the Alaï Mountains, commanding them to give me a friendly welcome, to provide
yurts (tents) at certain places and times arranged for, to
furnish me with supplies of food and fuel, to send people
on in advance to clear the road through the snow, and
hew steps in the ice which coated the narrow and dangerous mountain-paths of the Alaï Mountains, and in general to render all needful assistance in guiding the caravan
and getting forward the baggage from station to station.
Mounted messengers were likewise despatched to the Murghab; besides which I also carried letters to the commandant
of that post, and to the Chinese officer at Bulun-kul near the
frontier. The jighits were further directed to accompany
me the whole way. In a word, I met with nothing but the
most generous assistance at Margelan in completing the
equipment of my caravan, and in making preparations for
my journey.

The route which I mapped out before starting led over
the Alaï Mountains by the pass of Tenghiz-bai, then up the
Alaï valley alongside the Kizil-su (river), climbed the Trans-
Alaï range, and went down by the pass of Kizil-art to the
lake of Kara-kul, over that lake, through the pass of Ak-
baital, and so on to Fort Pamir on the Murghab. The en-

tire distance amounted to over 300 miles, and was divided into eighteen short days' marches, with five days extra for rest, as set forth in the subjoined table:

From Margelan to Utch-Kurgan	23	miles
To Austan	15	"
" Langar	26½	"
" Tenghiz-bai	17	"
" Daraut-kurgan	16	"
" Kizil-unkur	14½	"
" Kur-gur (Kashka-su)	17	"
" Jipptik	16½	"
" Archa-bulak	13	"
" Bor-doba	18	"
" Kok-sai	18	"
" Kara-kul (north shore)	16½	"
" Kara-kul (south shore)	13	"
" Mus-kol	18	"
" Ak-baital	12	"
" Rabat No. 1	15	"
" Chicheckli	16½	"
" Fort Pamir	17	"

At each of the stations—Austan, Daraut-kurgan, Archa-bulak, Kara-kul, and Rabat No. 1—I proposed to rest one day, so as not to overtask the horses. This programme was carried out on the whole with tolerable fidelity. A few deviations in points of detail, rendered necessary by circumstances, were the only changes that were made.

I hired horses from an old Sart trader at the rate of a rouble (about 2s.) a day for each—seven baggage animals, and one saddle-horse for myself. It would have come cheaper to buy them, and sell them again in Kashgar. But, according to the agreement I made, I incurred no responsibility for loss or injury to the animals, and was under no obligation in the matter of feeding them or attending to them. These duties were performed by two men, who took with them three additional horses carrying supplies of forage. A jighit named Rehim Bai, an active, weather-beaten little fellow, who had braved wind and sun and cold throughout many a long journey in Central Asia, was appointed my

right-hand man. In addition to his experience of Asiat
travel, he was an excellent cook and spoke Russian. I ga
him twenty-five roubles a month, together with rations ar
"lodging." He had to provide himself with a horse ar
winter felts. But on this journey he came near to losing h
life, and left me at Kashgar.

When Rehim fell ill, his place was taken by one of tl
two horsemen who accompanied him, Islam Bai, whose hon

EN ROUTE FROM MARGELAN TO THE ALAÏ MOUNTAINS

was at Osh, in Fergana. Islam proved the better man of tl
two, and throughout the entire journey served me with
fidelity and devotion which merit the warmest praise. Tl
following pages will best show how great is the debt
gratitude I owe to this man. When he first came to me
was a perfect stranger to him, and he had no conception
the real object of my journey. Nevertheless, he willing
left his peaceful home in Osh to share with me all the da
gers and perils of a protracted journey through the heart
Asia. We travelled side by side through the terrible Dese

of Gobi, facing its sand-storms in company, and nearly perishing of thirst; and when my other attendants fell by the side of the track, overcome by the hardships of the journey, Islam Bai, with unselfish devotion, stuck to my maps and drawings, and was thus instrumental in saving what I so highly prized. When we scaled the snowy precipices, he was always in the van, leading the way. He guided the caravan with a sure hand through the foaming torrents of the Pamirs. He kept faithful and vigilant watch when the Tanguts threatened to molest us. In a word, the services this man rendered me were incalculable. But for him I can truthfully say that my journey would not have had such a fortunate termination as it had. It gratifies me to be able to add that King Oscar of Sweden graciously honored him with a gold medal, which Islam Bai now wears with no small degree of pride.

I left behind at Margelan a quantity of stores and equipments for which I had no further need, including the venerable Orenburg tarantass, which I had hitherto used, and my European trunks. In place of these last I bought some Sart *yakhtans*—that is, wooden boxes covered with leather, and so constructed that they could be conveniently slung on horseback like a pair of panniers. I purchased the needful saddles, furs, and Pamir boots made of felt and untanned leather, and laid in a stock of extra provisions. I also took with me two steel spades to dig out the snow with when putting up the tent; and ice-axes and pickaxes to help us up the steep ice-coated precipices. When we crossed over the frozen lake of Kara-kul, I intended taking soundings, and for this purpose provided myself with a new hempen cord, 500 yards long, with ten-yard lengths knotted off, and a sinker at the end. The plane-table stand was so constructed that, with the addition of a Caucasian *burkha* (cloak or mantle), it could be converted into a temporary tent in case we were surprised by a snow-storm.

On February 22d, 1894, the string of horses started in charge of the jighits for Utch-kurgan. One horse was laden with photographic materials, packed in two yakhtans

(boxes); a second carried my topographical and other instruments, books, and the medicine-chest; the third, the
ammunition-chests; the fourth and fifth, the commissariat
supplies; the sixth and seventh, my weapons and personal
belongings. Last of all, at the tail-end of the caravan, were
the three horses carrying forage for the others, one of them
almost buried from sight under two enormous bags stuffed
with straw.

Two guides on foot went on first, and directed the horses
wherever necessary. The jighits rode. As the long, im-
posing-looking caravan filed away out of the yard of the
governor's palace, I stood and watched it with not a little
pride. I did not accompany it, but spent that night at
Margelan, the last I was to see of European civilization
for many a month to come. That evening everybody in
Margelan assembled within the governor's hospitable walls
to bid me farewell. What a contrast to the evenings which
immediately followed!

At eight o'clock on the following morning, after a last
word in dear old Swedish with General Matveyeff and Lieutenant Kivekäs, both light-hearted sons of Finland, and a
hearty send-off from the hospitable governor and his charming family, I said good-bye to Margelan, and cantered away
after my caravan. I caught up to it at Utch-kurgan. The
distance was only 23 miles; and yet even in that distance
the contour of the ground rose 1100 feet, up to an altitude
of some 3000 feet above sea-level.

Utch-kurgan is a large village picturesquely situated on
the river Isfaïran, at the point where it emerges from the
northern declivities of the Alaï Mountains. I was received
with a flattering welcome. A mile or two outside of the
village I was met by the *volastnoi* (native district chief) of
the place, accompanied by his colleague, the *volastnoi* of
Austan, a place higher up in the mountains. The former
was a Sart, the latter a Kirghiz. Both wore their gala *khalats* (coats) of dark-blue cloth, white turbans, belts of chased
silver, and scimitars swinging in silver-mounted scabbards.
At their heels rode a numerous cavalcade of attendants.

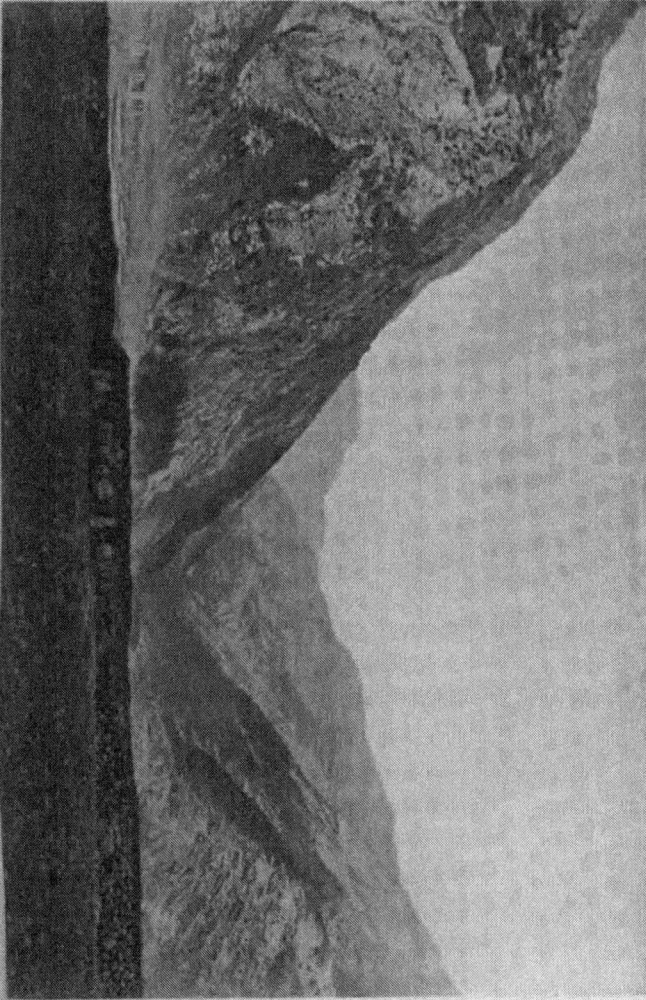

These dignitaries escorted me to the village, where a large crowd had assembled to witness my entry and enjoy the rare pleasure of a real *tamashah* (spectacle). After *dastarkhan* (refreshments) had been offered round, the caravan started again, escorted by the troop of horsemen.

The valley of the Isfaïran grew more sharply contoured as we advanced, and narrowed at the end to a width of only a few hundred yards. At the same time the path ascended, following in part the bed of the stream; though in places it ran along the face of steep, wellnigh precipitous slopes. The river has cut a deep channel through the coarse-grained conglomerates, and its waters, dark green in color, but clear as crystal, danced merrily along among the bowlders.

A few hours' ride brought us to our second halting-station, Austan. There the volastnoi of the place had got ready for us a comfortable yurt (tent) of white *kashma* (thick Kirghiz felt), decorated on the outside with broad strips of colored cloth, and furnished inside with Kirghiz carpets and — a crackling fire. Having rigged up a temporary meteorological observatory, and piled the baggage outside the tent, the men tethered and fed their horses, and then gathered round a fire in the open air. Here Rehim Bai got the first opportunity to exhibit his skill as cook. By the time I had completed my observations daylight had gone, and I set about arranging my bed for the night—not a very irksome task, however, seeing that the bed consisted simply of a piece of sacking stretched upon two poles, the ends of which rested on a couple of yakhtans (boxes).

The next day was dedicated to rest. The Kirghiz kishlak (winter village) of Austan, numbering about a hundred uy (tents), lay about three-quarters of a mile higher up the valley, surrounded by clumps of stunted white poplars. But the day was not spent in idleness: I made a short excursion from camp, and carried out several scientific observations. The Isfaïran brought down a volume of 280 cubic feet in the second. The temperature of the air at seven o'clock in the morning was 31.1° Fahr. (−0.5° C.); maximum during the day, 51.1° Fahr. (10.6° C.). The boiling-point of the water was at

.. altitude above sea-

. Margelan I had forgot-
_ .. outside the yurt at
. _ .. a curious way. On
.. the next stage to Lan-
.. miles farther on, a big
. came and joined himself
.. followed us faithfully
. . .y to Kashgar, and kept
. . every night. He was
was picked up on the

.. the track climbed steeply
.. horses clambered up one
Ere many minutes were
. that we could hear nothing
. .t a soft lisping murmur.
.. in and out of the heaps
. itself through the narrow
. .es it skirted the edge of a
. a side glen. Sometimes it
. fragments of rock. Every
. the side of the valley, and
. .ed of the stream; then up
.. abruptly as it had plunged

. . .t were cleft transversely by
. . so that the ruptured ends
.. the side-wings of a stage-set-
. .. and grand. Gigantic talus-
. .om the action of wind and
.. .eks of the mountains above,
.. .. the valley. The course of
. .ew scattered trees and bushes
.. Up on the mountain-sides
.. stunted *archa* (Asiatic juniper)
.. .e yawning precipices.

THE ISPAHAN VALLEY

Time after time we had to cross over the stream on wooden bridges which sagged and swayed at every step we took. One of these was known by the significant name of Chukkur-köpriuk—that is, the Deep Bridge. Seen from the lofty crest along which the path ran, it looked like a little stick flung across the narrow cleft far down below. Headlong down the mountain-side plunged the track ; then over the bridge, and as steeply up again, zigzag, on the opposite side. At every ten or a dozen paces the panting horses stopped to catch their breath. Again and again their burdens fell forward or backward, according as they descended or ascended, and had to be hitched right again. The voices of the men urging on the horses and shouting warnings to one another echoed shrilly among the hollows of the precipices. In this way we made our way slowly and cautiously along the narrow, break-neck path.

Shortly after crossing the Deep Bridge the road became paved with ice-slides and bordered with snow-clad slopes, which terminated a little lower down in a vertical wall, at the foot of which the clay-slates cropped out in sharp-edged slabs or flakes. The first horse of the string, the one which carried the bags of straw, together with my tent-bed, was led by one of the Kirghiz guides. But, despite the man's care, when he came to this spot the animal slipped. He made frantic efforts to recover his feet. It was in vain. He slid down the declivity, turned two or three summersaults through the air, crashed against the almost perpendicular rocks which jutted up from the bottom of the valley, and finally came to a dead stop in the middle of the river. The bags burst, and the straw was scattered among the rocks. Shrill shouts pierced the air. The caravan came to a stand-still. We rushed down by the nearest side-paths. One of the Kirghiz fished out my tent-bed as it was dancing off down the torrent. The others encouraged the horse to try and get up. But he lay in the water with his head jammed against a large fragment of rock, and was unable to respond to their exhortations. The Kirghiz pulled off their boots, waded out to him, and dragged him towards dry land. It was, however, wasted labor. The poor

brute had broken his back; and after a while we left him lying dead in the middle of the river, whither he had struggled
back in his dying agonies. The straw was swept together,
sewn up again, and packed on one of the other horses,
which carried it till we reached our night-quarters at Langar.

As soon as we got back to the track we went to work with
spades and axes and cleared away the ice, and then strewed
sand over the place from which we had cleared it.

The horses were led across this dangerous spot one by
one, and with every precaution for their safety. I need
scarcely say that I traversed it on foot.

Before we reached the end of our day's journey we were
suddenly overtaken by the twilight. The shades of night
crept thicker and thicker together in the deep, narrow gorge,
choking it with gloom. But after a while the stars began to
peep forth; and their keen glitter, piercing the obscurities of
the ravine, gave us a faint light by which to continue our
perilous journey. I have encountered a fair share of adventures and dangers in High Asia; but the three hours' travelling which still lay before us till we reached Langar were,
I believe, the most anxious of any I had hitherto experienced.
The first ice-slide was merely the forerunner of others to
come. They now followed one another in quick succession,
each more perilous than the last. Thus we walked, and
crept, and slid slowly on, beside the black abysses gaping for
their prey. This occasioned innumerable delays, for many
and many a time we had to stop to cut steps in the ice and
strew them with sand. Each horse required two men to get
him over these places, one to lead him by the halter, while
another hung on to his tail, ready to lash him if he stumbled
or slipped. Notwithstanding this, several of them did fall; but
luckily they managed to recover their feet. One fell and slid
several yards down the snowy slope, but fortunately stopped
in time. His pack was loosened and carried up the path;
the animal was helped to get back, and his burden was once
more lashed tightly on his back. I myself crawled several
hundreds of yards on my hands and knees, while one of the
Kirghiz crept close at my heels and held me in the more

VIEW BETWEEN AFSIAH AND LANGAR

perilous passages. A fall in any of those places would have meant instant death.

In a word, it was a desperate journey — dark, cold, awe-inspiring. The only sounds that broke the unearthly silence of the gorge were the piercing screams of the men whenever one of the horses fell, their shouts of warning when they drew near to one of these perilous passages, and the constant

MAKING A ROAD IN THE ALAÏ MOUNTAINS

roar of the torrent, which churned its way down through the foam-white rapids. It was an Asiatic river-spirit dashing a storm of music from her quivering harp!

When we at length arrived at Langar, weary, frozen, hungry, we had been toiling through the snow for twelve hours at one stretch. How welcome the two tents we found ready pitched for us there, with a brightly blazing fire in each!

8

CHAPTER IX

OVER THE TENGHIZ-BAI PASS

FROM Langar we travelled almost due south towards the pass of Tenghiz-bai. But before I go on to relate how we surmounted it, I must say a word or two about the principal passes which connect the valley of Fergana with the valley of the Alaï. There are five of them—namely, these, going east to west:

Talldik	. . . .	11,605 feet in altitude.
Jipptik	. . . .	13,605 " " "
Sarik-mogal	. . . .	14,110 " " "
Tenghiz-bai	. . . .	12,630 " " '
Kara-kasik	. . . . . .	14,305 " " "

This gives a mean altitude of 13,250 feet for the Alaï passes. It is noticeable that their absolute elevation increases as the chain advances westward; the difference in altitude between the passes and the valley, or the relative altitude of the passes, likewise increases from east to west.

The easiest of these passes is the one mentioned first—namely, Talldik. It has recently been levelled, and is now practicable for carriages and artillery. But it is closed by the snows the greater part of the winter. The second and third are very difficult, chiefly because of the avalanches, the violent winds, and the furious hurricanes of snow. The depth of snow on Tenghiz-bai varies very greatly from year to year. In normal seasons it does not amount to any great quantity, and for this reason it is the pass that is mostly used during the winter. It is the route followed by the post-couriers (jighits) who carry the mails between Margelan and Fort Pamir. Nevertheless it is no unusual thing for the

Tenghiz-bai pass to be closed during the last two or three weeks of February. In 1893 it was only closed for ten days. In 1892 it was impassable for a period of two whole months. And in 1891 the depth of the snow was so great, though for a shorter period, that junipers twelve or thirteen feet high were completely buried from sight in the snow-drifts.

February is the month in which avalanches fall and snow-storms rage with the greatest frequency. At that season the boldest Kirghiz hesitates to put foot inside the pass unless the weather is perfectly still and serene. All the same, hardly a winter passes without a fatal mishap of some kind. The numerous skeletons of horses, and even of human beings, which litter the track, might serve as mile-stones during the summer months.

The Kirghiz of the aul (tent village) of Daraut-kurgan, in the valley of the Alaï, told me a pathetic story of a man who came to that place from Utch-kurgan early in the year 1893, in order to spend Ramadan (the Mohammedan month of fasting) with some friends. On the way home he was overtaken, on March 23d, in the pass mentioned, by a violent buran (snow-hurricane), and was forced to stay there four days and nights squatting on the ground, with no other protection than his sheepskin coat. His horse died. His provisions gave out. When the snow-storm ceased, he found the way blocked in both directions. Nevertheless he pushed on, and, by dint of creeping, climbing, and wading, came, after two days and two nights of terrible labor, to the district of Kara-kiya, where he fell in with some of his own countrymen, who took charge of him, and fed him and nursed him. As soon as he had recovered a little he continued his journey to Utch-kurgan. But he died the very first night after getting home, overcome by the hardships and privations he had undergone.

I was also told that a caravan of forty men was over-whelmed that same winter in the Terek-davan pass by an avalanche, and killed to the last man.

On the night of February 26th I sent eight Kirghiz on in advance into the pass, with spades, pickaxes, and hatchets,

OVER T'

FROM Langar we t pass of Tenghiz-bai. surmounted it, I mus' passes which conne of the Alaï. Ther east to west:

Talldik   .
Jipptik   .
Sarik-mogal
Tenghiz bai .
Kara-kasik

This gives a m It is noticeable chain advances the passes and passes, likewise
The easiest namely, Talldik practicable for the snows th third are very violent winds, depth of snow to year. In quantity, and during the w couriers (jighi Fort Pamir.

followed up after
first difficult place we
found the Kirghiz
steps—in the ice; for the
surface, had melted during
the following night.
of the Kirghiz are truly
ordinary load is usually about
this load on their backs
distances down the mountain
the steep declivities; and
mountain-paths are generally
the edge of precipices, they
with almost inconceivable sure-
kiya, meaning the Black
name for the place. It is a nar-
perpendicular walls of rock,
shadows. Into those cavernous
penetrates. At this spot the
bridges. Underneath the up-
with the force and noise of a
region the hand of Nature has
Landscapes alternately wild,
romantic charm followed one
The eye commanded a truly
up and down the glen.
beg the valley bore the name
stream was spanned by four small
of these was a miserable con-
so rotten that my men were in
as they carefully led the horses
short distance farther on the glen
a newly fallen *kutshka* (avalanche
covered both stream and path. The
underneath the ice like a river
underground tunnel; while a new path, or
hewn across the sloping talus of
would have it, we chanced at this very

spot to meet a dozen or so Kirghiz from Kara-teghin, travelling on foot to Kokand and Margelan in search of work.
They stopped and helped us to repair the road.   But even
then. after all our efforts, the path was so steep that each
horse had to be actually pushed up by half a dozen men.

The glen narrowed rapidly towards its upper end, rising
with extraordinary steepness and becoming indistinguishable
from the mountain slopes.   At the same time the relative
altitudes decreased in proportion as the absolute altitudes increased.   The last portion of the way was tough work; avalanche succeeded avalanche at short intervals.   Almost every horse in the string fell once, some of them twice; and as
they were unable to get up again in the snow with the loads
on their backs, the baggage had to be taken off them and
then lashed on afresh.   In this way we were delayed time
after time.   The last ice-slide we encountered was so difficult
to cross that the horses could not by any possibility get over
it loaded; accordingly the Kirghiz unloaded them and carried
the baggage across on their own backs.   Indeed, they carried
it all the way to Rabat (Rest-house) — a little hut built of
stones and timber overlooking the glen below.   There also a
uy (tent) had been pitched.   I had walked the greater part
of the day, and was thoroughly tired.   The altitude was
9350 feet; and during the night I began to feel the symptoms of mountain-sickness—a splitting headache and an acceleration of the heart's action.   These symptoms, which were
caused by the sudden change from a relatively low to a relatively high altitude, continued all the following day; but passed
off after about forty-eight hours, leaving no ill effects behind
them.

On the following morning the Kirghiz road-makers and
Jan Ali Emin, aksakal (chieftain) of the Kara-teppes, who
had been in charge of the work, returned to Rabat.   At the
same time I and my men, fully realizing the risks of the undertaking, started on our journey up the pass, which was
now buried deep in snow.   The difficulties of the road were
almost inconceivable, and our labors trying in the extreme.
But by dint of persevering we managed to surmount all ob-

stacles, and came to a trough-shaped depression on the summit of the range, where the snow was fully six feet deep. A deep and narrow pathway had been trampled through the snow-drifts. But it was like a shaking bridge laid across a bog. One step off the path, and the horses plunged up to the girth in the snow; and it took all our combined efforts to dig them out again and get them back upon the "bridge." All this occasioned serious loss of time.

We now became aware of a group of sombre-looking peaks, split and weathered by wind and frost, towering above the eternal snows away in the southwest. It was a detached spur of the Kara-kir, pointing the way like a sea-beacon up to the dreaded pass of Tenghiz-bai. The track mounted up to the last summit by an endless series of zigzags, putting the horses' strength and climbing powers to the severest proof. But at length we reached the top of the pass safe and sound, and with all our baggage intact. There we rested an hour for tea, made meteorological and other observations, took photographs, and admired the entrancing scenery.

The spot at which we rested was shut in on every side by snowy crests, with bare, black pinnacles protruding here and there through their mantles of snow. Looking northward, we had the valley of the Isfaïran below us. We turned towards the southwest, and a magnificent panorama fascinated the eye. In the far-off distance were the sharply accentuated crests of the Alaï Mountains, and on the opposite side of the valley the system of the Trans-Alaï, its summits melting into the clouds, its flanks glistening with snow-fields of a dazzling whiteness.

The mountain saddle upon which we stood formed the water-shed between the basins of the Syr-daria and the Amu-daria. After recovering our breath in the clear, rarefied mountain air, we started to make our way at a leisurely pace down into the region where the head-streams of the latter river have their origin. The descent on this side was every bit as steep as the ascent had been up the northern face. The path was smothered under innumerable landslips and

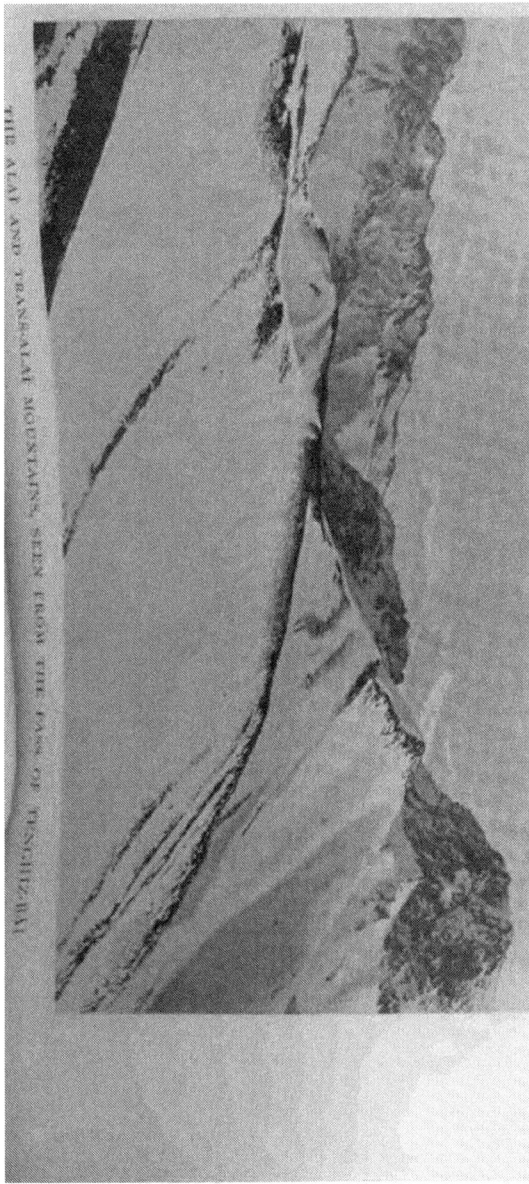

THE ALAI AND TRANS-ALAI MOUNTAINS, SEEN FROM THE PASS OF TENGHIZBAI

avalanches. Some of them had carried down with them in their fall vast quantities of earth and *débris;* so that we did not perceive them until the horses suddenly dropped up to the girth in the soft and treacherous ground. I measured one of the largest of these avalanches, which had fallen the day before. It was a quarter of a mile across, and had a depth of nearly seventy feet. The Kirghiz were not slow to congratulate one another upon having so fortunately escaped its clutches. The gigantic ice-slides rush down the mountain-side with such overwhelming force and momentum that, under the enormous pressure, their lower strata or under-surface become converted into ice, and anything living which should have the misfortune to be buried under it would be literally frozen fast in the middle of a block of ice as hard and as vitreous as glass. Once clasped in that icy embrace, a man would be hopelessly doomed. But in all probability the unhappy wretch who was thus swept away would be stunned by the fall, and would freeze to death before his consciousness returned.

Thoroughly exhausted by the exertions of the day, we halted in a little side glen called Shiman. Here the snow was several feet deep, and the Kirghiz were obliged to clear a space before they could get the tent erected. We passed the night hemmed in by a high breastwork of snow.

The next day we continued our march down the glen of the Daraut-kurgan. Every ten minutes or so we forded the stream, which raced along under arches and bridges of snow. Each time we did so, the horses were obliged to leap down the perpendicular bank of ice into the water, and then leap up again on the opposite side. Every time they did this, I was in a fever of anxiety lest any mishap should befall the animals which carried the ammunition and the photographic apparatus. However, everything passed off all right. The only incident was one of the commissariat horses plunging down a steep snow-slide, and rolling into the torrent. But we followed him down, unloaded him, hauled up the yakhtans with a rope, reloaded the animal, and then ploughed slowly on through the snow-drifts till another horse stumbled and fell.

At mid-day it began to snow. A thick mist came on, hiding everything from view, and preventing us from seeing where we were going to. One of the Kirghiz went on first and sounded the depth of the snow with a long staff, as sailors do when navigating unfamiliar waters. But there was this difference: whereas sailors aim to avoid the shallows, we sought for them, and for the firm ground under-

OUR CAMP AT DARAUT-KURGAN

neath them. Several times our guide dropped out of sight altogether in the snow, and had to crawl out, and try again in another place.

The glen we were following emerged into the valley of the Alaï near the spot where Khodiar, the last independent Khan of Kokand, had built the fort of Daraut-kurgan, a building with low clay walls, and a tower at one corner. Another hour's travelling brought us to the Kirghiz aul (tent-village) of Daraut-kurgan, consisting of about a score of tents (households) under the authority of the hospitable chieftain, Tash Mohammed Emin.

The origin and meaning of the name Daraut-kurgan are differently explained by different Kirghiz. Some maintain that it is composed of three words, *darah, utt,* and *kurgan,* the first common to both Persian and Kirghiz, and meaning "valley," the other two, both Kirghiz words, meaning "grass" and "stronghold" or "fort" respectively. Others declare that the name is a corruption of the Persian *dar-rau*, meaning "immediate" or "make haste on the road"; and go on to explain that Daraut-kurgan is intended to warn the traveller to make haste and get through the dreaded pass as quickly as he can.

To add to our difficulties, it began to blow a gale from the west. The snow still continued to fall, and the mist did not lift. The Kirghiz said that a violent snow-storm was raging up in the Tenghiz-bai pass; we might thank our stars we had got through it in time. And indeed it was a stroke of fortune to escape in the way we did. A day earlier and we might have been crushed under the avalanche; a day later and we might have been annihilated by the buran (snow-hurricane).

CHAPTER X

UP THE ALAÏ VALLEY

BEFORE I proceed with my itinerary I should like to say a few words about the Alaï valley, the huge troughlike depression which separates the Alaï chain from the Pamir plateau. Bounded on the north by the Alaï Mountains, and on the south by the Trans-Alaï, it is terminated at its eastern extremity by the massive mountain-knot of Mus-tagh-tau. Thence it stretches seventy-five miles westward, and is continued in the valley of Kara-teghin. Its breadth varies from three to twelve miles; the altitude sinks from 10,500 feet in the east to 8200 feet at Daraut-kurgan in the west. It is drained by the Kizil-su, which traverses it throughout its entire length, gathering up on the way the rainfall of the surrounding mountains. After quitting the Alaï valley, the river enters the valley of Kara-teghin, winds through it under the name of the Surkhab, and finally joins the Amu-daria, bearing a third name, the Wakhsh, at the point of confluence. The volume of the Kizil-su amounted to 780 cubic feet in the second at Daraut-kurgan. Add to this the volume of 175 cubic feet in the second contributed by its affluent, the Kara-su, and we get a total volume of eighty-two and a half million cubic feet in the twenty-four hours. The volume is greatest in the middle of summer, when the snows melt at the fastest rate. Indeed, for about six weeks at midsummer the flood is so powerful that it is impossible to ford the river at Daraut-kurgan. During that time all communication between the auls on the opposite banks is completely interrupted.

The volume of the stream is very much greater during the night than during the daytime. This is owing to the fact that the water from the snows, which are melted by the sun during the day, do not get down to the valley before darkness sets in. The flood begins to rise at about eight o'clock in the evening. At six in the morning it begins to fall again. It reaches its lowest level at eight, and maintains the same level all day long. In March, when I saw it, the water was as bright and as clear as crystal. But during the summer it is tinged a brick-red color by the sands and clays it passes through in its upper course. It is from this circumstance it gets its name of Kizil-su, which means the Red River. A similar circumstance has given the same name to its neighbor over on the other side of the mountains—namely, the stream which flows from the Terek-davan pass eastward to Kashgarand Lop-nor.

In the northern, middle, and eastern districts of the Pamirs—the districts through which my route ran—the downfall of snow is very unevenly distributed. Three sharply separated zones, dependent upon the configuration of the surface, may be distinguished. (1.) In the north, the valley of the Alaï, which becomes filled every winter with enormous masses of snow. (2.) In the east, the region of Sarik-kol, which receives a very much less quantity of snow. (3.) Lying between these two, the tract around the lakes Kara-kul and Rang-kul, neither of which has any outflow; there the snowfall is almost insignificant. It may be assumed that, as a general rule, the moisture-laden winds, which blow towards the lofty plateau of the Pamirs, discharge the greater portion of their precipitation upon the border ranges before they reach the central parts of the region. In these tracts it is only in sheltered spots, where the force of the wind is broken—for example, close to and around the passes—that any great quantity of snow falls. In all other places the thin, dry snow is quickly swept away by the wind.

One immediate consequence of the unequal geographical distribution of the snowfall is the unequal distribution, as well as the unequal size, of the rivers and glaciers. Both occur only in those regions where there is a plentiful snowfall. In the central parts of the plateau they are few and of

inconsiderable dimensions. Taking the results of my observations and measurements as a basis, I calculate that on an
average one cubic yard of snow out of the total quantity on
each square yard of land-surface goes to feed the rivers in the
form of water. The snow as it lies is of extraordinary density,
and only about one-fourth of its volume melts and becomes
converted into water. If we estimate that the aggregate
snowfall of the Alaï valley and the mountain-slopes which
surround it covers 2,870,000,000 square yards, we may reckon the aggregate volume of water which they yield at 19,500,-
000,000 cubic feet, or a solid cube of water measuring 2700
feet on each of its sides. This estimate can scarcely be considered excessive, when it is borne in mind that the volume
of the river during the period of high flood, in the middle
of the summer, is out of all comparison greater than during the colder seasons of the year. If we assume a volume
of 880 cubic feet in the second as the mean for the whole of
the year, the figures work out at an annual aggregate volume
of close upon 27,800,000,000 cubic feet. A calculation made
upon such insufficient data can obviously be nothing more
than an approximation. It is self-evident that the excess
precipitation must be set down to the summer rains.

During the winter violent westerly winds blow up the valley
of the Alaï with great constancy and regularity. Easterly
winds also occur, but are very rare. The high mountain-
chains on the north and south of the valley shelter it against
northerly and southerly winds, although it does occasionally
blow from the southeast. During the summer the air is
stiller, and the wind blows seldom, and then with but little
force. The west wind is called Kara-teghin *khamal*, the
east wind Irkestam *khamal*, and the southeast wind Murghab
khamal, after the various districts from which they blow.

In the valley of Fergana the spring rains come in the
middle of March. In the Alaï valley, on the other side of
the mountains, the same month is the season of the *sarik-
kar* or yellow snow, the name given to the last of the winter
snows. Why it is so called the Kirghiz were never able to
explain satisfactorily. But it is a fact that the name is in

common use all over the Pamirs. The most probable explanation is perhaps this: By that time, in certain quarters,
the snow has already melted, exposing the surface of the
ground. The dust which rises from those places is probably
caught up by the wind and blown upon the freshly fallen
snow, staining it a dirty yellow color.

I need scarcely add that the beginning of the winter
snows, and their disappearance in spring, vary in the various

AMID THE SNOWS OF THE ALAÏ VALLEY

districts. In the higher regions it snows all the year round.
In the Alaï valley the first snow falls in the end of Oc-
tober, and the last traces disappear about the middle of
April.

But to return to our journey. During the night between
February 28th and March 1st the wind howled and whistled
through the tent hour after hour, and at length rent several
narrow slits between the separate pieces of felting. In the
morning, when I woke up, the floor of the tent was braided
with ribbons of drifted snow; one of them ran diagonally
across the pillow on which my head rested. But what cared
I about wind and snow? I slept like a bear in his winter
lair. The storm continued to rage all the next day. The
wind, which blew from the west, whirled thick clouds of
snow as fine as powder past the yurt (tent) from morning
till night. In fact, every minute the tent itself threatened to

go, although we lashed it down with extra ropes, and supported it with additional stakes.

On March 2d we travelled as far as the winter village
of Gundi. But before starting in the morning we took the
precaution to send men on in advance to clear the path and
trample a passage through the snow-drifts. And fortunate
we did so, for the old track was completely obliterated by the
storm. We kept as close to the southern foot-slopes of the
Alaï Mountains as we possibly could, because in many
places on that side the snow had been swept clean away.

At Gundi we met with a misfortune. We had just got
the tent pitched and arranged, and had carried in the yakhtans, and the more perishable portions of the baggage, when

THE AUL OF GUNDI

Rehim Bai managed to give the quicksilver barometer a
knock, which smashed the delicate glass tube and set the
glistening beads of quicksilver rolling along the ground.
My costly and sensitive instrument, which I watched over as
tenderly as a mother watches over her infant, alas! it was
now useless, and might just as well be flung into a snow-
drift. I could no longer record its readings three times a
day, as I had conscientiously done hitherto. Rehim Bai was

dismayed at what he had done; but, as he really was not to blame for what had happened, I let him off with a mild wigging. What was the use of heaping reproaches upon him? That would not mend the barometer. Besides, I still had three other aneroid barometers and hypsometers.

With the idea of affording me some consolation for my loss, the men arranged a concert for the evening. One of the Kirghiz came into my tent, and squatting down began to play the *kaumuss*, a three-stringed instrument played with the fingers. The music was monotonous and of a melancholy cadence; but it harmonized well with the surroundings and the moods they inspired. In a word, it was typically Asiatic. I sat and listened to it with pleasure, giving my imagination captive to the music, the soft moaning of the night wind, the gentle crackle of the fire. How many and many a night did I not spend thus during the long years that followed, listening to the dreamy sounds of that primitive Kirghiz instrument! How many a dark, solitary winter afternoon did I not while away in this foolish fashion! In course of time I grew accustomed to the kaumuss, and derived as much pleasure from it as the Kirghiz did themselves. In fact, I grew fond of it. Its soothing music carried my mind away into the fairy realms of day-dreams; my thoughts flew far away to my home amid the dark pine woods of Sweden. And how sweet and pleasant a thing it is to dream yourself back among those who are near and dear to you! Many a night I was lulled to sleep by the measured tones of the kaumuss, played as an accompaniment to some melancholy Asiatic song.

March 3d. The storm had subsided, though the sky was still enveloped in clouds. The peaks of the Trans-Alaï range shimmered with the loveliest tints of gray, and white, and pale blue. Two hours of travel brought us to the little aul (tent-village) of Kizil-unkur, and another two hours to the pass of Ghaz, a low saddle among the southern spurs of the Alaï Mountains. All the way, even as far as Kashka-su, the river Kizil-su flowed close to the foot of the Alaï, as far from the Trans-Alaï as it could get. Our path lay close

alongside the right bank of the stream, which boiled along
at torrential speed in a sort of narrow cañon, now forcing its
way between mounds of red sand, now cutting a deep trench
through the conglomerate strata.

Then we gradually worked away from the Kizil-su. The
farther we advanced towards the east the deeper lay the
snow. The track was entirely blotted out by the latest
storm, and the snow-drifts were so thick that all day long

THE KIZIL-SU

four camels went on in front to trample down a path, or
rather a furrow, through them, along which the horses toiled
at a painfully slow and heavy pace. The wind continued to
sweep down on us in furious gusts, frequently smothering
the whole caravan in dense clouds of driving snow.

At length we came to the little brook of Kashka-su, on
the other side of which was the aul of the same name. To
get to it we had to ride over the torrent on a bridge of ice
and snow. There we found awaiting us a most comfortable
yurt (tent). Not only were Kirghiz carpets spread on the
ground, they were also hung round the walls; while the fire
which blazed in the middle of the tent scattered showers
of sparks in every direction, and crackled and shot out chips

of burning wood to such a degree that a man was told off to watch lest it should burn holes in the carpets.

On March 4th it snowed all day long. The landscape was shrouded in a thick mist, so that not a single feature could be seen. Sky and earth were one indistinguishable veil of white haze. The only relief to the eye was the long dark line of the caravan, shading off to a dull gray towards the head of the column and gradually fading away in the distance. Two camels led the way, their riders being instructed to find out where was the firmest ground. Ac-

CAMELS TRAMPLING A PATH THROUGH THE SNOW

cordingly they cruised up and down every rise and swelling of the path. But the snow was so deep that several times they dropped into it till scarce a vestige of them could be seen. Then, having scrambled out, they tried another place. The horses struggled on as best they could in the track of the camels, their packs and stirrups jolting and trailing against the banks of snow on each side of them.

At length we caught sight of a yurt on a hill-side—a black spot amid the universal whiteness. A short distance farther on we saw men engaged in putting up another tent. They were only about two hundred yards distant; but between us and them there was a ravine into which the snow had drifted to the depth of eight or ten feet, and it took us more than an hour to get all the baggage-animals safely over. The first which ventured to try to cross dropped through the treacherous surface, and was near being smothered in the deep snow.

It was as much as ever the men could do to free the horse
from his packs and haul him back again on to firm ground.
Then they set to work to dig out a path; but the snow was
so deep that they were unable to get through it. At length
the Kirghiz hit upon an ingenious device for overcoming
the difficulty. They took the felt coverings of the tent
and spread them over the snow. But there were not sufficient pieces to stretch right across, so, after a horse had advanced as far as he could get, the felts were lifted from behind him and laid down again in front of him. In this way,
but at the cost of extreme labor and great waste of time, we
managed to get all the animals safely across.

That district was called Jipptik. But the aul (tent-village)
of that name was two miles farther on, and the tents had been
shifted solely for our accommodation. Notwithstanding that,
it was anything but a comfortable camp. The fuel was insufficient in quantity, and, worse than that, damp, so that the
tent was filled with eddies of pungent smoke. The tent itself
was very speedily surrounded by high ramparts of snow.

March 5th. The night was bitterly cold. The thermometer registered a minimum of $-4.9°$ Fahr. $(-20.5°$ C.);
close at the head of my tent it was $14°$ Fahr. $(-10°$ C.)
at eight in the morning. Everything inside the tent was
frozen—canned provisions, milk extract, ink. Outside the
tent the poor horses, which had passed the night in the open
air, hung their heads dolefully, and tried to scrape away the
snow, which crackled in the frosty air every time it was
touched. The day, however, was fair, and about one hour
before noon the sun peeped through. Then the majestic outlines of the Alpine Trans-Alaï began to glimmer through the
fast vanishing mist, the topmost crests being still wreathed
in gauzy veils of cloud. Every now and again we caught a
glimpse of Kaufmann Peak (23,000 feet high), a pyramidal
summit which glittered like silver in the sunshine, and appeared to be overtopped by scarce any of its neighbors.

We waited some time for a band of Kirghiz, who, it had
been arranged, should come to meet us from Archa-bulak
and clear a track for us through the snow. But after wait-

ing some time and seeing nothing of them, our friend Emin, chief of the Kara-teppes, rode on in advance to see what had become of them, as well as to reconnoitre the ground. I confess it was not an encouraging sight to see his horse floundering through the snow-drifts, his flanks decorated with fringes of rime, while the breath gushed from his nostrils like light puffs of steam. For an hour and a half we

OUR HORSES ENDEAVORING TO FIND GRASS IN THE SNOW

watched him creeping like a black speck across the endless sea of white snows. Most of the time nothing was visible except the rider and the horse's head.

After an absence of a couple of hours Jan Ali Emin returned, and reported that it was impossible to advance farther; the snow was many feet deep, and his horse had been down several times. We held a consultation, as the outcome of which Emin and Rehim Bai rode over to the aul of Jipptik to beg assistance. The rest of us stayed behind in camp, literally snowed up on every side. At length, after some further waiting, we perceived a long string of horses and camels approaching from the north, the direction of the foot-hills of the Alaï. They were people from the aul, bringing us hay and fuel. When they came up, they strongly advised us to remain where we were till the following morning.

Early on March 6th we began to make preparations as

if for a military campaign.   Before daylight four men started on camels to trample a path through the snow-drifts.
The Kirghiz told me that some winters the snows were a
great deal worse than they were that winter.   Sometimes
they were piled up higher than the top of the tent, and inter-
communication between the auls had to be kept up by means
of yaks specially trained to do the work of snow-ploughs,
in that with their foreheads and horns they shovel narrow
tunnels or passages through the snow-drifts.

The task we had immediately before us was to cross the river
Kizil-su—by no means an easy thing to do.   Except for a deep,
rapid current in the middle, about ten or a dozen yards wide,
the stream was sheathed in ice, and the ice covered with heavy
masses of snow.   Moreover, the edges of the ice were unsafe,
being greatly eaten into by the water.   It was not at all a
pleasant sensation to sit on my horse's back when he came to
the edge of the ice above the ford and gathered himself together for a leap into the water.   If he slipped or fell, I felt
I was certain to get a cold bath, which in the temperature
that then prevailed would have been anything but agreeable;

JAN ALI EMIN RIDING THROUGH THE SNOW

worse than that—it would have been dangerous, seeing that
I was hampered with thick, heavy furs, which were a great
impediment to freedom of movement.   And even when the
horse had made the leap in safety, and was wading through
the ford, I only just escaped being seized with giddiness, for

the river boiled and foamed about him, and raced along so swiftly as almost to lift the animal off his feet. Unless I had kept a firm hand on him, he would have been swept off the ford into deep water, where he would have lost foothold and

CROSSING THE KIZIL-SU

been carried away by the current. Nevertheless, it is generally in the summer that mishaps of that sort occur.

Once over the Kizil-su, we struck obliquely across the valley towards the outer slopes of the Trans-Alaï Mountains, leaving the river behind us on the left. The ground was difficult travelling, owing to the great number of natural springs which gushed up in every direction. The water which oozed from them was partly frozen into huge cakes of ice; and where the temperature was somewhat higher, it trickled away unfrozen underneath the snow. This gave rise to soft, treacherous expanses of snowy brash, into which the horses sank at every step. From the character of the echo given by their hoof-beats we were able to tell what sort of surface was hidden underneath the snow. A dull, heavy sound meant hard frozen ground; a clear metallic ring indicated firm ice; while a muffled, hollow sound told us that we were riding over cakes or arches of ice.

Gradually as we advanced the surface became more uneven. We entered among the low foot-hills of the Trans-Alaï range, leaving the pass of Talldik behind us on the north. The snows grew deeper and deeper. After march-

ing ten hours we decided to halt, although the region around
was desolate in the extreme — not a blade, not a living creature to be seen. The men cleared the snow away from the
side of a low hill, and there stacked the baggage for the
night. The camels that were bringing the yurt from Jipptik
lagged behind on the road, and we had to wait a full hour
till they came up. In the mean time we kindled a fire, and
gathered round it close together in a circle, and tried to
warm our frozen limbs with tea. There were 47° of frost
Fahr. (−26° C.), and the least touch made the snow crackle
like parchment. I did not get under the shelter of the tent
until late that night.

I have already said that the governor of Fergana had sent
orders to the Kirghiz to have a tent and fuel prepared for us
at each stage of our journey against the day fixed for our arrival. The reason there was no tent ready for us when we

CROSSING THE KIZIL-SU (A SECOND VIEW)

reached Urtak, as this particular place was called, was due to
the following untoward circumstances. Khoja Min Bashi,
volastnoi (district chief) of Utch-teppe, which belongs to the
administrative district of Osh, had intended to meet me himself, and with that end in view set out to cross the Alai
Mountains. But in the pass of Att-yolli, near Talldik, he
had been overtaken by a snow-hurricane, and so prevented

from continuing his journey. In the same storm forty sheep
were buried in a snow-drift, their shepherd narrowly escaping
with his life. When he found himself stuck fast, the volastnoi managed to get six other men sent forward in his place
with the tent and fuel. But they had had hard work to force
their way through the pass, and after nine days' toil, and the
loss of one horse, were compelled to abandon both tent and
fuel. Four of them, struggling on, succeeded at length in
getting through to Jipptik, where they borrowed another

MARCHING UP THE ALAÏ VALLEY

tent and fresh fuel from the chieftain of the Kirghiz of that
place. When we at last met them in Urtak, they were very
uneasy about the two comrades they had left behind. One
of the four had got a frost-bitten foot, while another was
suffering from snow-blindness. He had been walking for
three days through the dazzling snows, and consequently had
overstrained his eyes. His companions did their best to
screen their eyes with tufts of horse-hair stuck between their
caps and foreheads, also with pieces of leather strap through
which they had cut narrow openings. Both invalids were
tended with the greatest care, and at the end of a couple of
days were all right again.

It was unusually late that night before we got to bed—
fully an hour after midnight before all sounds were hushed
in camp. At that time the thermometer registered −25.6°
Fahr. (−32° C.). It was my usual practice to sleep alone in

the tent, as it was not altogether pleasant to have the Kirghiz too close: they are seldom the sole occupants of their furs or felts. But intense cold is a pretty effective safeguard against the inconvenience I am alluding to. With such a low temperature I had not the conscience to let the men lie under the open sky. Accordingly, as many of them crowded into the tent and stowed themselves away on the carpets as could possibly squeeze in, till we lay as tightly packed as herrings in a barrel. Notwithstanding this, the temperature inside the tent sank to $-12.6°$ Fahr. $(-24.8°C.)$. The minimum during the night was $-30.1°$ Fahr. $(-34.5°$ C.$)$. The next morning when we woke a shower of ice flowers and icicles fell over us from the tent-roof. But I never saw the stars glitter with such matchless brilliancy as they did that night.

CHAPTER XI

OVER THE TRANS-ALAÏ

IT was eleven o'clock in the day when we got started on March 7th. We were all exhausted by the toilsome march of the previous day, and it was late when we turned in. Everybody therefore was glad to wait till the sun warmed the air before we set off again. Our Kirghiz guides led us through a series of low hills close alongside the Kara-su. This river gets its name of the Black Water from the circumstance that it has its origin, not in the snows of this highland region, but in natural springs; besides which, its water was so clear that in its deeper reaches it appeared to be almost black. We crossed over the stream two or three times on the brittle ice crust which spanned it from side to side. Underneath us we could hear the water gurgling and gulping with a clear metallic sound. There were not above two or three places where we could see the river flowing unhindered between the stones with which its bed was encumbered.

The snow-drifts grew deeper and deeper; so that the caravan could only make its way through them at a painfully slow pace. Towards the east we could see the termination of the Alaï valley, where the offshoots of the Alaï and the Trans-Alaï Mountains met together above a trough-shaped depression. The outlines of the latter chain now stood out in sharper relief, and its crest flashed back the dazzling coruscations of light which played about its snow-mantled shoulders. The chief tints were white and blue; and far, far above it sparkled the pure turquoise blue of the Asiatic sky. White gossamer clouds like bridal veils hovered about the summit of Kaufmann Peak and the neighboring altitudes. But what icy cold — what frigid brides!

The horses toiled on through the snow. The men had to be constantly on the alert, for the packs were always slipping round underneath the horses. Very often every man in the company was wanted to lend a hand to get them put straight again. At the more difficult places the characteristic cries of the Kirghiz—"*Bismillah!*" (In God's name!) or simply "*Haidah!*" (Get on!)—rang out shrilly upon the mountain air.

Our canine friend Yollchi thoroughly enjoyed himself. He tumbled like an acrobat over the snow-drifts. He rolled over and over in the snow, thoroughly cooling his thick, shaggy hide. One moment he would playfully catch up a mouthful of snow, the next he would race off swift as an arrow ahead of the caravan. The creature was half wild when he joined us; and I never succeeded in making him properly tame. Having been reared among the Kirghiz, he could never by any bribe be induced to come inside my tent. For the Kirghiz are Mohammedans, and look upon the dog as an unclean animal. The very dust off his feet would pollute the inside of a tent. I tried my best to wean Yollchi from such superstitious notions. But, do what I would, I could not get him past the tent door—neither by fair means nor foul. He had never once in his life set foot inside a tent, and obviously had made up his mind that he had no manner of business in such a place.

The climate in that part of the world is not without its peculiarities. While the sun is wellnigh burning one side of your face, the other side will be freezing. At noon, if the sky is clear, and there is no wind, it gets so hot that you are glad to fling off your sheepskins. But the moment the sun gets behind a cloud, or the shadow of a mountain comes between the sun and yourself, you begin to shiver with cold. After shedding your skin once or twice, your face gets as hard and dry as parchment, and you turn as brown as a Hindu. At noon on March 5th the thermometer registered 14° Fahr. (−10° C.) in the shade, while the black-bulb insolation thermometer showed 125.6° Fahr. (52° C.).

It began to darken while we were still two hours from the next camp. The horses travelled so slowly, and my back ached so from the heavy furs I wore, that, bidding Min Bashi accompany me, I left the caravan, and set off in the darkness to make my way as best I could over the pathless country. Min Bashi went on first. I followed in the track, or rather furrow, which his horse ploughed through the snow. It was a wearying ride, and, but that the stars shone brightly, would have been as dark as pitch. At last, however, we came to the solitary little hut of Bor-doba. Had there been a worthy Boniface in charge he would have been vastly amazed to hear two snow-smothered horsemen ride up to the door at that late hour of the night, fasten their horses outside, stamp the snow off their clothes and boots, and without further ceremony march into the house. To prevent any misconception as to the style of " house " it was, I will state at once that this rabat (rest-house) was merely an earthen hut, with a wooden roof supported by rough beams, and that the only provision for sleeping was a square bank of earth in the middle of the floor. This and a few similar huts have been put up by the direction of the governor of Fergana for the convenience of the mounted post-messengers who travel backward and forward between Margelan and Fort Pamir. This particular hut stood at the foot of a desolate hill, and from that circumstance gets its name of Bor-doba, a corruption of Bor-teppe, the Gray Hill. We both dropped straight off to sleep, and slept until the bustle and noise caused by the arrival of the caravan awakened us. Then we had tea made, and warmed ourselves over a glorious fire.

On the way to Bor-doba we saw the tracks of eight wolves, which had crossed over the valley in a scattered troop from the Alaï Mountains to the Trans-Alaï. Farther on they all struck into our track, which led through a narrow opening between two hills. The Kirghiz told me it was an old and well-known wolf-trail. The next morning at daybreak, when my men went out to see after the horses, they caught sight of seven wolves sneaking away in the direction of Kizil-art.

Wolves are very common in those regions. During the

10

summer they haunt the Alaï valley, and levy tribute upon
the Kirghiz flocks of sheep.   The Kirghiz sheep-dogs can
see them more than a mile off; but are frequently out-
witted by the wolves, who will hang about a flock for weeks
at a time, persistently spying out for a favorable opportunity
to seize their prey.   They are extremely bloodthirsty and
murderous; and if by any chance they light upon an unpro-
tected flock, will kill every sheep in it, leaving not a single

BOR-DOBA

animal alive.   Not many weeks previously a single wolf had
in the course of one night bitten to death 180 sheep belonging to a Kirghiz of Utch-teppe.   But woe betide the wolf
that has the ill-luck to be wounded by the Kirghiz, and falls
alive into their hands.   They force open his mouth, thrust
a short, thick piece of wood between his jaws, and lash them
all firmly together.   Another heavy piece of wood is fastened
to one of his feet, to prevent him from running away.   Then
they torture him to death.   On one occasion I was instrumental in putting an end to a horrible scene of this kind.

    When the great winter snows fall in the Alaï valley, the
wolves go up to the Pamirs, and range the districts around
Lake Kara-kul, preying principally upon the magnificent arkhari or argali (*Ovis Poli*)—*i.e.*, the wild sheep of Central Asia
—as well as upon the *kiyick* (goat) and hares.   In hunting the

wild sheep the wolves display remarkable craft and intelligence. Having enclosed the sheep in a wide ring, they begin to howl, so as to make their presence known, and gradually close in upon their prey. When they get near enough, they cut off two or three of the sheep and force them to take refuge on a narrow, outjutting crag, from which there is no return except into their jaws. If the crag is too steep for them to scale it, they patiently wait at the bottom until the wild sheep's slender legs become numbed from sheer weariness, and they roll down the precipice into the jaws of their ravenous persecutors. In the vicinity of Kara-kul we often saw flocks of arkhari quietly grazing a couple of miles from us. The Kirghiz used to discover them at a marvellous distance, so far off in fact that I, with my most powerful field-glass, could only just discern something of their movements. In various parts of the Pamirs travellers come across their skulls, bleached by the sun and still adorned with their huge curled horns. These are no doubt the sole remains of wolves' feasts.

According to the Kirghiz, two wolves can sometimes be dangerous to a solitary man. They told me many blood-curdling stories about wolves and their depredations up in those lofty regions of Asia. A few years ago a man was attacked and killed by wolves in the pass of Talldik, and when a day or two afterwards the Kirghiz went to fetch down his body, there was nothing left except the bare skeleton. On another occasion a Kirghiz perished in a buran in the Kizil-art pass. A week later the man's corpse was found in the snow; but the horse which he rode had been entirely devoured by wolves. Only the previous winter one of my Kirghiz guides and a jìghit (Sart messenger) were surrounded by a dozen wolves. Fortunately they were armed, and shot two of them. These were immediately devoured by the rest, after which they all took to flight.

At Bor-doba we rested a day. I employed it in making scientific observations. For one thing, we cut a vertical section three feet deep through the snow, and found it was deposited in six separate layers, showing different degrees of

purity and consistency. The bottom layer was 8¼ inches
thick, of a dirty appearance, and almost as hard as ice. The
top layer, 17 inches thick, was soft and pure as wool. It is
reasonable to suppose that the different layers or strata of
snow corresponded to different periods of snowfall, and that
those which lay underneath were pressed together by the
weight of the superimposed layers; so that during the winter of 1893–94 about six vertical feet of snow must have
fallen in the place where we made our section. The temperature of the air at three o'clock in the afternoon was 7.5°
Fahr. (−13.6° C.); the black bulb insolation thermometer
gave a reading of 115.9° Fahr. (46.6° C.). Nevertheless, at a
depth of 1¼ inches in the snow the temperature was only
−8.5° Fahr. (−22.5° C.). This tends to prove that the differences in the daily range of temperature were scarcely sensi-
ble at even that slight depth, or distance, from the direct
action of the sun's rays. (The minimum of the preceding
night was −18.8° Fahr. or −28.2° C.). As we went down
towards the surface of the solid ground—that is, deeper—measuring from the crust of snow, we found that the temperature
gradually increased. For instance, at a depth of 17 inches it
was 12.2° Fahr. (−11° C.); at 23 inches, 17.6° Fahr. (−8° C.);
at 25½ inches, 18° Fahr. (−7.8° C.); at 27½ inches, 21.7° Fahr.
(−5.7° C.); and on the ground, or at a depth of 36 inches,
24.1° Fahr. (−4.4° C.).

The ground was frozen as hard as a stone. But with
pickaxes and hatchets we made a hole two feet deep and put
down a thermometer; it registered 30.4° Fahr. (−0.9° C.).
Taking the whole series of observations together, I came to
the conclusion that the solid earth freezes to a depth of a
little over three feet and a quarter; which agrees with the
results I obtained in other parts of the Pamirs. From what
the Kirghiz told me, I inferred that the frozen ground thaws
through to the bottom during the summer.

On the morning of March 9th all the Kirghiz fell upon
their knees in the snow and prayed to Allah to vouchsafe
them a safe journey through the dreaded pass of Kizil-art.
I fully prepared myself for a terrible journey, for in the pass

of Kizil-art the snow-hurricanes are wont to swoop down upon the unsuspecting traveller out of a perfectly cloudless sky; but to my surprise I found it much easier than the pass of Tenghiz-bai, especially as we were favored with the best of weather. Bor-doba lies at such a great altitude that the climb thence to the pass, which crosses the highest ridge of the Trans-Alaï, was not especially steep. The torrent which races down from the pass in spring and summer was now frozen up, and its bed choked with sheets of ice, which, being polished bright by the wind, reflected the blue sky

SOME OF OUR PACK-HORSES

like a mirror. For the most part the range consisted of reddish sandstones and clay-slates; the former varying from brick color to blood-red in tint, the latter being dark green, light green, and gray. The bottom of the valley was thickly strewn with *débris* and disintegrated rocks, brought down from the higher regions of the mountains.

The gradients grew steeper as we approached the summit of the pass, and the snows lay deeper. But we reached the top (14,015 feet) without any mishap; though when we got there we were assailed by an icy northern wind, which penetrated sheepskins and felt boots alike.

On the very highest point of the pass stood the burial-cairn of the Mohammedan saint Kizil-art, a mound of stones, decorated with the religious offerings of pious Kirghiz—namely, *tughs* (*i.e.*, sticks with rags tied round them), pieces of cloth, and antelopes' horns. Arrived at this shrine, my men again

fell upon their knees, and thanked Allah for having preserved them on the way up to the top of the dreaded pass.
They told me that Kizil - art was an *aulia* or saint, who in
the time of the Prophet travelled from the Alaï valley to the
countries of the south to preach abroad the true faith.   In
the course of his journey he discovered this pass, to which
he gave his own name.   He is said to be now buried on the
highest point of it.   Others of the Kirghiz gave a much
more probable explanation of the name—namely, that the
cairn has simply been built in commemoration of the saint.
Further, they fully believe that, if the holy Kizil-art had not
discovered the pass, it would be impossible, even at the
present day, to travel across the Pamirs from this direction.
Tradition has also preserved the memory of his six brothers,
all of them holy men like himself.   Their names were Mus-
art, Kok-art, Khatin-art, Kolun-art, Ghez-art, and Ak-art.   The
suffix " art " is one out of several Kirghiz words meaning
" pass," and each of these six names is applied to a pass in
the mountains of the Pamirs.

CHAPTER XII

LAKE KARA-KUL

ON the southern side of the range there was at first a good deal of snow; but it soon began to get thinner. At the end of a march of eight hours' duration we came to the little caravanserai of Kok-sai. The name of this place is indelibly engraven upon my memory. It was there I recorded the lowest temperature it has been my lot to observe in the course of all my journeyings through Asia. The quicksilver thermometer fell to −36.8° Fahr. (−38.2° C.), that is, almost as low as the freezing-point of mercury.

South of the pass of Kizil-art the landscape changed its character entirely. There was a far smaller quantity of snow. Over large areas the surface of the earth was bare and exposed, in others buried under sand and the *débris* of disintegrated rocks. The mountains were softer and more rounded in outline, and their relative altitudes were less; while their several ridges or crests were separated from one another by broad, shallow, trough-shaped valleys. The region around Lake Kara-kul, between the passes of Kizil-art and Ak-baital, possesses no drainage outlet towards the Amu-daria; and the products of disintegration are not carried away by the streams, but remain and help to level up the natural inequalities of the surface. In other words, the distinction holds good here which Baron von Richthofen lays down as obtaining between regions which have no drainage outlet and peripheral regions which have a drainage outlet.

All day long on March 10th we rode towards the south-east, crossing in the early part of the day an open trough-shaped valley, girdled by low, snow-clad mountain ridges of moderate height. In the valley itself there was very little snow. What there was lay in thin, scattered patches. Before us on the right the valley opened out wider, and swelled up into a series of low, rounded hills. On the left a spur ran out southwestward across the valley, terminating in a single isolated cone. Continuing on up this gradually rising ground, we came, at the end of another four hours' march, to the little pass of Uy-bulak, from the summit of which we had a grand panorama towards the southeast. Far down under our feet we could see the northeast corner of Great Kara-kul, cased in a panoply of ice and mantled with snow. All round it stood a ring of giant mountains, draped from head to foot in one unbroken garment of dazzling snow. Within the pass the snow was once more 15 to 16 inches deep, and coated with a curiously hard, dry crust, tough as parchment, and so strong that the horses frequently went over it without breaking it. It was just as though we were travelling over a huge, tight-stretched sheepskin.

From Uy - bulak and the foot of the mountains a broad steppe sloped downward at an almost imperceptible angle towards the northern shore of the lake. Except in a few places, it was almost entirely covered with snow, which, under the force of the prevailing westerly and northwesterly winds, had assumed a strangely odd appearance. It resembled a number of small parallel dunes, or the wrinkled folds that come into cream when it is poured out on the ground and left to freeze. Several clumps of *teresken*, a hard, dry, scrubby shrub which yields excellent fuel, were scattered about the steppe.

The sun set at six o'clock. At the moment of his disappearance the shadows of the mountains on the west side of the plain raced across it so swiftly that it was difficult for the eye to follow them. Then they slowly mounted up the flank of the mountains on the east side, till nothing but the topmost pyramidal peaks were left glowing in the evening sunshine. A quarter of an hour later, and the entire region was dimmed with the twilight. The mountains on the east stood out like pale, chilly spectres against the background of the

GREAT KARA-KUL, SEEN FROM UY-BULAK.

rapidly darkening sky; while those in the west were like a
black silhouette thrown upon the brighter — light blue and
mauve tinted—atmosphere behind them.

We halted not far from the shore of Great Kara-kul, taking shelter in an earthen hut, where we passed the night in
warmth and comfort.

On the morning of March 11th I set off to cross the
lake towards the southwest, taking with me a specially se-
lected portion of the caravan—namely, two Sart jighits, two
hardy Kirghiz — all of us being mounted, with two pack-
horses carrying the baggage. We also took with us provisions and fuel to last two days, as well as a *teghermetch* (a
small conical Kirghiz tent), an iron bar, axes, spades, and the
sounding apparatus and line. Before leaving the rest of my
people I arranged with them to meet us at the next camping-station, not far from the southeast corner of the lake.

Kara-kul is a saline lake, with an area of 120 to 150 square
miles, and is shut in by mountain-chains of considerable elevation. But on the north, east, and southeast the mountains
recede sufficiently far from its shores to leave room for a
strip of steppe-like plain, two or three miles in breadth. Its
Kirghiz name, which means the Black Lake, is so far appropriate, in that in summer its waters do appear dark when
contrasted with the mountains which hem it in, for even in
that season broad patches of snow often continued to lie on
the ground. Its maximum length is about twelve miles; its
maximum breadth about ten. A peninsula jutting out from
the southern shore, and an island lying almost due north of
the peninsula, divide the lake into two basins — an eastern,
which is extremely shallow, and a western, much the larger,
and going down to abysmal depths. The object of my first
day's investigations was the eastern basin.

About two and a half miles from the shore we came to a
halt. The iron bar and axes were immediately brought into
requisition. It cost us an hour's hard labor to break through
the ice, for it was pretty nearly three feet thick. The ice
was hard and transparent, and brittle as glass. The last
stroke of the iron bar made a hole through which the water

gushed and boiled up till it filled the pit we had made in the
ice to within an inch or two of the top.　It was clear as crystal, but of a greenish-black color, and bitter to the taste.　We
let down the sounding-cord, which was divided off into lengths
of ten yards.　But very little more than the first length passed
my hands.　With the help of the measuring-tape I found th
the lake had a depth of nearly 41¼ feet.　The temperatu
of the water was 31.3° Fahr. (−0.4° C.) in the hole, and 29—
Fahr. (1.2° C.) at the bottom of the lake.　As soon as we had
finished the hole, which was nearly four feet across, the ice began to crack in every direction all around with loud repor-t
while a series of curious sounds issued from underneath it
quick succession.

We went on another two and a half miles, and made another sounding-hole.　Then we struck across the ice toward
the little island I have mentioned, hewing a third hole on
the way.　We landed beside a narrow creek, and rode across
the island till we found a suitable camping - ground.　The
Kirghiz said the island had never before been visited by human beings.　We pitched the small yurt (tent) we had brough
with us, and immediately in front of the entrance made a fire
of teresken fagots.　Then, having taken our supper, we spent
a raw, cold, disagreeable night, with the temperature down to
−20.2° Fahr. (−29° C.), at an altitude of 13,000 feet above
the level of the sea.

We woke up early the following morning, frozen, numbed
and out of humor.　We rode across the ice about three miles
due west from the island, then stopped and set about sounding the depth of the western basin.　The normal tension of
the ice was of course the same in every quarter.　Our riding
over it naturally disturbed the equilibrium by increasing th
downward pressure.　As we moved along, every step th
horses took was accompanied by peculiar sounds.　One
moment there was a growling like the deep bass notes of an
organ ; the next it was as though somebody were thumping a
big drum in the " flat below "; then came a crash as though
a railway-carriage door was being banged to ; then as though
a big round stone had been flung into the lake.　These

TAKING A SOUNDING THROUGH THE ICE OF GREAT SALAKEE

sounds were accompanied by alternate whistlings and whinings; while every now and again we seemed to hear far off submarine explosions. At every loud report the horses twitched their ears and started, while the men glanced at one another with superstitious terror in their faces. The Sarts believed that the sounds were caused by "big fishes knocking their heads against the ice." But the more intelligent Kirghiz instructed them there were no fish in Kara-kul.

MAKING A SOUNDING-HOLE IN LAKE KARA-KUL

Then when I asked *them* what was the cause of the strange sounds we heard under the ice, and what was going on there, they answered with true Oriental phlegm, "*Khoda billadi!*" (God alone knows!) Anyway, if the faithless Lady Ran* were hatching mischief against us, she strangely miscalculated her power. The ice did not break; it would have borne the whole of the city of Stockholm.

That day too we were favored with splendid weather— not a speck of cloud, not a breath of wind. There were nearly three inches of hard snow on the ice, which prevented the horses from slipping. How different all this was from the discouraging accounts given me in West Turkestan. There they told me that Kara-kul was never free from snow-

* The goddess of lakes in the old Scandinavian mythology.

hurricanes, that every flake of snow which fell was instantly swept away, and that I might look to have the entire caravan blown bodily across the glassy surface of the lake. Besides all this, they assured me I should have to put up a tent and hew my sounding-hole inside it; instead of which we did the work in the open air and in bright sunshine.

During the course of the day we rode across the lake from the north side to the south, making four other holes on the way.

The results of the soundings are embodied in the subjoined table; the Roman numerals indicating the bore-hole, the first column the depth of the lake in feet, the second and third the temperature at the bottom of the lake on the Fahrenheit and Centigrade scales respectively, and the fourth the thickness of the ice:

Eastern Basin

	Ft.	In.	Fahr.	C.	Ft.	In.
I.	41	3	34.2°	1.2°	2	11¾
II.	42	9	34.9°	1.6°	3	5¾
III.	62	10	35.2°	1.8°	2	6

Western Basin

	Ft.	In.	Fahr.	C.	Ft.	In.
IV.	726	5	38.1°	3.4°	1	7
V.	748	5	38.3°	3.5°	1	6
VI.	756	3	38.3°	3.5°	1	4½
VII.	256	3	35.8°	2.1°	1	8¾

These figures show that the eastern basin is shallow, while the western is very deep. A glance at the map, or better still at the lake itself, suggests that the contour of the lake bottom and its shores should be what the actual measurements proved it to be. The eastern basin is bordered by a tract of steppe - land, which slopes gently down towards its shore. The western basin is overhung by high, steep mountains. The lake is fed by several small brooks, which have their origin in natural springs in the vicinity, and from the melting of the snows on the mountains around. The springs are especially plentiful at the eastern end of the lake, and form large pools or marshes. One other deduction may be drawn from the table given above, though it is so self-evident as scarcely to need particularizing. It is this: with every increase in the depth of the lake, the temperature rose and the ice grew thinner.

Shortly after passing a little promontory, we saw before us the long fjord or gulf which cuts deep into the southern shore. It presented a striking picture; for, while the declivities came down at an angle of twenty degrees on the west, there was on the east a flat shelf sloping up gently towards the foot of the mountains, and in the background, at the head

A SMALL ISLAND IN LAKE KARA-KUL

of the fjord, a semicircle of the snow-clad giants of the Pamirs. Judging from what I could see of the configuration of the ground, I hardly think that the southern half of the fjord can exceed 160 feet in depth.

We cut our last sounding-hole right in the middle of the mouth of the fjord. As soon as we got through the ice, three of the men begged to be allowed to ride on in advance with the horses to Ak-tam, the place near the southeast corner of the lake where we had agreed to spend the night, so that they might get the tent ready against my arrival. I and the jighit Shir remained behind to take the soundings. By the time we had finished, it was dark; yet not so dark but that we could see to follow the trail of the other men who had gone on to camp. We tracked them obliquely across the fjord, but lost the trail when we touched the shore. We rode a long time across the peninsula, which I have mentioned before, scrambling over sand and stones and other products of disintegration. In a little the crescent of the moon appeared above the horizon, and shed down its cold, pale beams upon the desolate scene. And desolate indeed it was—not a sound to be heard, not a vestige of a living creature to be seen. Every now and then we stopped and shouted—no answer. Once we came across the trail in a scanty snow-drift. But the next moment the moon was shrouded in the night-mist, and we lost it again. After riding for fully four hours, we came to the shore of the eastern basin. But we saw no sign of horsemen, no signal-fire, no appearance of a camp.

The other men had, it was evident, travelled another way. The question was—which way? We rode on another hour, trusting to chance to guide us. But it was all to no purpose; we could not find those we sought. We determined therefore to halt for the night. The spot where we came to this resolve was a level expanse of sand, dotted with thin patches of snow. We tethered the horses together by a halter to prevent them from running away. The poor creatures, which had had no food all day, hungrily scraped at the sand with their hoofs; but they found nothing except the tough, hard roots of teresken. At these they tugged greedily. Having made the best preparations for spending the night that our resources admitted of, we sat close together, and talked till an hour after midnight, firing one another's fears with grewsome wolf stories. Shir said, however, that if danger threatened us from that quarter the horses would be our best protectors, as they would be certain to give us warning.

Having thoroughly tired ourselves with talking, we squatted down Kirghiz-fashion in our sheepskins—i.e., on our knees, with our backs to the wind. I made a pillow of the portfolio or satchel which contained my maps, sketch-book, thermometers, and so forth. But I was not a Kirghiz. I found it impossible to sleep in that attitude. Every now and then Shir dropped off and began to snore; but I could not sleep a wink. I tried the position we Europeans are accustomed to, but was soon chilled through by the cold, and had to rise and move about to get warm again. From time to time the horses nuzzled against us, as if to remind us that we had forgotten to give them their supper.

Fortunately for us the night wind was not too fresh, and the temperature only fell to 4.1° Fahr. (−15.5° C.).

About six o'clock in the morning day broke, and we mounted into the saddle, hungry and stiff with cold. We rode southward for an hour, till we came to a place where

THE STONE HUT AT AK-TAM

there was a litlle scanty yellow grass, left by the last flock of sheep which browsed over the spot in the autumn. While the horses grazed for an hour or two, I and Shir got a good sleep, for the sun was up and kept us warm.

Having mounted again, we pushed on still towards the south. On the way we met a solitary Kirghiz, travelling on foot from Rang-kul to the Alaï valley. As with most of his race, his eyes were as sharp as a hawk's; he had discovered us nearly two miles before meeting us. I and Shir found our comrades at the end of another hour's riding. Our first concern was to thaw our stiffened limbs and warm ourselves with hot tea; then, while the horses were eating their fodder, we despatched our breakfast, consisting chiefly of mutton and tinned provisions.

March 14th. The country rose from the Kara-kul very

gradually towards the south.   Before we had travelled far,
we rode into a broad valley, stretching between two parallel
mountain-ranges, which ran north and south, and were
sheathed in snow.   As a rule, a larger quantity of snow falls
every year in this valley than around Great Kara-kul, though
the depth seldom exceeds four inches.   Thick clouds hung
about the mountain-tops; everywhere else the sky was perfectly clear.   About noon, however, the wind got up, and it
soon blew with great violence.   For close upon five hours
we rode steadily towards the south-southwest; but coming
to a bifurcation of the valley, we turned to the left and
struck out towards the south-southeast.   Just where the valley divided, we saw, conspicuously crowning a low hill, the
masar or tomb of the Kirghiz saint Oksali, built of slabs of
stone and decorated with horns and tughs (sticks with rags
and pieces of cloth tied round them).

The valley into which we turned was the valley of Mus-
kol, which led up to the pass of Ak-baital.   There was but
little snow on the ground; but as we advanced, the surface
became more and more thickly strewn with disintegrated
débris.

Upon my arrival in camp I was met by four Kirghiz,
wearing their gala *khalats* (coats).   They had been sent
from Fort Pamir to welcome me, and had been waiting five
days, with a tent and supplies of food and fuel.   They told
me that my long delay had begun to make the Russian officers at the fort uneasy.   As a matter of fact, we had been
seriously delayed by the enormous quantities of snow we
met with in the Alaï valley.

The word Mus-kol signifies "ice valley."   Soük-chubir,
the place where we encamped, might very well mean Cold
Siberia, for the usual name for that region in Turk is
Chubir (Siberia).   Whether this last interpretation is correct
or not, and it is not quite certain that it is, both names may
with good show of reason be said to be appropriate.   For
the region thereabouts is characterized by an excessive winter cold; while the valley is distinguished for a remarkable
natural phenomenon, which I will now proceed to describe.

The little stream which traverses the valley of Mus-kol has its origin for the most part in natural springs. During the winter the water gradually freezes and spreads across the valley in huge "cakes" or sheets of ice. They resemble small frozen Alpine lakes, and their surface is so glassy bright that it reflects every dimple of the sky and every angle of the mountain crests. In certain seasons these ice-sheets do not entirely melt away during the course of the summer. The largest I saw was nearly two miles long and more than half a mile broad. We rode half way across it in order to examine its thickness. The lateral strain upon the ice, and the pressure of the water from beneath, give rise to long narrow ridges, which are sometimes thrust up to the height of several feet, and are cleft by fissures going right through them from top to bottom. With the axes and iron bar we cut a transverse section through one of these ridges, and found it was merely a crust about eleven inches thick. Below it was a hollow arch, $9\frac{1}{2}$ inches in height; and then came the water, three feet deep, going down to the sandy floor of the valley. The water was clear as crystal and of a light-green color; the thermometer gave its temperature as $31.6°$ Fahr. ($-0.2°$ C.). Looking down through the open section we made, I perceived that the still, transparent water was arched over in both directions by a long tunnel, and that the under surface of the ice-arch was decorated with frost-work, crystal pendants, and stalactites, all shimmering with the loveliest hues of blue and green.

There were three of these ice-lakes. On the edge of the smallest of the three, close beside the spot where we pitched our camp for the night, were two typical ice-volcanoes. Two springs gush out of the level ground. Late in the autumn, when the temperature permanently falls, the water which wells from them freezes. Meanwhile the springs continue to bubble up all the while the water continues to freeze. In this way two cones of ice are formed. One was $16\frac{1}{2}$ feet high, and had a circumference of 225 feet; the other measured $26\frac{1}{4}$ feet and 676 feet in height and circumference respectively.

Four deep fissures radiated from the crater of the smalle volcano, which was about fifty-five yards distant from th other. At the time of our visit they were all half filled witl ice. The cone was built up of an innumerable number o thin layers of light-green ice, each layer representing a sepa rate freezing. The mouth of the crater was closed by whit ice, full of air-bubbles; but there was not at that time th least sign of water oozing out. It was an "extinct" volcanc

The larger volcano consisted of a double cone, one super imposed upon the other. The bottom one, which was buil up entirely of white ice, was low and flat, its sides inclinin at an angle of not more than five degrees. The upper con which was a dome of pure, transparent ice, rising at an an gle of 30 degrees, and measuring 70 feet in diameter, wa seamed throughout by a net-work of intersecting fissures some concentric, others radiating from the centre outward Here again the mouth of the crater was frozen over, compel ling the water to seek a new outlet through a side-fissure o "parasite" volcano. Although the water trickled out at a lively rate, it gradually froze before reaching the ice-lake, anc so became set into a sort of "ice-flow." Its temperatur was 31.5° Fahr. (−0.3° C.).

In the small ice-lakes it begins to freeze in the very be ginning of November, and the last of the ice does not thav and get down to Lake Kara-kul before the middle of June In one of them it never does melt entirely away, being f vored by a shady, sheltered position; so that when the nev ice begins to form in the end of September some of the ol ice is still left.

We were surrounded on all sides by glacial landscapes only, unfortunately, mists and snow-storms prevented me fron taking photographs of them. Looking towards the west along the longer axis of the ice-lake, it was easy to imagin we were gazing down a narrow fjord or sea-gulf; the horizo was wreathed in mist and seemed to lie at an immense dis tance away. To right and left were mountain-chains; but i was only the slopes nearest to us which emerged out of th haze.

On March 15th we rode all day long up the valley of Mus-kol, traversing it right through from one end to the other. At its upper extremity to which the ascent had been very gradual, we halted for the night, close to the northern en-

A REST ON THE PASS OF AK-BAITAL

trance of the pass of Ak-baital. The next day brought us a hard climb of ten hours' duration right over the pass, which rises to the pretty respectable altitude of 15,360 feet. A sharp snow-storm, waxing for a time into a hurricane, gave us a chilling welcome in the pass. The ascent was tough work for the horses, chiefly in consequence of the extreme rarefi-cation of the air. They had to exert themselves to the utter-most, and frequently stopped to gasp for breath; and despite our utmost care often fell. The pass consisted of two dis-tinct ridges, separated by a stretch of almost level ground, which took us a good half-hour to ride over. It was cov-ered with snow to the depth of 12 to 16 inches. On the summit of the pass we rested a short while, although there was a keen sou'wester cutting through it. The temperature

there was 12.2° Fahr. (−11° C.), and water boiled at 184.3°
Fahr. (84.6″ C.).

The caravan started down the eastern side of the pass,
which was at first extremely steep, in a thick mist. But, the
steep upper slope passed, the country fell away at an easy
gradient all the way to Kornei-tarti, our next camping-
ground. In the Ak-baital pass another of our overworked
horses fell dead. One of the Kirghiz bought the skin from
Islam Bai, the leader of the caravan, for two roubles (4s).

Kornei-tarti, meaning "the Trumpet Blast," is a narrow
glen, half choked with detritus, partly products of denudation, partly large stones and rocks, through which meandered
a little brook; though at the time of my journey this last was
covered with a hard crust of ice. The bottom of the glen
was one unbroken expanse of snow; but on the mountain-
sides there was little, except in the declivities which faced
north. Of vegetation there was not a trace. We went on
steadily steering for the southeast and east-southeast, the
country retaining the same characteristics as before. At
Ak-gur (the White Grave), where a conspicuous spur jutted
out into the glen, we were met by Kul Mametieff, a Tatar,
whom the commandant of Fort Pamir had sent to act as my
interpreter. He was dressed in full uniform, and wore half
a dozen medals on his breast, and brought with him a letter

KIRGHIZ CAMP—BREAKING UP CAMP

eloquent of friendly greetings from his master. We continued to ride on till we came to Togolak - matik (Round Caldron Valley), or the junction of the valley of Rang - kul with that of Ak-baital.

On the 18th we accomplished the last stage of this portion of our long journey—namely, the lower extremity of the valley of Ak-baital, and the part of the valley of the Murghab which we had to traverse to get to the Russian outpost on the Pamirs. The first thing we noticed, upon catching sight of the fort at a distance, was the Russian flag flying from its northwest corner, proclaiming the sovereignty of the Czar over the "Roof of the World." When we drew nearer, we saw that the ramparts were beset with soldiers and Cossacks to the number of 160, drawn up in line. They gave us a cheer of welcome; and at the main entrance I met with a hearty reception from the commandant, Captain Saitseff, and his officers, six of them in all. They conducted me to the room in their own quarters which had been ready for me a whole week. A yurt was set apart for the use of my men.

As soon as I got my baggage stowed away, I went and had a good bath, and then joined the officers at mess. It was a meal not soon to be forgotten. I delivered the greetings I had brought from Margelan. I had a thousand and one questions to answer about my adventurous ride across the Pamirs in the middle of winter. Then, when the Cossack attendants served round the fiery wine of Turkestan, the commandant rose, and in a neat speech proposed the health of Oscar, King of Sweden and Norway. If ever a toast was responded to with real sincerity and gratitude, it was when I stood up to return thanks for the honor done to my king. If ever there was a place where joy reigned supreme, it was surely here on the " Roof of the World," 11,850 feet above the level of the sea, far removed from the bustle and noise of the busy world, in the very middle of Asia — a region where our nearest neighbors were the wild sheep of the mountain crags, the wolves which prowl over the snowy wastes, the imperial eagle which soars through the endless spaces of the sky.

CHAPTER XIII

POPULATION OF THE RUSSIAN PAMIRS

THE greater part of our route across the Pamirs led, as we have seen, through uninhabited regions. The Russian districts of the Pamirs had in October, 1893, a population of not more than 1232 persons. But the Alaï valley and the valley of Sarik-kol possessed, relatively speaking, a denser population. Administratively the Alaï valley is divided into two portions, the western half belonging to the *uyäsd* (district) of Margelan, the eastern half to the *uyäsd* of Osh. The information which I derived from the Kirghiz chiefs who dwell in those regions is not perhaps absolutely reliable, but it is sufficiently near the truth to deserve consideration.

Scattered through the Alaï valley there were, they told me fifteen kishlaks or winter settlements, aggregating a total of 270 yurts (households or families), who in part remained there the whole year through, in part migrated to the higher regions during the summer. The number of tents in the larger auls was estimated as follows: in Daraut-kurgan, 20; Kok-su, 120 Kizil-unkur, 50; Altyn-darah, 5; Tuz-darah, 45; Kashka-su, 20; and Jipptik 10. Ethnologically the inhabitants of these settlements were said to fall into the following groups: Teit-Kirghiz dwelt at Daraut-kurgan, Altyn-darah, and Tuz-darah; at Kashka-su, Teit and Chal-teit; at Jipptik, Choy-Kirghiz; at Kok-su, Naiman Kirghiz; in Kara-teghin, Kipchaks, Naiman Kirghiz, and Kara-teit. The greater portion of these people migrate every summer to the neighborhood of Lake Rang-kul, where, after the snows have disappeared, the grassy steppes furnish good pasturage for their sheep. A portion of them also winter, as we have seen, in the Alaï valley. There too, in the end of May or beginning of June the prosperous Kirghiz of Fergana bring *their* flocks to graze on the plentiful grass which springs up along the borders of the Kizil-su. They pitch their *ycylaus* or summer camps on the banks of the river, and amuse them-

THE KIRGHIZ BEG OF THE AUL OF MURGHAB

selves with their *baigas* or games on horseback, feast, marry —in a word, make summer holiday. The greater portion stay only a couple of months, none longer than three months. The rest of the year they spend in their kishlaks or winter-

quarters in Fergana.   During the summer there are about
150 yurts at Kashka-su.

The Kirghiz who go up to the Pamirs from Osh and
Andijan travel by way of the Talldik and Jipptik passes;
those who belong to Margelan and Kokand prefer the pass
of Tenghiz-bai.   This last is also the route which nowadays
is chosen by the large number of Tajiks who travel on foot
every summer to Fergana in search of work.   The Alaï
valley is also an important link in the chain of communication which connects East Turkestan with Kara-teghin and
Bokhara, and so with the pilgrim road to Mecca and Me-
dina; so that during the warmer months of the year many
a trading-caravan and pilgrim-train passes up and down the
valley.

The portion of the Pamirs which belongs to Russia is
divided between two *volasts* (arrondissements) embracing in
all seven *eminstvos* (communes):

1. The volast of the Pamirs consists of five eminstvos:
Kara-kul, with 131 inhabitants in October, 1893; Murghab,
with 253; Rang-kul, with 103; Ak-tash, with 239; and Alichur, with 256.

2. The volast of Kuh-darah includes only two eminstvos—
namely, Sarez, with 95 inhabitants, and Kuh-darah, with 155.
The inhabitants of the volast of the Pamirs were almost
exclusively Teit-Kirghiz; of Kuh-darah almost exclusively
Tajiks.   The total population, grouped by sex and age, embraced 320 men, 369 women, 342 boys, and 201 girls—a total
of 1232.

These statistics were given me by Captain Saitseff.   His
predecessor, Captain Kuznetsoff, took a census of the district under his authority in October, 1892, with the following result:—a total of 1055 people—255 men, 307 women,
299 boys, and 194 girls.   Captain Saitseff's figures thus
show an increase of 177 during the year.   But the increase
was partly due to immigration.   The Kirghiz who dwelt on
the other side of the Chinese and Afghan frontiers were
attracted into Russian territory by the improved conditions
of living, the result of the Russians' wise and humane treat-

ment of the native populations of Asia. The regions most
frequented during the winter months were those around
Rang-kul, Kosh-aghil, and Ak-tash.   There were also several
auls (tent-villages) in the Alichur Pamirs, some even in the
Pshart valley, south of Kara-kul.   The little aul of Murghab
lay a short distance east of the fort.

Captain Kuznetsoff estimated that the 1055 Kirghiz occupied 227 yurts (tents), and that their live-stock consisted of
20,580 sheep, 1703 yaks, 383 camels, and 280 horses.   The

TAJIKS FROM ROSHAN

Tajik population of the western Pamirs he estimated at
35,000.

The eastern slopes of the Pamirs—that is, the tracts lying
east of the Sarik-kol range—belong to China. With regard
to them, there exist of course no reliable statistics.   The beg
of Su-bashi (south of Little Kara-kul) told me that in the
environs of that lake there were some 300 Teit-Kirghiz
dwelling in about 60 yurts. He himself was chief of 286
yurts, most of which, however, lay on the east of the great
mountain of Mus-tagh-ata. All the Kirghiz of the Pamirs,

irrespective of the tribe to which they belong, are called by
their kinsmen in Fergana by the one common appellation of
Sarik-kolis, or people of Sarik-kol.

The statistics which I have just given demonstrate how
thinly the Pamirs are inhabited. Nor could anything different be expected, considering the characteristics of the region—
the intense cold, the frequency and fury of the snow-storms,
the few pasture - grounds and their scanty supplies of grass.
Of the two self-contained internal drainage-basins, Kara-kul
and Rang-kul, the latter only has a settled Kirghiz population.
The Kara-kul Kirghiz are true nomads. At the period of my
visit to the lake their tents were pitched some little distance
away on the south and southwest; its shores were entirely
unoccupied. The grazing - grounds in the vicinity are frequented during the spring, summer, and autumn. But there
is no grass during the winter; it is cropped too close by the
sheep in the latter part of the autumn. Sometimes the Kirghiz from Rang-kul migrate to the steppes round Kara-kul
for the summer grazing.

THE AUTHOR AND THE RUSSIAN OFFICERS AT FORT PAMIR

CHAPTER XIV

GEOGRAPHICAL SUMMARY

BARON VON RICHTHOFEN divides the whole of the Asiatic continent into three distinct regions of very unequal extent—the Central, in which the rivers drain into inland lakes; the Peripheral or border lands, in which the streams make their way down to the seas which wash the coasts of the continent; and the Transition or Intermediate tracts, which partake of the characteristics of the other two. The subdivision also holds good when applied to the Pamirs. Here, too, there are three similar geographical districts—a central district draining into lakes Kara-kul and Rang-kul, a peripheral draining to the Amu-daria (and so into Lake Aral) and to the Tarim (which empties into the lake Lop-nor).

The most remarkable feature in the region of internal drainage is the process of levelling-up which goes on unceasingly. The detritus which results from the disintegrating action of the weather, and the more or less mechanical agency of wind and water and gravity, is constantly being carried down from the mountains all round its borders towards the lower parts of its depressions, and being deposited there. In this way the natural inequalities in the configuration of the ground are being gradually smoothed away. Although, broadly speaking, this process is going on in the tracts around Lake Kara-kul, it is also true that there are very great differences in the relative altitudes in that same quarter. For instance, the lake lies at an elevation of 13,000 feet above sea-level. It has been sounded to a depth of 756 feet—a remarkable depth, considering that Kara-kul is a saline lake in the centre of Asia. And near its western margin the mountains tower up to an altitude of 4000 feet above the surface of the lake. Here there is an enormous field for the process of levelling-up to work in. But the soundings which I took in the lake proved that it *is* also operative there, for the bottom was covered with fine mud.

The mountain - chains which encircle the depressions of Kara-kul and Rang-kul attain to relatively great heights, and the passes which cross them are seldom much lower than the crests. The pass of Kalta-davan, for instance, has the same absolute altitude as Mont Blanc—namely, 15,780 feet; the pass of Kizil-art is 14,015 feet; of Ak-baital, 15,360 feet; and Chuggatai, 15,500 feet. The lake of Rang-kul, which lies 12,240 feet above sea-level, marks the lowest point of the depression. The area which falls between the passes just named amounts to about 2100 square miles, an area which is approximately equal to that of the basin of Issyk-kul.

The traveller who journeys from Fergana to East Turkestan cannot help observing that the character of the country which stretches from Kizil-art on the north to Ak-baital on the south, and is bordered by the Chuggatai range on the east, is totally different from the tracts which immediately surround it. It is not a highland region ; but a high-level plain, bounded on the north and south by latitudinal chains, and on the east by a meridional chain. Surveying the region from the summit of the Kizil-art pass, I was struck by the low angle of inclination and the soft, rounded forms of the mountain-slopes ; and noticed that the hills which diversified it were piled up, as it were, on the level ground, instead of striking off as sharply defined ranges in definite directions. The entire region bears witness to the enormous power of the forces of denudation exercised unceasingly over a vast period of time. *Débris* and fragments of rock, from the size of pebbles to the largest bowlders, strew the ground in every direction. The lower flanks of the mountains are buried under detritus and mounds of disintegrated materials. On every hand, in fact, I saw convincing proofs of the destructive power of frost and rain and snow. Hard bare rock was nowhere visible, except near the crests of the ranges, in places where the wind is able to work unchecked.

The valleys of this high-level plain or plateau are broad and almost level. They rise at such a gradual inclination towards the outer ring of mountains that they often seem to be perfectly horizontal. Each of them is as a rule traversed by a little mountain-stream, which is fed partly by natural

A TRANSITIONAL LANDSCAPE ON THE PAMIRS—ONE OF OUR CAMPS

springs, partly by the melting snows, and which empties itself into one of the two lakes, Kara-kul or Rang-kul. The scenery is frequently grand, but always depressingly monotonous, more especially in winter. In that season there is not a living creature to give animation to the desolate wilderness. A powerful field-glass will sometimes enable you to see a distant flock of arkhari (wild sheep) or kiyick (goats). Of human beings or human dwellings there is not a glimpse. Pastures are few, and the grass scanty. In a word, the landscape, with its barren, naked surfaces, puts you in mind of a typical lunar landscape.

Unlike similar tracts of Asia which possess no drainage

12

outlet, the depression of Kara-kul does not suffer from ac-
cumulations of sand.   The explanation of this, no doubt, is
that the finer products of denudation are swept up by the
constant violent wind-storms which prevail in that region, and
are carried away to be deposited in parts of the continent
where the atmospheric conditions are permanently calmer.
Sand-storms and dust-storms are indeed by no means a rare
visitation of the Pamir plateau.   It is very probably to them
that the so-called " yellow snow " owes its origin ; for an examination of the snow-drifts to which that name is given reveals the presence of extremely fine particles of yellowish soil.

The most powerful agencies of disintegration in this part
of the world are the winds and the enormous and sudden variations of the temperature.   I saw striking evidences of their
power on the little island in Lake Kara-kul, in huge blocks
of syenite and clay-slate ground, scooped out, polished into
the most fantastic shapes.   The variations of temperature
are enormous, not only in winter, but also in summer.   At
Fort Pamir, at seven o'clock in the morning of January 11th,
1894, the thermometer recorded a temperature of $-36°$ Fahr.
$(-37.8°$ C.); one hour after noon it was 53.6° Fahr. (12° C.)
in the sun—a difference of nearly 90° Fahr. (50° C.) in the
course of only six hours !   The amount of radiation is almost
inconceivable.   At a time when the temperature of the air
was just at the freezing-point, the black bulb insolation thermometer actually registered 133° to 136° Fahr. (56° to 58° C.).
These stupendous forces labor on unrestingly century after
century, wearing down the solid structure of the continent—
in this an imperfect image or analogue of the earth itself,
which is but the last surviving wreck of substances which
have been in process of formation and re-formation through
countless æons of time.

This region of exclusively internal drainage is girdled round
by a zone of what Von Richthofen calls Transitional areas.
On the north it is bounded by the Alaï Mountains, on the
east by the chain of Sarik-kol, on the south by the Hindu-
kush, while its western limit is marked by the line of 73°
E. long.   According to Von Richthofen, the definitive char-

acteristic of a region belonging to the Transitional zone is the fact that the erosive power of the water, and the resultant action of the violent alternations of temperature, have in more recent times broken a new path for the drainage streams, so that instead of seeking an interior, landlocked basin, they are now able to find an outlet to the rivers which eventually discharge into the sea ; or, *vice versa*, they cease to send their waters oceanward, but turn them instead towards an interior basin which makes no contribution to the seas around the continent.   A Transitional region is therefore one which retains the typical features of the region to which originally it definitively belonged.

The Transitional zones of the Pamirs bear a very close general resemblance to the self-contained drainage-basin of the Kara-kul.   Erosion is not yet sufficiently far advanced to enable the streams to carry off all the products of disintegration which cumber the valleys, the contours are soft and rounded, the valleys themselves broad and shallow.   The tendency of the active disintegrating forces operative in the Pamirs is to convert it into a Peripheral region.   For instance, in the southwest the little brook of Kok-uy-bel, a feeder of the Murghab, which in its turn goes to augment Lake Aral, has extended its remotest arteries to within about six miles of the brook of Mus-kol, which discharges into Lake Kara-kul. The springs which give origin to the Kok-uy-bel lie only a trifle higher than the level of the lake ; so that, geologically speaking, the Kok-uy-bel may perhaps to-morrow be converted into an outlet from the lake, through which its waters would gradually flow away till it became empty.   Simultaneously with this change, the Kara-kul depression would begin to lose the characteristic features of an independent area of internal drainage, and would gradually assume those of a Peripheral region.

A typical Peripheral region is one which through the agency of erosion has lost its former character of a high-level plain or plateau, and assumed the more definitely marked aspect of a region in which Nature's fingers have carved and moulded with powerful effect.   Its outward contours are very

much steeper and wilder, the relative altitudes greater; the
plateau is cleft almost to its foundations by gigantic trenches
or fissures radiating outward; the valleys or glens which cut
into it are deep and narrow, revealing the internal structure
of the mountains; while along their bottoms the torrents foam
and race through confined, gorge - like channels, over huge
bowlders of stone which have crashed down from the heights
above.

On the west side of the plateau the turbulent head-streams
of the Amu-daria—namely, the Murghab, Ghunt, and Pänj—
in many places force their way between vertical walls of rock, as
though they were traversing a tunnel through the mountains.
Such places are absolutely impassable except to the native inhabitants of those regions—namely, the clever Tajiks.   There
are places above certain of the streams where these people
have driven wooden pegs into the sides of the perpendicular
crevices, and with the sureness and nimbleness of apes clamber up from peg to peg, bearing heavy burdens lashed upon
their backs.   It is surprising what skill they show in availing
themselves of every jutting piece of rock, every ledge and
cornice, every crack and chink in the precipitous cliff-wall.

The border regions of the Pamirs are distinguished for the
striking geographical homologies they present.   On the north
the river Kizil-su flows between the two parallel mountain-
chains of the Alaï and the Trans-Alaï.   On the east the Sarik-
kol valley, between the Mus-tagh and Sarik-kol ranges, is
traversed by the Ghez-daria and the Yarkand-daria.   On the
south the Wakhan is hemmed in by the Wakhan chain and
the Hindu-kush, which both run in the same direction.   The
Pänj too on the west likewise flows between parallel ranges
of mountains, though they are of a less imposing altitude.
The valleys through which these several streams descend from
the Pamirs to the lower regions exhibit features of a Transitional character.   On the one hand, while they resemble the
deeply trenched valleys on the outer borders of the plateau,
with their large rivers in full flood all the year round, on the
other hand they possess many features in common with the
level plains of the central areas of depression.   Although

strictly speaking, according to Von Richthofen's definition,
the Ghez-daria and Yarkand-daria belong to the central area
of depression, the districts through which they flow, and which
their muddy streams to some extent help to mould and level
up, exhibit the characteristics of a Peripheral zone.   The
drainage-basin of the Ghez-daria embraces four lakes, the two
largest being Bulun-kul and Little Kara-kul.   The Ghez-daria,
as well as the Kara-su, an affluent of the Yarkand-daria, are
fed principally by the snows and glaciers of Mus-tagh-ata; so
that in spring and summer their currents swell to streams of
very respectable dimensions.   On April 28th the Ghez-daria
had a volume of 850 cubic feet in the second, and we had
some difficulty in crossing it.   Later on in the summer it
cannot be forded at all.   These two strong torrents have made
an irresistible assault upon the Mus-tagh range; both have
cut their way through it.   The Yarkand-daria is the chief
contributary of the river Tarim; indeed, it furnishes the greater portion of the volume of its waters.

Summarizing in broad, general terms, we may say that
the Pamirs may be grouped in two sharply contrasted divisions—an eastern half, which is principally a plateau-land
such as I have described, and a western half, consisting of a
system of latitudinal mountain-chains disposed parallel to
one another.   There can be no doubt that at one period the
entire region was strictly a plateau, and that it is being rapidly broken down by the agency of erosion.   Indeed, it is not
more than a generation ago when the Pamirs were universally considered to be a plateau pure and simple.   We know
now that they form a gigantic quadrilateral, embracing within its confines surface configurations and types of scenery of
the most diverse description.

On the Pamirs, as in other parts of the world, the bounda-
ries of different climatic regions are determined by the
outstanding physical features.   Over the central areas of
the region the amount of snowfall is exceedingly small; but
the cold is intense, the night temperatures being below
freezing-point all the year round, with the exception of a
couple of weeks in the middle of summer.   In the Alaï val-

ley, on the contrary, the climate is relatively milder, but at
the same time the snowfall is enormous.   Even in the valley
of Sarik-kol the quantity of snow which falls every year is by
no means inconsiderable.   It follows therefore, as a direct
consequence of the unequal distribution of the snowfall, that
the rivers of the Pamirs carry down very unequal quantities
of the drainage - water.   For instance, at the time of my
journey the Kizil-su had a volume nearly four times as great
as the Murghab (or Ak - su), the chief head - stream of the
Amu - daria; besides, the measurement of the latter was
taken a month later than the measurement of the former.
The volume of the Kizil-su was 950 cubic feet in the second;
the volume of the Murghab only 250 cubic feet.

The ethnological and linguistic divisions of the Pamirs
coincide pretty accurately with the physical divisions.   The
population of the plateau proper are almost entirely Kirghiz,
relatively few in number.   Farther west, the Peripheral districts of Darvaz, Roshan, and Shugnan are inhabited almost
exclusively by Tajiks, and the population there is relatively
much denser.   Nor is this a merely accidental difference.
The Kirghiz are nomads.   Their wealth consists of flocks
of sheep, yaks, camels.   As the seasons change, they move
from one pasture-ground to another.   Hence they naturally
prefer the level stretches of the plateau to the deep, narrow
glens and steep mountain-sides of the Peripheral regions.
The Tajiks, on the other hand, are a settled population,
their conditions of life being totally different from those
under which the nomad Kirghiz live.

The separate linguistic areas are almost necessarily coincident with the ethnological areas.   The Kirghiz give their
own Turki names to the geographical features with which
they are brought into relation.   The Tajiks call the same
objects by names borrowed from *their* language, which is
Persian.   By way of illustration I may mention that nearly
all the rivers which flow towards the west are generally
known by their Kirghiz names in the upper part of their
course, and by their Persian (Tajik) names in their lower
course.   Thus we have the Ak-su known lower down as the

Murghab, the Gurumdi known as the Ghunt. In one district there are two small streams flowing together side by side. One has a Kirghiz (Turki) name—Kok-uy-bel, because the glen through which it flows is frequented by Kirghiz. The other bears the Persian name of Kuh-darah, because there is a Tajik village close beside the entrance to its valley.

CHAPTER XV

FORT PAMIR

FROM this brief geographical summary I pass to the little Russian outpost of Fort Pamir, and a brief account of the very pleasant time I spent there between March 19th and April 7th, 1894.

Fort Pamir, situated on the right bank of the Murghab, at an altitude of 11,800 feet above sea-level, was built as a check upon Chinese and Afghan aggressions upon the territories of the former Khans of Kokand. Although the Russians conquered the khanate in 1875 and 1876, for some time they bestowed but little thought upon the region of the Pamirs. It was only thinly populated and very difficult of access, and possessed nothing to invite attention. General Skobeleff, for as far-sighted as he was, never seems to have given it a thought. But when the neighboring powers began to stretch out their hands towards it, Russia awoke to the necessity for energetic action. Colonel Yonnoff's famous expedition was the first result of the change of policy on the part of the St. Petersburg authorities. It was an expedition which opened up political questions of a grave and delicate character; which, however, were satisfactorily terminated by the labors of the Anglo-Russian Boundary Commission in the summer of 1895.

As regards Fort Pamir, I may mention that it was built by the men of the fourth battalion of the Russian army of Turkestan in the year 1893, between July 2d (O.S.) and October 30th. The outer wall, which forms an oblong, was constructed of sods and bags of sand, and encloses a fair-sized court-yard, around which are ranged the officers' quarters, and a long earthen structure, covered in with

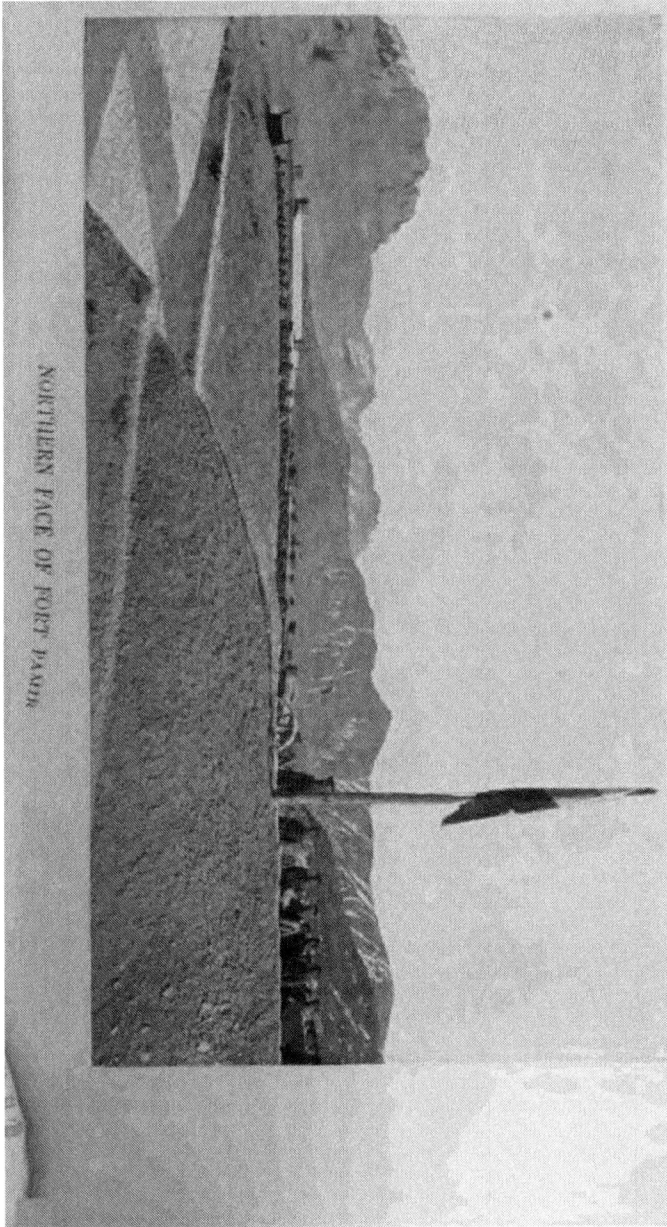

NORTHERN FACE OF FORT PAJO

beams, and containing barracks, kitchens, hospital, bath-
rooms, workshops, and so forth. The commissariat stores
and ammunition are kept in yurts. There is also a little
meteorological station, where observations are taken three
times every day. In the corners of the longer side which
faces the north are two platforms, each furnished with a battery of Maxim-Nordenfeldt machine-guns. The fort occupies a commanding position on a terrace of conglomerate,
which overlooks, but at some distance away, the right or
northern bank of the Murghab. Between the two extends a
marsh or morass, out of which gush a great number of
springs of clear water. Fort Pamir is a striking testimonial
and proof of the energy and spirit of the officers who built
it. For it was anything but an easy task to erect such a
structure at that high altitude and at such an immense distance from the resources of civilization. Every inch of timber and every ounce of other building material had to be
transported on horses' backs all the way from Osh in Fergana, pretty nearly by the route I have described. The
months in which the work was done were unusually stormy;
furious hurricanes of blinding snow, mingled with fine sand,
being of frequent occurrence. Part of the time both officers
and men dwelt in Kirghiz yurts, which were again and again
blown over by the wind.

Within the last few years a new route has been opened to
Kashgar, and the merchants of that town now resort to the
southern Pamirs, where they traffic with the Kirghiz, barter-
ing the wares they bring with them for sheep. They then
drive the sheep down to the market-towns of Fergana, where
they make a good price of them; and so return home to
Kashgar by way of the passes of Terek-davan and Talldik,
with a substantial profit in their pockets.

The commandant of Fort Pamir, Captain V. N. Saitseff,
was a settler of long standing in Turkestan. As aide-de-
camp to General Skobeleff he took part in the campaign
against Khiva in 1873, and in that against Kokand in
1875–76. Besides being commandant of the fort, he was also
governor of the Kirghiz population of the Pamirs.

Of Fort Pamir I have none but the happiest recollections.
I reached it at the end of a long, toilsome journey through
an uninhabited and difficult mountainous waste, and was received in that little outlying fragment of mighty Russia with
open arms, more like an old friend or long-standing acquaintance, by a group of officers who, I have no hesitation in saying, were as amiable, as courteous, as generous a set of men
as it is possible to meet with.   And, without undue self-love,
I can flatter myself that my arrival formed a not unpleasing
diversion in the lonely and monotonous life which the garrison of the fort are compelled to lead during the greater portion of the year.   For all winter through, ever since September of the previous year, not a soul had been near the
fort except the Kirghiz.   As soon therefore as the Russian
officers learned, from the mounted couriers I sent on in advance, that I was approaching, they hurried up to the battery
platforms, armed with every field-glass that could be got in
the fort, and swept the horizon northward until my caravan
came into sight.   And when I rode in through the gate, I
was received with the warmest of welcomes by every man
of the garrison.

Fort Pamir often reminded me of a ship at sea.   The
outer walls might be likened to the bulwarks; the wide,
open, sweeping valley of the Murghab to the sea; and the
court-yard to the deck.   Up and down this latter we used to
walk day after day, stopping every now and again to gaze
through our powerful field-glasses towards the far-distant
horizon — a view which never varied in its dull lifelessness
except on one day in the week.   That was Tuesday, when all
eyes were early on the alert for a single, solitary horseman, the
post-courier (jighit), who brought the eagerly expected mails
from far-off Russia.   His arrival was the great event of the
week.

When his horse trots in through the gate, every man of
the garrison hurries out to receive him.   The commandant's
adjutant makes haste to open the mail-bags.   Everybody
stands around in anxious expectation.   The adjutant draws
forth the letters, newspapers, post-parcels from those they

INTERIOR OF FORT PARMA, LOOKING SOUTH

love, now, alas! so far off. He distributes them to the happy
recipients. Joy reigns supreme, except in the bosoms of the
unhappy beings for whom this Asiatic Father Christmas has
brought no heart-warming gift. For three post-days in succession I was counted among the unenvied ones. This was
because of the alteration in my route. All my letters were
sent on to Kashgar, with the result that for a period of four
whole months I never received a single letter from home.
The contents of the mail-bags distributed, the rest of the
day is spent in greedily devouring the welcome home news.
Evening comes. Officers and men meet for dinner, each in
their own quarters. But all alike pursue one common topic
of conversation — the events which have been happening
recently in the great world of politics and human action
from one end of the world to the other.

Our day was generally spent in the following manner:
Every man had tea (first breakfast) in his own room. At
noon precisely a signal by roll of drum called us all together
for a substantial breakfast. After that we had tea again in
our private quarters. At six o'clock a fresh drum-signal reminded us that dinner was ready. After dinner we broke
up into little groups, to each of which coffee was served
round. We then talked until late into the night; and towards midnight I and the commandant used to have a snack
of supper.

Drill filled up most of the morning hours. The soldiers
and Cossacks were also during the course of the day instructed in certain of the sciences which have a bearing
upon military matters. But my time was for the most part
occupied in more peaceable pursuits; for one thing, photog-
raphy. In the evening, when I developed my plates, I was
usually surrounded by half a dozen closely interested spectators, who never tired of watching how as by a wizard's
"pass" the frigid mountain scenery and its half-wild inhabitants imparted life and meaning to the photographic
plates.

Among other things we measured the volume of the water
carried down by the Murghab, and set up a gauge-post in the

river, upon which one of the officers might observe the rise and fall of the current during the coming spring and summer. We also measured the depth to which the crust of the earth is frozen in winter; and industriously compared notes upon what we had seen and observed. The soundings I made in Kara-kul awakened the liveliest interest. Nobody had expected that the lake would go down to anything like a depth of 756 feet.

One of my friends in Margelan told me that Fort Pamir was an earthly paradise. I asked him " Why ?"

He replied, " Because there are no women there !"

Although I am very far from sharing his opinion, I am bound to confess it would not be easy to find a circle in which contentment, cheerful spirits, and the tone of light and easy comradeship are better preserved than they were at Fort Pamir. Nobody cared a rush about appearances. The officers went about in threadbare uniforms and with their boots unpolished. Nobody wasted time on the niceties of the toilet. Directly we heard the dinner-bell, or rather drum, we went straight into the mess-room without stopping to don such superfluous articles as collar and cuffs. No need to furbish up all the pretty sayings a polished man of the world feels it obligatory upon him to whisper in the ear of the lady he takes in to dinner. In a word, everybody at Fort Pamir was perfectly free, subject to no irksome social restraints. Cossacks prepared and cooked the food we ate. Cossacks waited at table. Cossacks rubbed us down in the bath-room, acted as house and chamber maids, even washed our dirty linen. There was not the faintest glimpse of a petticoat to be seen inside Fort Pamir. The only creatures of the female sex within its walls, so far as I was able to ascertain, were a female cat, a couple of bitches, and some hens. But to call Fort Pamir a paradise because no woman brightened it with her lovely smile — that is a doctrine I certainly cannot subscribe to.

Captain Saitseff enjoyed the full sympathy and esteem of his officers, and maintained the strictest discipline and good order among the men under his command. The long

THE JHONTS' TENTS AT FORT PAMIR

dreary winter, during which the little garrison had been straitly shut up within the walls of their fort, like a band of Polar explorers compelled to winter in their ice-bound vessel, had not occasioned the least slackening of discipline, the least indifference or discontent among either officers or men. Nevertheless the immediate approach of spring, which was indicated by the increased warmth of the sun's rays, by the melting of the snows on the mountains, and of the ice

RUSSIANS AND KIRGHIZ AT FORT PAMIR

on the lakes and rivers, seemed to reawaken several dominant interests. It was a season when every day brought fresh opportunities for scientific observation. Already the birds had begun their summer migrations. Small flocks of ducks and geese of a great variety of species were on the wing from their winter-quarters in India to their summer haunts in Siberia. The Murghab was apparently one of their favorite resting-places, where, alas! several of them entered upon a rest that was destined to prove unexpectedly long. The Cossacks spread their nets in the river. Others

of the garrison took their sporting-rifles and stalked the wary
arkhari or wild sheep (*Ovis Poli*), and not seldom brought
home a pretty well filled bag.

The relations between officers and men were in all respects excellent. On one occasion, when thirty time-expired
men were setting off to return to their homes in Osh, it was
quite touching to see how, in orthodox Russian fashion, their
superiors kissed each man three times on the cheeks. Their
rifle on their shoulder and their knapsack on their back, the
men set out right cheerfully to tramp the long 280 miles
which should bring them to their more genial homes in the
warm valleys of Fergana.

Sunday was given up to all kinds of games and dancing.
The music was but poor, being limited to a concertina, two
drums, a triangle, and a couple of cymbals; but the performers went to work with a will, and made the very most of
their resources, while the cleverest of the Cossacks danced
their national *kamarensky* with such spirit that the dust

THE CONGLOMERATE TERRACE ON WHICH FORT PAMIR STANDS

whirled up around them in clouds. Then, when the sun set,
and the west wind, which at regular intervals during the day
had swept past the fort with an angry howl, subsided, there
rose upon the rarefied mountain air a succession of Russian

songs, sung by some seventy fresh, strong voices. They were partly folk-songs with a melancholy cadence, partly soldiers' ditties of a livelier character. The last Sunday of my stay at Fort Pamir was closed by a musical evening of this kind. The atmosphere was still and calm, the air cold;

LANDSCAPE NEAR FORT PAMIR, LOOKING NORTHWEST—RUSSIAN OFFICERS RETURNING FROM A HUNT

the stars glittered with indescribable brilliancy; and the gentle murmur of the Murghab stole upon the ear in the pauses of the singing. The soldiers sang with much feeling, as though their hearts were touched by memories of their far-off native land; and their officers and myself listened with genuine sympathy, as their fresh, warm voices melted away into the lofty regions of immeasurable space.

CHAPTER XVI

FROM THE MURGHAB TO BULUN-KUL

ON April 7th, 1894, after partaking of a substantial breakfast, I bade adieu to Fort Pamir, though I was escorted a
good distance on my way by the commandant and his officers. Arrived at the little torrent of Ak-baital, we found
some of the Cossacks awaiting us with tea. Then, having
thanked my Russian friends for the splendid hospitality they
had shown me during those never-to-be-forgotten days—a
last shake of the hand from the saddle, a last wave of the
cap, and away I spurred towards the north, followed by the
interpreter of the fort, the Tatar, Kul Mametieff, whom the
commandant sent with me as a guard of honor.

Just as daylight was fading we came to the twin lakes
Shor-kul and Rang-kul, which are connected by a narrow
sound. There we took up our quarters for the night, camping in a *yulameika*, a tall, conical tent with no smoke-vent.
Meanwhile my right-hand man, Rehim Bai, had fallen ill, and
all the way to Kashgar was totally unfitted to discharge his
regular duties. We had to transport him thither like a bale
of goods on the back of a camel. His place was taken by the
man of whom I have spoken before—Islam Bai; and it was
during this part of my journey that I first learned to know
and value that excellent man's many excellent qualities.

The snow lay in scanty patches; but both lakes were sealed
with thick sheets of ice. Strange to say, however, the sound
between them was open water, and swarmed with wild duck
and wild geese. The configuration of the ground—grassy
plains sloping gently down towards the lakes — suggested
that the lakes themselves were shallow.

Next day I sent the caravan by the nearest road to the little fort of Rang-kul, while I myself with four men started across the ice of Rang-kul to take soundings. We only chopped out two holes, and found that the lake was as a matter of fact extraordinarily shallow, the two measurements giving 5 feet and 6½ feet respectively. The ice, on which was a thin sprinkling of snow, was 3 feet and 3½ feet thick where the two sounding-holes were hewn. There was a small open channel close alongside the shore. The temperature of the water in the sounding-holes was 31.6° Fahr. (−0.2° C.); at the bottom, which was covered with loose slime and mud, mingled with decayed vegetable matter, it was 37° (2.8° C.). The vegetable matter consisted almost exclusively of algæ and sedges. The word *ranga* is used to indicate the sedge *Carex physoides*. All the same, it is more likely that the lake derives its name from the wild goat which frequents that region, and which is known as the *rang* and the *kiyick*.

The word Shor-kul means "salt lake," and its waters were both salt and bitter. It was pretty evident that, while Rang-kul was fed by fresh springs and streams, Shor-kul derived its supplies from Rang-kul through the little sound already spoken of; and that evaporation went on to a very much greater extent in the former, leaving the saline concentrates behind it. In the eastern end of Rang-kul there was a long narrow island, barely a dozen feet high, but with perpendicular shores of soft, grayish-blue clay, much eaten into by the waters of the lake. Vast numbers of wild geese are said to breed there every spring as soon as the ice melts.

The soundings taken, we rode straight across the lake, and on to the fort, garrisoned by about twoscore Cossacks under a commandant. We stayed there two days. We left the fort on April 11th, riding almost due east towards the little pass of Sarik-gai, which crosses a spur of the northern mountains. On the west side of the hill we were approaching, the wind, mostly coming from the west, had heaped up enormous masses of sand, shaping them into gigantic dunes or billows with a slightly corrugated surface. On the other side of the pass we descended into the broad, open, level valley of Naisa-tash, in which were two Kirghiz auls (tent-villages). We took up our quarters in the one which stood farthest east. It consisted of five yurts (tents), occupied by nineteen individuals of the Chighit tribe, ten of them being men. They spend the winter and summer beside Lake Rang-kul; but cross over into the valley of Naisa-tash for the spring grazing. Their wealth in live-stock embraced 400 sheep, 40 yaks, 7 camels, and 3 horses.

On the following day, April 12th, we were to cross the provisional frontier-line between the Russian and Chinese Pamirs. Ever since we left Rang-kul we had seen glittering immediately ahead of us the snowy crests of Sarik-kol. That lofty range we had to climb over. Out of the several passes which lead over it I chose the one known as Chuggatai, 15,-500 feet in altitude. We struck off towards the northeast. The inclination increased the farther we advanced, until at the foot of the pass it became very steep and difficult. The track too was not at all easy, being strewn with large blocks of gneiss and clay-slate, still draped for the most part with snow. On the summit of the pass, which had a high, sharp pitch like a house-roof, we halted to rest; and while resting were surprised by a violent hail-storm which came out of the southwest. The temperature was 5° Fahr. below freezing-point (−2.8° C.).

The descent towards the north, on the other side of the range, was equally as steep as the ascent had been; and it cost us a wearisome march to reach the first aul of Chuggatai —a little collection of four yurts with twenty-four inhabitants. But we pushed on to another aul of six yurts a short distance lower down. There we made our first camp on Chinese territory.

I speedily learned that all sorts of wildly extravagant rumors were flying about the neighborhood concerning me. It was said that I was a Russian, coming, at the head of three-score Cossacks armed to the teeth, to make a hostile raid into Chinese territory. My arrival had therefore been looked forward to with not a little apprehension. But when the Kir-ghiz saw me ride up alone, accompanied by only a small band of their fellow-believers, their fears quickly subsided, and they carried from Shu King Sheng, the Chinese ambassador at the Court of St. Petersburg, addressed to the Dao Tai of Kashgar, they withdrew their opposition, but stipulated that, immediately we came down from the mountain, Kul Mametieff should take the shortest road back to the Russian Pamirs. On the other hand, a Kirghiz *allik-bashi*, a non-commissioned officer who nominally commanded fifty men, was bidden to go back at once, having no pass. I then proposed to send Rehim Bai on a camel direct to Kashgar, for his illness was assuming a critical phase, and he was in urgent need of rest and comfortable quarters. But to this Tura Kelldi Savgan would not agree; for if, said he, Rehim Bai were to die on the road, his death would involve the Chinese authorities in difficulties. It was only by promising to return to Bulun-kul when I came back from my ascent of Mus-tagh-ata, and not make for Kashgar by any other route, that I finally succeeded in overcoming the last of their scruples. Even then I had to leave behind in their hands one of my men as a hostage, together with one-half of my baggage. This compact made, I announced that it was my intention to return their visit without delay; but both officers declared that they had no authority to admit a European inside the fort in the absence of the commandant, Jan Darin, who had gone to Kashgar. But Jan Darin would soon return, they said.

In this laborious way we parleyed backward and forward for five mortal hours. When at last they rose to go, I thought to make a good impression upon them by presenting them with a Tula *kinshal* (dagger) and a silver drinking-cup. They protested, it was not at all the right thing for me to offer *them* presents after such a *recherché* dastarkhan; that it ought to be the other way on, seeing that I was their guest. But in the end they suffered themselves to be persuaded, saying they hoped to have an opportunity to return my presents when I came back from my trip up the Mustagh-ata. Having taken their leave in due form, they galloped off in a whirlwind of dust, through which their white horses, their scarlet uniforms, their glittering weapons were

for a long distance dimly visible. And we never saw a
glimpse of the gentlemen again; although they indicated
their presence by forbidding the Kirghiz of the neighborhood
to furnish me with supplies of mutton, fuel, and other necessaries.

The rest of the day was spent in making preparations for
the ascent of Mus-tagh-ata. I decided to take only four men
with me—namely, Kul Mametieff, Islam Bai, and the two
Kirghiz, Omar and Khoda Verdi. Four pack-horses were
got ready to carry the necessary baggage — provisions, bed,
furs, presents, medicine-chest, photographic apparatus, scientific instruments, and several other indispensable articles.
Everything else was left behind in the care of Khoja, the
Sart, who was also charged to look after Rehim Bai. The
more comfortable quarters I succeeded in getting for the invalid had done him no good. The winter journey over the
Pamirs had completely broken him down. His cheeks were
white and hollow, his eyes big, and with a vacant, glassy stare
in them. His friends would scarcely have recognized him,
he was so changed. He offered a he-goat to Allah, and declared that he felt a little better in consequence.

In the evening we were honored with a visit from some of
the Chinese soldiers from the fort. They begged to be allowed to peep into one or two of my commissariat boxes and
yakhtans (packing-cases). We afterwards learned that up at
the fort they believed all my boxes were packed full of Russian soldiers, who in that way were being smuggled across
the frontier. The fact that each and every trunk I had was
only capable of holding at the most about one-half of a soldier did not in any way help to allay their suspicions. I
opened two or three, and after that they appeared to be
easier in their minds. During the night the Chinese placed
sentries all round my tent; but they had the good feeling to
post them at a distance and out of sight. It was plain they
had received orders to keep us under surveillance, and find
out what was my real purpose in visiting this remote corner
of the vast Chinese empire.

Whichever way we turned, we had a magnificent view be-

... ... on the opposite side of the little lake of ... ... the sublime snow-clad mountain mass of Ak- ... ... Mountain," the northern continuation of ... ... to the left of it was the beginning of the ... ... to the right the broad trough of Sarik-kol. ... ... foreground, and only a short distance from our ... ... the Kirghiz aul of half a dozen yurts; while ... ... the slopes around were dotted with long-haired ... ... as they grazed. To the south lay the be- ... ... the narrow glen called Kum-yilga, the "Sand

CHAPTER XVII

MUS-TAGH-ATA

It was April 14th when we set off to climb the great Mus-tagh-ata. Immediately after we started we were met by a violent storm from the east, which drove clouds of fine drift-sand straight into our eyes. Having passed the two little lakes of Bulun-kul and taken a distant glance at the fort, we turned up the broad valley of Sarik-kol. For fully an hour we were followed by a big black yak. We wondered whether he was trained to play the part of spy; but eventually he grew tired of keeping up with us, and stopped.

The valley of Sarik-kol is a gigantic trench, piercing to the heart of the stupendous Pamir plateau. Sometimes narrow, sometimes expanding to a considerable width, its bottom is littered with huge bowlders of gneiss and other rocky *débris*, all polished smooth by the action of water. At one place we came to a colossal erratic block of gneiss split clean in two, in such a way that we were able to ride between the two halves as though we were going through the gateway of a mediæval town. The valley itself was hemmed in on both sides by lofty mountains, the flanks of which were thickly strewn with crumbled and disintegrated rocks. Scantily supplied with pasture-grounds, it was uninhabited except for a single, solitary yurt. On the whole it sloped up gradually and easily towards the foot of Mus-tagh-ata.

We soon perceived that we were no longer travelling in the Russian portion of the Pamirs. When we came to the end of our day's march, we found no yurt ready pitched for us by Kirghiz sent on in advance. We were now, plainly enough, on the Chinese side of the frontier. We were no longer to be indulged with such luxuries and comforts. How many a

14

night after that did we not sleep under the open sky! Such was our fate on this the first night of our trip. We endeavored to make the best of circumstances, by looking about for a hollow that was in some degree sheltered from the wind. We found one in a part of the valley called Kayindehdala (the Birch Plain). A singularly inappropriate name, for the ground was stony and barren, and there was not a single specimen of the graceful green lace-work which drapes the birch to be seen. Very possibly, however, the name is a survival from a time when those trees did grow in the locality.

We encamped under the shelter of a huge block of gneiss, which leaned over a little towards the south. Round the front of it somebody had built up a low wall of stones, which afforded some measure of protection against, at any rate, the worst of the wind. We piled the baggage all round us, spread out our carpets, and made our camp as comfortable as we could; and when shortly afterwards our ears were greeted with the bubbling of the soup over the fire of tereskèn fagots we were as happy as kings. But the wind whistled in through the crevices between the stones, and dust and sand kept swirling round us in eddies, so that our teeth gritted every time we took a mouthful of food. Once during the evening it snowed a little, but about ten o'clock the weather changed with marvellous suddenness. The atmosphere became calm, and the sky clear. Then the moon came forth and poured her light into our grotto, and lit up the desolate scene, deepening the oppressive silence and making the valley appear ten times more dreary and awe-inspiring than it was before.

April 15th. The farther we went towards the south the more broken grew the surface. We came to the little Alpine lake of Bassyk-kul, with its fantastic shore-line, leading me to think that its deep inlets must have been carved out by the most capricious of the brownies. The middle of the lake was crusted with ice, brittle and porous; but close in beside the shore we saw open water. It was pure, limpid, and sweet to the taste. At a short distance from the lake I observed an old Chinese inscription, engraved on a block of gneiss that was deeply embedded in the ground and surrounded by a rough wall of stones. Close by were two other gneiss bowlders, both bearing signs of having been subjected to the smoothing, polishing action of glacial ice. On one of them I just discerned traces of an inscription similar to that on the stone already mentioned, but most of the lettering had been obliterated by the wind and its powerful ally, the drift-sand. The place where the stones were was called Tamga-tash, or the Signet Stone.

A low hill in the vicinity gave us a distant view of the Little Kara-kul, a beautiful Alpine lake imbosomed in deep mountains, whose reflections played upon its surface, constantly changing its waters from blue to green and from green to blue. The ice was all gone, except for a small strip near the southern shore. A fresh breeze was blowing off the lake, ruffling its surface with foam - tipped waves, which chased one another in endless succession, and finally broke against the shore with a rhythmical and harmonious murmur.

The path gradually approached closer to the lake until it was only separated from it by a chain of low hills, the surviving remnant, as I discovered on a second visit, of an ancient moraine. That I should come back again to that lake, I little dreamed at the time I first saw it; and yet I did come back, and its lovely shores grew dear to me! How many a lonely evening did I not lie and listen to the mysterious tidings which those melodious wavelets whispered, and which there was none to interpret! And how many a time did I not feast my eyes upon those giant mountains, which mirrored their snowy crests in the transparent waters of the lake of Little Kara-kul! But I shall have occasion to relate my recollections of the place in a subsequent chapter, and therefore I hasten on with my journey.

In some places the cliffs, along which the path ran, had crumbled away, and we were obliged to scramble down as best we could, and ride through the water along the ridge of commingled *débris* and gravel. On the south of the lake we struck into the broad valley watered by the stream Su-bashi, where large herds of shaggy yaks were busy plucking the young spring grass. In the mean time the wind had quickened up into a veritable storm. Dense clouds of dust and sand, and even fine particles of abraded rock, blew straight into our faces, with such violence that we were sometimes compelled to stand still and turn our backs to the storm. When we came to the fort that guards the valley, we found the Chinese as busy as bees unpacking and inspecting a fresh consignment of stores which had just come in for the garrison. But we were met by a stalwart horseman, Togdasin Beg, chief of the Kirghiz of Su-bashi. He received me politely and in a friendly spirit, and conducted me to his large and handsomely appointed yurt. This man subsequently became one of my best friends among the many I made in Asia.

As soon as we got our tent in order we were honored by a stream of visitors, who kept coming all the evening. First there were all the Kirghiz of the neighborhood. Then we had the Chinese soldiers of the garrison, among them some Dungans (Chinese Mohammedans). All the sick too of the valley came to me begging for medicine. One old woman said she had the Kokand sickness. Another patient suffered from toothache. A third had a pain in his nose. One of the Dungan soldiers experienced an uncomfortable feeling in his stomach when a storm was blowing. And so they went on. I treated them one and all in the same simple fashion, by prescribing for each alike a small dose of quinine. And on the principle that the bitterer the remedy the more efficacious it is—a principle which is thoroughly believed in by all Asiatics—they went away universally satisfied.

The next day we were entertained at tea by the notables of the Kirghiz auls and by certain of the Chinese soldiers. In the evening Togdasin Beg came to my tent by invitation, and was entertained with a liqueur and the harmonies of a musical-box, which so enraptured him that he declared he felt twenty years younger. He said he had never enjoyed anything so much since the days when the great Yakub Beg ruled over Kashgar. Somewhere about twenty years earlier, he told me, the Sultan of Turkey sent a large musical-box as a present to Yakub Beg.

Ever since I left the Alaï valley my thoughts had been constantly running upon the ascent of Mus-tagh-ata, and I neglected no opportunity of gathering from the Kirghiz all

TOGDASIN BEG

the information I could at all bearing upon the project. But every man I talked to, without exception, assured me that it would be utterly impossible to reach the top. The precipices and yawning chasms would prove insuperable obstacles to progress. The flanks of the mountain were sheathed in ice as bright and smooth as glass. On them and on the summit storms roared without cessation; and if I were so venturesome as to defy the giant, he would bid the winds sweep me away like a grain of sand.

But Mus-tagh-ata is truly a magnificent mountain. Whenever the Kirghiz pass it, or first catch sight of it in the course of a journey, they fall upon their knees and say their prayers. They declare that it is the abode of threescore and ten saints. Nay, they assert that it is one gigantic masar or burial-mound of saints. Within its interior dwell, among others, the souls of Moses and Ali, the son-in-law and nephew of the prophet Mohammed. When Ali lay at the point of death he prophesied to those about him that as soon as the breath was gone out of his body a white camel would come down from heaven and carry him away. As he said, so it came to pass. When he was dead the white camel appeared, took the holy man on its back, and hastened with him to Mus-tagh-ata. The Kirghiz are firmly convinced that Moses' soul also abides in that mountain; and for that reason they sometimes call it Hazrett-i-Musa, or the Holy Moses.

The Kirghiz of Su-bashi told me this story about the holy mountain: Many hundred years ago an aged *ishan* (holy man) went up the mountain by himself. And when he came a certain way up it he found a lake and a little stream, with a white camel grazing on the shore. There was also a large garden planted with plum-trees, and under the plum-trees there walked to and fro a number of venerable old men dressed in white garments. The holy man plucked some of the fruit and ate it. Then came one of the venerable inhabitants of the garden and said to him that it was well he had done so; for if he had despised the fruit, as all those aged men had done, he would have been condemned like them to stay on the mountain, walking up and down the garden, to the end of time. Then came a rider on a white horse and caught up the holy man, and galloped with him down the steep mountain-side. And when the ishan came to himself he found that he was down in the valley, and could only remember dimly all the marvellous things he had seen.

There is also another legend associated with this part of the world, dating from the time when the famous Khan Khoja ruled over all the lands that lie between Kashgar and Manas, in Dzungaria. The Chinese sent two emissaries to Khan

Khoja, offering him peace; but he refused to accept it.   One
of the emissaries he killed, and cut off the ears and nose of
the other, and so sent him back to the Emperor of China.
This put the Emperor beside himself with rage.   He bade
his men fill three big cooking-pots with nails.   Then he had
the nails counted, and took a vow that he would send against
Khan Khoja as many soldiers as there were nails in all three
pots.   Khan Khoja had an army of 70,000 men, and for one
whole month he lay encamped near Manas over against the
innumerable host of the Chinese.   But at last battle was
joined, and Khan Khoja was defeated with the loss of
38,000 men; whereupon he marched back to Kashgar with
the remnant of his army, and from Kashgar pushed on to
Bulun-kul, where another battle was fought.   Again the
Khan was defeated, and again he retreated, going as far as
the lake of Little Kara-kul.   There he was once more hard
pressed by the Chinese; but at the critical moment, when
things again began to look desperate for him, a band of forty
horsemen, giants in size and mounted on raven-black horses,
galloped down Mus-tagh-ata, and, flinging themselves upon
the Chinese, decided the battle in Khan Khoja's favor.

Now there was in his army the *palevan* (hero) Chum Kar
Kashka Bater, and he was counselled by his master never, so
long as he was engaged in fight, to look behind him.   If he
obeyed, he would always be victorious; but if he disobeyed,
he would perish.   In three fights Chum Kar obeyed his
master, and so overcame his adversaries; but in the fourth
he glanced behind him, and in the moment he did so was
struck by an arrow and slain.   The hero's masar, or tomb,
stands on a dominant buttress of the west flank of Mus-tagh-
ata.   One of the glaciers of the mountain commemorates the
hero's name to the present day.

But the Chinese soon gathered another army, numbering
as many men as the stars in the sky, and came and fell upon
Khan Khoja near the lake of Little Kara-kul.   Thereupon
the forty horsemen withdrew and rode back up Mus-tagh-ata—
an ending, by-the-way, strangely at variance with all the im-
aginative tales I am acquainted with!   Khan Khoja's evil star

still remained in the ascendant. He was worsted again, and fled to Rang-kul and Kornei-tarti. But the Chinese pursued after him and compelled him to give battle once again. His army was routed and scattered like chaff, so that at last the Khan was left alone with none but his trumpeter to bear him company. Then the Khan bade the trumpeter sound his trumpet. Instantly the scattered fragments of his forces were gathered around him. But they were far too weak to stand against the Chinese, who drove them before them, pursuing them over hill and valley until they had slain nearly all of them. When Khan Khoja at length came to Yeshil-kul (the Green Lake), he had but fifty faithful followers left. There he went up alone into a high mountain; but when he looked down his men were surrounded by their enemies, the Chinese. Khan Khoja gave them a sign with his hand, and they flung themselves into the lake. Then, lo and behold! a new marvel happened. They would not sink, and the Chinese shot at them as though they had been shooting wild duck or other game. But Khan Khoja took up a handful of dust, muttered a prayer over it, and cast it over the lake. In a moment the heroic fifty disappeared beneath the waves. The Khan himself fled to Badakshan; but the shah of Badakshan cut off his head and sent it to the Chinese. His body was taken possession of by certain of his friends, and by them sent to Kashgar, where it lies buried in Hazrett-Apak.

The Kirghiz tell further, that on the top of Mus-tagh-ata there exists an ancient city named Janaidar, which was built in the days when universal happiness and universal peace reigned throughout the world. But since that time there has been no intercourse between the people of Janaidar and the inhabitants of the earth. Consequently the former still enjoy an existence of unblemished happiness. In the city of bliss there are fruit-trees which bear magnificent fruit all the year round, flowers which never wither, women who never grow old and never lose their beauty. The choicest pleasures of life are as common there as bread; death, cold, and darkness are banished from its confines forever.

In a word, Mus-tagh-ata resembles Mount Demavend in Northern Persia, and other strikingly conspicuous mountains, in being invested with a halo of mystery and made the centre of a tissue of fantastic legends and stories. The half-wild Kirghiz look upon it as a holy mountain, and regard it with profound reverence and fear. No wonder, then, the European does not escape the magic glamour of its spell!

Mus-tagh-ata, the loftiest mountain of the Pamirs, and one of the loftiest mountains in the world, towers up to the height of 25,600 feet, and like a mighty bastion overlooks the barren wastes of Central Asia. It is the culminating point in a meridional chain, the Mus-tagh or Ice Mountains, a chain that is worthy to rank with the stupendous ranges which converge upon the Roof of the World—the Himalayas, Kwen-lun, Kara-korum, Hindu-kush. The unchallenged pre-eminence of Mus-tagh-ata over the peaks which cluster around it is proved by its name, which means the Father of the Ice Mountains. And the name is very appropriate; for truly, like a father, it lifts its white head among its children, which in their turn are all clad in white robes of snowy purity and sheathed in breastplates of ice. The silvery sheen of the great mountain flashes like the gleam of a light-house to a vast distance across the desert ocean. Many a time have I gazed wonderingly upon it from afar off. Many a month have I wandered on its rugged flanks. Many a night and many a day have I been, as it were, spellbound by the weird mystery of its fascinations.

Upon questioning the Kirghiz of Su-bashi as to the possibility of climbing the patriarch of the snows, I found they were not so discouraging in their opinions as were their kinsmen in the inner parts of the Pamirs. They were all quite willing to accompany me, and ready to further my purpose to the utmost of their ability. All the same, they prophesied that the attempt would be a failure. Hunters who had lost their way while pursuing game into the higher reaches of the mountain had become giddy through breathing the "heavy" air. Even the agile and sure-footed wild sheep had been known to recoil in terror from the brink of

the icy precipices when driven out towards them by a posse
of hunters.   Nor was the imperial eagle able to swing himself up to the topmost pinnacles; his wings grew numb before he could reach them.

As a consequence of all this we planned a formal and
elaborate campaign against the giant, and resolved, cost
what it would, to conquer him.   Our plan was to lie in am-
bush and keep a close watch upon him, and seize the first
careless moment—*i.e.,* take advantage of the earliest favorable days as regards weather—to deliver our attack.   We decided to establish a third depot at the highest possible point,
and therefrom make our reconnaissances and take measures
for advancing farther.

CHAPTER XVIII

AN ATTEMPT TO CLIMB MUS-TAGH-ATA

In the course of a long exploring journey the traveller's plans are often upset by annoying difficulties and hinderances, causing him to deviate from the route he laid down beforehand, and compelling him to abandon objects which he had set his heart upon attaining. I encountered a reverse of this character in my attempt to scale Mus-tagh-ata. It was my desire, as it was also my intention, to climb to the summit of the mountain, examine its geological structure, its coat of ice-mail, and the gigantic glaciers which plough their slow way down its rugged sides. But alas! Instead of carrying out this plan, and achieving the proud consciousness of standing far above the heads of all peoples and princes in the world, and having five continents under my feet, with only a few Asiatic mountain-peaks above me, I was compelled to return, with my strength broken and my eyes bandaged, and seek a warmer climate.

However, on the morning of April 17th I found a picturesque troop awaiting me when I stepped outside my yurt. It consisted of half a dozen weather-worn Kirghiz, enveloped in sheepskins and carrying alpen-stocks in their hands, with nine yaks—big, black, good-natured, phlegmatic creatures—and two sheep. Some of the yaks were loaded with the needful provisions—spades, a pickaxe, hatchets, ropes, furs, felts and felt carpets, the photographic apparatus, and other stores. The indispensable scientific instruments and field-glasses were carried by the Kirghiz in satchels. The remaining yaks bore saddles on their backs. As soon as we were mounted, and had taken leave of Togdasin Beg, the caravan put itself into motion, and slowly began the ascent, in a south-southeast direction. The yak is guided by means of a cord drawn through the cartilage of the nose. All the same, the animal goes pretty much his own way, no matter how strongly his rider may protest. It is his wont to march doggedly on, with his muzzle close to the ground, breathing so hard that you can almost imagine your ears are buzzing with the sharp drone of a steam-saw tearing its way through timber some distance away.

At a place called Kamper-kishlak, or "Old Woman Village," we passed a glacier, with light-green ice in its crevasses, and a gigantic bowlder of gneiss, split in two, immediately underneath its terminal moraine. According to tradition, the place derives its name from the fact that once when the Shah of Shugnan waged war against the Kirghiz, the latter all fled, with the exception of one old woman, and she hid herself between the two halves of the huge piece of rock.

The ascent was very steep, and nowhere afforded firm footing, the slopes being thickly strewn with gneiss blocks of every conceivable size and shape. The mountain is indeed built up almost exclusively of gneiss and crystalline slates; although in the mounds of detritus higher up I picked out fragments of black porphyry and micaceous schists, the latter showing signs of having been subjected to great pressure. I also found the last-mentioned rock in solid masses at the altitude of 16,500 feet.

Coming towards evening to a place that was free from snow, as well as sheltered from the wind, we halted there at an altitude of 14,500 feet, and pitched our simple camp. It consisted merely of a few felt carpets, supported by the alpen-stocks and tied with a rope. Then one of the sheep was slaughtered, while the Kirghiz prayed "*Allahu akhbar, bismillah errahi man errahim!*" (God is great. In the name of God the Merciful, the Righteous!) and before the flesh was cold it was plunged into the melted snow which filled the cooking-pot. The fuel with which our fire was made was nothing better than yak-dung. But later on in the evening we were joined by another Kirghiz, who brought us two yak-loads of teresken, and then we very soon had a

plendid fire roaring away. Around it we gathered to eat
ur plain evening meal. The lively flames darted backward
nd forward like a giddy dancer, now skimming the lips of
ne of the spectators with a coquettish kiss, now singeing
ne beard of this or the other frozen Kirghiz, in a way that
ave rise to a good deal of merriment. The moon rose
om behind the shoulder of Mus-tagh-ata encircled by a

MUS-TAGH-ATA SEEN FROM THE NORTH

right halo; the fire gradually died down; and we slept the
eep of the just under the open sky on Hazrett-i-Musa's
Holy Moses') mountain.

The following day, April 18th, the weather was unfavorable, the sky being wreathed in clouds; besides which, it was
cold and windy. Nevertheless, we made up our minds to
go on. The Kirghiz preferring to walk, we took only three
yaks with us to carry our belongings. By innumerable sharp
zigzag curves we worked our way up the mountain-side, which
grew steeper and steeper with every yard. The yaks kept

plodding on, showing extraordinary sureness of foot; but their halts were many and long. At length the clouds lifted, and revealed to our gaze a panorama for which the only appropriate epithet is magnificent. The valley of Sarik-kol lay spread out before us like a map. To the north we caught a glimpse of Little Kara-kul and Bulun-kul. On the southwest the view was shut in by the mountain-chains on each side of the Murghab; while far down underneath our feet, towards the west, the tomb of Chum Kar Kashka crowned what appeared to be a little knoll of insignificant height, though we knew that, seen from the valley below, it was in reality a big mountain.

At length we came to the glacier of Yam-bulak, and there made halt to rest a while. We were then 15,900 feet above the level of the sea, and consequently stood higher than the tops of all the mountains of Europe. The glacier moves with the majesty of a king out of its castle portals—that is to say, a deep, wide dislocation of the strata; but no sooner does it get plenty of open ground before it, than it spreads out to twice or three times its former width, at the same time growing of course thinner. All its moraines—terminal, lateral, new and old—together with the glacial stream, and its deposits of steely blue mud—from the splendid coign of vantage we occupied we had a bird's-eye view of them all.

Having attained the altitude of 17,500 feet, we found water boiled at 180.5° Fahr. (82.5° C.), that the aneroid indicated 15.6 inches, and the thermometer read 23.9° Fahr. (− 4.5° C.). There we were overtaken by a buran so furious that we were compelled to stop where we were for several hours. Even when we did venture to make a fresh start, we were obliged to proceed with the utmost caution; for the freshly fallen snow completely hid the treacherous cavities and projecting rocks which diversified the surface.

When, after sundry hardships and adventures, we at length returned to camp, we found pleasing evidence of Togdasin Beg's friendliness; for he had sent us a yurt, together with a fresh supply of provisions and fuel.

April 19th we were visited by a snow-storm, even at the

altitude of our camp. Since, then, it was evident, we might possibly have to wait some time for favorable weather, I sent Kul Mametieff down into the valley to bring up a sufficient supply of provisions to last us several days.

Meanwhile, taking Islam Bai and two of the Kirghiz with me, I made a little excursion to the edge of the Yam-bulak glacier. The rest of the Kirghiz, who the day before had complained of a splitting headache and feelings of nausea, were allowed to stay behind in camp and rest. It was altogether a most interesting and instructive trip. We obtained an accurate topographical chart, profiles, various measurements, and a dozen photographic views. Armed with rope, ice-axes, and alpen-stocks, we started from the side of the glacier, and ventured some 350 yards across its surface, until stopped by a crevasse sixty feet deep. I inferred from certain protuberances of the ice about 100 feet in height that the minimum vertical thickness of the glacier was probably 150 to 170 feet. During this venturesome expedition we leaped over several yawning crevasses, though not without observing the well-known precautions of ice-craft.

That evening I determined to move the yurt round to the southern face of the mountain, and make another attempt to get to the top from that side. But my plans were unexpectedly thwarted; for, like an evil spirit, my old inflammation of the eyes (iritis) suddenly seized me, causing me excruciating agony. I applied the remedies I had with me, but all to no purpose. The next day the pain was so intense that I was obliged to leave my men and ride down to Su-bashi. Thus ended my ambitious hopes. The members of the expedition were paid off, and the company dissolved. And Mus-tagh-ata, which glittered in the glorious sunshine, a magnificent sight for those who had eyes to see withal, was for the time being left to enjoy his solitary state in peace.

But despite the warmer climate and the rest I granted myself, the inflammatory symptoms rather increased than got better; so that at the end of a couple more days I decided it would be wiser to go back to Bulun-kul, where I had left the half of my baggage, with six horses, in charge of two men.

When I set out from the aul I was followed by the sincere sympathies of all its inhabitants; nay, even some of the Chinese soldiers came to express their sorrow at my ill-fortune. As the caravan filed off, they all stood silently by, as though assisting at a funeral. And this melancholy impression was still further deepened when at the end of about an hour we were overtaken by a band of soldiers, who had been prevented by their military duties from coming to see me off. They now wished me *bon voyage*, and escorted me on my way for about half an hour, singing songs in my honor, but songs of such a doleful character that I really began to fancy the caravan *was* a funeral procession, and that the singers were the hired mourners and I myself the corpse.

And in truth it was a melancholy journey—that which we began on the morning of April 25th. I had taken strong doses of salicylic acid and morphia, and felt both deaf and brain-sick. My left eye was covered with a bandage totally impervious to the light; while my right eye, which was well, but extremely sensitive to the light, was protected by glasses doubly darkened. In spite of my condition, by dint of riding ten hours at a stretch, we accomplished the entire distance to Bulun-kul in one day. Upon reaching Little Kara-kul we were assailed by a snow-storm, which continued to increase in violence as the day wore on, so that by the time we arrived at Bulun-kul it was not only quite dark, but the country was again clothed in its winter vestments. Without a moment's delay I despatched a messenger to Jan Darin, who had now returned from Kashgar, begging him to oblige me with a decent yurt. The answer brought back was, that Jan Darin was drunk, and could not be disturbed. I had, therefore, to make the best I could of the miserable yurt of which I have before spoken, although the snow swirled in through the holes in the sides. Notwithstanding this, I intended stopping there two or three days, because the inflammation continued to get worse.

But my plan was roughly knocked on the head; for about noon on the 26th a messenger came from Jan Darin, saying that if I hadn't gone by an early hour on the following

morning he would help me on my way with his soldiers.
We had no choice, therefore, but to obey orders. But I will
hasten to add, in exculpation of the Chinese, that throughout
the whole of my journey, this was the solitary occasion on
which I met with insolent treatment at the hands of a rude
and unpolished mandarin, for during the course of the suc-

OUR CARAVAN IN THE VALLEY OF THE GHEZ-DARIA

ceeding years I saw the Chinese character from a very different side, and found them a truly amiable race of men.

On April 27th I sent Kul Mametieff back to Fort Pamir. He was subsequently honored with a medal by King
Oscar of Sweden and Norway. In addition to that, His
Majesty paid a similar compliment to more than one of the
Russian officers stationed at the fort, in recognition of the
distinguished services they had rendered me; so that it
would scarcely surprise me to learn that the Russians take
me for a prince in disguise!

At Tar-bashi (the Head of the Narrow Passage) we turned
off eastward, so as to descend the deep valley of the Ghez,
which eats its way far into the heart of the Mus-tagh chain.
I am sorry to say I know little about the road we followed,
for I rode with my eyes almost completely blinded by bandages. I can only say that we reached our first night's station, Utchkappa (the Three Stone Huts), down steep, break-

15

neck paths.   The next day we had to traverse an extremel
difficult gorge of the Ghez - daria.   The current was ver
strong and clung close to the foot of the high crags whic
shut in the valley on the right.   The path wound down th
face of the almost vertical cliffs, being protected on the oute
or river side by a breastwork of stakes and poles latticed t(
gether with withes.   My men thought they would prefer t
go down by the bed of the stream.   But the leading horse
came within an ace of losing their foothold in the deep, swil
current; and that sent the men back to the path.   On w
struggled, slowly, contending against serious difficulties, unt
two of the horses stumbled and refused to advance anothe
step.   This compelled us to return once more to the rive
bed.   We proceeded with the utmost caution, and final]
succeeded in getting through the gorge.

I judged it wisest to trust my packing - cases only to tl-
best of the horses, and this necessitated unloading and loa
ing up again, which wasted a good deal of time.   Each pac
horse was taken through by two mounted men, who he
themselves in readiness to whip him on if he happened
heel over.   It was a very queer feeling came over me whe
I moved down into the turbulent current, neither seeing t}
bottom, nor yet knowing whether it was covered with loo:
gravel or big cobble - stones, whether it was deep or shallo v
One thing, however, was imperative—namely, to keep fast t
the ford, or I should get a bath; and a bath in such a plac(
seeing that I was riding with my feet in the stirrups, woul
have been dangerous, for only a few paces distant the cliff
closed in upon the river, and drove it plunging down i
cataract.

From that point onward we crossed and recrossed the
stream several times, sometimes wading through fords, sometimes being obliged to trust ourselves to bridges of a more
or less precarious character.   One of these bridges formed
the prominent feature in a very picturesque piece of scenery;
for one end of it rested on a big round bowlder which choked
the bed of the river.   The valley descended at a very steep
inclination, and the river tumbled down one cataract after

another. But as we went down, the narrow passages of the gorge, such as the one I have already described, were choked with thick mist, completely shutting out the prospect, although the bare cliff walls gave back the echoes with a singularly penetrating sound. The ground was extraordinarily rough and stony. Gigantic blocks of gneiss were half embedded in the stupendous conglomerate precipices which overhung the path; but so loosely fixed, that every moment

THE GHEZ-DARIA

I fancied they must break away and crash down upon our heads. In truth, I was considerably relieved when we had passed the last of these perilous places.

By this the temperature had completely changed. We now perceived for the first time that the season was spring. The minimum during the previous night was 31.8° Fahr. (-0.1° C.). At mid-day it was 46.4° Fahr. (8° C.); by two o'clock in the afternoon it had risen to 52.9° Fahr. (11.6° C.); by three o'clock to 55.4° Fahr. (13° C.); by four o'clock to 58.1° Fahr. (14.5° C.); and by eight o'clock in the evening to 59° Fahr. (15° C.); the temperature steadily rising as we descended. We rested for a while at Köuruk-karaol (the Bridge-Watch), where on April 29th the minimum was as high as 39.2° Fahr. (4° C.).

The district which we had now reached was in ill-repute, because of the Chinese and Kashgarian robber-bands, which infested it. I therefore judged it prudent to post sentries during the night, with orders to keep an eye especially on the baggage and the horses. My men advised me to have my weapons handy and ready for use. But the night passed as quietly as other nights had done; the robbers did not molest us.

The following day we again had a difficult crossing. One of the pack-horses, ridden by Khoja the Sart, stumbled and fell, and narrowly escaped drowning. In a moment every man of my company was in the water, heedless of clothes. But it cost them a vast amount of labor to rescue the animal and the stores it carried. Khoja went head over heels into the water, and got an involuntary bath. As on the previous day, we were obliged to cross the stream time after time, sometimes by means of fords, at others over what were in many cases dangerous bridges. At length, however, the valley began to widen out, and as it did so we began to come across patches of scrub. At noon the thermometer showed 66.2 Fahr. (19° C.). We were getting to lower elevations and a warmer climate. Everything was shrouded in a thick yellow mist; moreover, my eyes pained me a good deal, so that I saw but little of the picturesque country we were passing through.

April 30th was the last day we spent among the mountains. Before the morning was over they began to decrease rapidly in elevation, till they were little better than insignificant hills, and finally they fell away and became lost in the distant haze which hung over the trumpet-shaped entrance to the valley. The surface grew leveller, and yielded a good supply of grass, which caused the horses to lose all sense of discipline. The poor animals, whose bellies had been sadly pinched during the journey across the snowy mountains and barren wastes of the Pamirs, snatched greedily at the appetizing pasture as they went along. We crossed three more small bridges, the last of them a particularly dangerous one. We narrowly escaped losing one of our horses there, which put its foot through the thin planking. The baggage having been taken off the animal's back, all hands set to work to haul him up again. That done, the men mended the bridge by filling up the hole with turf. After that we left the Ghez-daria on the left, and travelled on to Tash-melik (more correctly Tash-balik—Stone Fish), where

BRIDGE OVER THE GHEZ-DARIA

there was a small Chinese fort, the commandant of which would not allow us to proceed until he had first seen and examined my pass. The last night of our journey was spent at the village of Terem (Arable Land), and on the evening of May 1st we reached Kashgar. There I was warmly welcomed by my old friend Mr. Petrovsky, Russian consul-general, and his secretary, Mr. Lutsh.

CHAPTER XIX

REMINISCENCES OF KASHGAR

I REMAINED fifty days in Kashgar, waiting till my eyes got well. This time I employed in working out the results of my journey up to that point, in arranging and tabulating my observations, and plotting out my maps. The rest was indeed very welcome — in fact, absolutely necessary. I thoroughly appreciated the hospitality of my friend's house, where I was surrounded by all the comforts and conveniences of civilization. Consul Petrovsky is the most amiable man in the world, in every way a right excellent host. His intellectual conversation was as instructive as it was elevating. For he is a thorough man of science to his finger-tips. During the years he has been stationed at Kashgar he has made many discoveries and observations of the greatest value for history and archæology. Some day he intends to publish them to the world. His library contains a selection of the best books that have been written on subjects connected with Central Asia. He has also a laboratory fitted with the most costly instruments and scientific appliances. It would be absolutely impossible to have a better base than Mr. Petrovsky's house for a series of exploring journeys in the interior of Asia.

I have already described Kashgar and the vicinity in my former book, *Genom Khorasan och Turkestan*. Suffice it, therefore, to say here that the old town stood there on the banks of the Kizil-su, every whit as gray and solitary as when I first saw it in 1890. I add, however, a few words about the Europeans and Chinese with whom, during this visit, I was brought into contact.

The members of the consulate embraced Mr. Petrovsky

nd his wife, his secretary, two military officers, a revenue
fficer, and a troop of half a hundred Cossacks.

Adam Ignatieff, a Roman Catholic Pole, who went out to
Kashgar ten years ago as a missionary, was still there, a
standing guest at Mr. Petrovsky's table. He was a fine old
man, with a smooth-shaven face and snow-white hair, was
dressed entirely in white, wore a rosary round his neck with
a cross dependent from it, and looked like a cardinal out of
office. We used to rally him over the dinner-table; but he
met all our allusions, even the most embarrassing, with a jovial
smile, and resented nothing so long as he got his full number of drams. The only person who put faith in his pretensions to missionary zeal was himself. For during all the
ten years he had been in Kashgar he had not made a single
proselyte; indeed, he had made no serious attempt at conversion. He boasted that he had converted one old Sart
woman on her death-bed; but the malicious declared that the
old woman was already dead when he converted her.

During the following winter Adam Ignatieff often used
to visit me in the evening; and many were the lonely hours
he thus helped to shorten by his conversation. We would
both sit over the fire till well on into the night, and he
would relate to me the various episodes of his adventurous
life. He told me how, during the Polish Rebellion, he had
helped to hang a Russian priest; for which deed he was
banished to Siberia, and remained there about thirty years.
He was of noble blood, and belonged to the family of Dog-
villo. But he was then living half a wastrel in Kashgar, a
lonely man, forgotten, friendless, with none to care for him
or take any interest in him, with none to shed a tear over
his grave when the end of his days should come. Nevertheless, he was always cheerful, always friendly and jovial,
perfectly contented with his lot. And so we used to sit,
talking over the fire, like a couple of hermits.

I also found in Kashgar another old friend in Father
Hendricks. He was in all respects a remarkable man, who
had been domiciled in the town quite as long as Adam
Ignatieff. A Dutchman by birth, he had been twenty-five

years in Asia, spoke twelve different languages, and followed closely and with interest the affairs of the world; he was, in short, a man of wide culture, endowed with no small share of talent—in this respect the exact opposite of Adam Ignatieff. He made his home in a Hindu caravanserai, a miserable hovel without windows, and lived in a state of the greatest poverty, apparently long ago forgotten by his friends in Europe, for it was seldom, if ever, that he received any letters. It was, however, a real pleasure to talk to him. He was both amusing and ready witted, sang French songs with the same verve that he recited his Latin masses, and was a thorough original, if ever there was one. To see him striding at a smart pace through the Mohammedan bazaars, with his long cloak, his broad-brimmed hat, his staff, his long beard, and his big spectacles, always put me in mind of a gray-friar monk. Solitary, solitary, solitary—such was the burden of his life's song. A solitary man, he recited punctually every day the masses which none came to listen to; solitary he sat on the platform beside the door of his hovel and read, heedless of the bustle of the caravans that came and went; solitary he dressed the scanty fare which his poverty permitted him to eat; solitary he wandered about the roads of an evening—always and everywhere a solitary, lonely being. It was always a pleasure to me when I fell in with him. Many an hour we sat together philosophizing over life, for I too was just as lonely a man as he.

There was also a third missionary in the town, a Mohammedan, who had been converted to Christianity and baptized by the name of Johannes, or John. He had studied the Koran in Erzerum, in Turkish Armenia, and from the minarets of that city had cried to the faithful, "*La illaha il Allah, Mohammedeh rasul Ullah*" (There is no God but Allah, and Mohammed is His Prophet). After being converted to Christianity, he spent two years at a mission school in Sweden. At the time of my visit to Kashgar he chiefly occupied himself with translating the Bible into Turki and the dialect of Kashgar, and with playing Swedish psalm tunes on a violin in the evening.

Such were the happy destinies of the champions of the Cross in that remotest of Chinese cities! I felt truly sorry for them. Their energies were wasted, their labors fruitless, their lives empty, hard, and of no account.

During my first visit in Kashgar, I had the good fortune to come in contact with two pleasant English gentlemen—the famous traveller Captain Younghusband, and Mr. Macartney. The former had in the interval returned to India. The latter still dwelt in Kashgar, occupying a comfortable house in a splendid situation close to the garden of Chinneh-bagh. On more than one occasion he entertained Father Hendricks and myself with splendid hospitality. Mr. Macartney was the Agent of the Indian Government for Chinese affairs in Turkestan. He had had a first-rate training, and spoke fluently the principal languages of Europe and the Orient, being especially distinguished in Chinese. In fact, he was too good for his post. He was capable of rendering his country substantial services in a more distinguished sphere of action.

I will now turn to the more eminent of the Chinese with whom I had relations during my stay in Kashgar.

The highest official in each of the nineteen provinces of China is the governor; and with him are associated the vice-governor, the head of the provincial treasury, the judge, and the procurators. Now, whereas the first four exercise authority over the whole of the province, the functions of the last official, the procurator or *Dao Tai* (the Man who Shows the Right Way), are limited to a smaller district or subdivision of the province. For instance, in the province of Sin-chiang (Sin-kiang), which embraces the whole of East Turkestan, Ili, a part of Dzungaria, and a part of Gobi, there are several dao tais. Urumtchi, the capital of the province, has one; Ak-su has another; there is a third at Kashgar; and so on. The dao tai's sphere of authority is therefore less extensive than the spheres of his colleagues; but within his own sphere his actual authority is in several respects superior to theirs, seeing that he enjoys the power to check and regulate their action, as well as to make representations to the central government, if he considers them lacking in the performance of their duty. The position he occupies is in many ways similar to that which was occupied by the Russian provincial procurators in the time of the Empress Catharine II.; but with this fundamental difference, that, whereas the functions of the Russian procurators were limited to protesting, the Chinese dao tai possesses, under certain circumstances, the power to command.

My friend Shang, Dao Tai of Kashgar, exercised authority over a very extensive region, stretching northeastward towards the boundary of the procuratorship of Ak-su, and embracing Kashgar, Maral-bashi, Yarkand, Khotan, Keriya, and Cherchen. His duties are principally civil; but they also extend into the domain of military affairs, in that he acts as paymaster to the troops and inspector of commissariat. The district of Sarik-kol, on the Eastern Pamirs, is administered, like the similar frontier districts of the Russian and Afghan Pamirs, by military officers. The Dao Tai of Kashgar is able to exercise a certain measure of influence upon the conduct of affairs in Sarik-kol; for he is authorized to give advice and furnish intelligence, but is not allowed to issue direct commands.

When a young man, Shang was nothing more than a simple clerk to a mandarin; but having distinguished himself at the time of the first revolt in Dzungaria (1864), he rapidly mounted the ladder of promotion till he attained his present high position. Although no Adonis, he was from top to toe a thoroughly high-principled gentleman. On ordinary days he was wont to flit his saffron yellow body about in a little blue cart; but for ceremonious occasions and functions of high solemnity he came out in magnificent attire—namely, a robe of blue and black silk, in the ample folds of which golden dragons played hide-and-seek, while golden lions of fantastic shape climbed up a bewildering tangle of interlaced garlands. A mystic button on his silk skull-cap proclaimed that he was a *darin* or mandarin of the second class. To complete his gala costume, he wore round his neck a long chain of hard fruit-kernels, polished and carved on the outside.

Upon arriving in Kashgar, one of my first duties was of course to go and pay my respects to this high and influential official. He received me in a singularly polite and cordial fashion. He lived in a straggling *yamen* (official residence), consisting of a labyrinth of square court-yards, with mulberry-trees planted in the middle, and wooden verandas running round the sides. The pillars which supported the verandas were decorated with Chinese ideographs, and the walls of the building with mural paintings, representing for the most part dragons and other fantastic animals. The Dao Tai himself received me at the first door, and with an affable smile conducted me as far as the audience - chamber, where we took our seats on opposite sides of a little square table, and drank

SHANG, DAO TAI OF KASHGAR

tea together and smoked out of silver pipes. Soldiers, armed with long-shafted halberds, kept watch beside the door, and a group of respectable yellow - skinned functionaries, with well-preserved pigtails and buttons in their black silk caps, stood like a circle of lighted candles all round the room, keeping as silent and motionless as statues all the time the audience lasted. The Dao Tai himself wore the insignia of his lofty dignity. With the view of repaying honor with honor, I had put on my best "dress" suit of broadcloth, and went to his palace riding a horse as white as fresh-fallen snow and escorted by a troop of Cossacks.

For two hours we conversed together, or rather competed which should excel the other in paying compliments. The Dao Tai asked me how I liked his tea. I answered "*Choa*" (good), that being the only Chinese word I knew. Thereupon he clapped his hands and said, " By the memory of my fathers, what a marvellously learned man my guest is !" A little later he told me that the river Tarim, which flowed *out* of Lop-nor into the desert, reappeared again several thousand *li* (quarter of a mile) distant, and formed the great river Hwang-ho of China. At this I gave him as good as I got: " What a well-informed man Your Excellency is! You know everything."

But I also let him hear a little plain truth as well. I told him how I had been received at Bulun-kul, the first place I entered on the Chinese side of the frontier; expressing my astonishment that I should have been treated with such discourtesy in face of the pass and letters of introduction I carried, and declaring my intention of making representations on the subject in higher quarters. Upon hearing this, the Dao Tai's face clouded, and with some show of emotion he begged me not to lodge a complaint; he would himself teach Jan Darin a lesson. I promised, therefore, that for that once I would let the matter drop; for of course I never had any intention of doing what I said. But I have found that the only way to deal with the Chinese is to be positive in your statements and peremptory in your demands if you wish to avoid being made ridiculous by their fantastic exaggerations.

Towards the close of our interview the Dao Tai reminded me that Kashgar possessed two chiefs—himself and the Russian consul-general. The Mohammedans declare that Mr. Petrovsky is the true successor of the Jagatai Khans (who ruled over Kashgar from the death of Jenghiz Khan to past the middle of the sixteenth century). He pointed out that, since I had taken up my quarters for a time with the Russian chief, it would only be right that I should also grant his Chinese colleague the honor of entertaining me for, at any rate, a few days. I thanked him very, very much for the honor, but declined.

The next day the Dao Tai returned my visit, coming with all the pomp and circumstance of Oriental display. At the head of the procession rode a herald, who at every fifth step sounded a gigantic gong. He was followed by several men armed with switches and whips, with which they dusted the jackets of everybody who had not the good sense to get out of their way. The great man himself rode in a little covered cart, with three windows and two high wheels, drawn by a mule, which was shaded by an awning, held up by rods fixed to the shafts. On both sides of this state chariot walked attendants bearing huge parasols and lemon-colored standards, inscribed with Chinese ideographs in black ink. The rear of the procession was brought up by a troop of soldiers, mounted on beautiful white horses, but wearing such fantastic uniforms as would have astounded even Doré.

CHAPTER XX

A CHINESE DINNER-PARTY

I CANNOT part from my Chinese friends in Kashgar without adding a brief account of a Chinese dinner-party which I shall never forget. I had scarcely recovered from dining at the house of Tsen Daloi, a kind of mayor of the city, when I had the honor to be invited, along with the staff of the Russian consulate, to a similar function at the palace of the Dao Tai.

I recollect something about an ancient Greek deity who swallowed his own offspring. I have read in Persian legend about the giant Zohak, who devoured two men's brains every day at a meal! I have heard rumors of certain African savages who invite missionaries to dinner and give their guests the place of honor inside the pot. I have been set agape by stories of monstrous big eaters, who at a single meal could dispose of broken ale-bottles, open penknives, and old boots. But what are all these things as compared with a Chinese dinner of state, with its six-and-forty courses, embracing the most extraordinary products of the animal and vegetable worlds it is possible to imagine? For one thing, to mention no more, you need to be blessed with an extraordinarily fine appetite—or else be a Chinaman—to appreciate smoked ham dripping with molasses.

When a Chinaman issues invitations to dinner, he sends out one or two days beforehand a tiny card of invitation contained in a huge envelope. If you accept the invitation you are supposed to keep the card; if you have not time—that is, if you decline—you are expected to send it back. If the banquet is appointed for twelve o'clock, you need not go before 2 P.M. Should you, however, appear punctually, you will

find your host taking his mid-day siesta, and see neither
guests, attendants, nor signs of dinner. When things are
sufficiently advanced in your host's house, he sends off another messenger, who comes and shows you his master's calling-card. This is to be interpreted as a signal that you may
now begin to dress yourself, though you need not bustle
about it.

We too of the consulate made a truly gorgeous show as
we rode in procession to the great man's palace. The place
of honor at the head of the procession was filled by a Sart
from West Turkestan, the aksakal (chief) of all the merchants,
subjects of Russia, who dwelt in Kashgar. He wore a red
velvet khalat (coat), decorated with two or three Russian gold
medals. Close behind him rode a Cossack, carrying the silk
banner of the consulate, red and white, with a little blue cross
stitched diagonally across the corner. Consul-general Petrovsky and I rode in a sort of landau, escorted by two officers
and by Adam Ignatieff, in the long white coat with the cross
and rosary round his neck. Last came a dozen Cossacks in
white parade uniforms, curbing in their snorting horses with
a tight rein.

Thus arrayed in holiday magnificence, we rode, under a
broiling hot sun, at a gentle pace through the narrow, dusty
lanes of Kashgar, across the market-place of Righistan, with
its hundreds of tiny stalls, shaded by thatched roofs, each supported by a slanting pole, past mosques, madrasas (Mohammedan theological colleges), and caravanserais, across the " flea "
bazaar, where old clothes are on sale, coming occasionally
into collision with a caravan of camels or a string of donkeys
laden with small casks of water, and entered at length the
Chinese quarter of the city, full of quaint shops, with up-
curling roofs, painted dragons, and red advertisement signs.
Finally we drove in at the great gates of the Dao Tai's yamen
(residence), and were there received by His Excellency in
person, surrounded by a band of beardless and wrinkled
military attendants dressed in their gayest attire.

· We had not got further than the preliminary "appetizer"
when the presence of Adam Ignatieff started His Excellency

off on the subject of the missionary activity of Europeans in China. He spoke in terms of great admiration of the Christian missionaries, praising their self-abnegation and disinterested zeal for the well-being of their fellow-men; but, speaking with marked emphasis, he went on to add that he felt bound to look upon them as the authors and instigators of discord, setting members of the same family at variance, undermining the time-honored ordinance of domestic subordination, dividing the population into two hostile camps. I ventured to remind him of the murder of two Swedish missionaries in Sung-po, of which I had just heard; but the Dao Tai professed total ignorance of the affair.

Our host then conducted us and his Chinese guests to a little pavilion in the garden, where dinner was to be served. Chinese etiquette prescribes that the host shall touch his forehead with the cup each guest drinks out of, and thereupon present it to him; similarly with the chopsticks each guest eats with. The Dao Tai also shook each chair, to prove that it was in a sound condition, and passed his hand over the seat as if to brush away the dust. This performance over, we took our seats round the big, red, lacquered table. Next came in a string of servants, each bearing a little round porcelain dish with some preparation of food upon it. They put down the dishes along the centre of the table. There were dozens of them; and the first supply was followed by others, time after time. In front of each guest stood still smaller dishes, containing spices, sauces, and soy.

If the guests neglected to help themselves, the host occasionally sent them portions of the delicacies which lined his own dishes—such as the skin, fins, and cartilage of different varieties of fish found in the seas and rivers of the Chinese empire, fungi, salted mutton fat cut into long strips, lizards (salamanders), ham with a great variety of widely different adjuncts, besides a multitude of strange preparations, the real constituents and names of which remained mysteries to me. As for tasting them, I really had no confidence in their suspicious appearance, still less in the rancid odors they gave off. The culminating triumph of the feast was smoked ham in molasses, washed down with tea and Chinese brandy, strong and boiling hot. The greater part of the numerous dishes served at the banquet had been brought from China proper, and consequently, owing to the vast distance, at a very considerable cost. Evidently His Excellency, who at ordinary times lived very plainly himself, was desirous to show us every mark of respect. But I am sorry to say we scarcely did justice to the skill of the Chinese cuisine, although a Brillat - Savarin would no doubt have gone into raptures over it.

The only person who worthily upheld the honor of Europe was Adam Ignatieff; but he did wonders, exciting the amazement of the rest of us, and even the admiration of the Chinese themselves. With punctilious conscientiousness he partook of every one of the forty-six courses, and, with the rosary still round his neck and the cross on his breast, drank seventeen cups of brandy, stuff which to my throat was as hot and burning as sulphuric acid poured upon iron-filings. And at the end of the three hours that the banquet lasted he rose every whit as sober as when he took his seat at the beginning.

The conclusion I came to about Chinese state banquets was that you require a certain amount of time to become accustomed to the many unfamiliar dishes which are put before you. All the same, several of them were excellent, some even quite delicious. Undoubtedly the most delicious of all was the soup made from the edible nests of the swallow, or, more correctly, swiftlet—a dish which is seldom served in this far-off region because of its extremely high price.

On one of the walls there were painted two or three black flourishes. I inquired what they signified, and was told they meant " Drink, and tell racy stories." There was no need for any such admonition, for the spirit which reigned over the company was so hilarious, and we transgressed so wantonly against the strict rules of Chinese etiquette, that the Dao Tai and his compatriots must surely have blushed for us a score of times had not their skins been from infancy as yellow as sun-dried haddocks.

16

We were entertained all through the dinner by the melodies of a Sart orchestra, consisting of drums, flutes, and
singers; while the monotonous music was occasionally enlivened by a couple of dancing boys, as though we were not
dizzy enough without their gyrations.

As soon as the last of the six-and-forty courses had disappeared, the guests, following the rigorous law of custom, instantly rose to take their leave. That moment was one
which I had long been anxiously waiting for; for I was dying
for a cigar and a glass of sherry with iced water, to banish
the recollection of one of the most extraordinary banquets it
has ever been my lot to be present at.

As we drove home, the streets, the market, the bazaars
were silent and empty. The only persons we saw were a
few solitary wanderers — a dervish or a leprous beggar.
The sun set behind the airy contours of the Terek-davan
pass. The twilight lasted only just long enough to make
the bare announcement that a new night was approaching.
Then the Orient lay down and dreamed again on its own
grave.

I shall not easily forget the many happy hours I spent in
Consul Petrovsky's society. It is always a pleasure to me
to go over them again in my thoughts. For, as I have
already said, he was really an extraordinary man, both in the
matter of experience and general culture. I owe him a very
deep debt of gratitude, not only for his unstinted hospitality
but also for the extremely valuable advice he gave me, drawn
from the storehouse of his wide experience. He has lived
twelve years in Kashgar, and no man possesses a more intimate knowledge of that region than he does. To many it
may seem like transportation for a well-educated man to have
to spend so many of the best years of his life in a place like
Kashgar. But it was nothing of the sort to Mr. Petrovsky
He had learned to like the place; and he had an inexhaustible
fund of interest in its historical and archæological treasures
which he had unearthed. There was one thing about Mr
Petrovsky which had for me an especial attraction. He was
always cheerful, always in excellent good humor; for, when

you come to think of it, what is there that can give greater
or truer pleasure than to associate with people who see life
and the world in bright colors, and are perfectly contented
with the lot destiny has shaped for them? At the same time
he was both philosopher and critic. With biting wit and
scathing irony he would lash the minor follies of the world,
more especially everything that savored of toadyism and
servility. Throughout all my travels I have met no man
who made a deeper or more real impression upon me than
Mr. Petrovsky; nor is there any I would so gladly meet again
and yet again.

In a word, I had a splendid time of it in Kashgar. I was
quartered in a cosey little room in a pavilion in the consulate
garden, and after breakfast used to stroll backward and forward under the shady mulberry and plane trees, along a terrace which commanded a wide view of the desolate regions
through which I was shortly to journey on my way to the Far
East. I had constant company in a colony of swallows, which
had built their nests under the projecting eaves, and which
were quite at home, flying freely in and out of the open doors
and windows, for, the summer air being warm, the doors and
windows stood wide open all day and all night long. On
Easter morning I was awakened by the clear, melodious echoes
of a church bell, which the day before had arrived from Na-
rynsk, and was hung in the chapel of the Russian consulate.
I spent my time there working all day, and wrote two or three
geographical papers. Altogether, it was in every way a delightful existence, and just suited me down to the ground. I
heard the wind whispering in the tops of the plane - trees.
What it really said I knew not; but I loved to dream that it
was bringing me greetings from home. Little did I know
then that I had still three whole years of hard travel before
me in the heart of Asia!

My life was, however, anything but solitary. Apart from
the staff of the consulate, the place swarmed with Orientals
—Sarts and Kirghiz—who came in and out on business or
pleasure. Then there was a crowd of Mohammedan servants, and a Chinese interpreter, to say nothing of hens and

chickens to the number of three hundred, turkeys, geese, and ducks, a monkey, four parrots, and more than a dozen dogs. I was on good terms with the whole menagerie, with the sole exception of the monkey. His favor I could not succeed in winning, even when I resorted to such tempting delicacies as apples and pears.

During my seven weeks' stay in Kashgar I often discussed my plans of travel with Mr. Petrovsky, especially how my

GARDEN OF THE RUSSIAN CONSULATE IN KASHGAR

journeys ought to be arranged, so that I might visit each region in the season most favorable for reaping a successful harvest of observations. The result of our conversations was a total alteration of the original idea with which I left Europe. Instead of exploring all the regions I had set my mind upon in one continuous and unbroken journey, as I had at first intended, I decided to carry out my purpose in a series of longer or shorter expeditions, all starting from Kashgar as a centre. By that means I should be able to carry my observations to a place of safety as I made them, to develop my photographic plates, pack and send off home my collections,

as well as have an excellent base at which to make preparations for each fresh expedition.

I intended my first journey to be to Lop-nor, that being
the object upon which my heart was most set. But in the
beginning of June the weather underwent a sudden change.
Summer—the Asiatic summer—was upon us almost before
we were aware of it. The sky glowed like a gigantic furnace.
The temperature rose to 100.4° Fahr. (38° C.) in the shade;
the black bulb insolation thermometer showed 150.8° (66° C.).
The queen of the night was powerless to infuse coolness into
the superheated atmosphere of East Turkestan. And every
afternoon the desert wind blew in across the ancient capital
of Yakub Beg, dry, burning, impregnated with fine dust, filling the streets with a stifling, impenetrable haze. And as
the summer advanced, the heat would increase, as well as grow
more intense the nearer we travelled towards the middle of
the continent. I thought of the superheated atmosphere,
heavily charged with dust, vibrating above the dunes of drift-
sand; I thought of the whirlwinds which every afternoon
drive up and down the banks of the Tarim; I thought of the
1000 miles of long, difficult marches across the unending,
waterless deserts, and—I shuddered. It was only the other
day, as it were, that I had been living in nearly forty degrees
(Fahr. and C.) of frost high up on the Pamirs. I should be
all the more sensitive to the burning heat of the desert. At
the eleventh hour, therefore, I resolved to spend the summer
in the higher regions, and continue my observations in the
Eastern Pamirs, and wait for the winter or the spring before
starting for Lop-nor.

CHAPTER XXI

FROM KASHGAR TO IGHIZ-YAR

WE left Kashgar on the evening of June 21st, 1894. The caravan consisted of half a dozen pack-horses, laden with provisions, instruments, khalats (Kirghiz coats), cloth, colored handkerchiefs, and bag-caps, intended as presents for the Kirghiz; these articles being valued among them almost as much as money. Besides these things, I had my tent-bed, winter clothing, felts, weapons, and ammunition. The only reading I took with me consisted of certain scientific books, and half a year's issue of a Swedish journal, as old as the hills, but none the less delightful on that account, when every line conjured up dear old Sweden before my mind's eye.

My companions were the Evangelical missionary Johannes; Islam Bai, from Osh in Fergana, the successor of Rehim Bai; the Taranchi Daod (David) from Kulja, who acted as my interpreter of Chinese; and Ekbar-khoja, caravan *bashi* (leader), from Fergana. It was from the last named I hired my horses. In addition, I was to be provided every day with two Kirghiz guides, to point out the road. The Dao Tai's good offices exceeded all expectation. Not only did he give me two big bright-colored letters of introduction of a general character, he also supplied me with an official proclamation to the commanders of Sarik-kol and Tagharma, to the effect that I was of a rank equivalent to a mandarin of " the second button," and was accordingly to be received and treated as such. In sharp contrast to their former behavior towards me, the Chinese local authorities were now anxious to do all in their power to serve me.

The sun's rays were still very hot, although it was nearing sunset, when the caravan moved off between the poplars and

willows which line the broad high-road, one of the great public works of Yakub Beg.   It being market-day, the road was
enlivened with a brisk traffic.   There were mandarins of different "buttons," driving along in their little blue carts, each
drawn by a mule bedizened with trappings and bells; there
were small troops of Chinese officers and soldiers in gay uniforms, all mounted.   But not the least striking features were
the huge, picturesque *arbas* (carts) crowded with Sarts or
Chinese on their way to Yanghi-hissar or Yarkand.   Each
vehicle was arched over with a tunnel-like roof of straw, and
drawn by four horses, hung all over with bells of various sizes;
one horse being harnessed between the shafts, the other three
a considerable distance in front, pulling by means of long,
roughly made ropes.   These clumsy but serviceable vehicles
are the diligences of East Turkestan.   By them, for the extremely modest fare of ten Kashgar tengeh (about 2s. 3d.),
you can ride all the way from Kashgar to Yarkand, a distance
of four long days of travel.   We met one caravan of mer-
chandise after another.   Along the sides of the roads were
swarms of beggars and cripples of every kind and degree,
water-sellers with their big earthen-ware jars, bakers and fruit-
dealers displaying their wares on tiny stalls; while a swarm
of sun-browned urchins paddled in the muddy water that
stagnated in the ditches by the road-side.   We passed a line
of saints' tombs; the monument which the Russian consul-
general, Mr. Petrovsky, erected in 1887 to the memory of the
murdered Adolf Schlagintweit, now undermined by the spring
floods; and Yakub Beg's ruined castle of Dovlet-bagh (the
Garden of Riches).   We crossed the Kizil-su, a reddish-brown
mud stream, crawling underneath the double-arched bridge.
Finally, leaving the Chinese town, Yanghi-shahr, on the left
hand, we struck the desolate, lifeless country, which stretched
away southward and eastward, flat and boundless, as far as
the eye could see.   By that time, nine o'clock in the evening,
it was quite dark.   We therefore stopped in the village of
Yiggdeh-arik, and rested and took our suppers, till the moon
should get up.   It was two o'clock in the morning when we
arrived at Yappchan, the object of our first day's march.

On June 22d the temperature was so high (91.6° Fahr. or 33.1° C., at 1 P.M.), that we preferred to stay in the shade; but towards evening it grew cooler, and we resolved to start again. We had not advanced very far when we were met by a beg, followed by two attendants. He had been sent by the *amban* (Chinese governor) of Yanghi-hissar, bearing greetings from his master, with expressions of welcome into his district. He was at the same time ordered to furnish me with provisions, and do everything that lay in his power to help me in my journey. After escorting us a piece of the way, the beg rode back again, in order to find out and get ready a suitable place for tea. The avenues of trees and cultivated fields became more and more interspersed with belts of sand as we advanced. Two hours after leaving Yappchan I saw sand-dunes nearly twenty feet high. They stretched from north-west to southeast and from north to south; but were so overgrown with vegetation that they offered no impediments to traffic.

After stopping a short time for tea in the village of Sogu-luk, where a party of Chinese were making a fearful hubbub, we continued our journey in the dark towards Yanghi-hissar, and arrived there early the next morning. An apartment had been allotted to us in the Hindu caravanserai; and the caravan created quite a commotion when it filed in at the gate, for all the guests of the "hotel" were sleeping in the court-yard under the open sky.

Later on that same morning, June 23d, I was awakened by a mandarin of inferior rank, who brought fresh greetings and protestations of eternal friendship from the amban, together with a sheep, two pullets, a sack of wheat, another of maize, a bundle of grass, and a fagot of firewood. All day long I had three begs sitting outside my door, ready to run my errands at the slightest hint. And in this friendly spirit I continued to be treated by the amban during the whole of the forty-eight hours I remained in his town.

In return for his obliging kindness, I presented him with a revolver and a knife. Thereupon he sent me a complete Chinese dinner, consisting of a number of remarkable but delicious dainties, arranged on dishes and in tiny cups, grouped round a whole roasted pig, which was placed on a big tray with a leg to it. At the same time he expressed his regret that, being indisposed, he could not give himself the honor of helping me to consume the good things he had sent. This message furnished me with the welcome opportunity to reply that, as I was quite unable to do justice to such a bounteous spread all by myself, I felt called upon to send it back to him. For I strongly suspected that all these unusual attentions were merely an artifice to put me under such strong obligations of gratitude towards the astute amban, as almost to compel me to conform to his wishes. His real object was to turn me aside from the route I had chosen for getting up to the high plateau—namely, the glens of Keng-kol and Tar-bashi. That route lay through his district; and it ran counter to the wishes of his worship the amban that I should travel through the country over which he exercised rule. He feared, and with justice, that I should map it out, and so open it up to European travellers, from whose presence it had hitherto been tolerably free. Indeed, he directly advised me to follow the route *via* Yarkand, alleging that the mountain-torrents were now so greatly swollen that I should run very serious risk, and if my baggage were to suffer injury or get lost, he would be held responsible for it by the Dao Tai.

Meantime I had learned from other quarters that donkey-caravans had actually crossed the torrents. Moreover, the time of year was the reverse of favorable for going all the way round by Yarkand, where pestilence always rages in the summer. When the amban learned that it was still my intention to pursue my original plans, he sent offering to supply me with guides. Then, finding no other pretext for keeping up communications with me, he inquired the best way to proceed in order to make water run uphill for purposes of irrigation. I replied to his inquiry by making a paper model of a windmill, and adding explanations of its purpose and the way to use it.

On the outskirts of Yanghi-hissar I noted the first indi-

cations of the proximity of a mountainous country, in certain minor irregularities of the ground. For example, a
narrow ridge, about half a mile long and from 60 to 80 feet
high, stretched away eastward from the town. It was so
evenly and regularly formed that it might easily have been
mistaken for an old fortified wall or rampart had it not been
built up of sand and conglomerate. On the north of this
ridge lay the greater part of the town, with its houses and
bazaars embowered in gardens. On the south of it there
was nothing more than a single row of clay huts with low
flat roofs. Along the foot of the ridge was the cemetery,
every tomb being surmounted by a small dome. When the
sun was at its fiercest, the place gave off the offensive smell
of a charnel-house.

But the prospect from the town was both fine and extensive. Mus-tagh-ata shut in the southwest like a steel-blue
wall, its white battlements inviting us to cooler climes. Between Yanghi-hissar and Mus-tagh-ata the face of the country was dotted with low hills. But in the opposite quarters—
that is, towards the east and north—there was nothing but
the desert, as level and unbounded as the ocean. The town
possessed nothing whatever to interest a stranger, its few
mosques and madrasas (theological colleges) being totally
destitute of architectural pretensions. One of the latter was
built, I was told, sixty years ago by Halim Akhun. Its façade, ornamented with blue and green tiles, and flanked by a
couple of small towers, overlooked an open square with a
muddy pond in the middle. There was also a typical Central Asiatic mosque, small in size, with a colonnaded veranda
along the front, showing simple decorative designs, painted
inscriptions, and streamers; and associated with this was the
masar (saint's tomb) of Kara-chinak. The court-yard of the
mosque was planted with venerable poplars, with stems of
a mighty girth. By an ingenious contrivance one of them
was made to do duty as a sort of minaret. Lastly, I will
merely mention the masar of Supurga Hakim; it had a
green cupola and four small towers.

On the whole, the town was a rural sort of place, abun-

dantly filthy, its streets narrow and dusty, its bazaar protected against the burning heat of summer by wooden roofs
and straw mats.   The men went about for the most part
naked from the waist upward.   The small boys were entirely naked.   The little girls had their heads and feet bare,
but wore one garment — a bright red skirt.   The women,
who seldom go veiled, frequently sat at the stalls in the
bazaars, or in the open squares, with baskets of fruit at their
feet.   As a rule, they were not blessed with good looks.
Like their sisters in other parts of East Turkestan, they
wore their black hair in two long thick plaits.

The Chinese quarter of the town, which, like the Chinese
quarter of Kashgar, was called Yanghi-shahr (the New
Town), lay close beside the Mohammedan quarter, and was
defended by a lofty crenellated wall with towers and a moat.
It was there that the amban of the town had his yamen
(residence), with its train of bareheaded Chinese in long,
white tunics and wide, blue trousers.

The Indian caravanserai, where we put up during our stay
in the place, was built round a square court-yard, with a pil-
lared veranda along each of its sides.   Its principal inhabitants were half a score Hindus from Shikarpur, importers of
cloth from India by way of Leh, Karakorum, Shahidula, and
Yarkand.   But their chief business was money-lending; and
by exacting exorbitant rates of interest they had so completely got the people into their power, that the greater portion of the proceeds of the harvest flowed into their pockets.

But I must not linger longer in Yanghi-hissar.   The
mountain-breezes are wooing me; and there is a great deal
to do before I can permit myself to indulge in rest.   I was
unable to persuade our host, Odi from Shikarpur, to accept
any return for the hospitality he showed me.   But I in
some sort satisfied my conscience by making him a present
of the amban's sheep and firewood, together with a knife
which I added out of my own stores.   Kasim Beg escorted
us as far as the canal of Mangshin-ustang, which has a
volume of 280 cubic feet in the second.   There he dismounted, bowed, and took his leave; his place being taken

by another beg, Niaz, who accompanied us throughout the whole of the journey. About six o'clock in the evening we were assailed by an extremely violent whirlwind, which came out of the northwest, and filled the air with dense clouds of dust and sand. The gust only lasted five minutes, and was shortly afterwards followed by a heavy pelting rain, which wetted us to the skin before we were able to reach shelter in a hut by the road-side. But it brought a compensating advantage in that it purified the air and settled the dust.

From the village of Kara-bash (Black Head) we directed our march due south, leaving on our left the high-road to Yarkand. For a pretty considerable distance eastward the country was diversified with ranges of low hills of sand, clay, and conglomerate. The route we followed was excellent riding, being a perfectly level steppe, diversified by a few scattered knolls. We rested two hours in Sughet (the Willow-Tree), then started again in the night; but it was so pitch dark that we had to be guided through the narrow lanes of the village by a man carrying an oil-lamp. It was about two in the morning when we arrived at the kishlak (winter village) of Ighiz-yar (the High Terrace). There we took up our quarters in a finely situated court-yard.

The amban of Yanghi-hissar had despatched a man on before into the mountains to prepare the way for us. We met this man, Emin Beg, on June 25th, returning with the intelligence that the torrents had really become much swollen during the past few days, but that nevertheless they were not so high as to offer any serious impediment to the progress of the caravan. As a reward for his welcome news I invited him to take tea with me, and let him enjoy the rare treat of listening to a tune on the musical box. One of the inhabitants of the place strummed a *setar* (zither), and a mollah read aloud passages from the Koran to a group of the faithful.

One *tash* (five miles) south of the village there is an iron-mine known as Kok-bainak. The ore occurs in strata of loose earth or clay, and is dug out and carried to Ighiz-yar to be smelted. Both the appliances and the process of extraction are of the most primitive description; the furnace being only about six feet high, with three feet interior diameter. It is housed in a little hut built of planks and sun-dried clay. After the furnace is half filled with charcoal, the ferruginous earths are thrown in, till they cover the charcoal to the depth of six or eight inches. The fuel is then lighted, and half a dozen men squat on their haunches in front of as many holes made near the bottom of the furnace, and blow into it with goat-skin bellows, in order to intensify the draught. They keep up at that nearly all day long, from time to time examining, by means of an iron rod inserted through a hole in the side of the furnace, how the smelting is progressing. Towards evening the molten metal comes running out at the bottom of the furnace. After every burning the furnace of course requires to have the slag and ashes raked out, so that it may be clean and ready for a fresh batch of ore. The metal thus obtained is of such a miserably poor quality that it cannot be forged. It is only fit to be converted into the more primitive agricultural implements. It is no use for horseshoes. One entire day's smelting yields 5 *chäreck*, which are sold in Yanghi-hissar for 30 tengeh (6*s.* 8*d.*). One chäreck is equal to 12 *jing;* and one jing equals 1½ Russian pounds or 1¼ pounds avoirdupois. The owner of the furnace, the *yuz-bashi* (chief of one hundred men) or village chieftain of Ighiz-yar, manages the business himself, personally superintending the smelting, and paying each of his seven work-people at the rate of only six *da-tien* a day; the *da-tien* being a Chinese bronze coin equal to less than half a farthing in value.

CHAPTER XXII

THROUGH THE GORGE OF TENGHI-TAR

OUR spirits were high when we left Ighiz-yar early on the morning of June 26th; for immediately before us we saw the valley of Tazgun opening its arms to welcome us. The mountains themselves, now brown, now gray, were barely visible, their contours being blurred by the great amount of dust which obscured the atmosphere; but at their feet we could just discern two of the kishlaks or winter villages, snugly ensconced amid groves of green trees. But as we drew near to the entrance of the valley the outlines of the mountains gradually came out more distinctly into view, at the same time seeming to creep closer together. The valley of Tazgun is very narrow, so narrow even at its entrance that it could easily be defended by the little fort of Ighiz-yar-karaol, with its garrison of only twenty-four men. On the other side of that post the population are exclusively Kirghiz nomads, who climb up to their summer grazing-grounds on the plateau by paths which strike upward from several of the side-glens of the Tazgun valley. Passing one of these glens, Mahmud-terek-yilga (the Glen of Mahmud's Poplar), I caught a glimpse at its head of a mountain covered with glittering snow. The air was pure and mild; so we pitched upon a shallow grotto in the syenite cliffs of Tokai-bashi for our camping-ground for the night.

Our camp was near the junction of two glens, Käptch-kol and Keng-kol. We struck up the latter; and as the torrents which coursed down both glens contributed about equal volumes to the river Tazgun, we now had to deal with a current only half the volume of that in the Tazgun valley. The glen of Keng-kol (the Broad Glen) did indeed contract as we advanced; yet not so much but that there was space for several small meadows and pasture-grounds, frequented in summer by the Kipchak Kirghiz, who spend the winter lower down near the entrance to the valley. There were still a few isolated poplar-trees to be seen, for the vegetation was by no means meagre. The cliffs on each side of the glen consisted of syenite, porphyry, and black clay-slates, very much weathered, so much so indeed that in many places the bottom of the glen was completely covered by their *débris*. Otherwise the surface was soft soil.

At the aul of Keng-kol (11,000 feet) we were hospitably received by the aksakal (white-beard—*i.e.*, chieftain) of the place, Abdu Mohammed, who gave up to me a portion of his own large yurt. We were detained at that place all day long on June 29th by violent showers of rain. The aul (tent-village) numbered twenty-one inhabitants, who spend there the three summer months of every year. Every evening the sheep and goats are driven to the aul to be milked; and are then shut up for the night in large fenced-in folds, guarded by fierce, long-haired dogs, to protect them from the wolves, which abound in that district. Whenever the dogs bark during the night a man hurries out towards the point where danger threatens, and by loud shouts endeavors to frighten the wolves away.

About noon a troop of men and women, dressed in holiday attire, came to the aul. They were on their way to the funeral of a boy in another aul lower down the valley. But some of them thought they would have a pleasanter time of it with us; and therefore stayed behind when their companions continued their journey. The company in my host's yurt was thus augmented by a dozen men, eight women, and seven children; and yet it was so roomy that we were not at all crowded. They were a lively set of people too, as a single picture will show. One man played the *dutara* (a two-stringed instrument of music); others sat about in little groups chatting. Some of the women, wearing enormous white head-dresses, ate bread and drank milk out of big wooden bowls. The children ran about and played. Our hostess was engaged in suckling her infant, a boy of about one

month old, leaning over his cradle to do so. The head of
the family, old Abdu Mohammed, was the only individual
who heeded the obligations of religion. He alone punctually
observed the hours of prayer. None of the rest heeded
them, but went on laughing and talking. There was the
usual fire in the middle of the tent.

There was a good deal of humus and luxuriant herbage in
the vicinity of the aul of Keng-kol, which was situated on
the right bank of the stream. Immediately opposite to it, on
the other side of the river, the bare rock cropped out in several places, consisting of clay-slates, alternating with a hard
species of crystalline rock. The stream was at that time
very insignificant ; but the water was limpid, cold, and whole-
some. In consequence of the recent rains, it was expected
to rise soon to flood-level. The rainy season in that valley
is coincident with May and June. Snow never falls except
during the four winter months.

During the following days the ground became more broken
and variable as well as wilder in character. Our route led
out of the glen of Keng-kol into that of the Charlung, one of
the tributaries of the Yarkand-daria. The pass connecting
the two glens, like the two streams which flowed down from
it in opposite directions, was called Kashka-su (the Many-
colored Stream).

The little glen, which led up to the pass out of the Keng-
kol valley, was extremely narrow, and rose at a steep angle.
Owing to the great variations in the contour of the ground,
I was obliged to take frequent measurements, in order to calculate our rate of marching and the distance marched. I
found that, to ascend this glen, it took the pack-horses 4½
minutes to climb a quarter of a mile; and our day's march
varied from 12 to 20 miles.

Although the black clay-slates cropped out visibly on both
sides of the pass, on its culminating ridge there was not a
trace of bare rock to be seen. The contours were, on the
contrary, gently rounded off, the ground being covered with
humus and luxuriant grass. At the time of my visit the latter was being grazed by large troops of horses belonging to

Sart merchants of Yarkand. The top of the pass afforded a splendid view of the deep-cut glens on both sides of the ridge, and of the snow-clad mountain-peaks in the far distance. The two streams which carried off the rainfall on each side of the watershed were about the same size. The feeders of both have eaten their way deeply into the flanks of the mountain, giving origin to many fan-shaped corries or gullies. The altitude of the pass was 13,000 feet above sea-level.

The path on the other side of the pass went straight downward, due south, towards the little aul of Koi-yolli (the Sheep-Path), consisting of six yurts, and so on to the karaol (watch-house) of Chihil-gumbez, a collection of stone and clay houses, stables, and yurts, besides a cemetery with a small chapel crowned with a cupola (*gumbez*). The inhabitants numbered only 13; and, like those of Keng-kol and Charlung, were Kipchak Kirghiz. The watch-house stood at the junction of three routes—those, namely, which come from Yarkand, from Keng-kol, and from Tagharma. A great many caravans and mounted men pass the place in the course of the year; indeed, I was told that the daily average of travellers was ten.

On July 1st we went over another pass, Ter-art (the Leather Pass), 13,250 feet, which closely resembled Kashka-su, except that the ascent and descent were even steeper. On the crest of the ridge the clay-slates stood out almost vertically in sharp fantastically shaped snags, flakes, and slabs. The spaces which intervened between the separate summits were frequently filled with mounds of detritus, which in their fall had exposed the planes of fracture of the inky-black argillaceous rocks. The descent on the other side was through a remarkably wild and striking ravine, traversed by a little rippling mountain-brook. Its sides were walled in by bare clay-slates; the bottom littered with huge masses of conglomerate, consisting of broken schists and white, coarse-grained syenite, embedded in yellow soil and sand, through which the torrent had carved out a deep channel for itself. Rushes and grass grew between the blocks of syenite. Another rivulet came down a side glen,

I.—17

Borumsal, greatly quickening the vivacity of the Ter-art. Eventually the glen widened out; but after it did so, became every now and again almost blocked by terraced ridges of conglomerate several hundred feet thick. About three o'clock in the afternoon the southwest wind brought up a slight mist; this gradually thickened, and towards evening changed into a drizzling rain, which searched through everything, so that we were glad to find shelter in the aul of Pasrabat (the Low-lying Station), a place of three yurts 9460 feet above sea-level, inhabited by 13 Kessek Kirghiz.

But although so small, Pasrabat is so far important that it lies on the road connecting Kashgar, Yanghi-hissar, and Yarkand with Tash-kurgan, the principal Chinese stronghold in the Eastern Pamirs. For this reason it boasts of a small fort. The stream of Pasrabat runs into the Taghdumbash-su, which in its turn becomes an affluent of the Yarkand-daria.

Several times during the night I was awakened by the rain, which beat with a loud pattering upon the roof of the tent, and occasionally came through upon me, sprinkling me all over. The next morning the neighboring glens were again shrouded in thick mist. As soon as I got up I had an animated discussion with the Kirghiz, as to whether we should go on or stay where we were. They advised me to push on, being afraid that if the rain continued, though only one day longer, the mountain-torrents would rise so high as to be impassable. But my *karakesh* (owner of horses) was of opinion that the day was already too far advanced; we should not get to the biggest stream we had to cross between Pasrabat and our next station until after dark. Accordingly we decided to remain where we were.

This gave me an opportunity to take certain observations as to the volume of water carried down by the stream. By this the rainfall of the past day or two had begun to come down from the mountains, and the flood had already risen very considerably. Yesterday it was clear as crystal; to-day it was gray and muddy, and boiled along tumultuously among the stones. The breadth of the torrent increased to

53 feet, its depth to a maximum of 21.6 inches, its volume to 250 cubic feet in the second. At mid-day the temperature of the water was 50.9° Fahr. (10.5° C.). The variations which the current underwent during the course of the day will show how sensitive these mountain-brooks are to precipitation and temperature. By three o'clock in the afternoon the water had sunk .6 of an inch. This was owing to the fact that the highest rills which fed the stream froze during the night. But at five o'clock, by which time that morning's rains had got down to Pasrabat, the stream rose 1.38 of an inch. At seven o'clock it was 6.3 inches above the height of my first measurement; but in consequence of the steepness of the banks, the breadth had not increased more than about 3¼ feet. The noisy brawling of the current, now of a brownish-gray color, sounded duller and heavier than in the earlier part of the day; for the stones and pieces of rock which protruded above the surface in the morning, checking the flow of the water, and causing it to splash up into the air, were now entirely submerged. Now that the outpour of the rains had got down as far as our camp, the volume was more than twice as great as in the morning, being 495 cubic feet in the second. At the same time the temperature was 49.5° Fahr. (9.7° C.). By eight o'clock the current had risen yet another .8 of an inch, and the temperature had fallen to 48.9° Fahr. (9.4° C.); another hour later the figures were .4 of an inch and 48.4° Fahr. (9.1° C.) respectively. All this goes to show that, as the volume of the water increased, it took a proportionally longer time for it to attain to the temperature which prevailed in the lower valleys.

At seven o'clock next morning the flood stood at about the same level as when I took my first observation; but during the night the temperature had fallen to 45.5° Fahr. (7.5° C.).

That day, July 3d, we had an unusually trying day's march. At first the glen was of medium breadth, and tolerably rich in grass, bushes, and willow-trees. Every now and again the conglomerates stretched pretty far up the mountain-sides, forming rampart-like walls, with covered galleries,

excavations, and grottos, but so precipitous that they looked
as if every moment they would crash down into the glen.
But after we passed the end of the side glen of Yam-bulak
(the Grotto Spring) the main glen became very narrow, and
its bottom choked with disintegrated *débris*. The torrent
too dwindled a good deal, having lost two or three of its
principal contributaries.

At Yam-bulak there was a hut by the way-side, and our
eyes were charmed by the sight of the fresh, white flowers
of the wild-rose. Beyond that point the glen was called
Tenghi-tar, a very suitable name, although a pleonasm; for
tar means "narrow" and *tenghi* "narrow glen-path." Here
the coarse crystalline rocks predominated again; the sharp
pinnacles and needles of the mountains in the argillaceous
formation being replaced by more rounded domes and flat—
tened tops. The glen was, as I have said, choked with
débris, nevertheless vegetation thrived; the beech, wild-rose,
and hawthorn being the most noticeable species.

Finally the glen contracted to a wedge-shaped trough,
carved, as it were, out of the mountain-side. The path grew
more and more difficult. We wound a hundred, a thousand
times in and out round the fallen bowlders; and every now
and again crossed the stream, its water once more clear and
limpid. The glen was closed by an upheaval of gneiss, over-
lain sporadically by conglomerate strata. At a spot appro-
priately named Issyk-bulak, a triple hot spring gushed out
from beneath a large block of conglomerate. The water,
though not particularly copious, burst forth with a splash,
and had a disagreeable sulphurous odor. It colored the
stones upon which it fell brown and yellow; nevertheless,
luxuriant green grass and other vegetation grew only a little
way lower down. A column of steam rose above the
springs, the water having a temperature of 127° Fahr. (52.8°
C.) at the point where it emerged. The torrent, which raced
down the glen, passed within eight yards of the springs.
Ten yards above them its water was 54.5° (12.5° C.); but ten
yards below them as much as 66.2° (19° C.).

Two minutes farther up the glen we discovered another

hot spring, very similar to the first, except that it was much smaller and its temperature 125° (51.7° C.). Above this spring the temperature of the glen torrent was only 54° (12.2° C.). My reason for quoting these trivial details of varying temperature in the stream is this. In winter the torrent never freezes below the hot springs all the way to Yambulak; while above them it always freezes.

Above the hot springs the glen contracted still more, and at length became a veritable ravine, only a few yards wide, the air cold and clammy as in a cellar, the rocky sides perpendicular, the stream filling up nearly its entire width dashing itself against the bowlders, flashing up above them in spray, plunging down small waterfalls. Near the entrance to the gorge lay the carcass of a dead horse, a warning to us to keep a watchful eye upon our own animals. And indeed there was need of it; for the ascent was painfully steep. But, as some compensation for that, the scenery was grand and wild. When we shouted, and we had to shout pretty loud to make ourselves heard, the echoes were dashed from side to side against the hollow cliffs. Above our heads there was only a narrow strip of sky visible. Every minute almost the gorge appeared as if it would come to a sudden stop, the cliffs seemed to meet and join. But no; it was only a fresh bend in the glen. We turned the corner, and lo! another splendid prospect opening itself out before us. And so this remarkably picturesque gorge went winding on, a narrow, sinuous gap excavated through the granite and quartzite rocks by the furious little torrent.

It was anything but an easy task to get our heavily laden pack-horses safe and sound through this long and difficult defile. For the greater part of the way we were obliged to ride up the bed of the torrent; and the tossing spray prevented us from watching the horses' feet. The inhabitants of the district had filled up the lowest pools with blocks of stone, large and small, thus making a sort of bridge or causeway. But at the best, these pieces of road-making were only so many new pitfalls of peril. The water had scooped out and carried away all the smaller, softer materials which had to fill up the spaces between the bigger blocks; ... causeways were now full of gaping holes, into ... horses frequently slipped and nearly broke their ... or three of them actually fell off the causeways ... away dashed the men into the stream to get them up ... and rescue the cases and bales. All the way up my ... was in my mouth, for fear the horse I rode should give ... an unwelcome bath. One spot in particular I recollect ... well. It was a very ugly place. A number of big ... and stones, with brightly polished, slippery surfaces, formed ... of sill stretching obliquely across the bed of the torr... A couple of men ... up each on to a large bow l- ... and, seizing hold of ... ing-cases and hauling away ... em, helped the horses ... ber over.

At length, however, the path grew better. For at a spot ... led Tarning-bashi-moynak (the Pass at the Head of the ... rge) the glen was divided into two widely differing halves ... a mountain-spur, which pr... ed from the left. At its foot ... torrent shot down to such great depth that it was quite ... possible to advance. We ... efore climbed up and over the crest of the projecting spur, getting a magnificent view of the glen both ways, up and down, from the top. In striking contrast to the deep narrow gorge we had left, the glen ahead of us widened out into a broad, level valley, with gently sloping hill-sides and rounded eminences above them, plenty of vegetation, and a practicable path alongside the stream. A little higher up the rock formation on the left hand was again conglomerates; but on the right syenite, its surface so smoothly polished that I could not help fancying it had been worn away by water or glacial ice. Upon looking back, I perceived that the spur before mentioned was overtopped by a double-crested mountain, covered with perpetual snow. The Kirghiz called it Kara-yilga-bashi (the Head of the Black Valley). The portion of the glen above Tarning-bashi-moynak was called Tar-bashi (the Head of the Narrow Gorge), showing how sharply the Kirghiz are wont to discriminate between regions of dissimilar formation and character.

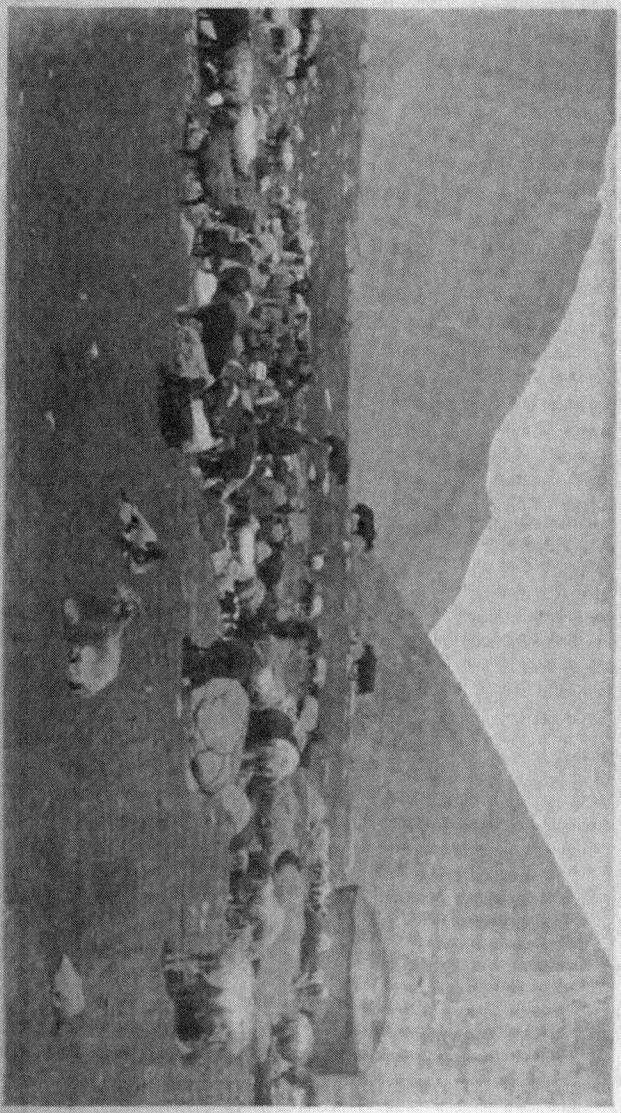

CATTLE AND SHEEP NEAR KARA-TEGA

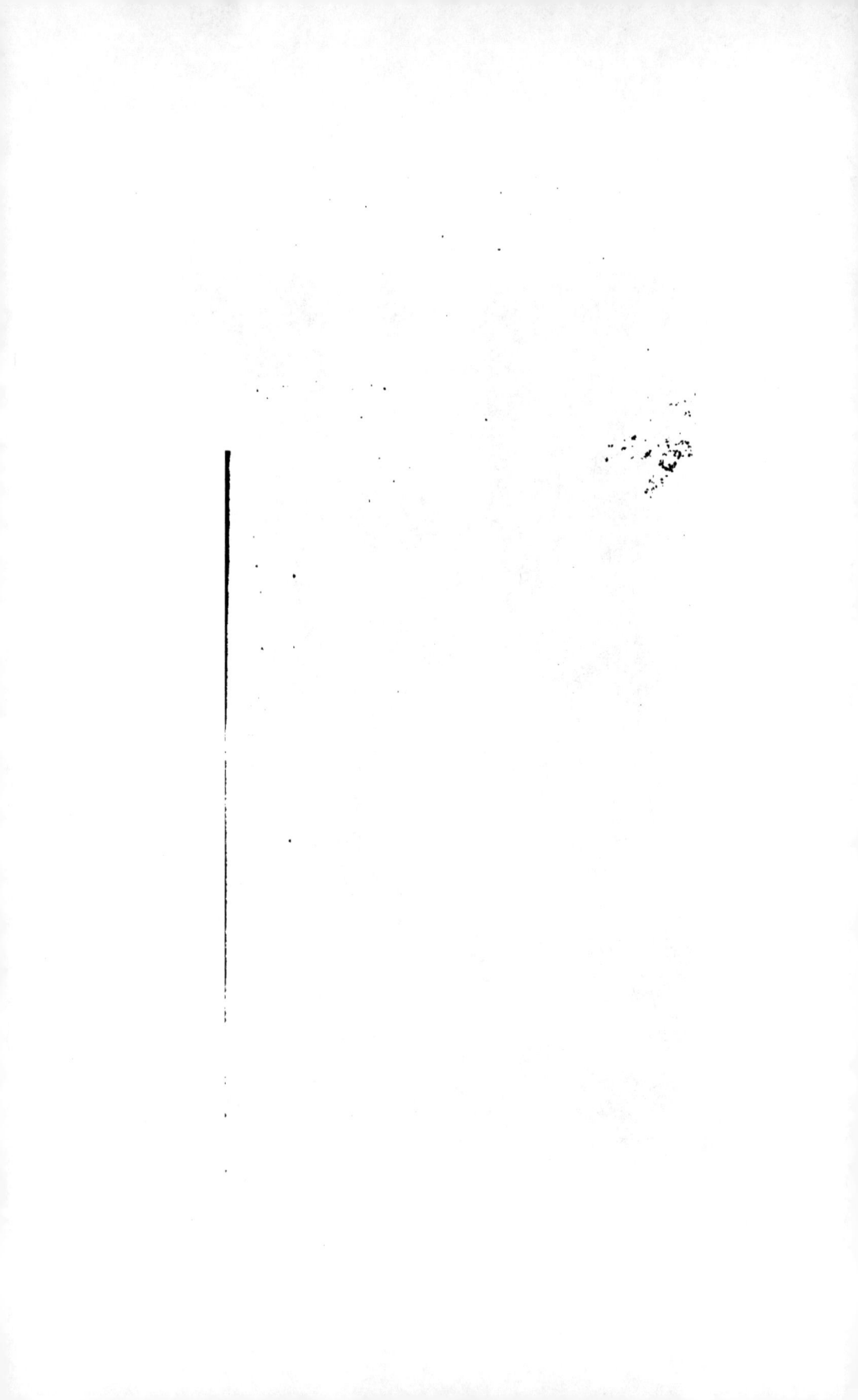

By this we had nearly reached our camping-place for the night, Bulak-bashi (the Head of the Springs). The yuz-bashi (chieftain) of the place, an old beg, received us with the friendliest courtesy, and at once ordered a comfortable yurt to be got ready for our accommodation. At this place I observed a very remarkable phenomenon in connection with the stream of Tar-bashi. When we arrived, its current was low, and perfectly limpid; but at half-past three in the afternoon we suddenly heard a distant rumbling sound. The noise grew rapidly louder and louder. Then, foaming like a white surf-roller, down rushed the flood, born of the melted snow and ice in the higher altitudes, and of the recent rainfall in the lower. How lucky we had got through the gorge! Otherwise the whole caravan would infallibly have been swept away. But we only just cleared it in time! This was what the Kirghiz were anxious about at Charlung.

Since leaving Ighiz-yar we had crossed over the broad, far-stretching easterly spurs of the Mus-tagh range—a confused jumble of crests, peaks, and intervening valleys. From the valley of Keng-kol we had crossed over into the glen of Charlung, and from the glen of Charlung into the glen of Pasrabat, climbing up and down two passes of relatively minor significance on the way. At the place where the Tenghi-tar, one of the head-feeders of the stream which descended the glen of Pasrabat, broke obliquely through the crystalline mountain-chain, we had traversed an extraordinarily romantic gorge, which, having cut out its channel to a great depth, recalled the characteristics of the typical Peripheral region of which I have before spoken. Above the gorge the glen had widened out; the enclosing mountains assuming at the same time a gentler inclination and falling to a relatively lower elevation—a typical Transitional region in miniature. We now began to enter upon a typical high-plateau or Central region. I had ascertained that the volume of water in the mountain-streams generally increased towards four o'clock in the afternoon, and went on increasing until well on in the evening; proving that the snows which are melted by the mid-day sun do not get down to the glens until several hours

later.   The streams were lowest about noon and a couple of
hours afterwards, and attained their maximum during the
night.   But these general variations are subject to irregular
oscillations, caused by the irregularity of the rainfall.   It is
these deluge-like floods which do the real work of erosion, a
fact evidenced further by their thick, muddy-looking water.
During the early part of the day the stream gradually deposited the detritus it caught up on its way down, and so became clear again.

Bulak-bashi was a place of six yurts, inhabited by thirty
Kessek Kirghiz.   They are stationary there all the year
round, being commissioned to keep karaol (watch) upon the
passes, to lodge and help Chinese travellers journeying over
them, and to carry to and fro the Chinese post.   Both at Bulak-
bashi and at Pasrabat there were therefore three postmen stationed, each three being paid 25 chäreck (nearly 6 bushels) of
wheat from Yanghi-hissar and 20 chäreck (nearly 5 bushels)
from Tash-kurgan.   Since leaving Yanghi - hissar we had
passed six watch-houses—Ighiz-yar, Tokai-bashi, Kashka-su-
bashi, Chihil-gumbez, Pasrabat, and Bulak-bashi.   Two of
the men belonging to the aul last named were looked upon as
bais—*i.e.*, rich men ; each owned about one thousand sheep,
two hundred goats, one hundred yaks, thirty horses, and the
same number of camels.   The winters were said to be very
cold in that glen ; and while the head-feeders of the stream
remain frozen, which they usually do for two or three months,
the stream itself dries up.   Snow falls during five months in
the year, but seldom lies more than knee-deep.   The rainy
season, properly so-called, begins in the middle of May ; there
is rainfall also in the summer and autumn.

July 5th was one of our heavy days : we crossed over the
main chain of the Mus-tagh system.   The night before was
still and sparkling bright.   The thermometer dropped below
freezing - point ; and even at a late hour in the morning the
edges of the brooks and pools of stagnant water were fringed
with ice.   The upper extremity of the glen widened out more
and more.   The mountains which fenced it in, outliers of the
principal crests we had on both sides of us, grew flatter and

A KIRGHIZ AUL IN THE EASTERN PAMIRS

flatter. The gneiss rarely cropped out in continuous masses. The little brooks came rippling down the glens on both sides of the valley one after the other, as though emerging from the side wings of a stage. The valley stream, being at this point nearer its sources, attained its greatest volume about noon, and its waters were not yet muddy. As we passed several of these small side glens, we saw at their upper ends the main mountain-ranges, clothed with glittering mantles of snow. The only places immediately overlooking the valley itself on which snow still remained were the slopes which faced north, northeast, and northwest. The floor of the valley was in great part a carpet of luxuriant herbage, on which several herds of yaks were grazing, and in part was littered with *débris* and fragments of rock from the mountains above.

A short time afterwards we came to an oval, caldron-shaped valley or *cirque*, surrounded by a ring of mountains partly covered with snow. Immediately ahead of us rose a ridge of considerable altitude; and soon, to the north, we perceived the pass of Yanghi-davan (the New Pass), which leads to Yam-bulak, but is only used when the Tenghi-tar route is impassable. In the middle of that open, dish-shaped valley lay two small lakes, each about 500 yards long. They are fed by the melting of the snows around, and their waters, clear as crystal, are the source of the Chichekli-su, a little brook which runs down into the glen of Shindeh, and so on to Pasrabat and the Yarkand-daria. The name Chichekli is likewise given to the low saddle which serves as the watershed between the glen of Tar-bashi and the glen of Chichekli.

From the caldron-shaped portion of the glen the track swung up a relatively easy slope to the pass (15,065 feet) of Kityick-kok-moynak (the Little Green Pass). A little farther on was another pass, the Katta-kok-moynak (the Big Green Pass), equally easy, although it attained 15,540 feet in altitude. Between the two a small fan-shaped valley gathered up a number of mountain-rills, and out of them formed an affluent to the Chichekli-su. Both passes were on the top of low, rounded domes, where, except for a few scattered patches of gneiss, the bare rock was not visible, being effectually covered with humus.

CHAPTER XXIII

THE PLAIN OF TAGHARMA

THE passes just mentioned formed the culminating points of the route. On the other side—that is, towards the west—the path descended very abruptly, going down alongside a little brook, which, like the Tenghi-tar on the east side, has excavated a deep, narrow passage through the solid rock. It cost us an hour's hard work to get down. The more sheltered spots harbored patches of ice and snow, across which we sometimes rode. The glen, which was called Därshett, gradually widened out, and at last we perceived the end of it—a rocky gateway giving access to a broad plain. Against the far-off background of the plain stood out in clear relief a bluish-white mountain-wall, denticulated at the top. It was the Mus-tagh chain. But we still had a detached spur of no great elevation to surmount. On the other side of it there burst upon our view the wide, level plain of Tagharma, deliciously green, and bathed in the brilliant afternoon sunshine. On our right lay the Chinese stronghold of Beshkurgan (the Five Forts), surrounded by a rectangular wall, and garrisoned, it was said, by a *lanza* or troop of 120 men. As soon as we had crossed the river Tagharma, we were met by the begs and yuz-bashis. They greeted us politely, and told me they had been directed by letters from the Dao Tai to place themselves at my disposal.

The plain of Tagharma is in reality an elevated steppe, carpeted with the greenest of green grass, and abundantly watered by running streams, which gather their water from the snow-fields on the mountain summits around, and unite to form the Kara-su (the Black Water), a tolerably large stream, or the Tagharma-su (the Apple-Mountain Water), which effects a junction with the Yarkand-daria by wav of Tash-kurgan. A large number of Kirghiz dwelt on the plain; the yeylaus (summer camps) of the district enjoyed an excellent repute.

July 6th was a day of rest. The heat was very oppressive at noon, the thermometer registering 89.6° Fahr. (32° C.) inside the tent, and 127.4° (53° C.) outside in the sandy soil. The black bulb insolation thermometer rose as high as 160.4° (71.3° C.). Not only does the plain itself, in virtue of its great extent, absorb an enormous quantity of heat, it is also open towards the south and slopes in that direction. The sky was as pure as crystal, except that a very few light, fleecy clouds hovered about the mountain-tops. The atmosphere trembled and vibrated with the heat that was radiated upward. A fine gossamer-like haze hung over the surface of the ground. Our camp was situated at an altitude of 10,620 feet.

The rainfall in the plain of Tagharma presents a strong contrast to the rainfall in the glens by which we had penetrated through the mountain-spurs of the Mus-tagh. In the former the quantity of rain which falls is inconsiderable. When it does rain, it comes in gusts lasting about a couple of hours at a time. The season for it to come is the spring. The amount of snowfall is also small, and is spread over barely three months. The winters are extremely cold; but, owing to the clear, dry atmosphere, the newly fallen snow disappears very quickly.

The great amount of radiation, and the plenteous natural irrigation, foster vegetation to an extraordinary degree. The plain was carpeted with luxuriant grass, thick in bottom growth, diversified by moist, verdant tussocks, and enlivened by the music of running brooks and springs. Herds of grazing yaks and sheep roamed all over it; and here and there the eye caught glimpses of the cosey Kirghiz auls. In the valleys farther east we had experienced frost at night. On the plain of Tagharma even the nights were warm. And not warm only: they were also silent and tranquil—not even the soft whispers of the brooks reached our ears. But the mosquitoes were very troublesome, keeping us awake a long time.

The Kirghiz, who inhabit the plain of Tagharma, remain there winter and summer alike. They counted eighty yurts, fifty being occupied by Kessek Kirghiz and thirty by Teit Kirghiz. On an average there were four persons to each yurt. Besides these, there were twenty families of Tajiks at Besh-kurgan and Sarala. But the majority of the Kirghiz were poor. All together, they owned scarcely more than 2000 sheep and 200 yaks; several of them possessed barely half a dozen sheep, some none at all. On the other hand, the Tajiks were reputed rich. These people are not nomads, but permanent dwellers in houses of clay. Their chief occupation is agriculture; their principal crops being wheat and barley. At the same time they breed sheep and other domestic flocks, a single individual frequently owning as many as one thousand sheep. The Kirghiz say they were much better off a score of years ago, when Yakub Beg was ruler in Kashgar. In his time they enjoyed much greater freedom, and were allowed to drive their flocks and herds westward to the grazing-grounds on the Pamirs; whereas now the Chinese jealously forbid them to cross the Russian frontier. Our host, Mohammed Yussuf, was beg of all the Kirghiz of Tagharma.

Wild animals were numerous in that region, and embraced the wild goat, hare, and other rodents, the wolf and fox, the partridge, wild duck, wild geese, and several species of *Natatores* and *Grallatores*.

On July 7th we continued our journey, aiming west and northwest for the foot of the Mus-tagh-ata *massiv*, having on our right hand that part of it which is called Kara-korum (the Black Stony Region). Our route lay alongside the Kara-su, which derives its waters from glacial streams and natural springs combined, and, after gathering up the drainage of the plain of Tagharma, effects a junction with the Yarkand-daria. We passed the ends of several old moraines and a great many erratic blocks of gneiss, proving that glacial action was once far more prevalent in this region than it is at the present time.

In the middle of the plain, at a place called Gedyäck (the

Violin), there was a picturesque *tu*—that is, a mound of stones, with a branch of a birch-tree fixed in it and hung round with the skulls and horns of wild sheep and tekkes (wild goats), the tails of horses and yaks, pieces of white rag, and other religious offerings of the Kirghiz. Several smaller birch poles were stuck into the stone heap round about the larger one; and the whole vicinity was littered with horses' and antelopes' skulls. Immediately in front of the mound was a fair-sized block of gneiss which had been hollowed out by water or ice. The cavity was black with smoke; and the explanation given me was that pilgrims were in the habit of leaving in it offerings of lighted candles or oil lamps, when they came to the *tu* to repeat their prayers. In that same spot too a little side glen, called Kayindeh-masar (the Holy Tomb of the Birch), opened upon the plain from the west. The name is derived from the burial-place of an important saint, situated in the middle of a little grove of birch-trees. It is also one of the principal burial-places of the Kirghiz; a legend running to the effect that it was the resting-place of the hero Khan Khoja in one of his warlike excursions. The *tu* has been built in the middle of the public road, as an intimation that there is a burial-place in the vicinity; also as a sign that the great saints' masar of Mus-tagh-ata rears aloft its snow-white head immediately above it.

Away to the right we now saw for the first time several of the glaciers with which we were to become more intimately acquainted during the course of the summer.

On July 8th there remained but one day's march between us and Su-bashi, our first goal. After that we proposed to surmount the easy pass of Ullug-rabat (the Large Station), which divides the valley of the Sarik-kol into two portions—a northern, which sends off its drainage waters to the Ghez, and a southern, which drains into the Yarkand-daria. It was a splendid day. The mountain-peaks on our right stood out bold and clear-cut, their glittering snow-fields contrasting sharply against the limpid, light-blue sky; the only flaw upon its pearly purity being a few light feathery clouds far off towards the south. In a word, the still, soothing peace of

I.—18

the Sabbath rested upon the whole face of the country, so
that it was pure joy simply to sit still in the saddle and quietly observe it.

We reached the summit of the pass at one o'clock, and
from a cairn of stones there (13,875 feet altitude) were able to
get a general survey of our surroundings. The large glaciers
radiated westward from the central *névé*, the ice at their fract-
ured edges and in the crevasses glistening a beautiful trans-
lucent blue. The spaces between the glacial arms were filled
up with stupendous crags and pinnacles of rock, coal-black
in color below the snow-line. We were too close in to the
mountain to be able to see the majestic dome which crowns
it. That can only be seen to advantage a long way west of
the place in which we were then; for instance, its noble proportions can be seen clearly and distinctly from the Murghab.
There was an almost equally fine view to the north, where
the valley of Sarik-kol inclined a little towards the northwest,
so that the Mus-tagh chain shut in the view on that side.
The dominating feature on the south and west was the Sarik-
kol chain, curving in towards the Pamirs; but in certain
places it was obscured by the undulating country between—
a country diversified by knolls of sand, gravel *débris*, and
earth, gradually merging one into the other, overgrown with
scanty patches of tussock grass. In the immediate foreground, on the north, was the tolerably level plain of Su-
bashi, having at its upper end the karaol (watch-house) of
Irik-yak, garrisoned by seven Kirghiz, whose duty it was to
watch the two passes Mus-kurau and Tock-terek. The latter
possessed two approaches, in one of which, that called Kara-
tock-terek, there was an isolated hill of fine-grained granite,
which has been subjected to great pressure, and showed a
fluidal structure, interspersed with veins of pegmatite or
coarse-grained granite. The glacial current, which came
down at the same point and flowed into the Tock-terek, was
very turbid, owing to the quantity of detritus and glacial mud
it held in suspension. It had also a bigger volume than the
stream it joined. The latter, not being of glacial origin, was
clear.

At the bottom of the northern slope of Ullug-rabat we came upon an aul of nine yurts, and shortly after that upon another of five, both standing on the brink of the stream, and both owning large flocks of sheep pasturing in the neighborhood. At the first aul (tent-village) I was met by Togdasin Beg, who gave me a flattering welcome. He led me to his own aul, where the yurt I occupied before still stood in the same place; at the moment, however, it was occupied by nearly a dozen dirty, ill-smelling Chinese soldiers, who gaped their fill at me, shouted, laughed, and touched and poked their fingers at my several packages. Then came the secretary of Shi Darin, the commandant, requesting to see my passport. He saw it, and was satisfied. Thereupon I invited him to partake of tea. He did so, and made himself tolerably agreeable.

Togdasin Beg asserted that the garrison numbered sixty-six men, but I question whether there were more than a dozen; at any rate, I never saw more, and if there had been more, they would certainly have come to my yurt, for their curiosity was insatiable. Togdasin had simply counted the horses, and then jumped to the conclusion that there was a corresponding number of men. But in that part of the world the Chinese have a most extraordinary way of enumerating their troops. They are not content with counting the soldiers only, but reckon in also their horses, rifles, shoes, breeches, and so forth; so that the resultant total is a long way above what it ought to be. They apparently go on the supposition that the rifle is at least as valuable as the man; and by an analogous train of reasoning they argue that a man is of little use if he has to travel on foot, that he cannot go about naked, and so on. Hence they count in the whole kit, rifle, breeches, and all. By this peculiar process of arithmetic they fancy they deceive the credulous Kirghiz, as well as the Russians on the other side of the frontier, into believing that their garrisons are very much stronger than they are in reality. Woe to the Kirghiz who should presume to count the soldiers of the Celestial Empire by the same common rule as that by which he counts his sheep! A short time before my visit in that

quarter a Kirghiz yuz-bashi (chief of 100 men) was asked
Mi Darin, commandant of Tash-kurgan, how many men th
were at Su-bashi. The chief replied, " Thirty." Thereuj
Mi Darin wrote to his colleague, Shi Darin, asking if
statement was correct. Shi Darin promptly sent for
yuz-bashi, and beat him, asking him how he dared to cou
the garrison, or even presume to think about its size.

The Chinese troops at Su-bashi were armed with hal
dozen English rifles and an equal number of Russian; exc
for these, their principal weapons were Chinese bows a
lances. The European rifles were in bad condition, not h
ing been cared for. I myself saw two or three of the troc
stick their rifle-barrels downward into a muddy brook and u
them as jumping-poles to get across with. Less than a doz
of their horses were really serviceable animals; the oth
were nothing better than sorry caravan horses. Drill, ri
practice, or other military duties are seldom perform
Togdasin told me that the entire garrison, the commanda
included, spend days and days smoking opium, gamblii
eating, drinking, and sleeping. These frontier garrisons a
relieved at irregular intervals from Kashgar, Yarkand, a
Yanghi-hissar; and three or four times a year are suppli
with provisions by means of caravans from the same tow
The Kirghiz pay no taxes to them, but are under the oblig
tion to supply half a dozen sheep every month, for which t
Chinese pay at the rate of about one-half or one-third of th
real value.

CHAPTER XXIV

AMONG THE KIRGHIZ

I GRADUALLY learned to have much sympathy with the Kirghiz. I lived among them for four months a solitary European, and yet never once, during all that time, felt lonely. The friendship and hospitality they showed me never wavered. They shared with willing pleasure in the hardships of my nomad existence; and some of them were at my side in every sort of weather, took part in all my excursions, all my mountain ascents, all my expeditions across and to the glaciers. In fact, I won a certain measure of popularity in the valley of Sarik-kol. The people came from far and near to visit me at my camping-stations, bringing me presents of sheep, wild ducks, partridges, bread, yaks' milk and cream. And almost invariably, when I drew near to an aul, I was met by a troop of horsemen and escorted to the beg's yurt, given the place of honor near the fire, and offered dastarkhan (refreshments).

But the little ones entertained me most. Many of them were such sweet, pretty little things, as they ran about with a colored cap on their head, and not a stitch else on them, unless it were their father's huge skin boots, that I sometimes found it hard to tear myself away from them. At the first glance of such a strange apparition as my spectacles and my strange clothes they generally fled and hid behind their mothers, or concealed themselves in their favorite hiding-places in the yurt; but the offer of a lump of sugar quickly won their confidence. On their part, too, the Kirghiz soon understood that I regarded them as friends, and felt at home among them. I lived constantly in their yurts, ate the same food they did, rode their yaks, wandered from district to dis-

trict as they did—in a word, became to all intents and purposes a full-blooded Kirghiz. They often used to say to me :
"*Siz indi Kirghiz bo oldiniz*" (You have become a Kirghiz
now).

Three months earlier I had experienced nothing but kindness at the hands of Togdasin Beg, chief of the Kirghiz of
Sarik-kol, and their intermediary with Jan Darin at Bulun-kul.
On this the occasion of my second visit he welcomed me like
an old acquaintance, showing me every attention, and honor-
ing me with the choicest delicacies of the Kirghiz *cuisine*.
He asserted that a day or two's rest in his yurt was absolutely
indispensable for me before I went on to visit his neighbor,
Mus-tagh-ata, a chieftain who from a sublimer tent commands
authority over a greater race of subjects. I was very glad to
accept his insistent hospitality, for I wanted to engage men
and yaks for the summer. For July 11th my host planned a
grand surprise. Being anxious to show me the full glory of
Su-bashi and the neighboring yeylaus (summer camps), he
made arrangements for a *baiga*, or "mounted games"; which,
although as but a drop in the ocean when compared with a
parade of imperial troops, nevertheless, for romantic and
fascinating effects, probably exceeded anything household
troops can produce.

During the course of the morning the flower of the man-
hood in the district rode towards the higher-lying auls in the
plain of Irik-yak, where the games were to take place. On
they rode, troop after troop. Towards noon I too went in
the same direction, escorted by a body-guard of forty-two
Kirghiz wearing their best khalats. And what varieties of
color! Khalats of every conceivable shade, check girdles,
daggers and knives, baldrics with jingling vade-mecums—a
piece of steel for striking fire, an awl, tobacco-pouch, etc.,
head-coverings of every variety, mostly, however, small, round,
black, close-fitting caps (*calottes*), embroidered in red and
yellow and blue. Closely surrounded by this gay holiday
throng, I involuntarily felt, in my plain gray travelling-suit,
like a dervish among better folk. The sole ornament which
gave a little brightness to my outward man was my compass

KIRGHIZ MOTHER WITH HER BOYS

chain, which, without much stretch of the imagination, the Kirghiz might easily have taken to be pure gold. Of the elders none made such a brave show as Togdasin Beg and Togda Mohammed Beg, chieftain of the Kirghiz who dwelt on the east side of Mus-tagh-ata. The former wore an orange yellow gala khalat, edged with gold brocade, which I had brought him as a present from Kashgar the day before. Chance seemed to have played the chief part in determining the choice of attire in the case of the latter; for the colors were decidedly loud—a long navy-blue khalat, girdled by a broad light-blue sash, and a violet bag-cap with a gold ribbon round it. The wearer was a tall and strikingly typical Kirghiz, with oblique, narrow eyes, prominent cheek-bones, thin black beard and coarse mustaches, and rode a big coal-black horse of some foreign breed. Add to this the scimitar which dangled at his side in a black scabbard, and you have a picture of a true Asiatic Don Quixote.

We drew near to the upper villages, in and about which the bands of horsemen grew thicker and thicker. I was conducted to the place of honor in the middle of the plain, where I found awaiting me Khoat Beg, a fine old chieftain, one hundred and eleven years old, surrounded by five of his sons —gray old men they were, too—and a score of other horsemen. Although the aged patriarch's back was a little bent under the burden of his years, he nevertheless sat his saddle with as firm a seat and as proud a bearing as any among them. He wore a violet khalat, lined with fur, brown skin boots, and a brown turban. He had striking features—a large Roman nose, short white beard extending under the chin, and deep-sunk, gray eyes, which seemed to live more in the memories of the past than in the actual observations of the present. His people manifested the greatest veneration towards him, some of the begs hastening to throw themselves from their horses in order to pay their respects to him — all which he took with the imperturbable majesty of a god. The old man had formerly been Chong Beg (principal chieftain) over the Sarik-kol Kirghiz, a dignity which had passed from father to son in his family through seven generations before him, partly as independent chiefs, partly under foreign domination.

When not absorbed in his own meditations, the old man was very talkative, and plainly enjoyed telling what he could remember of past times and his own family circumstances.

He had seven sons and five daughters, forty-three grandchildren, and sixteen great-grandchildren.   Nearly all of them

A KIRGHIZ BAIGA

lived together in one community, a large aul (tent-village), which in summer was pitched beside Lake Kara-kul, and in winter near Bassyk-kul.   His eldest son, Oshur Beg, an unusually facetious old man, who gradually attached himself to me, told me that his father, Khoat Beg, in the course of his long life, had had four Kirghiz wives, two of whom still lived, old women of ninety, besides one hundred Sart wives, whom he bought at different times in Kashgar, and whom he successively discarded when he grew tired of them.

Khoat Beg took such a strong fancy to my spectacles that he asked me to give him them; but as I could not do without them I told him that, as he had managed to get along without such things for one hundred and eleven years, I thought he might do without them a little bit longer. I afterwards made him presents of cloth, caps, and handkerchiefs. Later on in the autumn the old chief was to go with one of his sons to Yanghi-hissar, climbing a pass which came within about 350 feet of the altitude of Mont Blanc. He was going to look at some land he owned there, as well as to indulge in a little merrymaking before the beginning of the long winter sleep.

A he-goat, in the literal sense of the word a scape-goat, was dragged in front of us. A Kirghiz sliced the animal's head off with a single sweep of his knife, and let the blood flow until it ceased of itself. The carcass was, so to speak, the prize of the subsequent mimic warfare, the object of the contestants being to obtain possession of it.

A man came forward, caught up the sheep across his horse, and rode away with it. We waited a few minutes. Then we saw a troop of horsemen approaching at a furious gallop. Eighty horses' hoofs rang on the hard ground—the grass gnawed off to the very roots by the sheep. The din was deafening. Wild, shrill shouts mingled with the jingling of the stirrups. On they came, enveloped in a cloud of dust. The foremost horseman flung the dead goat immediately in front of my horse's fore-feet. Like a horde of Huns or a band of robbers they dashed past us, away across the plain. But wheeling smartly round, they were soon back again at the spot where we stood. The person who is thus honored with having the dead goat flung down before him is expected to testify his sense of the favor conferred in some tangible fashion, either by offering dastarkhan — which is what the Kirghiz usually do—or by the present of a handful of silver *tengeh* (about 2¾d. each), which was what I offered on this occasion.

We had barely time to draw back before the wild troop were upon us again. They flung themselves upon the still smoking carcass of the goat, and began to struggle for it as though they were fighting for a bagful of gold. All I could see of them was an indistinguishable confusion of horses and men enveloped in a cloud of dust. Some of the horses fell ;

    ai ;d; others shied. Holding fast to their saddles,
ʼiders leaned over towards the ground and snatched at
carcass as they swept past it. Some fell off and were
ʼly trampled under foot. Others clung underneath their
ses' bellies. All grasped at the goat, tugging and hauling
the wildest disarray. The stragglers in the gallop, the
arrivals, all plunged headlong into the *mêlée* as though
would ride right over the mass of struggling horsemen.
men shouted. The horses whinnied. The dust rolled
ı clouds. The contestants were allowed to practise
n artifices, such as pulling at another man's bridle,
ag his horse over the nose with his whipstock to
him back, or even dragging one another out of the
e.

    ꞓ confusion was still worse confounded by a couple of
mpions who rode yaks with sharp horns. As these strong-
ʼd animals pushed their way into the *mêlée*, they kept
g the horses with their horns. This made the horses
  and kick. The yaks, irritated by the kicks, thrust
tnemselves in all the more stubbornly, till the contest began
to look remarkably like a bull-fight. At length one of the
men got a firm hold upon the goat's skin. He snatched the
body up, clasped it tight between his knee and his saddle,
and, bursting out of the throng, galloped away like the wind,
describing a wide circle round the plain. Hard after him
raced all the others. They disappeared from sight in the
distance. Two or three minutes passed. Again the dull
thud, thud of scores of horses' hoofs beating the ground.
Straight down upon us they charged, oblivious of all hinderances. Another moment and they would have ridden over
us and crushed us. We could not get out of their way. But
when within two or three yards of us they wheeled sharply
off, still going at a headlong pace. Once more the goat, now
bruised into an indistinguishable mass of flesh, was flung at
our feet, and then the struggle began again. This went on
time after time.

    I remarked to Khoat Beg that it was a good thing for us
old folk to be safe outside the scrimmage. The old chief

KIRGHIZ CHILDREN

laughed and said he fancied it must be wellnigh a hundred years since he was my age. I let him surmise that, in point of fact, he was nearly four times as old as I was.

Meanwhile Togdasin Beg became so excited by the mimic battle that he flung himself into the thick of it, and actually succeeded in gaining possession of the goat, and made his horse leap to one side. But getting a few Chinese hieroglyphics wealed across his face and nose in crimson, he became as quiet as a lamb, and, pulling his horse in beside ours, was content to sit still and remain an onlooker.

While the sport lasted most of the participators in it took off their khalats; indeed, some of them had the right side of the upper part of their body naked. With but very few exceptions every man came out of the contest with some sort of wound or scratch. Several of them had their faces so bloody that they rode off to the nearest brook to wash themselves. Nor were limping horses a rare sight. Caps and whips lay scattered all over the ground, and, the game at an end, I saw their owners wandering about over the battle-field looking for them. To tell the truth, it amazed me there were no serious mishaps. The reason of there being none is that from their earliest years the Kirghiz grow up on horseback, and so become habited—become skilled in all that belongs to horsemanship. This exciting and dangerous sport being concluded, the chief men present were invited to dastarkhan in the tent of the nearest beg. There we were entertained by the musicians of the neighborhood to a "chamber concert."

I had been obliged to dismiss my interpreter, the Taranchi Daod. He turned out to be a self-willed individual, and was not very accurate in his Chinese interpretations. Immediately after arriving at Su-bashi he added to these accomplishments by beginning to gamble with the Chinese, and in one day lost 40 tengeh. When, therefore, I sent back the kara-kesh (horse-owner) I hired at Kashgar, together with his horses, Daod received his orders to go with him. Thus of the men who left Kashgar with me the only one remaining

was my faithful Islam Bai. I now further engaged two trust
worthy Kirghiz—namely, Yehim Bai and Mollah Islam, both
of whom did excellent service during the journeys of the
summer. In addition to these men, I employed others for
shorter periods, as well as horses.

CHAPTER XXV

LITTLE KARA-KUL LAKE

I HAD chosen Little Kara-Kul lake as a suitable starting-point for my summer's cartographical labors and excursions, and accordingly journeyed thither on July 12th, to take possession of a yurt which had been put up by agreement on its southern shore.

On the way, near a few small auls, we witnessed another baiga, which was, if possible, more turbulent than the previous one. A rider came tearing past with a live goat on his saddle, chopped its head off at one blow, and with the dripping body dangling against his horse's side began to career wildly round the auls. Hard after him followed the rest. But the man had a first-rate horse, and it was not until the third round had been completed that he was caught, and the goat taken from him and dashed at my feet, raising a cloud of dust. One or two of the men got ugly tumbles, and a yuz-bashi scraped his face against the ground, but went on, however, scarred and bloody, as if nothing had happened. After taking dastarkhan (refreshments) we rode down to the lake, followed by the tumultuous troop, who still continued their mimic contest; and we were not sorry when soon afterwards they disappeared, and we were left to settle down in peace in our lonely tent.

This was pitched close to the shore, and in front of it spread the blue waters of the little lake, disappearing in the mist. Togdasin Beg and a few other friends came with us and were invited to tea. They stopped until it began to grow dark; and the festive feeling was enhanced by a musician, who performed on a stringed instrument called a *kau-muss*. The victor of the baiga came to see me, and pre-

I.—19

sented me with a can of *kumiss* (fermented mare's-milk); it was sour and cold, and tasted excellent. The only drawback to our camping-ground was the myriads of mosquitoes swarming over the flat shore of the lake, which was intersected in all directions by pools and arms from the glacier stream.

July 13th was our first working-day by the lake. As we found that the south shore, permeated as it was by stagnant water, would probably be unhealthy for a lengthened stay, we decided to move to a suitable spot on the east side; and accordingly the next day the men packed up our goods and chattels, and we moved over. I myself took a couple of Kirghiz with me and mapped the outline of the lake with the plane-table and diopter, continuing the work till I reached the new camping - station. On the way I paid a short visit to old Khoat Beg, who was encamped there with six yurts.

At the southeast corner of the lake, in a narrow opening in the rock, we saw the Sarik-tumshuk-masar (the Saint's Grave on the Yellow Cape), decorated with yaks' tails and rags. A clear spring gushed out at the base of the steep schistose rocks with a temperature of 47.1° Fahr. (8.4° C.).

Our steps now bore directly along the shore, where the ruptured ends of the stratified schistose rocks fell sheer into the lake, often necessitating our riding in the water.

On our left stretched the lake, its surface varying from a pretty light green to deep navy blue, blotched here and there with streaks of dirty yellow mud brought down by the streams. On the west shore rose the huge rocky wall of the Sarik-kol chain, with its out-jutting promontories just visible through the hazy atmosphere.

When I arrived at the new camp, everything was in order; the yurt had been put up close to the shore, on a little patch of luxuriant grass between it and the mountain, and there our horses were contentedly grazing.

Yolldash (the Travelling Companion), a wretched Kirghiz dog, which, like the late Yollchi, had joined our expedition as a volunteer, and was greatly valued by my men, had already made himself at home and was guarding the tent. When we first made his acquaintance, he was travelling with some Chinese horsemen, who had visibly reduced him to the brink of starvation. However, when the dog saw us he thought that, no matter who we might be, we should surely be better than the Chinese, so he turned back with us. I thought the creature so starved and miserable that I wanted to send him away. But my men begged so hard for the new member of the expedition that I gave way; and he followed us faithfully for a long while. He had a fine time of it now, ate as much as he liked, and enjoyed the sole right to the remains of our meals. He soon picked up, and grew into an unusually good and handsome dog. He was the best of watch-dogs and the best of companions, and when, later on, we made a second visit to the Russian Pamirs, he became a great favorite among the officers on account of his liveliness. By degrees he grew to be such a companion to me that I could not do without him, and when, about a year later, he died of thirst in the Takla-makan Desert, the parting was really bitter.

We bought a sheep, which we now proceeded to kill, and all had a good meal. Islam roasted a *chisslik* (steak or chop); the Kirghiz provided us with yak's milk; rice and tea we had ourselves, so that we could not have fared better.

That evening the sunset was beautiful, and threw a peculiar light on the clouds and western mountains, which were illumined with various shades of gray and yellow. The wind had been in the north, but towards evening went round to the east; and the waves, which broke against the stony beach with a sleepy, melodious murmur, were crested with dancing white horses. The moon soon rose over this beautiful picture; and, the temperature being pleasantly warm (62.6° Fahr. or 17° C.), we were able to enjoy our new camp, which was called Yanikkeh, to the utmost.

The following is a series of notes from my diary just as I wrote them down:

"July 14th. After the first meteorological observation of the day had been taken, we made a little botanical trip in the neighborhood and collected algæ from two or three lagoons along the shore.

" About one o'clock a violent squall passed over the country, with sharp gusts of wind and rain, which, however, did not last long. The white-crested waves were driven up to a considerable height, and dashed noisily against the beach. The sky was heavy and black with rain-clouds, chasing each other to the south. During the forenoon the mountains had been shrouded in the usual dust-haze, but the rain cleared the air, so that we could now see the white snow-fields of Mus-tagh-ata shining through the broken clouds with dazzling brilliance. The surface of the lake passed through the most won-

WEST SHORE OF LITTLE KARA-KUL.

derful changes of color; near the western and southern shores it was such a bright green that the boldest impressionist would not have dared to paint it as it actually was. Farther out it was striped with violet, while near the eastern shore the water was dark blue. Gray and gloomy stood the mountain giants, keeping guard over the little Alpine lake which lay cradled between their lofty crests. There was a flat stretch of fine pasture along the south shore, but on our side, with the exception of the little meadow where we were encamped the mountains rose sheer from the lake.

" It was not till the afternoon that the weather permitted a short topographical excursion in the neighborhood; even then we were overtaken by sharp showers of rain, and heard the thunder rumbling among the clefts of Mus-tagh-ata. We wandered through a typical moraine landscape, where wide tracts were strewn with mounds of grit and bowlders of all sizes; nearly all the latter being of different kinds of gneiss and schist, chiefly crystalline mica-schist.

"These collections of gravel and grit sometimes formed continuous ridges, sometimes isolated cones. Not seldom they formed *cirques*, fifty to two hundred yards in diameter, with a rampart round, the last sometimes completely closed, sometimes with a single opening. Some of these *cirques* had a cone, others a cavity, in the middle.

"Several bowlders were very highly polished, or striated; and everything tended to show that we were in a tract from which a glacier had once receded. One of these bowlders particularly attracted my attention, and was chosen as a topographical fixed - point on account of its dominant position. Its surface, two yards long and one broad, was smooth and polished, and on it was roughly but characteristically depicted six *tekkes* (wild goats). The brown gneiss rock had been scratched away with a sharp stone, or perhaps an iron tool, and the design stood out in relief in dull gray. The Kirghiz could tell me nothing about the picture, except that they thought it was very old.

"We discovered that the north end of the enormous moraine fell sheer down to a river, which was almost entirely fed by the melting of the glaciers and snow-fields. The stream was called the Ike-bel-su (the River from the Two Passes), and flowed through the Sarik-kol valley, then broke through the Mus-tagh chain, and under the name of the Ghez-daria (as I have already mentioned in a previous chapter) reached the plains near Kashgar.

"From the summit of the moraine we had a splendid view over the upper reaches of the river, rolling down its current as if issuing from a rocky portal between the lofty snow-covered mountains. On through the valley it wound, sometimes narrow and foaming, sometimes calm and broad, with grass - grown banks, on which were two or three Kirghiz auls.

"When we again returned to camp over another part of the moraine-ridge, we found that the Kirghiz had procured another big yurt, and in it my men settled down with the kitchen paraphernalia.

"Immediately southeast of the camp there was a dominant mountain of black schist, called Kara-kir (the Black Peaks) and as it seemed to promise a splendid point of vantage for surveying the neighboring country, I wished to ascend it as early as possible, which we did on July 15th.

"The panorama which unfolded itself to my view when we reached the top exceeded my most sanguine expectations. The long moraine-ridge, with its labyrinth of cones and grit-mounds, appeared from that elevated point of view to dwindle to insignificance, and the green-banked ribbon of the Ike-bel-su winding through the gray scenery formed a particularly marked feature in the landscape. But the sublime grandeur of the Mus-tagh-ata, whose white crests were visible between the clouds, completely dwarfed everything else. Fantastic, inky-black rocks broke up through the expanses of snow, some attaining an altitude of 20,000 feet; and above them again towered the spotless dome. The east side of the mountain was so precipitous and irregular that I perceived at once from its shape it must be quite inaccessible. The northern versant presented a confused medley of rocks, snow-fields, and glaciers. On the other hand, the western declivities were particularly even and rounded, towards the summit the angle being only twenty-two degrees; while on the east side the inclination varied from thirty to forty-eight degrees.

"The Tegherman-tash-su (the Millstone Brook), which fell into the Ike-bel-su, was divided at its mouth into five arms, flowing over a talus slope or sort of sloping delta, partly formed by its own glacial *débris* and mud.

"In the southwest we saw the broad, level valley of Su-bashi, with its river also forming a delta, and its marshes and innumerable miniature lakes laced like beads on a mat.

"In the west also there was a grand panorama. The bright surface of Little Kara-kul, lying between the massive mountain-chains, immediately underneath our feet, appeared quite small in comparison with their overwhelming masses. Its light-green surface contrasted forcibly with its own dark-green grassy shores, and with the gray mountain-walls broken here and there by moraine deposits. Sometimes the grass trenched a little upon the lake; but it was nowhere broad, except on the southern shore. The light fleecy clouds were reflected in the water as their shadows glided over it. The turbid yellow flood of the Su-bashi, which debouched on the south, wound through the lake like a dirty ribbon. Immediately in front of us, near the west shore, there was a little island, the only one in the Kara-kul, if we except a few small green plots which have become detached from the grassy southern shore. On the other side of the lake the Sarik-kol chain faded away towards the north and west.

"The northern shore of Little Kara-kul was a moraine wall, a continuation of that already described; that is the reason why the outline of that shore was so very irregular. The moraine was intersected by a stream which issued from the lake, which was also conspicuous from its green grassy banks; farther down it united with the Ike-bel-su. In the northwest, beyond the Kara-kul, we could see the two basins of Bassyk-kul.

"About mid-day we were again overtaken by a storm of rain and hail, but continued our way till we were sent home by really bad weather. I now felt that I had pretty well taken my bearings; I had my programme clear, and knew how and on what plan the mountain should be attacked.

"Every evening after dark I held a *levée* in my tent. The Kirghiz came from far and near, and always brought with them welcome gifts of sheep, partridges, new bread, fresh yak's milk and cream; in return for which they received money, pieces of cloth, caps, knives, etc., which I had brought from Tashkend for the purpose. In a short time we had a whole circle of friends, and felt quite at home in the place. During our later excursions we never passed an aul without going into one of the yurts, and we were always pretty sure to find one or two old acquaintances. Our chief friend and protector, however, was Togdasin Beg, who often came to see us, and procured everything for us that we wanted, such as yaks, horses, tents, and the like.

"The whole day on July 16th there was a thick fog. In the morning the lake presented a curious sight, as the mist completely hid the farther shore from view, and we seemed to be standing on the brink of a boundless sea.

"I bade a couple of my Kirghiz undress and wade out into the shallow water, to collect some of the algæ which grew along the shore. Yolldash was also carried out, and given a thorough and much-needed bath. The water was not so cold but it could be used for bathing purposes. At one o'clock it was 63.7° Fahr. (17.6° C.), but it cooled off considerably during the night. At seven in the morning of the same day it was 53.2° Fahr. (11.8° C.). On clear days the water soon became warm in the shallow places, though naturally only the upper layers. By mid-day on July 16th, for example, the radiation rose to 138.2° Fahr. (59° C.), although the atmosphere was not clear; but at the depth of 4 inches the water was only 82.4° Fahr. (28° C.), which shows how impervious even such a thin layer of water is to the direct heat of the sun.

"We made an excursion to the confluence of the Kara-kul stream with the Ike-bel-su. At the north end of the lake we found a large semicircular creek or bay. It was shallow, and grassy near the shore, although the moraine came down to within 50 or 100 yards of it. Near the mouth of the river the grass was broader and more luxuriant; but the mosquitoes swarmed over it in thick clouds, by no means enhancing our comfort.

"The Kara-kul stream issued from the lake through a trumpet-shaped creek, studded with erratic blocks projecting above the surface of the water; shortly afterwards it widened out into a small basin, called the Su-karagai-kul (the Water-Pine Lake). North of this, but not connected with the river, was another small sheet of water called the Angher-kul (the Duck Lake). Both basins were bordered with grass and marsh-land, interspersed between the moraines through which the river cut its way.

"A little farther on the gradient suddenly became so steep

that the river broke into cataracts over the stony *débris* which littered its bed, though its banks were in places still lined with narrow strips of grass. On it foamed, its channel becoming more and more deeply eroded, until it emptied itself into the Ike-bel-su. Near its mouth the velocity decreased all of a sudden, as if the river had encountered a serious check. Sometimes its water was as clear as crystal, sometimes foaming white, sometimes deep blue, until finally it mingled with the main stream, which was turbid and gray from the glacial mud, and possessed twenty times its force. The bed of the Ike-bel-su was excessively deep, the river having energetically carved its way through conglomerates 150 to 300 feet high. It was absolutely impossible to cross it. I put down the breadth at 27 yards, and the velocity was 5½ feet in the second.

" A deafening roar echoed between the perpendicular walls; the water dashed a yard into the air every time it encountered an obstructing stone, and the spray rose in clouds; but the foam was hardly distinguishable, being as gray as the flood itself.

" A few yards below the confluence of the Kara-kul, its clear blue water, which was pressed towards the left bank, totally disappeared. Its effect was only visible a short distance, while its foam disappeared at once. With such violence and momentum did the enormous masses of water plunge on their way that we could feel the ground vibrating under our feet.

" The Kara-kul river had a temperature of 61.9° Fahr. (16.6° C.); the Ike-bel-su of 57.9° Fahr. (14.4° C.). Thus the water which came direct from the glaciers was four or five degrees colder than that which lingered in the lake under the sun's rays, although the lake itself received similar cold glacial streams. After depositing its glacial mud in Lake Kara-kul, the stream became perfectly clear.

" Between the two water-courses the great moraine-bed sent out a tongue, thickly studded with chains of hills, ranged sometimes in rows, sometimes in circles, crescents, and amphitheatres. They belonged to the terminal moraine, which was still standing, showing how far the tongue of the Ike-bel-su glacier, which has now disappeared, reached at one time.

"On my return I had a visit from Oshur Beg, Khoat Beg's son, who brought me two live wild geese caught at Bassyk-kul, and bread, milk, and butter.

"July 17th. There was a south wind blowing this morning, and the water on our shore was not quite clear, the waves

OUR CAMP AT YANIKKEH, EASTERN SHORE OF LITTLE KARA-KUL

having brought sedimentary matter from the mouth of the river. The beach round the creek exhibited plain indications of the effect wrought by the waves under the influence of the south wind. The water washed up an even wall of sand all round the creek, leaving also a belt of dry seaweed. We started out on an excursion, but were overtaken by such a violent north-northwesterly gale that we were obliged to turn back. This region is notorious for its winds. Those which come from the north and south are the most violent, as they sweep unhindered through the meridional valley. In accordance with the configuration of the country, the east winds are more irregular and squally, while from the west, or Pamirs, it seldom blows at all.

"Yes, indeed, the wind often put our patience to the test; it curtailed or prevented the carrying out of many plans, and the whole summer long we were very much dependent on the caprices of the weather. On unfavorable days there was nothing for it but to sit in the yurt and write, or work out my sketch-maps. It was always refreshing to hear the monotonous song of the waves on the beach. To-day, too, the lake was greatly perturbed; long white-topped waves crossed it diagonally, and cast up sand and seaweed on the beach, so that the water was muddy for ten yards or more out into the lake, before the fresh green-blue color supervened again. A thick mist came on by degrees, enshrouding the Kara-kul, so that nothing except the two points on either side of our creek were visible, and they seemed to be much farther off than they were in reality. When one white crest after the other came rolling in from out of the mist I had the feeling of standing by the open sea.

"Along the beach, near our camp, there were two small lagoons, one behind the other. The outer lagoon was connected with the lake, whence a deep narrow channel conveyed water to it every time the waves broke. The inner lagoon was separated from the outer by a strip of land six or seven yards broad, intersected by a narrow but deep channel, so that even there the water was churned up by the wind. The outer lagoon was separated from the lake by a grass-grown wall of earth a yard in height, which threatened to give way under the continual beating of the waves. It was evident that the lake had at one time overflowed our present camping-ground. The bottom of the lagoon was covered with fine sand and algæ, and in its sheltered waters were tadpoles and water-spiders.

"In the afternoon it rained hard, but about six o'clock suddenly cleared. All at once we heard a rushing sound, as if a gale of wind were approaching from the northwest. The noise grew louder and louder, came nearer and nearer. On the now calm and shining surface of the lake a dark blue

ıme visible on the opposite shore. It rapidly
our side. The wind howled and lashed the wa
ıext moment a hail-storm broke over us. It c
ıw moments; but the ground was white with l
quarter to half an inch in diameter. They s
the sharp shower of rain which followed.

CHAPTER XXVI

LITTLE KARA-KUL LAKE

(Continued)

" IT was not necessary to stay long by the Little Kara-kul to perceive clearly its geological formation.   I soon saw that it was a moraine lake, formed by the damming of the valley by the moraine of the Ike-bel-su glacier, the remains of which are now pierced by the rivers that issue from the lake.   The basin, or part of the valley dammed by the moraine, is filled with glacier and spring water, which bring down with them large quantities of sediment, and this, in conjunction with the drift-sand, is gradually choking the net-work of lake streams. The day will no doubt come when they will be effaced alto- gether, and the Kara-kul river will flow through the valley in   a continuously eroded bed.   The lake was undoubtedly much larger at one time, when the river flowed at the top of the moraine, and had not yet succeeded in digging down through it.   The number of bowlders still cumbering the bed of   the river and lying in its broad mouth—fragments of the former medial moraine—testify to this ; as do the lagoons just described.   That the whole valley was once cut off by the now defunct glacier we have unmistakable proof in the number of gravel-mounds, ridges, and bowlders which lie scattered about on every side.

" The material, consisting of fine-grained mica schist, crys- talline schist, pretty, fine gray gneiss, coarse-grained gneiss with felspar crystals, and red varieties of the same, etc., is similar to that which I found in the higher regions of the Mus-tagh-ata.   The gneiss bowlders, which are spread over large areas, could only be brought thence, and the force which brought them such long distances from the solid mountain

could only be ice. Indeed, they exhibit unmistakable signs
that this was the case: they are rounded or hollowed out like
bowls, and are much striated or polished by attrition.

"July 18th. I had now completed my work on the east
shore of the Kara-kul, and determined to move on to another
camping-ground. I therefore ordered the men, under Islam
Bai's supervision, to break up camp, and move the tent and
baggage to a suitable spot on the shore of the lake Bassyk-
kul. Meanwhile I myself went on a topographical trip, accompanied by one of the Kirghiz, intending to make for the
new camp in the evening.

"We crossed the bed of the moraine higher up than formerly, and then went down to the aul of Keng-shevär, a place
of four yurts, lying on the left bank of the Ike-bel-su. The
tents were surrounded by splendid pasturage, and several of
our friends lived there and received us with great cordiality.
According to custom, the oldest inhabitant of the aul came
forward to meet the guest with both hands to his forehead,
and then showed me the way to his yurt, which had been
hastily set to rights. A piece of carpet and one or two
cushions were placed on the seat of honor, opposite the entrance, and there I was invited to sit down by the fireside.
The other inhabitants of the aul dropped in one by one and
seated themselves round the fire, on which was boiling an
iron pot containing tea. Tea and milk were served in bowls
of wood or Chinese porcelain, and conversation was soon in
full swing. Sometimes the men's wives, with their high,
white, turban-like head-gear, and some of the young girls,
were also present; but they did not take part in the conversation. They only affected importance with regard to the
fire, which they fed with *tesek* (dried yak-dung), and attended
to the management of the household generally. These visits
were always pleasant, and had, further, the great advantage
that I was able to glean valuable information as to ways and
tracks, climate, the migrations of the Kirghiz, their manner
of living, and the like.

"Our hosts told us that they spend the summer only at
Keng-shevär; in the winter, this part being exposed to wind

and snow, they move on to the Shuveshteh kishlaks (winter villages), which are situated farther up and are more sheltered from wind and weather.

"The Ike-bel-su presented quite a different appearance seen from this little tent-village to what it had at the outlet of the Kara-kul stream, being 200 feet broad, and the velocity about three feet in the second. At the only place where it was possible to ford it, we let a Kirghiz ride over, and found that the maximum depth amounted to 3¾ feet; but the bed was tolerably level and did not vary much. The volume was 2440 cubic feet in the second, which is remarkable for a river chiefly fed by glaciers. The water was said to be lowest about four o'clock in the afternoon; but it rises towards evening, as the glacial streams, which do not reach the river before that time, then give up their tribute. There were several low islets in the river, more or less grass-grown, of which one divided it into two arms. In winter the bed is dry, or has, at most, a few narrow rivulets of frozen water; but by the beginning of August the stream falls so considerably that it is possible to ride over it at several points without danger. A little way below the aul a projecting spur of the moraine forces the river to make a sharp bend to the right. The result of this is a little lake-like basin, into which the water eddies; after that it continues its way in a deep, wide channel, breaking through the moraine-wall with a roar that can be heard at some distance.

"Opposite Keng-shevär, on the other bank, there was an aul with seven yurts. As its inhabitants pastured their sheep during the day on the left bank, the animals had all to be brought back across the stream in the evening, and it was very amusing to see what a difficult business it was. A number of men on horseback took each a couple of sheep across their saddles and rode in a long string through the river; but, as there were many sheep, it took a considerable time before the whole flock was safely landed on the other side.

"But we had to think of getting back before dusk came on and put an end to our map-making. We therefore set our course over the moraine, where we again found many pretty

cirques with vegetation in the middle. In such situati
grass grows comparatively well, as it is sheltered by the ri
like formation of the moraine, which also retains any r
that may fall. We reached the new camp on the shore
the Lower Bassyk-kul by way of the Angher-kul. In t
middle of the former lake there was an island, with a morai

MUS-TAGH-ATA FROM BASSYK-KUL, LOOKING SOUTH-SOUTHE
Erratic Blocks (Gneiss) and Moraines in the foreground

cairn sticking up in it. Our two yurts were pitched or
patch of grass, and around us lay a new domain to be explor
　"Our first day at Bassyk-kul was anything but a succe
The wind blew; it poured with rain from morning till nig
the heavy drops pattering incessantly on the tent-coveri
Open-air work was out of the question; but happily I had
much back work to make up that the involuntary confi
ment was rather welcome than otherwise. Togdasin Beg p
me a visit, and was regaled with tea and Chinese brandy,
latter specially brought for such occasions, and was furth
more entertained with tunes on the musical-box, which ne

failed to arouse the Kirghiz' intense astonishment and liveliest interest. Our mountain friends were most impressed, however, by the Husqvarna rifles. They found the mechanism so complicated that they declared no human hands could have constructed it, and that it must have been made by Allah himself.

"Togdasin Beg told me that the Chinese garrison in the Sarik-kol valley was following all my movements with some uneasiness, and was kept informed daily by Kirghiz spies of what I was doing and where I was going. They wondered, if I were an *oruss* (Russian) or *Ferenghi* (European), how long I meant to stay, what my real motive was in making maps, and why I hacked pieces of stone out of the rocks. They had been ordered to watch the frontier towards the Russian Pamirs, and now a stranger, whom they supposed to be a Russian, had made his appearance, and was proceeding, unhindered, to find out how the land lay. Thanks, however, to the passport which the Dao Tai had given me, they never molested us.

"Heavy blue-black rain-clouds swept down the many lateral valleys which strike off from the Sarik-kol chain towards the open country, in which were the two Bassyk-kul lakes. Everything was enveloped in a thick Scotch mist, darkening the otherwise magnificent landscape with gloom. Every now and again a fragment of the glacier or mountain-side became visible through the mist, which clung to the surface of the ground and drifted off to the south. The Kirghiz assured me that such continuous rain as that of to-day was unusual. The patch of grass on which we were encamped was transformed into a swamp, and we were constrained to dig deep ditches round the yurt, with branches running towards the lake, to protect ourselves from the wet. In the evening it cleared up, and the atmosphere became perfectly still. The lakes lay like dark mirrors in which all the fantastic projections of the mountains were clearly reflected.

"During the ensuing days I explored the country round our new camping-ground, and mapped the west shore of Little Kara-kul. First of all we followed the shore-line, and

I.—20

where the rocks fell sheer into the lake we rode through the water, on the disintegrated terraces at their base. Then we made short excursions from the lake to the neighboring mountains, where we often had decidedly disagreeable passages to traverse. There was one point which was especially suitable for studying this remarkable and beautiful Alpine region. Each of the twenty-one glaciers of the Mus-tagl chain was visible with the field-glass, clearly lit up, so that every detail was distinct. The slopes of the chain were draped with dazzling white snow except the rocky pinnacles which projected highest. In places, however, particularly in the lower regions, the snow was tinged a dirty yellow, due to dust brought thither by the wind. On the summits the snow formed a continuous covering, closely following the relief of the underlying mountains; but in several places its lower edge was broken, the snow having slid down over the precipices. Otherwise the tendency of the snow is to gravitate towards the gathering-basin of the glaciers, whence it is gradually dispersed by the ice-streams. These are sometimes narrow and compact, sometimes hive-shaped, sometimes thin and spreading, but always covered with gravel and bowlders, which cover the belts of ice between the transverse crevasses, and give the glaciers a striped appearance. Some of the glaciers are so covered with moraines that it is only with difficulty they can be distinguished from their surroundings.

A trip to the isthmus between the two small lakes showed that they were separated from each other by a decayed, and much broken, moraine-wall, beside which we found erratic blocks measuring as much as 1000 cubic meters or more cubic feet, and with beautifully polished surfaces. It was possibly the oldest of the terminal moraines of the former second glacier.

On one occasion when we were returning from a trip of this kind, Yehim Bai, who was carrying the topographical instruments, lost a brass diopter, and I gave him to understand that if the missing instrument were not found he would be in disgrace. He forthwith started off to go over the ground again, and see if he could find it. An acquaint-

ISSYK-KUL AND ISSYK-KUL-DEN-KIASI-DAVAN

ance, whom he eventually met, told him that an extraordinary metal thing had been found and taken to the Chinese commandant, Jan Darin, at Bulun-kul, who thought he could put a spoke in my wheel by retaining it. I sent off a messenger at once to inform Jan Darin that he would have to settle the matter with the Dao Tai if he did not return me the instrument. I received the diopter back immediately.

"I spent a whole day in investigating the country between the Lower Bassyk-kul and the Ike-bel-su. A small stream issued from the lake, and flowing through fairly luxuriant grass-land, littered with fragments of the moraine, joined the main stream a little way north of the river Kara-kul. The Ike-bel-su had decreased considerably in volume the last few days, owing to the fall in the temperature; but here, too, it raced between perpendicular or oblique conglomerate walls, in the sides of which round gneiss blocks were partially embedded, looking as if every moment they would topple down into the river.

" On July 24th examined the upper basin of the Bassyk-kul. About the middle of the south shore a promontory, formed by a spur of the mountain, fell almost sheer into the lake so that none but foot-passengers could get round it. We, being mounted, were obliged to make our way through a pass over the ridge.

" This little pass, called Bassyk-kulden-kiasi-davan (the Mountain-Path Pass of Bassyk-kul), was situated not more than two hundred feet above the lake, but had steep approaches, and its summit commanded a fine view. At our feet basked the little lake, washing the promontory on three sides; we also saw its small islands and shoals, its submarine moraine elevations and erratic blocks, still half immersed in the water, and the small deltas which form at the mouths of the streams that entered it from the western valleys. On the isthmus between the lakes was the crumbling moraine-wall, in the middle not more than eight or ten feet above the level of the water. Just at that low spot there was a marsh; nevertheless, all visible connection between the two lakes was en-

tirely wanting. The Kirghiz told me that even in the spring
and summer, when the increase of water from the western
valleys is sometimes considerable, the rise of niveau is never
very perceptible, and no water ever flows over from the upper
to the lower basin.

Hastily surveyed, it might be supposed that the lake possessed no outlet, and that it was therefore salt. The water,
however, was perfectly fresh and clear. A glance at the map

THE LOWER BASSYK-KUL AND THE MUS-TAGH CHAIN

reveals a satisfactory explanation of this. The lower lake, it
is true, does not receive any visible affluent, but out of it flows
a tiny stream. The lake must therefore receive an invisible
influx, and this naturally comes from the upper basin, whose
surplus water percolates under the isthmus moraine to the
lower lake, and thence finds its way to the Ike-bel-su. Bassyk-kul was situated 12,221 feet, and Little Kara-kul 12,201
feet, above sea-level.

"Several subsidiary chains branched off from the main
Sarik-kol range, and their *yilgas* or side-glens all opened tow-
ards the lake. The most important were the Kara (the Black),
Yellang (the Bare), and Khamaldi (the Gusty) yilgas. The

last-named has its own stream, running into a creek; while the streams from the first two united with several other small watercourses, and formed one, which again, just before reaching the lake, divided into two arms with a delta between. The sediment brought down by these several streams has been deposited in long narrow tongues and islets of mud; and beyond them again lay a group of moraine islands.

" In the three glens which I have just mentioned there was more or less good pasturage; the yaks, however, have to put up with the inferior qualities, as the better grass is reserved for the sheep. Here the Naiman Kirghiz of Khoat Beg's aul spend the three coldest winter months. Through the Kara-yilga a path leads up to the Sarik-kol pass, Kok-ala-chukkur (the Green-Chequered Depths), and thence to Lake Rang-kul. It can, however, only be traversed by yaks or by people on foot, and is seldom used, except occasionally by Kirghiz going to the Russian Pamirs, without permission from the Chinese authorities.

" At 4 o'clock it again began to rain; and the wind blew from the north. We rode back towards the west shore of the lake by following the little Kara-yilga stream, which was now dry, with the exception of small pools in the deeper holes. An hour and a half later we observed a most extraordinary phenomenon. A slight rushing sound was heard from up the bed of the stream. Then a brownish gray wave of water appeared suddenly round a bend, and foamed down among the stones, first slowly and gradually, filling the deeper parts, and winding between the steep excavated banks, along which there was a narrow belt of vegetation. This onrush of water takes place regularly every evening at this time of the year; it is glacier water from the Sarik-kol chain, which only reaches the lake towards evening.

" On July 25th we broke up camp at Bassyk-kul and went to Keng-shevär, whence I intended beginning the exploration of Mus-tagh-ata. On our way thither we passed an unusually fine circular moraine, about a hundred yards in diameter, situated on the south shore of the Bassyk-kul. In the middle there was a tiny round pool, surrounded by a ring of white salt deposit, which in its turn was girdled by a belt of vegetation; outside of all was the moraine-wall, with its one opening towards the lake. Although the pool was on a level with the lake, and quite near its shore, so that it was fair to assume a subterranean connection between them, the water in the *cirque*, which was called Shor-kul (Salt Lake), was absolutely salt. The Kirghiz told me that sheep which drink of it get cramp and die.

"At Tamga-tash we met Togdasin Beg, bringing me a sheep and a can of yak's milk as presents. He accompanied us to Keng-shevär, and stopped the night there. The sheep was killed in the evening, and the inhabitants of the aul were invited to the feast; but we were disturbed during the proceedings by a violent whirlwind, which threatened to carry away the yurt. All the guests scrambled to their feet and seized hold of the tent-poles, while two or three other men anchored the tent with ropes and supports."

CHAPTER XXVII

AMONG THE GLACIERS OF MUS-TAGH-ATA

THE following day we rode up the northern flank of Mus-tagh-ata, and crossed the huge ridge on the left side of the Ike-bel-su. The gradient was steepish before we reached the top, which rose and fell in long, sweeping undulations, but otherwise was fairly level, the surface being covered with sand, gravel, and small bowlders, with here and there a few tussocks of grass and clumps of *Ranunculaceæ*. On the other side of the summit we again reached the Kara-kul watershed, whence a brisk little rivulet from the glen of Köntöi flowed down to the lake through a broad, shallow bed. Beside this stream, at a height of 13,530 feet, were the Kotch-korchu yeylaus (summer grazing-grounds), which we chose as our first starting-point for exploring the glaciers.

The Kirghiz belonging to the aul had come there three months previously, and intended to remain three more; the six winter months they spend in the Köntöi-yilga. There exists among the Kirghiz a traditional agreement by which each family or clan possesses its own kishlaks and yeylaks; a rule which cannot be broken without a general convocation being held. The inhabitants of this place, like most of the Sarik-kol Kirghiz, belonged to the Kara-teit tribe. Their aksakal, or chief, Tugul Bai, was ninety-six years old, sound in mind and body, and with pleasing manners. The active life they lead in the open air hardens the Kirghiz to such an extent that as a rule they live to a very great age.

To-day again there were torrents of rain and the thunder echoed among the mountains. Shortly afterwards we heard a rushing sound, which our host explained was always audible after heavy rain; it was the rain-water streaming over the precipices.

My first business at Kotch-korchu was to pay and dismiss the two Kirghiz, Nur Mohammed and Palevan, who had done good service hitherto, but knew nothing of the glacier world up above, neither had they any yaks. In their stead I engaged a couple of Kirghiz belonging to the place, and had their yaks out on parade in the evening; yaks being the only riding animals which can make their way at all in these high glacial regions.

On July 27th, mounted on a splendid black yak and accompanied by a couple of Kirghiz as guides, I steered my course eastward towards the first glacier to be explored, Gorumdeh. We rode quietly along over country sloping towards the north, and cut through by three small glacier streams. Leaving on the right some angular, inky-black rocks, we discovered behind them a small glacier, excessively steep at its upper end, but of no very great extent. Farther to the east there were several similar prominent outcrops of rock, huge ragged masses of mountain, between which the glaciers thrust out their finger-like projections towards the north. The largest of these was called Gorumdehning-bashi (the Head of the Stony Tract); its stream, which gathered up glacier water from all the other brooks, flowed through a deeply excavated channel and farther down united with the Ike-bel-su.

I contented myself with mapping the left lateral moraines of the Gorumdeh glacier while riding up. For this purpose I only used the compass now for mapping. The distances I measured by adding up the yak's steps, allowing for the errors due to our irregular course, and after having previously measured how many steps on the uneven ground corresponded to a hundred yards.

The lower part of the Great Gorumdeh glacier was so encumbered with gravel and other detritus that it was often difficult to distinguish it from the neighboring rocks. How steep this stream of ice was will be understood when I state that the point of the tongue inclined at an angle of fully nine degrees. But after that the slope of the glacier-trough de-

many-branched babbling brook that came foaming down one
of the outermost moraines, forming a delta of sediment and
débris at its foot, over which its arms again divided.

This stream seemed to issue from one of the smaller
glaciers; but although its volume was as much as 70 or 100
cubic feet in the second, the tarn had no visible outlet, nor
did it rise above a certain level, as the surplus water that issued from underneath the moraines flowed into the general
glacier-basin. The tarn could not exist at all between moraine-walls of such coarse material were it not that the sedimentary matter which it brings down itself forms a sort of
foundation for the water to rest upon.

From the tarn we rode up in a southerly direction, between two gigantic moraine-walls. The trough between them
was overgrown with sparse tufts of grass, wild rhubarb, and
other plants, and was well named Gultcha-yeylau (the Pasture
of the Wild Sheep); for here, and far out on the glacier, we
found the tracks of wild sheep.

As the moraines farther on became worse and worse, consisting exclusively of cyclopean blocks of naked rock, we left
our yaks and made our way on to the glacier on foot. After
passing the last lateral moraine, which, by-the-by, was still in
course of formation, we reached the firm ice. At first it was
covered with gravel and bowlders to such an extent that the
clear ice-pyramids only peeped out at intervals. The lateral
moraine, carried on the back of the glacier, was 500 yards
in breadth, and ceased somewhat abruptly where the white
ice began. This formed a chaos of pyramids and mounds,
which, however, had no sharp edges, but were much rounded,
and caked with a layer of soft, wet ice, chalky white and resembling snow. This was, of course, the result of ablation,
or the destructive influence of the atmosphere and warmth
upon the ice, which was then working everywhere with great
activity. The sound of trickling, dripping water was audible
in all directions among the bowlders and stones, in the crevasses, and in small pools on the surface of the ice. The glaciers rumbled and cracked; every now and again we heard
the ringing echo of smaller bowlders and gravel falling into

the gaping fissures, and in the distance the rushing sound of the glacial torrents, which, now that the sun was high, were fed abundantly from every side. The material brought down from the mountain consisted for the most part of the same gray gneiss which we had previously observed down by the lakes. Gigantic blocks such as those that lay beside the Bassyk-kul were, however, absent. The smaller fragments of stone, by reason of their greater power of absorbing heat, had sunk down in holes in the ice, and lay at the bottom in a little pool of water. The larger blocks, on the other hand, protected the underlying ice from melting, and therefore formed glacier tables resting on platforms of ice.

A glance northward, that is to say, down the glacier, showed us, to the left, the gray masses of the lateral moraine, with only occasional glimpses of the ice showing through; to the right the white corrugated surface of the naked glaciers, with the two medial moraines gradually merging into one, the biggest I saw on the Mus-tagh-ata; and in the background the deep depression which marked the continuing line of the glacier, and through which probably the Gorumdeh formerly streamed to the Ike-bel-su glacier, although the old terminal moraine has been entirely swept away by the glacier-stream.

Lastly we went down to a place near the tongue of the glacier, which was split into two portions by a small lake of clear water. The highest altitude we reached on the glacier was 14,700 feet above sea-level.

To the south was the vast *firn* or root of the glacier, a gathering-basin into which the snow slid down from the surrounding precipices, leaving step-like platforms behind it.

On July 29th we again broke up camp and got under way for a new base of operations—namely, a spot more conveniently situated for the investigation of the glaciers which streamed out towards the west.

We started in a south-southwesterly direction, and made our way up the grass-grown slopes. The weather was cold and misty, with an occasional snow-storm. At length we reached the pass of Sarimek (the Pass of the Yellow Elbow), an important feature in the country, as it forms the passage

Plains of Tagharma

SKETCH MAP OF MUS-TAGH-ATA

over a gigantic spur of the Mus-tagh-ata which stretches to the northwest, dividing the glaciers and streams of the northern declivities from those of the western. The pass was strewn with gravel and small bowlders, and on its southern face were fissured rocks of an unusually hard, dark crystalline schist inclined at an angle of thirty-eight degrees to the north.

If, standing on this pass, we turned towards the massive knot of Mus-tagh-ata, the following picture from left to right, or from north to south, unfolded itself to view: First of all, the rocky buttresses, foreshortened, with a small snow - clad glacier; then, between two arms of the mountain, both in part thickly carpeted with snow, there was another small glacier, fairly clean at the top, but at its lower extremity strewn with fine gravel, so that the blue ice in the fissures was only visible here and there. In the middle of the glacier transverse crevasses predominated, at its lower end longitudinal crevasses. The tongue of the glacier was girdled by gigantic moraines crumpled up into several ridges. Between the third rocky buttress and that part of Mus-tagh-ata which we were on in April, and high up on the mountain-side, there was a deep gorge, into which the Sarimek and Kamper - kishlak glaciers poured their streams, while they in their turn were separated by a huge snow - clad wall of rock. The former glacier was encumbered with moraines; the latter was shining white. Finally, in the south, the pass of Ullugrabat; and in the west the entire Sarik-kol chain, with its thinly scattered snow-fields. It was partly hidden by particularly beautiful white cirrus-clouds, which contrasted strikingly with the steel-blue, wintry sky over the Pamirs in the background.

The descent from the pass was very steep; we rode down the gully of a stream which issued from the right-hand side of the Sarimek glacier, and raced merrily along its stony bed, tumbling down falls and cataracts as it went. We left the terminal moraine with its imposing front, crossed some streams, and reached a small patch of water-soaked greensward, where I collected several new species of plants. A herd of kiyick, or wild goats, were peacefully grazing there; but upon catching sight of us, instantly sprang up the mountain-side. We

then crossed five more brooks, fed with glacier water. Between them low elongated ridges ran down to the Sarik-kol
valley, forming black and gloomy continuations of the rocky
buttresses which, like radii or ribs, divided the glaciers one
from another.

Some of the men, who had gone on ahead with the cara-

SARIMEK AND KAMPER-KISHLAK GLACIERS, LOOKING SOUTHEAST

van, were already camped when we arrived, having chosen a
piece of lush, well-watered grass, that afforded splendid pasturage for the yaks.

That evening it snowed hard, and the next morning the
mountains were covered with a thin sheet of snow.   The
Kirghiz said that winter was already coming in the mountains, and that it would get colder and colder every day.

On July 30th winter was upon us in full severity. It snowed
the whole day, heavily and ceaselessly; sometimes the entire
landscape was enveloped in dense clouds of driving snow, so
that not a trace of the mountains, or of the valley lying deep

down below them, was to be seen. It was dark, cold, and gusty, and the inhospitable mountain received us at Yam-bulak - bashi much as it had done the April previously. There was no prospect of any excursion that day, for we could not see many steps in front of us for the snow-storm, and my winter wardrobe, consisting of a sheepskin coat, fur cap and waistcoat, and *valenkis* (Russian felt boots), was not yet unpacked. In order not to be hampered with too much paraphernalia, I had this time only brought a small yurt with me; and in this I sat the whole day, writing and drawing, with a cup of hot tea every now and then to keep me warm. The men crowded together in their great sheepskin coats, and sat crouched under the shelter of a block of gneiss, listening to Mollah Islam, who was read-ing aloud out of an old book of tales. As the snow-storm in-creased in violence, I made them come into the tent, and let them continue their reading. Towards evening it ceased to snow; but heavy gray clouds swept through the deep valleys, trailing their long fringes and draperies behind them. Every now and again flying fragments became detached from them, and sprinkled the rocks with their white powder. In the evening we had a visit from the aksakal of the aul of Yam-bulak, and half a dozen other Kirghiz, who came to bid us welcome, and brought a sheep with them as a present. They were regaled with tea and bread, as usual, and were given an equivalent for their sheep.

When the weather eventually cleared, all the mountains reappeared in a garb of dazzling white, and we were sur-rounded by a thorough winter landscape. The white mantle, however, did not reach down to the bottom of the Sarik-kol valley, because at this time of the year the snow changes to rain at a lower altitude.

The weather being favorable on July 31st, we were able to start on our scramble over the Yam-bulak glacier. Its surface was perfectly white, being covered with soft, wet, sticky snow. Small glacial streams, with a temperature of 31.5° Fahr. (0.29° C.), rippled cheerily over the ice. We struck a south-south-easterly direction across the uneven ice-sheet towards the

I.—21

right-hand lateral moraine, which was from three to seven feet thick, and sent out long crescent-shaped offshoots towards the central parts of the glacier. There were also a few small glacier tables, or ice-pillars, 14 inches in height; and a crevasse, 6 feet wide and 32 feet deep, which would have put an end to further advance had it not hung so far over at the

THE YAM-BULAK GLACIER AND ITS PORTAL IN THE MUS-TAGH-ATA

edges that we were able to get across it. The ice in its sides was of the purest blue, and heaps of snow lay at the bottom. The glacier was for the most part covered with a thin layer of soft, wet slush, caused partly by the newly fallen snow, partly by the destructive agency of ablation. The beautiful transparent blue ice was only visible in the fissures, and in the channels where the small glacial streams flowed over the surface of the glacier. These streams, with their delightfully babbling, crystal-clear water, were none of them large; for usually they were soon swallowed up by some gaping crevasse.

After we had advanced some 440 yards on the glacier, probably a third of the whole way across, the ice became per-

fectly impracticable, a maze of hummocks and pyramids, crevasses and streams, these last running in deep trenches sunk
between the irregularities of the ice and partly hidden by
snow-bridges.

Looking upward from this point towards the rocky part of
the mountain situated between its perpendicular buttresses—
i.e., towards the east—we perceived even then that the glacier
trended in three different directions—namely, to the east, the
south, and the west; or, in other words, forward and to both
sides. Immediately after leaving the upper reaches of the

ON THE YAM-BULAK GLACIER, LOOKING EAST

mountain it streamed over a fairly steep fall, and then across
broken ground. Its lower part was therefore excessively cut
up and fissured by transverse crevasses. The offshoots of
the right-hand moraine, consisting of gneiss and innumerable
varieties of schist, reached as far as the spot where we were
standing. There, too, we again found some glacier tables,
one on a pillar nearly four feet high and leaning over very
much to the southwest, where the sun, as usual, had most

power to undermine it. There also, from a very narrow
outlet, a glacier stream issued. We heard the water purling
softly at the bottom, fifty feet or more down.

On our return to the moraine, where we left the yaks tied
to the bowlders, we came across a place where the marginal

VIEW FROM THE YAM-BULAK GLACIER, LOOKING WEST

moraine was broken off, so that the edge of the glacier lay
naked and flayed, so to speak. Its sides rose up to a height
of forty feet, at an angle of sixty-four degrees, and down the
glassy face ran numerous tiny streamlets, the head-waters of
the Yam-bulak-bashi. In a couple of small moraine-pools at
the edge of the glacier the water was a gray-green color, and
had a temperature of $31.2°$ Fahr. ($0.46°$ C.).

Our expedition proved that the glacier differed very much
in appearance from what it was in April. The crevasses
were not so deep, being partly filled with material which had
fallen in; nor were their edges so sharp; while the surface
was in general softer and more rounded. Shortly put, everything tended to prove that the glacier was in a condition of
great activity, and that all the agents of ablation were at work
to level down its outer form and fill up its depressions.

We afterwards followed the right lateral moraine to the tongue of the glacier; but had not reached it when a violent gale sprang up from the south, accompanied with hail, which stung us in the face, and compelled us to seek shelter under some overhanging rocks.   The hail was followed, as usual, by torrents of rain, and it was only after waiting an hour that we were able to proceed.

Immediately in front of the tongue of the glacier we made a halt.   It was a confused jumble of pyramids, ridges, and huge fragments of ice, all greatly weathered.   The face resembled four icebergs, two large ones in the middle and two smaller ones on either side, separated from each other by crevasses, and set up, as if on purpose, facing the southwest sun, which beats on them and destroys them.   From the right-hand side a little stream flowed through a glacier portal only 24 inches high, which, at a distance, looked like a narrow fissure between the sill or ground-moraine and the ice.   The water in the stream was gray and muddy from the abraded materials it held in suspension.   It foamed and bubbled along the ice and among the moraines.   Here, too, a number of small brooks and streamlets assembled on their way down to the glacier river, and fell in cascades of perfectly clear water not broader than a man's arm.   They spurted out from the top of the glacier-wall in veritable fountains and waterfalls, the fine spray which streamed off them being colored with all the tints of the rainbow.   One of the small terminal moraines seemed to indicate that it had advanced since our last visit in April.

In the evening the sides of the mountain were lashed by a violent hail-storm, which pelted the roof of the yurt, and compelled us to shut the smoke-vent and put out the fire. The hailstones were about a quarter of an inch in diameter, and as they were followed by snow, which fell in big, close flakes, the slopes and the moraines were soon covered again with their wintry mantle.   Yolldash, who was guarding the entrance of the tent, howled dismally out in the cold.   The bad weather continued the whole of the next day, August 1st, though mostly in the shape of rain, so that the snow quickly

disappeared; but it was a day lost, and there was nothing for it
but to stick to the tent and work out my last sketch-maps.

August 2d was devoted to the Kamper-kishlak glaciers.
The smaller of these ended at a considerable altitude, and
had piled up in front of itself an enormous terminal moraine,
500 to 1000 feet in height. This bore rather the appearance
of a huge mound of gravel, for the material which resulted

THE GLACIER STREAM OF THE YAM-BULAK GLACIER, LOOKING EAST

from attrition gradually fell and slipped down the steep
mountain-sides. The moraine mound inclined at an angle of
thirty-five and a half degrees.

It was now a question of getting up on the top of the
great Kamper-kishlak glacier, the left side of which we were
following, though riding on the moraine. The ascent was so
steep that we were obliged to leave the yaks and proceed on
foot, till we reached the solid mountain—hard crystalline
schist—on the left side of the rocky buttresses. The sky
was entirely clouded over; but the usual hail-storm did not

whiten the ground, as the hailstones rolled, hopping and jumping, into the numberless crevasses of the moraine, and when the shower cleared off the wet bowlders quickly dried in the arid air.

The glacier extended down its bed in the shape of a long, flat, narrow spoon, turned alternately up and down, and surrounded on all sides by moraine-ridges.   On the whole, its surface was level, with elongated, flattened undulations.   No transverse crevasses were seen ; but, on the other hand, there were two or three very long narrow ones running lengthwise down the middle of the tongue, and the whole of the left side of the ice was jagged by small fissures set close together at the edge.   When we got down upon the ice it became clear to me at once how the lateral moraine had been formed. Had I taken but one step, I should have slid twenty through the loose *débris*, which continued falling, like a landslip, down upon the lateral moraine.

Once over the fissures at the edge, it was an easy matter to walk on the ice, which was sheeted with a thick layer of snow.   This, however, sometimes concealed longitudinal crevasses, which we had to feel for with our alpen-stocks.   A block of gneiss, some 140 cubic feet in extent, had dropped through the ice by reason of its weight, instead of forming a glacier-table.   After we walked about six hundred and sixty yards across the glacier (its full width was some three-quarters of a mile), farther advance was cut off in every direction by a deep crevasse, a dozen feet wide and forty-five in depth.   Its sides were a deep blue, and from them hung long icicles.

On August 3d we started on a new excursion, namely, back again to the Yam-bulak glacier, to put in rods, by which, after a certain time had elapsed, we could tell at what rate the ice was moving.   It was by no means easy to find a stick long enough for this purpose, for there was not a tree or a bush to be found in the whole of the Sarik-kol valley, except half a dozen stunted birches at Kayindeh-masar, which, of course, could not be touched, as they were growing on holy ground. At length Yehim Bai succeeded in finding a bundle of *oks*, or poles used to support the dome-shaped roof of the yurt.

Equipped with these, we succeeded in getting nearly 580 yards across the ice, and putting in nine poles, some in small moraine-ridges, others in the ice itself, and their position was marked on a map drawn to the scale of 1:4480. It would have been better to have placed them in a straight line across the glacier; but this was impracticable, as the whole of the left side was absolutely inaccessible, and formed a projecting bump as compared with the right side. This is because the left half of the glacier is completely shaded by the mountain crests to the south of it during its entire passage between the enclosing walls of rock. Not a ray of sunshine, therefore,

BUILDING A KIRGHIZ YURT

reaches this part of the glacier until after it has emerged from the mountain's arms. The right half, on the other hand, even when in the gorge, is exposed to the direct rays of the sun, and therefore melts incomparably the quicker. This fact was plainly perceptible in the shape of the glacier, even after its issue from the passage, as the right half was about 130 feet lower than the left. After it emerged, the glacier tongue spread out to two or three times its previous breadth, and became correspondingly thinner, so that the process of melting goes on over a more extended surface, and the tongue soon shrinks to a comparatively narrow point.

The inevitable hail-storm came on at four o'clock. First of all, in the deep valley below us, we saw light clouds, like smoke, hurrying before the north wind. Then they swiftly ascended the mountain-side, and before we knew where we were had enveloped us in their disagreeable vapor. It grew dark and 'cold. The hailstones rattled on the ice, and we could do no work, only seat ourselves under the shelter of a lofty ice-pyramid, and wait. When we got back to the tent a long time afterwards we were very tired and half frozen.

The new day which broke promised fine weather by way of a change, and we had a glorious trip to the Kamper-kishlak glacier, the right side of which we had still to examine. On that side the glacier sent out a massive "spine," which almost touched the left flank of the lateral moraine of the Sarimek glacier. It consisted of a sheet of ice, nearly 100 feet thick, broken off almost perpendicularly at its face, and on the whole was remarkable for its great purity. There were no moraines on the front wall of the glacier worthy of the name; but there were occasional blocks of gneiss and mica-schist, the largest measuring as much as 850 cubic feet. This rudimentary terminal moraine was fed in a niggardly way by the fragments of rock we had seen scattered about over the surface of the glacier.

At the base of the glacier-wall there was a large grotto, a dozen feet high and nearly as many deep, which had manifestly been caused by the relative warmth of the earth. Four small glacial streams and several little rills dropped from the edge of the ice in pretty cascades. The largest had a fall of sixty feet, and had eaten into the edge of the ice, so that it did not come all the way from the top. Another had cut nearly twenty feet into the ice, and as the brash had got heaped up on top of it, the streamlet resembled a spring issuing from a hole in the level wall. It was a beautiful sight, to stand underneath the big waterfall and watch it shoot out into the air as if from the gutter of a house, split into a thousand drops that glittered like pearls in the sun. The ice was everywhere as soft as a sponge, so that we could actually make "snowballs" of it. Water was dripping, trickling in every direction; no matter which way we turned we heard the sound of bubbling and running water. The ice was courting destruction in venturing down to tracts whose climate it could not endure. Beneath the face of the glacier were large detached blocks and heaps of extremely rotten ice, which had broken off and were melting rapidly. When the grotto, just mentioned, has become sufficiently hollowed out, and the superincumbent mass of ice too heavy, the latter will crash down, and contribute to the more hasty decay of the glacier.

Keeping immediately alongside the ice, we then rode round the face of the glacier, and continued up its right side. At one point at the foot of the glacier, where a cascade splashed noisily into a pool of its own making, the Kamper-kishlak approached so close to the lateral moraine of its neighbor, the Sarimek glacier, that we could scarcely get through the narrow passage.

The surface of the glacier sloped at an angle of twenty-five and a half degrees, and was thus extraordinarily steep, as compared with the glaciers of the Alps, which often have an inclination of less than one degree in their lower regions. The two contiguous glaciers of Sarimek and Kamper-kishlak approached each other at right angles, and between them, near the rocky spine which divided their common *névé*-basin, a brook issued and helped to fill up the intervening space with mounds of gravel and patches of *grass*. The latter, however, was only in demand by the wild goats of the mountain.

We found that the left half of the Kamper-kishlak glacier, like that of the Yam-bulak, was much higher than the right half, and was further encumbered with huge moraines, while the right side had hardly any. This circumstance shows plainly that the stream of ice was trending towards the left wall of rock, where it pressed close against the foot of the mountain and derived its moraine material from near at hand. On the left side the ice lay underneath the moraine; while on the right the moraine lay underneath the ice.

CHAPTER XXVIII

MY SECOND ATTEMPT TO ASCEND MUS-TAGH-ATA

THE whole time we had been at this considerable elevation, an elevation not exceeded by many of the Alpine peaks, I had kept an eye on the Mus-tagh-ata, watching for a suitable opportunity to make an ascent; but the weather had invariably rendered it impossible. At one time it snowed and hailed; at another there was an icy north wind, which took away all desire to ascend to still higher regions, where the wind whirled up the fine snow in thick clouds like dust. At yet another time the clear sky and bright sunshine would tempt us to make a start; but suddenly bad weather would set in and upset all our plans for the day. Two or three times we actually had the yaks ready, and the loads distributed among their bearers, and were about to start, when a storm delayed us; and in order not to waste the day entirely, we gave up the Mus-tagh-ata and went some shorter excursion to the glaciers.

By this it was the 5th of August, and, as we had already discovered, to our cost, that winter was an early guest in those altitudes and that we had not much time to spare, we determined to be ready for a campaign the following day. The 5th was given up to rest. Solemn silence reigned in the yurt, and I was the prey of a presentiment that we should soon be hovering between heaven and earth. Our yaks, which had been worked very hard of late, were discharged, and returned home with their owners; while Mollah Islam procured fresh ones in excellent condition in their stead. Saddles, alpen-stocks, rope, provisions, and instruments were collected and packed in the evening. The day had been fine; but at dusk the usual hail-storm came on, accompanied by a gale of wind. The mountain, with its snowy wastes and white ice-fields, which a while ago had glittered in the still, bright evening air, was again enveloped in thick clouds, and towards evening the wind-gods whirled in a frantic dance round one of their loftiest thrones.

Leaving Islam Bai to take care of the camp, I set off, on August 6th, at half-past six in the morning, accompanied by Yehim Bai, Mollah Islam, and three other Kirghiz, and a train of seven splendid yaks.

The day was brilliantly fine; so absolutely clear was the atmosphere that the smallest details of the mountain could be distinguished even from its foot, and the summit seemed quite near, although the declivities deceptively hid the highest parts. Not a breath of wind stirred the air; not a cloud marred the serene purity of the heavens. At first we rode slowly, in the light of the rising sun, up the gradually ascending slopes of the Yam-bulak-bashi, then up the steeps in the shade of the rock, till the sun got so high that it beat full in our faces.

We made good progress, and by ten minutes past seven had reached the height of 14,760 feet. The steep declivities were now littered with gravelly material, of the same varieties as the solid rock higher up. The gravel was so closely packed that no vegetation was able to insinuate its roots. Two of the yaks had already "struck," and as they delayed us very much we left them behind. The Kirghiz preferred to walk and took it in turns to lead the big, handsome yak I was riding, which climbed up the sloping *débris* without any apparent effort. By eight o'clock we had reached the altitude of Mont Blanc, and a short distance above that, at 16,250 feet we reached the snow-line. At first the snow lay in smallish patches, with the *débris* exposed between them, then in a continuous sheet, through which individual fragments of rock protruded here and there. The snow was compact and coarse-grained, but had no hard crust. After we had ascended another six or seven hundred feet, the snow was caked with a thin crust, and lay so solidly packed that the men's soft leather boots left no footprint behind; but then, it

MUS-TAGHATA SEEN FROM THE WEST

is true, they were not provided with wooden soles. The snow crunched under the yaks' pointed hoofs; but the animals never once stumbled. The higher we went the deeper grew the snow, though it never formed drifts worthy of the name. From a quarter of an inch its depth increased to four or five, and at the highest point we reached it was just under fourteen inches. The continual wind, the excessive evaporation, and the dome-like shape of the underlying surface which exposed the snow to the action of the wind, made it difficult for snow-drifts to accumulate. The snow crystals glittered in the sun with a thousand dazzling facets, and although I wore double snow-spectacles, I suffered somewhat from snow-blindness. The men, who had no glasses, complained that everything seemed to be going round, and that sometimes the landscape appeared to be quite black.

We stopped to rest more and more frequently. I employed the time in making sketches, and in taking our bearings with the compass. We followed the edge of the rocky wall on the right-hand side of the glacier, and therefore had a glorious view over its entire surface, which glittered below us. Up in the *couloir*, where the rocky walls gradually became lower, according as the surface of the glacier rose higher, and where they diverged somewhat from each other, until they finally merged into the rounded ridge which connected the two culminating summits of the mountain, there was a splendid view of the distant trough-shaped depression.

In the middle part of the glacier longitudinal crevasses predominated, the largest ran exactly midway between the walls of rock, and stretched down towards the tip of the glacier's tongue. At three places in particular, where the ice glided over a natural depression, they were intersected by transverse crevasses; and the chequered system, with ice cubes and ice pillars, was the result. In one place the crevasses appeared to start from a common centre and radiate in all directions, as they were broad and gaping in the middle, but grew narrower towards their extremities. The glacier was probably about five-eighths of a mile broad, and its breadth everywhere tolerably equal. It appeared to be considerably steeper than it really was; but in this it was the eye that was at fault. The mountain summit was high above us, while the tongue of the glacier stretched a long way below us; and in the clear, attenuated mountain air the distance between these two points appeared to be quite short. No traces of striation or glacial scratches were perceptible on the perpendicular rocks, which towered 1300 feet above the surface of the glacier. This negative testimony does not, however, count for much; as if at any time such indications did exist, they would long ago have been obliterated by the weathering of the rocks, a process which is ceaselessly going on in these parts, mainly because of the enormous and sudden changes of temperature. The part of the mountain on which we then were had consequently a ragged, serrated edge, consisting of an unbroken series of rocky projections and undulations which had nothing whatever to do with the glacier, as they were exclusively the result of weathering.

The side of the mountain sloped here at an angle of twenty-two degrees towards the plain of Su-bashi, a gradient which was easily perceptible in the rarefied air. The snow became purer and more dazzling, and the icy crust cracked audibly. We advanced slowly, doubling one rocky projection after another, and skirting the bays or recesses between them, faithfully following the outline of the edge of the rocks; while new perspectives of exactly the same kind continued to appear one after the other the higher we ascended. At an altitude of 16,700 feet Mollah Islam and two of the other Kirghiz left their yaks in the snow, declaring that it would be better to walk. However, they did not get more than six hundred feet higher when they fell down from exhaustion and headache, and were soon dead asleep in the snow-drifts.

I went on with the two remaining Kirghiz and the two yaks. My beast was always led by one of them; the other yak they rode turn and turn about. They, too, complained of splitting headache, and were ready to drop from breathlessness. I did not suffer much from either of these symptoms, though I had a slight headache, which increased when we got higher up; but I was only attacked with breathless-

THE YAKS TAKING A REST ON THE LOWER SLOPES OF THE MUS-TAGH-ATA

ness when I got off the yak to make observations. The slight exertion of remounting the animal gave me violent palpitation of the heart, and I was almost choked by breathlessness. On the other hand, the yak's movements, which were now much more labored, did not affect me in the least. I had suffered much more at a far lower altitude on Mount Demavend, in Persia, but on that occasion I was on foot. The secret lies in avoiding bodily exertion as far as possible; for instance, you can ride up to a very considerable altitude without suffering much from that species of discomfort. In this ascent, however, all the Kirghiz were ill, a couple of them even declared they were going to die; while I, on the contrary, kept comparatively brisk the whole time. But the Kirghiz, in spite of my remonstrances, persisted in leaving their yaks behind, and what with struggling through the snow and climbing up the steep declivities, they exhausted the strength which they so greatly needed to withstand the enervation caused by the rarefaction of the air.

Meanwhile, a fresh wind sprang up from the southwest, driving the snow, which was as fine as flour, and without a crust, into eddies; while the sky became hidden by thick clouds. As we were all now rather done up, we determined to halt and take observations. Bread and tea were brought out, and fuel to boil the water for the latter; but we had only to look at the food, and we were seized with such a choking sensation that none of us would touch it. We suffered only from thirst, and looked longingly at the snow, which the yaks licked up in large mouthfuls.

The view which presented itself from this point (20,660 feet) was inconceivably grand. We could see right across the Sarik-kol chain far away to the picturesque snow-decked mountains of Trans-alaï and the Murghab. Only a few summits in the nearer parts of the Sarik-kol mountains seemed to exceed 16,500 feet in height. But in the Mus-tagh chain, which is a continuation of Mus-tagh-ata, there were on the north a couple of peaks which did not fall far short of the " Ice Mountains' Father " himself in altitude. The whole of the Sarik-kol valley was spread out like a map under our

feet, clearly visible from Ullug - rabat to Bulun - kul. Every
lake, except the Upper Bassyk-kul, which was hidden by intervening rocks, shone blue - green in the prevalent gray of
the moraine landscape, but from our position looked like insignificant pools. The Yam - bulak glacier pointed its icy
finger down the valley, and far beyond its outer extremity we
were able to distinguish the concentric semicircles of its former terminal moraine, long since dead. We could not have
obtained a better view anywhere of the glacier streams and
their beds between the out-stretched arms of the mountain
than from the spot where we stood.

The large rivers of the Yam-bulak and Chum-kar-kashka
glaciers ran parallel to the very end of the valley, which was
as gray as steel from their alluvium.

There still remained four other rocky buttresses above us,
and behind them the northern summit of the mountain, now
appearing quite near. The parts between it and the farthest
visible point of the mountain had a flatter perspective.

We now held a council of war. The day was drawing to
an end, and it was beginning to be cold in the wind (33.3°
Fahr. or 0.7° C. at 4 P.M.). Moreover, the Kirghiz were so
done up that they could go no farther; the yaks stood panting, with their tongues hanging out. We had reached the foot
of a dome-shaped elevation, which gradually merged into the
flat crown of the summit. On its slopes the snow lay in
more massive and more compact layers; and there were
cracks and displacements in it which pointed to a tendency
to avalanches. The Kirghiz warned me against attempting
this precipitous snow - slope. They declared it was ready to
fall; and that the yaks, owing to their weight, might easily
be the cause of an avalanche, in which case we should reach
the foot of the mountain quicker than we bargained for, although in a mutilated condition. They furthermore told
me that from the valley below avalanches were sometimes
seen falling on this very slope. The snow then soared up in
enormous clouds, rolled together, and slipped over the precipices, smothering them in clouds of fine powder, and when it
finally reached the valley it was partially turned to ice.

At the level which we had then attained the snow rested chiefly on a rock and gravel foundation, which was often exposed in the tracks made by the yaks. It only rested on ice close along the edge of the rocks, from which depended long icicles pointing straight down upon the surface of the glacier. On the top of the opposite or south wall, on the other hand, there was a thick sheet of pure blue ice, clothing the mountain as with a supple coat of mail and conforming to its every irregularity.

Though sorely against the grain, I now determined to turn back. We rapidly descended in our own footsteps and soon reached a more clement region, picking up the deserters and the yaks, which were still standing where we had left them, and reaching the camp at seven o'clock in the evening. There we found visitors awaiting us with gifts of provisions.

Apart from the splendid opportunity it afforded for taking our bearings, and apart from the observations I had made, this expedition convinced me that the northern summit of the Mus-tagh-ata could hardly be reached in a single day's climb. It would be better, therefore, on a future occasion to allow two days, camping the first night at a considerable height, and continuing the next day with our yaks well rested and with only a light equipment. The Kirghiz and Islam Bai were very keen to make another attempt, so soon as a good opportunity presented itself.

But we had still three large glaciers to examine farther east, and therefore struck camp on August 8th, and moved to Terghen-bulak. Mollah Islam and I made a detour round the western foot of the mountain. I wanted to see the Yam-bulak glacier-stream at the spot where it received its contributaries. Where we crossed it, it was 33¾ feet broad, 13¾ inches deep (maximum), and had a velocity of 7¼ feet in the second, and a temperature of 42.3° Fahr. (5.7° C.). On both sides of it there were gigantic moraines of gneiss and crystalline schist, in pieces varying from 5000 cubic feet to small fragments, with binding material of glacial clay, though without any signs of stratification. Along the path of the stream the soil was washed away from between the big blocks, so

that they encumbered its bed, causing waterfalls and cataracts. It was therefore no easy matter to get across the
stream with the yaks, as the water was so muddy they
could not see where to put their feet; and often I felt my
animal disappearing, so to speak, from under me, when it
stepped between two deceptive bowlders, round which the
current was foaming and eddying. It was a decided relief
to find myself riding up the opposite bank. A magnificent
view unfolded itself to the east, where the white glacier
tongue lay embedded between its gigantic moraines at the
foot of the mountain.

We rode from the tongue of the glacier, up along the left
lateral moraine, to the place where the ice issued from its
rock-bound cradle. The marginal moraine consisted entirely
of huge gneiss bowlders, most of them measuring about 350
cubic feet each; while the rock itself was a hard, dark crystalline schist, falling at an angle of twenty-one degrees towards
the north-northwest. The moraine, then, received its material from higher regions. It was evident from other circumstances that the lower rocks could not contribute to its formation; for between them and it there were a *bergschrund* or
fissure and a gravel-strewn declivity, which prevented the ice
from coming into contact with the wall of rock.

It was no easy matter to make our way through this labyrinth of gneiss bowlders. They were too big for the yaks to
clamber over; hence there was nothing for it but to dis-
mount, and let Mollah Islam go round with the animals, and
meet me at the base of the moraine. Alone, and followed by
my faithful Yolldash, I made my way as best I could, sometimes crawling over the rocks, sometimes balancing on them.
They were separated from each other by dark, chilly fissures,
in whose depths the water gurgled against the stones at the
bottom. At one time I managed to toboggan down the side
of a bowlder so successfully that I jammed my foot in between it and another rock, and had to take off my boot to set
myself at liberty. In other places I found it better to wade
through the water, under, and between, the blocks; and it
was with a feeling of intense relief that I at last succeeded in

extricating myself from that dangerous and gloomy labyrinth where I might easily have got lost if I had not had a compass. After many adventures I reached the slope at the foot of the moraine. Then looking back, to my dismay I beheld Yolldash on a huge bowlder, whining and howling dismally, and not able to move either backward or forward. Then he disappeared behind the bowlder. I heard him splash into the water, and finally he emerged from *underneath* the moraine, evidently elated, though slightly lame of one paw. At the same time he was annoyed with me for having decoyed him into such an awkward predicament.

After traversing a sloping piece of greensward, down which a fresh stream was flowing, we reached the tongue of the Chal-tumak glacier, which had the considerable inclination of 24.9°. Its surface was black with gravel, through which solitary white pyramids stuck up; but the side of the glacier was polished like steel.

It was twilight when we reached the new camp, where everything was in order. Not far off lay the aghil (aul or tent village) of Chal-tumak, consisting of four uys (tents). The chief, Togda Bai Beg, a handsome, refined-looking Tajik, came at once to pay his respects. He told me that the village had altogether twenty-five inhabitants, and that one tent was inhabited by Tajiks (Aryans, speaking a Persian dialect), and the other three by Naiman Kirghiz. He said that they lived in the neighborhood the whole year round, but wandered from yeylau (summer grazing-ground) to yeylau, stopping one or two months at each place. In winter it was terribly cold, and there were heavy falls of snow, making it difficult for the sheep to find pasture. After a continuous snowfall enormous avalanches were frequent, carrying down bowlders and *débris* with them.

The kind old beg gave us a sheep and a bowl of yak's milk, and was only sorry, he said, that his great age prevented him from coming with us on our mountaineering trips. He told us the old story of the sheikh, who went up Mus-tagh-ata and saw a white-bearded man and a white camel, and brought down from the top an enormous iron pot, which is now kept at a masar (tomb) in the Shindeh valley. We talked for a long time, chiefly about my plans; and it was late in the evening before the old man went back to his lonely home among the moraines.

The air was milder than usual. The night was bright and still; and the snow-fields gleamed silvery white in the moonlight. The moraines flung out their deep shadows, and underneath gaped the dark abyss of the valley through the weird stillness of the night. Every now and again the distant bleating of the beg's flocks, or the tinkle of running water, penetrated to our ears.

On August 9th we explored the left side of the Chaj-tumak glacier, riding up the moraine to a point on the flank of the mountain which gave us a splendid view over the glacier. It was quite regular in shape, and was intersected by a double system of crevasses, one transverse, the other longitudinal. This resulted in a series of ice-pyramids, and gave the glacier a chequered appearance. The stones and fragments of rock which fell from the moraine into the crevasses caused the intersecting lines to look like black stripes.

At the place where we were standing, the gneiss cavities had been some time or other polished by the ice of a former branch of the ice-sheet. This ice-sheet still covers immense areas on the side of Mus-tagh-ata, wrapping the body of the giant like a tattered mantle, hanging down the declivities in points and folds; while its edge is often broken off so abruptly that the beautiful, blue-green ice seen underneath the white snow with which it is capped produces quite a dazzling effect. It is of course only on the convex parts of the mountain that this glacial formation, which resembles the Norwegian glaciers, can be developed; for in the concave parts we found the usual Alpine glacial structure—a bowl-shaped *névé*-basin and a deep, narrow glacier-bed.

On the return journey we kept between the ice-pyramids and the lateral moraine, where a stream glided noiselessly along like oil flowing in a well-greased metal pipe. It had undermined the base of one of the pyramids so much that every minute it threatened to topple over.

TOGDA BAI BEG

Finally we paid a visit to Togda Bai Beg, who called to-gether the elders of the village and offered us dastarkhan (re-freshment). His aul lay on the bank of the glacier-stream, and was surrounded by pastures on which the camels, yaks, and horses of the aul were grazing, and where the women were at work milking the sheep. Several of these Tajik wom-en were pretty, and looked happy and good-natured in their picturesque but slovenly dress. They seemed to have fre-quent errands to the tent, and generally took the opportunity to have a good look at the strangers.

The view to the east was one of the grandest I have ever seen. In front of us the colossal mountain mass soaring up to a giddy height—to the ethereal workshops in which the eternal snow spins the delicate webs which it sends down the slopes of the mountain as offerings to the sun; where the winds gambol at their will; and where the stillness of death divides sovereignty with the bitter cold. Calmly and ma-jestically the glacier moved from between its mountain portals like a king issuing from his royal hall; and the moraines tow-ered above it like ramparts fencing round an impregnable castle. The turbid glacier-stream danced joyously down its stony bed, as glad as a school-boy off for a holiday, happy at escaping from the thraldom of the ice, and at reaching warm-er and more genial regions.

On August 10th we rode up beside the glacier-stream, on whose banks we were then encamped. It led to the right side of the neighboring Terghen-bulak glacier, from which, indeed, it derived the greater part of its waters; but it also received several affluents from the ice-sheet. The erosive power of the stream is enormous, and its bed was filled with round, polished stones. At one o'clock it carried 210 cubic feet of water in the second.

The right lateral moraine was about 100 feet high, and hid the glacier, except for a few detached pyramids nearly fifty feet high. The yaks toiled on cautiously and with their ac-customed phlegmatic unconcern up the deep gully between the moraines and an enormous gravel slope, which had ac-cumulated at the foot of the perpendicular wall of rock to the

north, and which was crowned by the massive ice-sheet.
edge partly overhung, and was in part broken off; and fr
it the icicles hung down their dripping tips to a distance
more than 30 feet. From the sharp edge of the rock, i
mediately underneath the ice, the glacier water spouted for
in innumerable cascades, large and small—crystal-bright j
which fell to such a depth that they were shattered to pe:
seed or powdered into a mist of rainbow-colored spray
fore they reached the bottom. The stronger gusts of w
dashed the spray against the rocks, down which the wa
then trickled, and finally found its way to the stream un
and over the gravel slope in a thousand tiny rills :
rivulets.

The Terghen-bulak was a triple glacier fed from th
sides. The middle ice-stream was much larger than the ot
two, and occupied much the greater area. A smaller :
joined it from the right; and its bed was sunk deeper in
mountain, so that the surface of the main glacier was con
erably higher than the surface of the branch. Between
two rose a huge shoulder of the mountain; and in the ar
between the two ice-streams, below the outermost point
the rocky shoulder, there was a triangular hollow, forming
it were, an eddy or backwater, such as may be seen at
bottom of the pier of a bridge in a river. On the left th
was a broad, clean offshoot from the ice-sheet, but it was o·
powered to such an extent by the bigger mass of the m
glacier that it was pressed in like a narrow wedge betwee
and the rocky mountain-arms.

The ice groaned and cracked; stones and bowlders rat·
down into the crevasses; and there were glacier-tables
their pedestals. From every direction came the sound
trickling, dropping water. The surface of the ice was
and rotten. Everything, in fact, tended to denote that
glacier also was in a condition of great activity.

As we were riding back down the mountain we sa·
couple of big gray wolves, which took to their heels am
the moraines. The animals seemed to be very commor
that region, and now and then were said to carry off a

calf, so that Togda Bai Beg was right to guard his flocks with a pack of savage dogs.

The same evening that chieftain prepared a little make-shift yurt, and other necessaries, for a two days' ascent of Mus-tagh-ata, which we thought of trying again the next day, August 11th.

CHAPTER XXIX

MY THIRD ATTEMPT TO ASCEND MUS-TAGH-ATA

WHEN we rose betimes the next morning, prepared to make a fresh attack upon the giant, the chill, night air was sweeping down off the mountain, and the minimum thermometer showed a reading of 23.4° Fahr. (−4.8° C.). Along the banks of the stream, and between the stones in its bed, there were pieces of ice, against which the water lapped and gurgled. On the whole, however, the stream had dwindled to an insignificant rill, muddier than usual, probably because the clear, glacial water had frozen in the higher regions. The weather was particularly favorable for an ascent; not a cloud was to be seen, and the slight breeze there was soon dropped. We intended climbing to a height of 20,000 feet, spending the night there, and continuing as high as we could possibly get the following day. For this reason we took with us the little tent, four large bundles of teresken for fuel, alpenstocks, ropes, ice-axes, fur coats, and provisions—all carried by nine strong yaks.

"Bismillah!" (In God's name!) cried the half-dozen Mohammedans, when we were ready, and we started leisurely up the mountain. I intended to exert myself as little as possible in order to save my strength for the following day, when the real climbing, with a light equipment, and only three men, would begin. My yak was therefore treated as a beast of burden from the very outset. A Kirghiz, riding or on foot, led him by his nose-rope the whole time, while another cudgelled him behind. For whenever the animal thought my plans were unduly ambitious, he stopped to cogitate, wondering what this perpetual scrambling was going to lead to. By this arrangement it was not even necessary for me to goad the yak, an occupation which in itself is very exhausting, and I could sit quietly with my hands in my pockets, only taking them out every now and again to look at the aneroids. The needles of these instruments had very little peace during the days we were vainly trying to scale the "Ice Mountains' Father."

Our little caravan struggled leisurely zigzag up the mountain-side, which terminated in a long level ridge on the left side of the Chal-tumak glacier. The yaks grunted and panted, and their blue tongues hung out of their mouths dripping.

The ridge was the same gravel-covered backbone we had reached on August 9th, and we took our first rest at the point where we halted then. Immediately south of this the ice-mantle threw out a projection with steep walls, and at its base the fallen pieces melted together into a sheet of ice. By one o'clock we had reached the altitude of 17,000 feet above the level of the sea. Here the snow lay in scanty patches in the crevices; it was only in the larger depressions and in the clefts at the edge of the gorge that it was heaped up in any considerable quantity. It was soft, sticky snow, which melted in the sun, and the ground was consequently wet where it had lain. The naked ridge finally tapered off and disappeared under the ice-mantle. The latter was not broken off abruptly, but was quite thin at the edge, so that we had no difficulty in getting upon it, and was covered with a thin layer of snow, which the yaks occasionally slipped through. But we soon got on deeper snow, and then they went as steadily as they had gone before over the gravel and *débris*.

Suddenly we heard a deafening crash and roar from the right-hand rocky wall on the other side of the Chal-tumak glacier. It was an avalanche which had slipped from the ice-mantle. Large blocks of blue ice were hurled from the edge, clashing together, and crumbling into fine white powder as they struck against the outjutting rocks; then they fell like flour upon the surface of the main glacier. The sound reverberated like thunder near at hand, the first echo being flung backward and forward many times between the

rocky walls before it finally died away, and was succeeded
by the usual silence. But a mist of powdered ice-needles
hung a long time in front of the glacier. Meanwhile w
had a splendid opportunity of observing how the glacier
worked. The ice-mantle kept slipping, slipping, ponderous
and massive, over the edge of the rocks. Again and again
it broke off at the crevasses and ice-falls, great blocks of ice
being precipitated into the depths below, and reaching the
main glacier in powder as fine as flour. This, nevertheless,
melted into its surface, and in that way built up a regener-
ated parasitic glacier.

From the same considerable altitude we also saw plainly
how the Chal-tumak glacier was fed from every side by fract-
ures from the ice-mantle.

Where the small patches of crystalline *débris* underlay the
snow, the latter was longer in melting; but about mid-day
the radiation increased to 112.8° Fahr. (44.9° C.), and the atmosphere was brilliantly clear and pure. The gravel was
succeeded by a layer of snow three to six inches thick, which
prevented the yaks from slipping, although the angle was as
much as twenty-four degrees.

Here we saw the tracks of four kiyick (wild goats). The
animals fled up the mountain in the direction of two swellings
of the ice; and in another place we found the skeleton of an
animal of the same species lying among the snow.

The naked ice-mantle stretched up before us in all its
dazzling whiteness. We knew, of course, quite well that it
would bear us; all the same, we felt as if we were venturing
out on thin ice when we stepped upon this unknown tract,
never before trodden by the foot of man, and where perhaps
the many dangers inseparable from a glacial landscape threatened us.

We soon found ourselves in a labyrinth of intersecting
crevasses, which, however, were as a rule not more than a
foot broad. We were obliged to steer a zigzag course in
order to evade them, since they generally widened out in
both directions. Sometimes we crossed them on snow-
bridges; in other places the yaks stepped across them with-

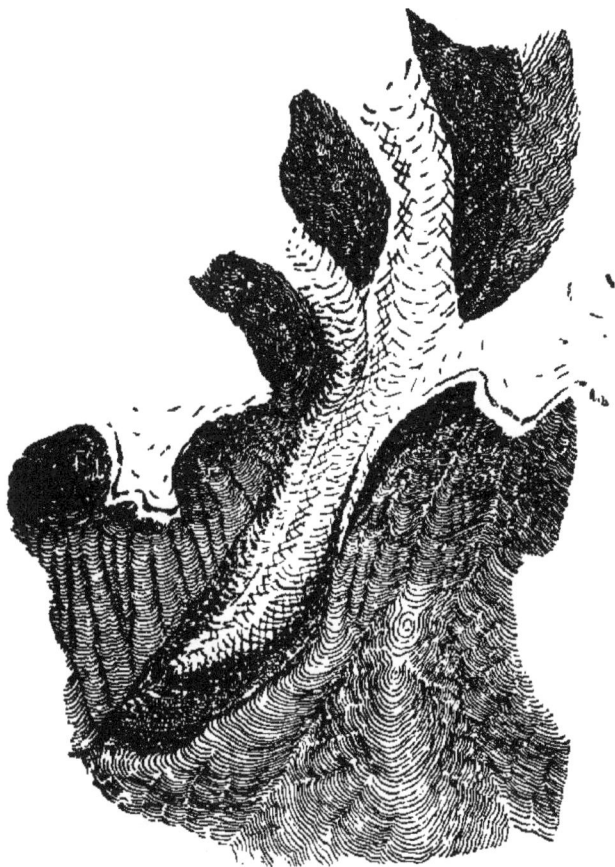

THE TERGHEN-BULAK GLACIER

ut difficulty. The Kirghiz declared that for safety's sake
·e had better follow the track of the kiyick; and we did so.
˙he bridges along their track sometimes held, but as often
s not the yaks went through, for although the snow had
ɹpported the light weight of the swift-footed wild goats,
 was not strong enough to bear the solid burden of the
ık.

Farther on we spent a whole hour in getting over a part
 the ice which was terribly cut up by transverse crevasses,
d where we had several nasty falls in consequence. As
ual, we had the yaks to thank that matters went as well as
ey did. When a yak put his fore-legs through the de-
ptive snow and fell into a hidden crevasse, he carefully
dged his muzzle on the other side, and so scrambled up
:ain.

The ice was now covered with a layer of snow eight inches
:ep; but it soon increased to fifteen and twenty inches, so
at the animals had hard work to shuffle and wade through
e hindering drifts; on the other hand, the crevasses were
ss frequent. Then for a long time the "going" was better.
he ice-mantle seemed to be evenly rounded off above us;
ɪt we hoped to find a passage between the lofty ice-swell-
gs, with their blue glistening edges, and the snow-sheathed
rfaces.

In several places the ice-mantle bulged up into bosses and
lls, and we went from the one to the other. We were just
ı the comparatively level summit of one of these up-swell-
gs when Mollah Islam's yak, which was being led by its
ᵛner at the head of the procession, suddenly disappeared,
ith the exception of its hind-legs and horns, and the teresken
gots. These still remained visible above the snow. The
ɔimal had fallen into a crevasse a yard wide, which had been
ɔmpletely snowed over, and was suspended over a yawning
bʏss in the ice. There it lay, grunting and puffing like a
ᵉature doomed; but by its immovability it showed that it
ɥlly realized the danger it was in. If it had moved ever so
ıttle it would have been precipitated into the crevasse, which
ᵉew narrower as it descended.

A long delay ensued in consequence. The Kirghiz twisted ropes round the yak's body and horns, and made them fast to the other yaks. Then both animals and men hauled as hard as they could, and the heavy beast was successfully hoisted up. A little farther on we nearly had a repetition of the same performance; only the yak stopped in time to save himself. Next it was one of the men who went through, and remained hanging at his armpits. After that we thought it was about time to call a halt, and make a reconnaissance of the ice, which was crossed and recrossed in every direction by pit-falls.

We found that the ice-cap on which we were standing was chequered throughout by crevasses running in all directions, intersecting each other and cutting off our advance on every side. Then, to make matters worse, we discovered a crevasse nine to twelve feet broad and eighteen feet deep, and at the bottom of it great masses of snow were piled up. We peeped cautiously over the edge and saw that the chasm extended in both directions, like an enormous trench. Northward it ran as far as the trough of the Chal-tumak glacier, and south-westward to the foot of one of the highest of the ice-swellings. To get over it or round it seemed equally impossible; so we stopped and held a council of war.

The layer of snow which sheathed the ice-mantle was ten inches thick, and stretched across the crevasses like a tar-paulin. It was only across the broader chasms that it was cracked or had fallen in. Where the yaks broke through they left gaping holes, which on our first looking into them appeared to be pitch-dark. But when our eyes became used to the darkness we saw that it was only a blue glimmer, and that the bottom of the chasm was buried in snow. The icy walls were of the clearest blue, and the glacier-water trickling down them froze into rows of long icicles hanging down the abyss. The deepest of these crevasses was twenty-two feet three inches deep.

Evening was coming on, and I was again constrained to beat a retreat, for it would have been useless to wait till the next day and then try to find another passage. It was

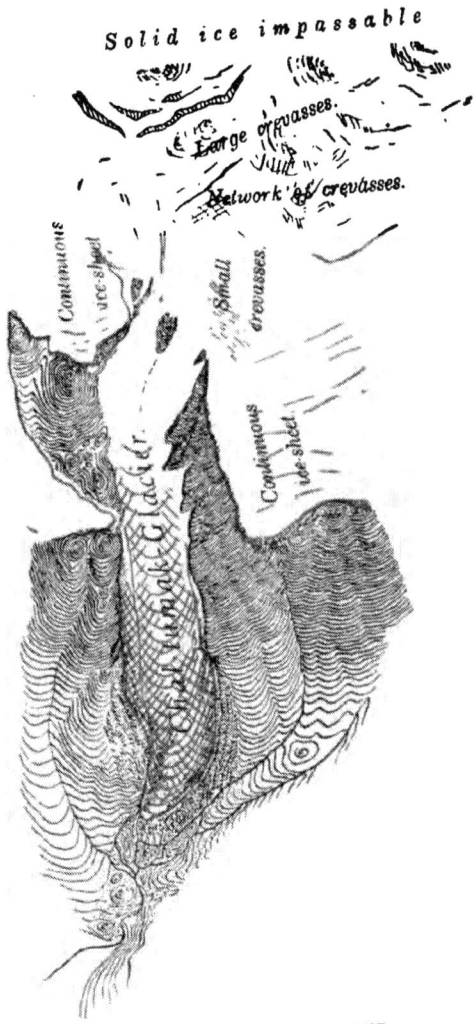

Solid ice impassable

Large crevasses.

Network of crevasses.

Continuous ice-sheet

Small crevasses

Continuous ice-sheet

Chal-Tumak Glacier

THE CHAL-TUMAK GLACIER

ly impossible to venture upon an ascent of Mus-tagh-ata
this side without special appliances, which were not at
lisposal. Above us towered the loftiest summit of the
ntain, and down its precipitous sides glided the eternal
treaming in part to the collecting-basin of the glacier;
vhere the declivities were convex and the ice-mantle was
ced by the relief of the underlying ground, it built itself
nto veritable terraces, walls, towers, and solid blocks of
nous dimensions. To get past these seemed, so far as
ould judge from the spot where we stood, altogether
nd the reach of human power.

ir first two ascents up beside the right wall of the Yam-
: glacier had taken us over incomparably more favorable
nd; we determined to try that route once more before
nally abandoned the project as hopeless.

e had only reached an altitude of 18,500 feet, it is true;
is a set-off, the trip had been attended with important
graphical results. We had got a splendid insight into
lisposition of the higher regions—the cylindrical shape
e mountain, and its covering of ice, which is so difficult
terpretation, and of the relation of the ice-mantle to the
al glaciers. The latter, which are in reality colossal ice-
ms, looked like insignificant white bands from that alti-
of no magnitude at all in comparison with the stu-
ous volume of the ice-mantle.

ı Sunday, August 12th, we rested; and, as was my wont,
d the Bible lessons for the day during the quiet fore-
, and afterwards studied Heim's *Gletscherkunde.* The
her was anything but inviting for an excursion. The
sphere was thick; it was blowing hard; and the moun-
were wreathed in thick clouds. All my men were away
ave, having been invited to a festivity of some kind by
la Bai Beg. Only Yolldash and I were at home, enjoy-
ur rest, which never was more delightful than when the
ner was bad, and the wind whistled and howled among
ocks outside. I never felt lonely amid those distant
ers, where one day was, on the whole, so like another—
I shall not say, as I might lay myself open to being

thought sentimental; but, anyhow, I had not much time to think about it, having more than enough to do. The only thing which disturbed me was that the summer was passing so quickly that I did not see any possibility of being able to carry out the whole of my programme. The days were always too short. As soon as I got my clothes on in the morning, the first thing was to read the meteorological instruments, while Islam Bai prepared breakfast. Our fare never varied, and consisted of the following courses: *chisslick* (mutton roasted over the fire on a spit), *ash* (rice pudding), and bread, which we sometimes procured from the Kirghiz and sometimes baked ourselves; and the whole was washed down with tea. I soon grew so tired of the chisslick that I could not bear the sight of it, and lived on rice and bread. And our fare was to be precisely the same for two years and a half, all the way to Peking. Occasionally I opened a tin of preserved food; but the supply was small, and the time long, and I had to be chary of these delicacies. Happily I never tired of rice and tea, and thrived on the simple diet. There was always plenty of yak's milk and cream for the tea, so that we had no need to economize in these products. I had brought a good supply of tobacco with me from Tashkend, chiefly consisting of pipe and cigarette tobacco, but also a few cigars; and I must confess that I felt very sorry for myself if I had not a pipe in my mouth while we were about our glacier work.

When the weather compelled us to remain "indoors," I always had plenty of work to do, such as sketch-maps, section or profile drawings, notes, etc., to work out. The inside of the yurt was so comfortable that it felt quite like home. In the middle of the "floor" there was a little fire, fed with teresken fagots and yak-dung; otherwise the ground was covered with felt rugs. Immediately opposite the entrance was my bed. The packages, generally, were arranged round the sides, and there, too, were the tins and boxes of provisions, guns, saddles, instruments, etc. I had only two meals a day: breakfast was served again at supper-time. When I got into bed I generally read, by the light of a dying candle, one of the Swedish newspapers of which I have already spoken. And then I turned over and slept like a log—no matter how boisterously the wind blew outside, or how desperately Yolldash howled at the wolves in the mountains—till Islam Bai woke me up in the morning.

CHAPTER XXX

MOONLIGHT ON MUS-TAGH-ATA

I HOPE I am not tiring the reader with these, perhaps, rather
monotonous descriptions of glaciers; but I have thought
proper to treat this subject somewhat exhaustively, as it
virgin soil, and every step I took was new. Only the Yar
bulak glacier had been visited before—viz., by Bogdanovitc
in 1889; but I made up my mind I would not leave th
mountain before I had mapped and examined them a
There are only two or three left, and those I will describe
briefly as possible.

We set apart August 13th for an expedition to the Chur
kar-kashka glacier, riding thither up the side of the enormo
lateral and terminal moraines of the Terghen-bulak glacie
and over very rugged country, covered sometimes with grav
sometimes with sparse vegetation. A swelling of the groun
starting from the vicinity of the former glacier, dipped do
into the Sarik-kol valley, where it was continued in the pa
of Ullug-rabat. This serves as an important water-shed,
that the glacier-waters from the Chum-kar-kashka glacier fl
to the left, to the Little Kara-kul, while the streams from t
ice-mantle farther south drain into the little lake of Gallch
töck, and thence, southward, to the Yarkand-daria. Besi
the lake stood an aul of six yurts, subject to the begs of Ta
harma.

This glacier resembled the Kamper-kishlak glacier, ar
like it, trended towards the right. The right lateral morai
was of relatively small size; the left of tolerable dimension
The tongue of the glacier was level and rounded, with n
crevasses worth mentioning; the only fissures that seemed to
be at all developed were those at the sides. Towards them,

CHAL-TUMAK GLACIER, LOOKING NORTH

and generally falling into them, ran a number of little streams of the clearest glacier-water. The largest was as much as $35\frac{1}{2}$ inches broad and 9 deep, and had a temperature of 32° Fahr. (0.02° C.). The ice along its channel, in which the water ran noiselessly, was polished and gloriously blue. Otherwise the whole surface was excessively soft and rotten, all the stones had sunk deeply into it, making gaping holes. The surface of the ice resembled a maze of upstanding needles or leaves, and we were able to walk on it without slipping, as easily as on snow.

Getting on to the glacier was easy enough. But getting down again from the left side was a very different matter; for the glacier was very much swollen, and the side abrupt and steep, forming a couple of high steps down to *terra firma*. We found innumerable small pools on the ice, a yard in diameter and about eight inches deep; they were covered with a thin crust of ice even during the daytime, so that we got an occasional foot-bath. Here also we put in measuring-rods, to find out the rate at which the ice was moving.

On August 14th we rode up along the left lateral moraine of the Terghen-bulak glacier, and then out on to the moraine which is carried on the back of the glacier. This we after-wards followed down to its face. The two lateral moraines were very large; but only began in the lower part of the glacier's course, where they appeared on the surface of the ice like small black wedges. Gradually, however, they became broader and broader, and finally, at the lower end of the glacier tongue, formed a stupendous mass of stones and *débris*.

The Terghen-bulak was hard at work. Rumbling and rattling sounds were heard continually. Large blocks of ice were precipitated with a deafening crash into the crevasses. New fissures appeared in all directions; and swift streams, abounding with water, flowed between the ice and the lateral moraine. The latter was 400 yards in breadth at the lower part of the glacier, and was at first wonderfully level, and easy to travel over. Afterwards it rose considerably above the

surface of the ice: but as the stones lay in a single thin st
tum, the ice projected through them in fine needles, "raze
backs," and pinnacles. This was due to the stones havir
gradually sunk into the ice, imparting to the surface a pecu
iar knotted and rugged appearance.

We managed to get entangled in a labyrinth of morair
ridges, pyramids, and ice-clefts. After crossing the morair
we went on over the middle of the glacier; and we had ma
adventures in the twilight, which quickly turned to darkne
The travelling was so bad that we preferred to walk, jum
ing over the crevasses and streams. The Kirghiz drove t
yaks before them, and it was a pleasure to see with what ag
ity the animals scrambled up icy slopes several feet in heigi
in which they were sometimes obliged to scrape out a st
before they could get foothold. At last we reached the rig
lateral moraine. There we discovered several small glacie
lakes on the ice. Owing to the sluggish movement of t
ice-masses they were always convex at their lower end. Ti
two lateral moraines stretched a good way farther down th
the middle of the glacier; for the ice they covered was she
tered from the sun, and consequently slower in melting.

Below the glacier-tongue we had to pass a succession
old terminal moraines, built up in front of it like rampart
and broken through by the united stream. It was now be
come quite dark, and I was obliged to follow closely in th
footsteps of one of the Kirghiz, in order to see where I wa
going. Another man goaded on the yaks; while a third wa
looking for one of the beasts, which had gone astray on i
own account among the moraines, and was not recovered u
til the following day. After much trouble and many detou
we managed to make our way back to camp without furthe
adventure.

One of the points in my summer programme was to rid
into the Pamirs; and as some of our stores showed signs
giving out, particularly the tea and sugar, I decided to con
bine this expedition with some "shopping" at Fort Pamir.

But, as a journey of this nature would probably occup
a whole month, and we could not be back at Mus-tagh-at

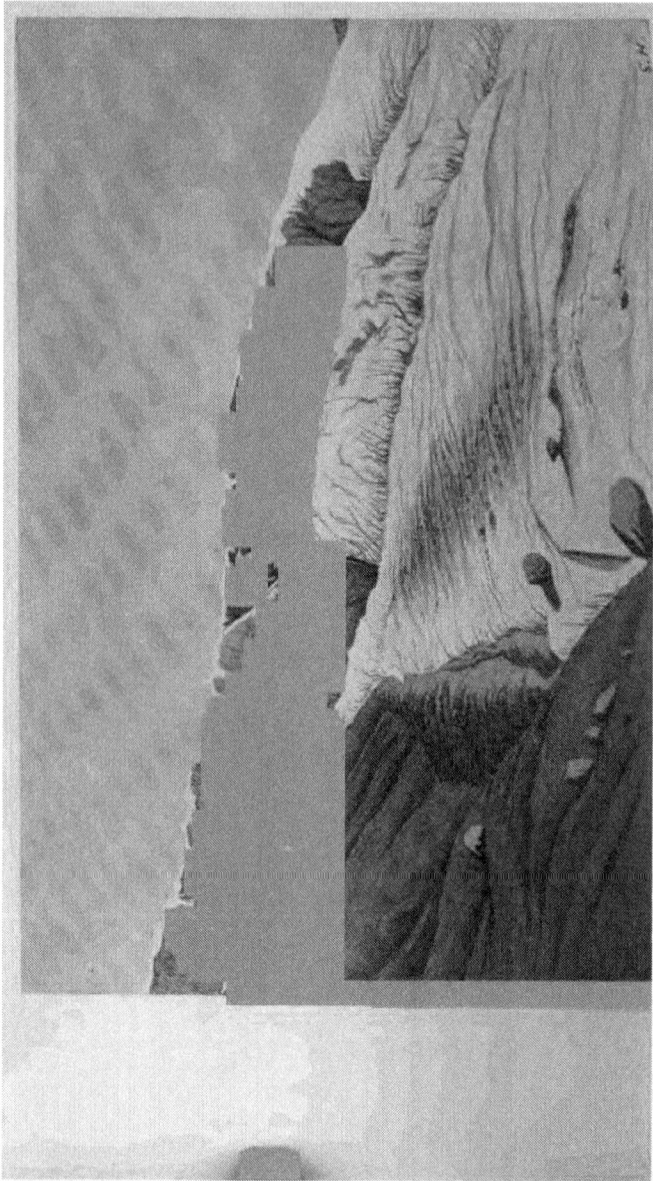

before the autumn, I wished, before starting, to try another ascent, divided, as I mentioned before, into two days' marches.

Accordingly, on August 15th, we wended our way back along the well-known path to our old camp; and although it blew and hailed in the evening, we made everything ready for a last attempt the following day.

Fully equipped for a two days' march, and accompanied by six Kirghiz, my faithful attendant Islam Bai, and ten yaks, I made a fourth attempt, on August 16th, to climb Mus-tagh-ata from the same point whence we had tried it previously, on April 18th and August 6th.

After reaching the snow-line, we followed our old trail, which was, at any rate, a guarantee against accidents. The path could be seen quite plainly, winding zigzag up the mountain by the edge of the rocks which fenced in the glacier-gorge on the right. The snow, not being deep, had melted away in large round patches in our former footsteps, exposing the bare gravel underneath. Higher up every footmark was filled with bluish green ice, and highest of all covered with a sprinkling of snow as thin as paper. In some places, indeed, the track was partly obliterated, though not so much but that we could see it; and naturally we followed it, as we knew by so doing we were safe from danger. It had actually never snowed here for ten days.

With Islam Bai and one of the Kirghiz I reached, at four o'clock, the point we had stopped at on the 6th. The other men followed more slowly, Yehim Bai riding at their head. As soon as we were all together again we held a consultation, and decided to spend the night where we were, as there a few small islands of rock protruded through the sea of snow. The ten yaks were tied to loose bowlders of schist, and the Kirghiz swept away the snow as well as they could from the sharp gravel beneath, and so cleared a place on which to put up the yurt. This was small, and very rough and ready, providing sleeping-room for three only. It had no *tunduk* or smoke-vent, as the poles met at the apex, and were simply thrust through a bundle of rope and rags to keep them in

place, Although we tried to level the ground as much
possible with a spade, the yurt still stood on a slope; and ʼ
had therefore to anchor it with strong *arkhans* (camel's-ha
ropes) to a couple of bowlders. A slight breeze sprang up
the evening and blew for an hour, driving clouds of fine snc
through the many cracks and crevices; so the Kirghiz banke
up a wall of snow all round the tent on the outside.

At first everything went well. We made a big fire
tereseken fagots and yak-dung, which warmed us and thawe
our stiffened joints; but, unhappily, the yurt was filled wiʈ
suffocating smoke, which made our eyes smart, and on
found its way out leisurely through the open entrance. Tʜ
snow inside the tent melted, it is true; but when the fiː
slackened it all turned into a mass of ice.

Meanwhile the Kirghiz began to complain, one after tʰ
other, of headache; and two of them were so bad that the
asked to be allowed to turn back, to which I consented tʜ
more readily as they were manifestly in no condition fe
further fatigue. As night approached other symptoms d
veloped, such as continual singing in the ears, slight deː
ness, a quickened pulse, and lower temperature than is nc
mal, combined with persistent sleeplessness, probably tʼ
result of the headache, which towards morning became v
endurable. Besides all this we suffered from slight attac
of breathlessness. The Mohammedans complained bitteː
the whole night. Our furs were oppressively heavy. A ɪ
cumbent position only increased the breathlessness; and
could plainly feel my heart beating violently. When the t
was ready there was no demand for it. And as the shad
of night came on, the depression of the Kirghiz grew vc
evident; for they were as little used as I to a night spc
more than twenty thousand feet above the level of the sea.

A grander camping-ground, however, I have never pitch
tent on than the snow-clad slopes of this, one of the loftiɪ
mountains in the world, at whose foot the glacier-tongu
streams, and lakes were already wrapped in darkness, and
the edge, too, of one of the most fantastic of glaciers—a fe
steps to the south and we should have fallen down an abʸ

twelve hundred feet deep on to blue ice that sparkled as bright as steel.

I had expected a picturesque sunset; but that evening it was nothing out of the common. The sun sank into clouds illumined by a fiery yellow flare, which glowed for a long time after the sun had set, and threw up the mountains of

THE RIGHT LATERAL MORAINE OF THE YAM-BULAK GLACIER, LOOKING EAST-SOUTHEAST

the Pamirs in sharp relief. The whole Sarik-kol valley lay for some time in darkness, while the sun was still shedding its last rays over the top of Mus-tagh-ata. But soon even our camp was shrouded in cold, dark shades. The top of the mountain glittered for a moment like the ruddy crater of a volcano, and then the light of the day was swallowed up in endless space.

I stepped out to see the full moon rise, and watch it dim the stars, which only just before had glittered so brightly in the deep-blue heavens. It was not far to the boundless realms of space; and the sovereign of the night rose with a splendor so dazzling that it was only by an effort of will that

I.—24

I was able to keep my eyes upon her. I seemed to be regarding a burnished silver shield suspended in the sunshine, or a gigantic electric lamp. Serenely yet majestically the moon sailed above the opposite wall of the glacier defile, with its grand, black, perpendicular rocks, the glacier itself being still in shadow in the depths below. Every now and again I heard the dull crack of a new crevasse forming, or the crash of an avalanche falling from the ice-mantle. The moon shed her silver light over our camping-ground in lavish measure, conjuring forth the most entrancing effects. The yaks were thrown up in dark, sharply defined relief against the white snow, their heads drooping low, silent as the stones they were bound to; every now and then they ground their teeth against the fibrous pad of their upper jaw, or crunched the snow under their feet as they changed position. The tent looked like some weird figure of a seated giant; the ring at the top of the poles being his head, and the frame hung with felt mats his body. The three Kirghiz who could not be accommodated inside the yurt made a fire between a couple of large rocks. When this died out they doubled themselves up in a kneeling posture with their heads on the ground, enveloped in their fur coats, and crowded together round the dying embers like bats in winter. From the yurt and the yaks long narrow shadows, intensely dark, streamed out across the northwest slope, in sharp contrast with the sparkling snow-fields, on which myriads of small ice-crystals glittered like fire-flies. All round the tent, where the snow had been trampled down, the light and shade alternated in small patches. On the steep slopes in the northwest the beautiful curves and noble outlines of the vast snow-fields, modelled by the capricious winds, were lit up with a magic glamour. But I looked in vain for the marvellous tints called forth on the snow-fields by the sun. The only alternation was of black and white — the silver of the moon, the gloom of the shadows, at once barren and monotonous like those on the surface of the moon herself, but at the same time grand, inthralling.

Although the Sarik-kol valley was vividly illumined by

the moonshine, it was not easy to recognize the landmarks in the prevailing gray of the gravel detritus. It was only with difficulty that I could distinguish the darker yeylaus (summer camps) of Kamper - kishlak, Yam - bulak, and Su - bashi, their pasturages watered by the glacier-streams. The outline of Little Kara - kul lake was but slightly marked. The

THE HIGHEST PART OF THE YAM-BULAK GLACIER

entire landscape, in this direction, right up to the crests of the mountains of the Pamirs, was an inextricable chaos, without any point to arrest the eye.

The scenery was most beautiful in the quarter of the moon. I stood as though chained to the spot in the crackling snow, and could do nothing but look, and look, and admire. A magic scene so grand that neither pen nor brush could depict it adequately! The architecture of Nature was conceived here on a bold and masterful plan—the blue glacier sunk between its black walls of rock, sheathed in mail of ice and snow—the five-headed mountain giant towering above

ore forcibly than ever man's littleness as compared with
the inconceivable magnitude of creation. I seemed to be
standing on the confines of space—cold, silent, boundless.

The inside of the tent showed the reverse of the medal.
Islam Bai and Yehim Bai were sitting in their fur coats as
near to the dying embers as they could get, uttering never a
word. We all froze, so that our teeth chattered; and, to add
to our discomfort, when we made up the fire the tent became
filled with stifling smoke. After the evening's observations
had been taken, each man crept into his fur coat and blank-
ets, the fire was allowed to die out, and the moon peeped in-
quisitively in through every slit and crevice of the tent.

The aneroid showed 14½ inches pressure, at a temperature
of 25.5° Fahr. (−3.6° C.). Water boiled at 176.9° (80.5° C.);
and the minimum temperature sank to 10.4° Fahr. (−12° C.).

It was a long, wearisome night, which seemed as if it would
never end. No matter how closely we drew our knees up to
our chins or crept together in our endeavor to keep warm, it
was impossible for mere physical heat to do battle against
the penetrating cold from outside; and we felt it the more in
that the southeasterly wind increased hour by hour during
the night. None of us could get a moment's sleep; at last,
towards morning, I fell into a sort of doze, but was awakened
by want of air. The men moaned and groaned as though
they were being stretched on the rack; not so much on account of the cold, however, as from the constantly increasing
headache.

At last the sun rose upon our misery; but the day that
dawned was anything but favorable. A southwest wind, almost violent enough to be called a hurricane, swept along the
sides of the mountain, smothering us in clouds of fine powdery snow. The three Kirghiz, having passed the night in
the open air, were half dead with cold, and could scarcely
drag themselves into the yurt, where a large fire was burning.
We all felt ill and depressed. Nobody spoke; nobody would
eat anything; and when the tea, which was not even properly
hot, was ready, I was so exhausted I could hardly lift it to
my lips. The yaks were still standing where we left them

the previous evening, motionless as statues. The top of the
mountain was shrouded in impenetrable clouds of blinding
snow; and to have continued the ascent on such a day, and
over ice probably seamed with crevasses, in the teeth of the
terrible buran, finally perhaps to lose our bearings in those
inhospitable regions, would have been to tempt providence
and court certain destruction.

I at once realized the folly of setting the mountain at defi-
ance. But as I wanted to see what sort of stuff my men

OUR CAMP NEAR YAM-BULAK-BASHI

were made of, I ordered them to prepare for a start. No
one of them uttered a word of grumbling. All rose at once
and began to strike camp; but they were manifestly greatly
relieved when the order was countermanded.

One peep through the tent-opening made us glad to creep
back again inside. There, at any rate, we had shelter from
the wind—a wind which penetrated furs, felts, and felt boots.
I earnestly hoped that by mid-day the gale would abate, and
we might continue our work. But, on the contrary, the storm
waxed more violent, and by twelve o'clock it was evident that

ay was lost. I therefore left the three Kirghiz behind to
strike the tent and load the yaks, while I and Islam Bai and
Yehim Bai, wrapping everything round us we could lay our
hands on, mounted our animals, and down the snow-drifts we
raced at a spanking pace. The yaks literally flung themselves
headlong down the declivities, diving like otters through the
snow, and in spite of their clumsy, heavy bodies never stumbling or slipping a step. To sit in the saddle was something
like riding a high sea in a rocking, pitching skiff. Under
such circumstances a man who was not sure of his seat was
likely to have a pretty bad time of it. Often I was obliged
to fling myself backward till my back touched the back of
the yak, and I had constantly to adjust my balance to his unexpected, but agile and dexterous, movements.

How glorious it was, when we had left the clouds of blinding snow behind us up above, and saw our camping-ground
far down below our feet, on a level with the top of the Fin-
steraarhorn!

We ate our dinner, of which we stood much in need, washing it down with steaming tea. Then, our vital energies restored, we were soon sleeping the sleep of the just, each in
his corner. But the whole of the following day we felt like
convalescents recovering from a long illness.

I had now attempted the ascent of Mus-tagh-ata four times,
but each time without success. I do not say, however, that
an ascent to the summit is an absolute impossibility. To
reach it up the face by which we forced a passage on August
11th is impossible—impossible, that is, without extraordinary
appliances, such as it would be absurd to think of using in
such a place. But by the route we followed on April 18th,
and again on August 6th and 16th, there were, as far as I
could make out with my field-glass, no insurmountable physical obstacles in the way; and any climber possessed of sufficiently strong lungs ought to be able to work his way up to
the northern summit. And although that is not the higher
of the twin peaks, it is connected with its loftier brother by a
slightly depressed *col.* Between and below the two extends
the *névé* or *firn* of the great Yam-bulak glacier; but how far

it admits of being traversed is another question. In all probability it is cut up with crevasses and covered with deep snow, so that it would require some days to effect a passage across. The barriers behind which the eternally Happy of the legendary city of Janaidar have intrenched themselves are indeed insurmountable!

Man's physical functions are influenced in no small degree by the rarefication of the air; and in order to ascertain in what way this acted, I registered in different altitudes the temperature of the body and the pulse in myself (29 years old), in Islam Bai, a native of Osh in Fergana (43 years old), and in the Kipchak Kirghiz Yehim Bai, from Shugnan (40 years old).

The following table shows the results of my investigations:

Date and Hour		Temperature Fahr.	C.	Pulse	Altitude
July 28, 10 P.M.	Myself	96.8°	36°	98	13,450 feet*
	Islam	97.5°	36.4°	92	(13,550 feet)
	Yehim	96°	35.6°	66	
July 29. 10 P.M.	Myself	95.9°	35.5°	88	14,440 feet
	Islam	97.3	36.3°	92	(14,100 feet)
	Yehim	95.5	35.3	74	
August 5, 9 P.M.	Myself	96.8	36	88	14,440 feet
	Islam	97.5	36.4	90	(14,100 feet)
	Yehim	97.9	36.6°	84	
August 6, 12 NOON,	Myself	95.9	35.5	86	17,390 feet
	Yehim	96°	35 6°	82	(17,200 feet)
August 11, 2 P.M.	Myself	97.2	36.2°	94	18,700 feet
	Islam	96°	35.6°	86	(18,600 feet)
	Yehim	96 6°	35.9	84	
August 16, 8 P.M.	Myself	95.6	35.3°	106	20,660 feet
	Islam	97.9	36.6°	98	(19,500 feet)
	Yehim	97.9	36.6°	116	
August 17, 9 P.M.	Myself	97	36.1°	102	14,440 feet
	Islam	97.9	36.6°	82	(14,100 feet)
	Yehim	98	36.7	84	

* The altitudes given in the paper I sent to the Royal Geographical Society are those repeated here in parentheses. They are not quite accurate, as in Kashgar I had not the means of applying the necessary corrections to my calculations. The figures which are not in parentheses give the corrected altitudes.

Although this table contains a number of exceptions, it would certainly seem to indicate that the temperature decreases, while the pulse quickens, according as the altitude increases. There would also appear to ensue a moment of sluggishness; for on descending from a considerable height the pulse continued for some time to beat more quickly than the normal rate. In my own case the temperature varied, as a rule, not much more than a degree, and my pulse remained fairly regular. This was probably due to the fact that I carefully avoided all unnecessary physical exertion, while my men, on the contrary, often walked. The greatest variation of the pulse was in the case of the Kirghiz, Yehim Bai. At 13,450 feet his pulse was 66, and at 20,660 feet it was 116; that is to say, it quickened at the rate of fifty beats in a little over 7200 feet. The irregularity in the figures of the table is no doubt attributable to several other causes, such as, for instance, greater or less physical exertion, greater or less susceptibility to the rarefaction of the air, accidental indisposition, and the like. Nevertheless, I always made a point of taking these observations after a rest of suitable length, so as to eliminate the effects of breathlessness, violent perspiration, and undue acceleration of the heart's action, as also to allow of recovery from the worst feelings of fatigue.

Our experience demonstrated, on the one hand, that it was impossible to reach the summit in one day, the horizontal distance of which from the western foot of the mountain is very considerable; and on the other hand, that it is not prudent to sleep at the height of 20,000 feet, because a night spent at such an altitude impairs the physical strength and induces a feeling of lassitude and depression. The best way to reach the top would, without doubt, be to wait for a clear, calm day in the beginning of July, to break up camp early from a depot situated 15,000 feet up; and from there make the final ascent in a single day. Should any such attempt be made, the yaks ought to be taken as high as they can possibly be got, and when they cannot be got any farther the ascent should be continued on foot. Unfortunately, I had no time to make a new attempt, partly on account of the advanced season of the year, partly on account of the stormy character of the autumn.

In any case, the western foot of the mountain is the best point of departure for making the ascent, because it is at an altitude of from 12,000 to 13,000 feet to start with, and the slope on that side is less steep. From the east, south, and north the mountain is inaccessible.

A bold Alpine climber in good training, and accompanied by a couple of hardy and experienced Swiss guides, would probably reach a considerable height, and possibly the northern summit itself. But even a Swiss guide, however well trained, would find himself in quite an unknown world, for the summit of the Mus-tagh-ata is directly exposed to the full force of the sun's rays, and exceeds the highest mountain in Europe by fully 9000 feet.

Farewell, then, Father of the Ice Mountains! Thou didst suffer me to kneel before thy snow-white footstool; but didst not permit me to behold thy august presence face to face and eye to eye. Farewell, thou mighty sovereign of the giants of the Pamirs, at once a corner-stone of the earth's loftiest mountain-range and the topmost pinnacle of the Roof of the World! At thy knees thy mighty children, the Kwen-lun, Kara-korum, Hindu-kush, and Tian-shan, kneel together hand in hand. Farewell, again, thou beauty-spot on the venerable face of our Mother Earth, whose cheek is furrowed with such deep and unfathomable wrinkles around thee! In my memory I still hear the rippling of thy mountain-brooks, bringing strange messages from those sublime regions which no mortal foot hath ever trod. Like the holy Dalailama, thou permittest none but thy chosen children to approach the sacred precincts of thy temple. Shed, then, thy saving light as from a lofty beacon-tower across the desert ocean which stretches to a boundless distance from thy eastern flank. Let the gleam of thy silver brow scatter the dust-haze of the desert hurricane— let the cool, refreshing airs of thy palace of eternal snows be wafted towards the weary traveller toiling through the burning heats of sun and sand—let the life-giving streams which flow from thy mighty heart abound in strength for thousands of years to come, and for thousands of years to come still maintain their fight against the all-devouring, all-devastating desert sands! Among the lights of Asia thou art, and always wilt be, one of the brightest, as thou art among the mountains of the earth one of the noblest, one of the most sublime!

ON August 18th I paid a last visit to the Yam-bulak glacier, to take out the sticks which I put in on August 3d for the purpose of measuring at what rate the glacier moved. The advance during the interval of fifteen days was scarcely perceptible. There was, however, a slight movement, most marked towards the median line of the glacier, where it amounted to close upon one foot a day. I made an interesting observation in the neighborhood of the lateral moraine. The glacier there spread out, giving rise to a back current near the edge of the ice, resembling in its origin and effects the backwater at the side of a river, although the time required for the movement to become perceptible must, in comparison with its extent, be very long indeed. The ice, which might be expected to pile itself up above the eddy, is easily kept down by the agents of dissolution.

The appearance of the ice had very much changed in the interval. On the occasion of our first visit it was covered with snow and hail. Now, on the contrary, it was fully exposed, with edges as sharp as knives, while all the stones had sunk into deep holes; and the ice was, as a rule, slippery and dangerous to walk upon.

On our return we observed a phenomenon which we had not remarked before. The pool beside the right lateral moraine was situated in a fissure, caused by an earthquake, which stretched all the way from the tongue of the great Kamper-kishlak glacier to the immediate vicinity of the scene of our measurements. For the most part it was single, but occasionally double, resembling a trench or dike, about sixteen feet deep and fifty to seventy feet across, with the bottom encumbered

with gravel, sand, and earth, which had gradually fallen into
it. Both edges were continuous and maintained the same
uniform level. Now the moraine showed a decided subsidence at the point where the earthquake fissure penetrated
beneath it. The Kirghiz told me that the fissure was caused
by a violent earthquake eighteen years ago (*i.e.*, 1876), when
Yakub Beg was still alive. It affected Tagharma, Tur-bulung, and the whole of the west side of the Mus-tagh-ata, but
was not felt at either Su-bashi or Kara-tash-davan. The lateral moraine had thus undergone no change for fully eighteen years. The fact that the earthquake was not felt at Su-
bashi, only two hours distant, shows that it was probably a
tectonic or fundamental shock of purely local extent. How
far it affected the glaciers, the Kirghiz were unable to tell
me. On the surface of the glacier itself there was naturally
no trace of any subsidence, since any rift that might be made
would necessarily soon be filled up. It would, however, have
furnished an ideal opportunity for the investigation of the
thickness of the ice and its inner structure. Earthquakes
are not relatively frequent in the vicinity of the Mus-tagh-ata;
slight shocks only being felt from every third to every fifth
year.

When I left Kashgar in June it was my intention to remain only two months in the neighborhood of the Mus-tagh-
ata. But I had rather under-calculated the time I should require, so that, when the two months expired, only half my
work was done, and I had no provisions left. I was compelled, therefore, to travel to Fort Pamir to procure a fresh
supply. As, however, I knew that the Chinese were watching me, and almost looked upon me as a spy, and as I did
not wish to fan their suspicions unnecessarily, I resolved to
cross the frontier during the night through an unguarded
pass, and return subsequently in the same manner, without
their having any idea of the excursion. I only took with me
two of the Kirghiz and my ever faithful Islam Bai; the rest
were dismissed. Then, with the assistance of Togdasin Beg,
we spread abroad the report that I had gone to Kara-korum.
on the southern flank of the Mus-tagh-ata.

On the evening of August 19th I carried all my baggage and my scientific collections to the tent of one of my Kirghiz friends, old Yehim Bai, who hid them safely behind his carpets and felts. After our return from Fort Pamir we learned that the Chinese, who were greatly astonished at my disappearance, had instituted a search after me. Hereupon Yehim Bai thought it advisable to transfer my baggage to a safer hiding-place, and concealed it under an enormous bowlder lying in front of the Kamper-kishlak glacier, at the same time taking the precaution to wrap the boxes in felts to protect them from the weather.

We made our preparations for the journey in Yehim Bai's tent. We had four capital horses. Having packed up carpets, felts, instruments, and other necessary equipments, and prepared provisions for three days, for we were going to ride through a wholly uninhabited district—a distance of about eighty miles — we sat a couple of hours round the fire, talking and drinking tea, and getting a good meal of the old, inevitable fare, mutton and yak's cream. But as soon as the moon broke through the driving clouds sufficiently to light up the silent country, we lashed the loads on the men's horses; and, at eleven o'clock of a windy night, rode, well wrapped in furs, in single file, down between the ancient moraines of the Mus-tagh-ata.

A ride of two or three hours brought us to the Sarik-kol valley; thence our path wound up the opposite side, and through the Mus-kurau glen to the pass of the same name situated in the Sarik-kol chain, the boundary mountains on the east side of the Pamir plateau. In this glen was the critical point of the journey—namely, a Chinese karaol (watchhouse), or sentry aul (camp), placed there for the purpose of guarding the frontier next the Russian possessions in the Pamirs. We rode past it in deep silence and at a slow pace, so near, indeed, that the Kirghiz with their eagle eyes were able to see the tents. But none of the guard challenged us: the dogs even did not bark, although we had Yolldash with us. My men were terribly alarmed, and their spirits only revived after we left the aul behind us; for they knew that, if they were caught, two or three hundred lashes on the bare back certainly awaited them.

At four o'clock on the morning of August 20th we safely reached the Mus-kurau pass. There I took some scientific observations; and there, too, we were overtaken by a furious

AN OLD KIRGHIZ FROM SARIK-KOL

snow-storm. From that point the surface gradually inclined towards the west. We rode through the broad valley of Nagara-kum (the Drum-Sand), the bottom of which was covered with fine yellow drift-sand; while over the slopes on either side it assumed the form of well-shaped dunes. The sand was brought thither by the west and southwest winds, the winds which nearly always prevail in the Pamirs. But as they are unable to surmount the plateau-rim of the Sarik-kol Mountains, they drop their sand in the valley and heap it up along the foot of the mountains. As the tract is entirely destitute of water, it is uninhabited in summer; but the Kirghiz visit it during those winters in which there is a sufficient fall of snow to provide them with water. We only saw water at one spot, Sarik-bulak (the Yellow Spring), where a tiny spring bubbled up out of the ground, affording nourishment to verdure of a fairly good quality. In that place we rested from 10 A.M. to 1 P.M.

Towards evening we emerged upon the broad plains of Kosh-aghil, plains as hard and as level as a pavement. The vegetation consisted of nothing but scattered teresken bushes, which in the gleam of the setting sun cast their shadows a long way across the ground. Our route led through the characteristic landscape of the Pamirs—broad, level, waterless valleys, bounded by low mountain-chains, rounded and greatly worn.

We reached the Murghab at dusk, now in the season of the summer floods swollen to a majestic river. We encamped on a little patch of meadow on the right bank, and spent the night in the open air.

One word more about my faithful Yolldash. He accompanied me again on this journey across the Pamirs. The hardest day's travel never drew from him so much as a growl. At night he kept the most vigilant watch over our camp, and was always in excellent spirits. Nor could he be counted among the cowardly ones of the earth. Whenever we approached an aul, off he would dash ahead like a flash of lightning, and pick a quarrel with the dogs of the place. Although he set on to right and left with a determination worthy of all praise, he was, of course, always beaten; yet he never displayed the slightest fear, even when outnumbered by half a score. Now, however, having to foot it all the way to Fort Pamir, he galled his hind-paws. The men therefore made him a pair of skin boots, which gave him a ridiculous likeness to Puss in Boots. It was irresistibly comical to see the

extravagant care with which he first made trial of his wonderful foot-gear.   At the outset he only used his fore legs,
and dragged himself along in a highly ungraceful sitting
posture; then he tried running on three legs, lifting each
hind leg in turn; but finally he found out that the boots
were practical, and were meant to protect his paws from
further hurt.

The following morning we crossed over to the other side
of the Murghab, and continued down its left bank — *i.e.*,
westward.   At length, after we had passed a succession of
spurs which projected into the valley *en échelon*, like the side
scenes of a theatre, the valley suddenly opened out before us
into the expansion through which it receives its tributary, the
Ak-baital, and in which Fort Pamir is situated.   We rode
hard all day.   About five o'clock we perceived the light blue
smoke slowly curling up against the darker background of
the mountains, and an hour later rode into the court-yard of
the fort.

All was silent and still; there were no officers about.   But
a Cossack sentry challenged, "Who goes there?"   I made
myself at home in the solitary fortress, and soon discovered
the reason of its being deserted.   It appeared that a young
lieutenant from St. Petersburg had been a guest at the fort
since the previous day, and in his honor a picnic was being
given by the officers in the neighborhood.   It was not long
before the whole party returned, my old friend, Captain Saitseff, at their head.   The younger officers who had been under
him the previous winter were now in the field, engaged in
active operations under General Yonnoff against the Afghans
in Shugnan; and their places had been filled by others, who
were to spend the winter at the fort under the command of
Captain Skersky, an officer of the general staff.

Two other changes had been made since my former visit.
The lonely fort, which one of my friends in Fergana called a
Paradise, because there were no women within its walls, was
now honored with the presence of the young wife of the new
commandant, Madame Skersky.   German by birth, and a lady
of an exceptionally sweet and amiable disposition, she did the

honors at table with exquisite charm. Tastes, as we know, differ; but in my opinion the fort was now infinitely more like paradise than it had been before. Threadbare tunics and dusty boots had given place to a more becoming exterior, while linen cuffs, blacking, and the little arts of the toilet-table afforded evidence of their existence; everything, in fact, bore witness to the ennobling presence of woman.

In addition, the fort had also started a band of twelve men, which played during dinner every day outside the windows of the mess-room. The mess-room itself had been rechristened. It now bore the name of *vayenny sobranye*, or "the military club," and its walls were papered with maps of the Pamirs and plans of the fort.

Fort Pamir is overlooked on the south by the latitudinal chain of mountains which divides the valley of the Murghab from the Alichur Pamirs, known as the Bazar-darah. Just at this point it makes a bend to the left, forcing the Murghab close in under the rocks, so that the river almost describes a semicircle, and in places sweeps along with great velocity.

The Cossacks had rigged up a boat by stretching oiled canvas over a light frame-work; and with it they used to lay their nets and cross the river to the fishing-grounds under the opposite bank. One day Captain Saitseff and I tried our luck in this improvised craft. We embarked a good way up the river, each taking an oar; then we let the boat drift with the current round the elbow, taking care to steer clear of some treacherous sand-banks near the corner. In certain places, where the water was forced through deep, narrow channels, the boat sped along at a giddy pace close to the cliffs. The panorama changed continually, and, owing to the numerous short twists and turns of the river, gave rise to the most curious optical illusions. Although the boat kept gliding onward all the time, the horizon seemed to keep moving backward and forward, so that while at one moment we had the opening of the Ak-baital valley on the one side of us, and at another straight in front of us, at yet another time we had to look well about us before we could perceive it at all. One moment the fort was on our right; shortly afterwards it had moved over to the left, until we were perfectly bewildered. The lapping of the water against the banks was barely audible, for the main current glided like oil along its bed, and the boat was carried on like an unresisting nutshell by the irresistible flood. Once or twice the frail craft scraped against the stones at the bottom, but no harm came of it, and after an hour's exciting work we landed, as wet as a couple of water-spaniels, in still water, a good way down the river, at a spot where it again widened out for a short distance.

On the other side of Shah-jan (the King's Soul), the place where the first Russian fort was erected a few years ago, 2½ miles below the present fortress, the valley of the Murghab contracts; at the same time the river becomes narrower and deeper, and increases in velocity. At that point stood a Kirghiz aul of six uys (tents), and there was the last safe ford, a passage that is always used by those going to the Western Pamirs.

When, on August 27th, I started for Yeshil-kul, I was escorted the whole of the first day's march (twenty-five miles) by Captain Saitseff and a young lieutenant. The Kirghiz misled us at Shah-jan by advising us to cross the river 6½ miles farther on, because, they said, the road on the right bank was the better, and the flood had gone down. When we arrived at the spot which they indicated as a safe ford, one of the Kirghiz was sent across first to show the way. But the river was four feet deep in the middle, and the man's horse lost its footing and was carried down stream. Fortunately it managed to touch the bottom again, and so reached the other side, but its rider was dripping wet up to the waist. After one or two more Kirghiz had ridden over, Captain Saitseff set his horse at the stream, and reached the opposite side in safety, but so wet that he deemed it prudent to take off his boots, which were full of water, and to strip wellnigh to the skin, and spread out his clothes to dry on a hill-side facing the sun. As I had no inordinate desire for a bath, I waited until the three camels came up, which were carrying our baggage, and, climbing on to the tallest of them, managed to reach the opposite bank without getting a stitch wet.

As soon as Captain Saitseff's clothes were dry we continued our journey, reaching the entrance to the valley of Ak-alkhar at dusk. There we encamped in the shelter of a huge isolated rock that stuck up out of the ground. Captain Saitseff had brought a good dinner with him, including a

A KIRGHIZ GIRL.

couple of bottles of claret; and by the light of colored Chinese lanterns and a blazing camp-fire we made a right good feast. Speeches were made on various topics, songs were sung without end, but to very halting melodies; in fact, the echoes of entire operas struck against the cliff walls, but, I must confess, in such inharmonious tones that had an oper-

atic singer heard us he would have been tempted to use his
legs rather than his voice. Happily our only audience were
the Kirghiz, who stood round us in a ring, looking very
much astonished, apparently under the impression that we
had taken leave of our senses on the way. Midnight was
approaching when our musical entertainment came to an
end, and we were overcome by the sound sleep which was
invariably ours.

The next day we halted at Ak-alkhar, for there Captain
Saitseff had sowed some barley and wheat, turnips and rad-
ishes; and all had succeeded beyond expectation, although it
was at an altitude of 11,000 feet. During the course of the
day I mapped part of the river towards the west, and afterwards we spent another jolly evening together, parting early
on the morning of the 29th, the Russians to return to Fort
Pamir, and I and my men to continue our ride up the valley
of Ak-alkhar.

In two days' marches we crossed the Bazar-darah chain
and discovered a new pass (15,970 feet), to which I gave the
name of Saitseff. It was only of secondary importance, as
it was difficult to cross, the incline being very steep and the
declivities covered with fine schistose gravel, in which the
horses had hard work to keep their footing. A barely
visible path showed that the sole frequenters of this pass
were kiyick, tekkes, and arkharis—that is to say, wild goats
and wild sheep.

On the southern side of the pass the country dipped gradually down through the defile of Mus-yilga to the broad valley of Alichur, inhabited by the population of 120 Kirghiz
uys (tents). This valley, in the longitude of Ak-alkhar, lay
about 2000 feet higher than the valley of the Murghab. Two
more days brought us to Sumeh, at the east end of the Yeshil-
kul (the Green Lake); on the way we passed Ak-balik (the
White Fish), or, as the place is also called, Balik-masar (the
Shrine of the Fish). Several springs gushed out of the
ground on the northern side of the valley, and converged
upon a small pool about ten feet deep and twenty yards or
so in diameter. The water was a deep blue color, constantly

varying its tints, but always crystal clear, and with a temperature of 39.2° Fahr. (4° C.). Up and down it swam a number
of fat fish, about a foot long and with black backs. From
the culinary point of view they looked particularly tempting;
we therefore made a long halt beside the pool for the purpose of catching some of them. We had neither rod nor
tackle. Still, what mattered that? With the help of some
pack-thread and the hook of a Swedish watch-chain, and a
piece of mutton for a bait, we soon hauled up three " beau-
ties." After we reached camp the men fried them in yak
butter for supper, and anticipated a splendid dish. But, alas!
our hopes were dashed; the fish were uneatable, having a
rank, disagreeable flavor. Yolldash, however, relished them;
though he apparently regretted his excesses later on, to judge
by the dismal howling he kept up all night.

On the left bank of the Alichur river we rode past a
simple grave, surrounded by a stone wall. It was the burial-
place of seven Afghan soldiers, who fell two years previously
in a skirmish with the Russians. Some rags of felt and the
poles of the tent they had lived in still remained. We took
some of the latter to make our fire of, in spite of Yehim Bai's
protests that it was sacrilege to plunder a grave.

The night of September 2d we spent at the rabat (rest-
house) of Sumeh, which consisted of three gumbez (hive-
shaped towers), built by Abdullah Khan of Bokhara; and on
the following morning we visited a hot sulphurous spring
which issued from the ground in the neighborhood, with a
temperature of 141.1 Fahr. (60.6 C.). In the same place we
also inspected a cube-shaped Chinese *tamga-tash* (seal-stone)
or inscribed stone, showing that there was a time when the
Chinese considered themselves masters of the Pamirs. On
its upper face there was a hollow space, in which a stone
tablet bearing an inscription was originally inserted; but it
has been removed to St. Petersburg.

We then continued our way westward along the northern
shore of the Yeshil-kul, over the vast gravel slopes which
have rolled down from the disintegrated hills above and
stretch down to the lake at an angle of thirty-three degrees.

At this point the Alichur valley became so contracted that the lake was barely two miles across, while its length was as much as fourteen.   The lake was undoubtedly very deep, for the water was a greenish blue color, and it had a temperature of 64.4° Fahr. (18° C.), though it was not so limpid as the water of the Little Kara-kul.   Its altitude was 12,460 feet.

Several side-valleys, with streams flowing through them, reached the lake along both shores.   The largest was known as Chong-marjanay; and although its volume, at the time we saw it, was not more than 105 cubic feet in the second, it had nevertheless formed a delta that projected some distance into the lake.

We halted on a small spit of low-lying land, Kamper-chick, close by the side of the lake, spreading out our felt carpets on the ground in a thick clump of bushes, which were already dry and bare of leaves.   Having made tea and eaten a very simple supper, I jotted down the experiences of the day in my diary by the light of an enormous fire, which lighted up the whole neighborhood; then, having wrapped myself in my furs, I fell asleep to the monotonous murmur of the waves.

On September 3d and 4th we explored the western end of the Yeshil-kul, a particularly interesting spot.   The south shore was overhung by a branch of the vast range of mountains which divides the Yeshil-kul from the country of Shugnan, and which bears in that region the common name of Kara-korum (the Black Stony Tract).   Its summit, near the western end of the lake, where the river Ghunt issued, was covered with snow; and we could even discern a rudimentary glacier, which in former times must have been very much larger, and, together with its moraines, must have completely shut in the valley in that quarter.   The Yeshil-kul was thus formed in the same way as the Little Kara-kul.   That is to say, it is the reservoir or collecting basin of the drainage of the Alichur valley, which afterwards passes out of it across, if I may so say, the moraine threshold; then, under the name of the Ghunt, it cuts its way through a narrow glen, steep and wild, and finally joins the river Pänj.   The moraine was composed of huge blocks of granite, and was excessively difficult to get across. I was at first astonished to find that the river Ghunt, which has the name of being as large as the Murghab, was but an inconsiderable stream, with a volume of scarcely more than 280 cubic feet of water in the second. But the mystery was soon explained: the greater portion of the current found its way *underneath* the moraine, where it was plainly audible as it hurtled along.

We returned to Fort Pamir through the Alichur Pamirs and over the pass of Naisa-tash. There the report reached

YESHIL-KUL, LOOKING SOUTHEAST FROM ITS WESTERN END

us that Togdasin Beg had been punished with three hundred lashes on the bare back for not having informed Jan Darin that I had crossed the frontier, and that the beg was lying half dead in his tent. As I was afraid that the Chinese might get hold of my possessions and the collections which I had left behind, we took cordial leave of the hospitable Russians and hurried back to the Mus-tagh-ata, *via* the Sarik-kol pass (14,540 feet). Arriving there unobserved on September 16th, we were met by the information that, after all, the report was false. Togdasin Beg was safe and sound, and came to see me that very evening; nor had the Chinese discov-

ered my possessions, although they ransacked everything belonging to the Kirghiz who had been in my employ. The
things were still safe in their hiding-place under the rocks.

While we were away winter had advanced with giant
strides. The snows had crept farther down the mountains,
and the whole of the Sarik-kol chain was covered with a
thin white veil. The streams had shrunk into rivulets, and
Nature seemed to be fully prepared for her long winter

ISLAM BAI AND TWO KIRGHIZ WITH THE PLANE-TABLE
ON THE CHUM-KAR-KASHKA GLACIER

sleep. The Mus-tagh-ata towered above us, icy-cold and
uninviting, so that we had not the slightest wish to molest
him further.

Instead of making any further attempt to storm the citadel
of the Father of the Ice Mountains, we travelled southward
along the foot of the mountain, my object being to finish my
cartographical work of the summer. On September 20th I
made a fresh trip over the Chum-kar-kashka glacier in quest
of the rods we put in on August 13th. The change in their
situation indicated only the very slightest movement; in the
middle of the glacier the greatest velocity amounted to slightly under 1¾ inches a day. This slow advance is probably
characteristic of all the glaciers of the Mus-tagh-ata, and is

consequent chiefly upon the long winter, the great amount of radiation, and the heavy evaporation. The movement due to gravity is to some extent neutralized, owing to the diminution in the mass and weight of the glacier through the agencies just mentioned.

The Chum-kar-kashka glacier is an important landmark. All its streams seek the Little Kara-kul, and finally the Kash-gar-daria; while the drainage of the region to the south of it flows into the Yarkand-daria. All the streams which we crossed in the further course of our journey had eroded fairly deep channels in the lower slopes of the mountain ; the which slopes consisted of detritus and old moraines, rounded and levelled down, strewn with occasional blocks of gneiss, and sometimes embellished with tiny meadows. On our left the rocky mountain - walls dipped abruptly under the detritus slopes, and were crowned by several sharp crests. On the same side, too, the Kok-sel glacier issued from an enormous couloir. The moraine was of an extraordinary size, and was strewn with gigantic bowlders of gneiss; while its stream was fed from several directions. We now found that the farther we went in a westerly direction the smaller were the glaciers and the larger the old moraines. This is no doubt due to the greater energy of the agents of dissolution on the southern than on the northern versant.

On September 21st we made a long circuit round the base of the mountain towards the east-southeast and east, as far as the glacier-stream of the Sar-aghil glaciers, and on the 22d we passed the Shevär-aghil and Gherdumbeh glaciers. Both these were inaccessible, owing to the insurmountable moraine-walls which surrounded them ; not even the yaks could climb them. The conformation of the mountain was in that quarter extremely rugged ; in fact, it was a sheer wall, with craggy contours and irregular ridges and cols, and the glaciers were so short that they seldom emerged from between the arms of the mountain. Its lower slopes presented the characteristics of an ancient moraine landscape, with *cirques*, ridges, erratic blocks, and pools ; and farther on they gradually merged into the plains of Tagh-arma. The next two fundamental rifts in

the central mass of the mountain were called Kara-korum.
They possessed no glaciers; but the ancient moraines at
their base were deeply excavated by running water, and the
entire region was strewn with gigantic fragments of a beautiful gray gneiss and smaller pieces of crystalline schist, among
which a number of hares were hopping about.

Finally we branched off to the northeast, entering the glen

KARA-KORUM, ON THE SOUTH OF MUS-TAGH-ATA

of the Tegherman-su. There we halted by the side of the
brook, in a pleasant camping-ground among the grass and
bushes; and there we rested over September 23d. The
minimum thermometer gave a reading of 41° Fahr. (5° C.),
showing that we had descended to lower regions. At 4 P. M.
the temperature of the water in the brook was 46.9° Fahr.
(8.3° C.), and it was pure and bright, and good to drink. The
volume of the stream was 70 cubic feet in the second.

It had been my intention to make the entire circuit of the
Mus-tagh-ata, from the Tegherman-su, in a north and north-

westerly direction till I came to the Little Kara-kul. Unfortunately the Kirghiz declared this project to be impracticable,
owing to the east side of the mountain being a labyrinth of
precipitous and jagged crests, which it was impossible to surmount even on foot.   In order to convince myself of this, I
made a reconnaissance to the source of the brook, and found
that the Kirghiz were quite right.   There was nothing for it,
therefore, but to go round the mountain by the old way, via
Gedyäck and Ullug-rabat, and on September 30th, 1894, we
reached our old haunts on the east shore of the Little Kara-
kul.

CHAPTER XXXII

BOATING ADVENTURES ON THE LITTLE KARA-KUL

THIS time we encamped beside the Little Kara-kul from the last day of September until October 9th, partly because we needed rest, and because it was unwise to pass directly from the higher-lying regions down into the warm valleys; and partly because I wished to take soundings of the lake, which would, I hoped, verify the observations I had made during our first visit in that region regarding the formation of the lake. Quite near our camp there was an aul of six yurts; and the first day after our arrival I consulted with its inhabitants, and with Togdasin Beg and some of my own men, as to the best way of taking the soundings. There were, of course, no boats. One of the Kirghiz had indeed *seen* a boat on the upper Amu-daria; the others had not the faintest idea what a boat was like, and could not even conceive how such a thing was made. Throughout the whole of the broad valley of Sarik-kol there were only six small birches, growing on the saint's grave of Kayindeh-masar; but to touch them would have been looked upon as sacrilege. Apart from those trees, there was not a bush within a hundred miles.

The only things to be found in our immediate neighborhood were raw hides and *obs*, or the slightly bent poles which support the cupola-shaped felt roof of the Kirghiz yurt. But how these materials could be turned into a boat the cleverest of the Kirghiz was unable to form a conjecture. I set to work and made a little model of a boat out of some oiled linen, with a mast, sail, rudder, and keel, and very well she sailed, greatly to the amazement of the Kirghiz. Togdasin Beg said bluntly that a thing of that kind on a large scale

would cost me my life, and I had better wait till the lake
froze, which he thought would happen in about six weeks'
time. The temperature at night had already fallen to 14°
Fahr. (−10° C.), and every morning the small lagoons on the
lake shore were covered with a thin coating of ice, which,
however, melted as the day advanced. The lake itself was
too rough to allow of ice being formed. During the whole
of the ten days we spent on its shores, full-fledged gales flew
from the south with swift, strong wings, racing one another
across the lake as if consumed with impatience to get to the
Bulun-kul; just as though there were not a single molecule
in the atmosphere, and the great Jan Darin, with the whole
of his lanza (garrison), sat in the vacuum gasping for breath.
But I was not dismayed. I had heard the sea-waves boil and
break before then, and preferred braving vigorous Æolus to
waiting till the ice formed.

I had the tent pitched barely two yards from the shore, so
that I might lie and listen to the music of the waves; and
the "dock-yard," where the boat-building was to take place,
was close beside the tent. Here we lay down the keel and
lashed the tough ribs to it with ropes, and in less than a
couple of hours the frame was ready; it was only six feet
long and three feet broad. A horse which had been so con-
siderate as to die the day before contributed his skin, and a
sheep also gave us materials. Thus things were beginning
to look more ship-shape. The finishing touches were added
in the form of a mast and a sail of scarlet cotton stuff. To
each side we fastened two inflated goat-skins, and another
was lashed at the stern, which somehow pointed suspiciously
downward. Our oars were made out of oks split at one
end, and a piece of goat-skin stretched across the fork. For
our rudder we took a spade, pure and simple, and fastened it
firmly to her stern.

It was a very queer craft which left the slip on October 3d.
Honestly speaking, she scarcely did credit to Swedish boat-
building, being entirely wanting in the noble lines and beautiful proportions for which our cutters are famous. On the
contrary, she was everywhere as warped and angular as an

empty sardine-box. As our brave craft, in which I was going to navigate the Kara-kul for a whole week, lay bobbing up and down near the shore on her inflated goat-skins, she put me strangely in mind of some unknown antediluvian creature hatching its eggs.

Togdasin Beg turned up early the next morning to inspect the monster. He pulled up at a respectful distance. His expression was indescribably comical, and seemed to say: " Why, you don't mean to tell me a *boat* looks like that? I never could have imagined such a thing!" Then, the next moment, an ironical smile crossed his lips, and he seemed to be thinking to himself—" What a crazy looking affair!" But he had the tact not to say anything, and I bit my lip to keep a straight countenance. Meanwhile I invited him to go for a sail later in the day. After some demur, he accepted the invitation. When it came to the point, he was far less afraid than his fellow-tribesmen.

On the day our boat was launched, the Kirghiz assembled from far and near; and there were even a score or so of women, with their big white turban - shaped head - dresses, peeping from behind a moraine - mound. I asked the old men if they thought Jan Darin would be able to keep from laughing if we put him on board, and sent him out on the lake. The idea tickled them so, they were ready to split with laughter.

In a word, the whole thing was a sensational event, a very uncommon *tamashah* (spectacle); and reports of it spread like wildfire over the whole of the eastern Pamirs. On our way back to Kashgar, we used to be asked at the Kirghiz auls where we halted for the night, even at great distances from the Little Kara-kul, if it were true that a stranger with wings had flown up Mus-tagh-ata, and later had flitted backward and forward across the lake? Mollah Islam even went so far as to compose a song, which was afterwards sung of an evening to the music of a *gedyäck* (violin), and no doubt will be handed down to posterity in the form of a legend.

It really was a supreme moment in my existence when the boat was launched. The Kirghiz followed its move-

ments with bated breath, and were astounded at my temerity
when I stepped in and went for a short sail in her, for it was
blowing hard. But the little craft, with her five goat-skin
bags, rode the water gayly, and Togdasin Beg was so encouraged by the sight that on my next trial-trip he willingly
accompanied me.

Never did bluer, purer, fresher waves rock a more ram-
shackle contrivance than ours: she seemed to feel about as
much at home on the water as a hen or a cat. No pride at
being the first to ride the waves of the Kara-kul; no exulta-
tion at being at such a sublime altitude above the level of
the sea! Anxiously she swayed on the crisp curling waves;
which seemed as if they took a malicious pleasure in playing
with her fears. Oh what a boat that was! A perfect menagerie of a boat! Her carcass compounded of horse and
sheep and goat; in character a mule; in her movements re-
calling the graceful gambollings of a cow. And yet she did
full honor to her descent: for she was as obstinate as a mule,
and when she dropped into the trough of the waves, she
kicked and plunged like a mustang. Oh that Irish pig of a
boat! She never understood when you called to her "Starboard" or "Larboard." "Right" and "left" were words
that meant to her the exact opposite of what ordinary folk
understand by them. To all the rules of navigation she was
perfectly indifferent, and you might labor at her tiller like a
galley-slave: she just deluged you with water and went her
own way. No matter whether we wanted to go south or
wanted to go north, she always imagined we had a head-
wind to face; and if we tried to tack ever so little, she was
bound to fall off, till she got wind and wave behind her. In
a word, she was every bit as stubborn as a yak!

As the wind blew constantly from the south, every time
we wanted to use our precious boat we had to tow her round
to the south shore, and then let her drift with the wind across
the lake, taking soundings as we went. This method was
inaugurated on October 4th, when the boat was towed by a
horse through the shallow water to the middle of the southern shore. Then I and one of the Kirghiz, Mohammed Tur-

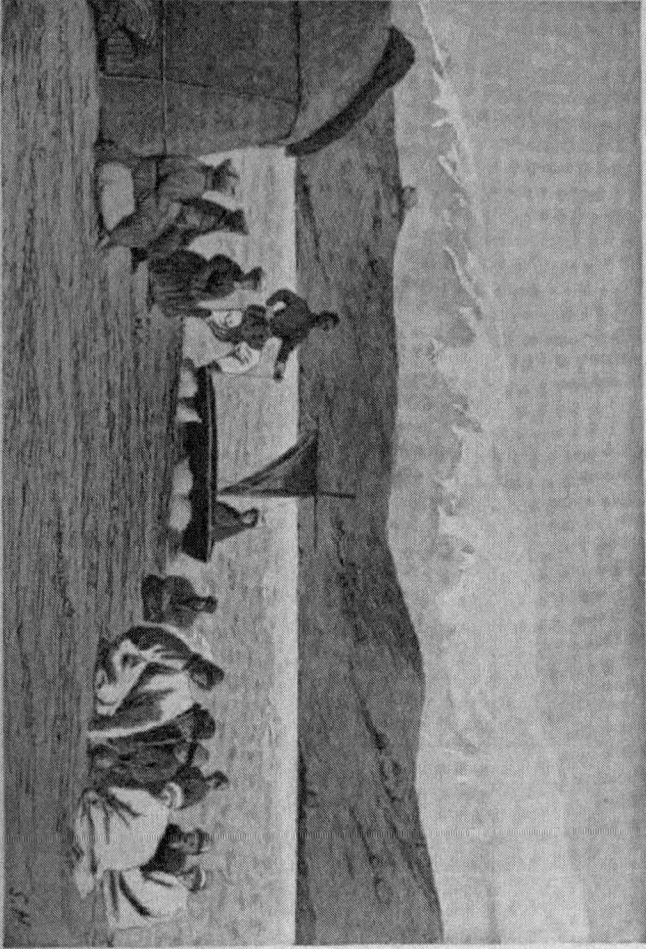

FREIGHT BOAT ON THE ...

du, got into her. There was not much wind; but it was cold, so that I was well wrapped up in my furs. Before we had got very far from the shore, one of those hurricane-like squalls from the south swept over the lake, ploughing up the water furiously before it. We lowered the sail and held fast to the sides, for the boat was plunging like a restive horse. Our situation was critical—the boat was drifting out to the middle of the lake, and it was a long way to either shore. I was steering, when all of a sudden she dipped astern, and a sea broke over us, half filling the boat and wetting us to the skin. The goat-skin bag which held up the stern had got adrift, and was floating off over the water on its own account. Every wave that reached us broke right over us, although I tried to take the sting out of them with the oar, while the Kirghiz Mohammed baled away for dear life.

Our position was really serious; particularly when both the starboard goat-skins began to collapse, the wind oozing out of them with a shrill hissing sound, and the boat took a list to starboard. The seas broke over us from all sides, leaping upon us like malevolent sea-trolls, with wild dishevelled hair.

Thus we drifted, tossing on the angry waves over unknown depths. I was afraid the other goat-skin bags would part company with us, or would lose their buoyancy before we reached the shore, and kept calculating whether or not I should be able to swim the intervening distance. Nor were my spirits raised by Mohammed Turdu becoming dismally sea-sick; he would assuredly have been as white as a sheet had he not already been as sunburned as any gypsy. He baled the whole time, and baled double measure: on the one side water and on the other— Poor fellow! he had never been in a boat in his life before, and had never heard of sea-sickness. He fully believed his last hour had come.

The Kirghiz crowded the nearest shore on horseback and on foot, expecting every moment to see the boat go down. But, happily, we succeeded in keeping her afloat; and it was with a feeling of indescribable relief that we at last saw she was gliding over shallow water. Safe and sound, but wet through, we finally reached the shore, hurried to camp, and kindled a huge fire, at which we slowly dried our clothes.

Our first sounding expedition was thus a complete fiasco. The only discovery we made was that the drift-sand contributed, in as great a degree, perhaps, as the glacial mud, to the levelling up of the lake-basin; for, while the glacier-streams only develop energy during the summer, sand-storms are a common occurrence all the year round. In the night, however, the drift-sand which drops from the passing storms is blown away across the slippery surface of the ice. Several times on the lake we were enveloped in clouds of sand so thick that we could hardly make out the shore-line; and in the evening, after the storm had subsided, the water was still muddy. The everlasting mutton broth actually crunched between our teeth when we took it at supper.

The following day we accomplished three good lines of sounding without any further adventure; and on the 8th set out from the western end of the southern shore. We began work late in the day, so as to let the wind settle a little first, and drifted gently across the lake, dispensing with the sail so as not to disturb the accuracy of the soundings. Hour after hour passed; then dusk came on, and it was quite dark when we reached shallow water. We were only a couple of hundred yards from the northern shore when suddenly a dead calm set in, and the next moment a violent gale from the north, which tossed the boat back into the lake as though it had been a mere nutshell. We felt that now we had the whole lake before us, and the night. Row as we might, we could make no head-way: the wind was too strong for us, and pitilessly drove us out to the very middle of the lake. It was pitch-dark until the moon rose and comforted us a little; while Islam Bai, who was uneasy at our non-appearance, made a large fire at the camp, which served us for a light-house. The north gale was, however, of short duration, and by dint of hard rowing we managed to reach camp about midnight.

One great advantage in navigating those waters was that we did not fear meeting other craft or being run down by careless roisterers returning home late of an evening. We

MY HORSE-SKIN BOAT IN A HEAVY STORM ON THE LITTLE KARA-KUL

were the unquestioned masters of the Little Kara-kul, and had plenty of sea-room to turn our boat in; for the lake was about two miles long, two miles broad at the south end, rather more than half a mile at the north end, and a mile in the middle.

I have made fun of our noble craft. Let me now say a word in its praise, as a sort of memorial on its grave. The completion of my soundings and the continuance of unfavorable weather put an end to our trips on the lake. I was sorry to have to take our pleasure-yacht to pieces, and return the various materials to their respective purveyors, instead of sending it to the Ethnographical Museum at Stockholm; for beyond a doubt it would have been one of the stars of the collection. It had, indeed, served to show the Kirghiz what sort of thing a boat is; but it is doubtful whether it impressed them with any exaggerated admiration of Swedish navigation.

Meanwhile we had ascertained the bathymetrical or depth relations of the Kara-kul, having taken 103 soundings altogether. All these I marked on an enlarged map, on which I afterwards drew out the curves of depth. The maximum depth was 79 feet in the southern half of the lake; in the middle it varied between 50 and 70 feet. Along the whole of the southern shore, where the glacial streams entered the lake, there was a fairly steep deposit of mud; whereas on the north the moraine sank down to the lake level at a gentle inclination. At the northwest corner, where the Kara-kul stream issued from the lake, numerous small erratic blocks of gneiss projected above the surface of the water. Close to the southeastern shore, under the steeper cliffs, the sounding-line touched bottom after uncoiling about 5 or 6 feet; whereas everywhere in the northern half of the lake it ran out to 1000 feet or more. Near the middle of the west shore there was a small island, Kindick-masar, every spring the breeding-place of innumerable wild geese. In the same quarter, too, we discovered two large shallow creeks, and some submarine dunes of drift-sand, formed in the shelter of certain projecting rocks.

With regard to the changes of color in the lake, the deeper parts were a deep blue, the shallow parts light green, and the strips along which algæ grew dark violet.

The Kirghiz were very decided in their statements that there were no fish in Little Kara-kul; and in point of fact I only found one, a small one, floating dead on the water. It was of the same species as those of which I collected specimens from the neighboring Bassyk - kul, and was probably dropped in Little Kara-kul by a bird.

The water was fresh, and good to drink. During our stay the temperature near the shore varied between 53.6° Fahr. (12° C.) and 37.4° Fahr. (3° C.), and in the middle of the lake, at the bottom, it was 46.4° Fahr. (8° C.).

In several places numerous small springs entered the lake in different parts; and in all such places there were open holes in the ice nearly the whole winter. Little Kara-kul freezes in the middle of November, and the ice begins to break up in the middle of April. The Kirghiz described the ice as resembling a sheet of looking-glass, so smooth that the wind sweeps away every particle of snow. They also told me that they could see broad woods and pastures (algæ) at the bottom of the lake through the ice, and that on winter nights the images of the stars twinkled as brightly as the actual stars did in the sky above.

Now that we had work to do every day, our life passed as quietly and peacefully as it did during our former stay beside the lake. Sometimes, when the day's work was done, and it was blowing hard, I used to go and sit on a rock by the shore, and imagine that the waves which came rolling in to my feet were beating against the wooded isles of the Skärgård at home; and a thousand memories of my native land would crowd in upon my mind, lighting up as with torches the dark night of my loneliness. I imagined myself a pilgrim resting in one of the most beautiful of Nature's temples, at the threshold of which the snow-capped mountain-giants kept watch and ward. At their feet lay the lake wonderful, set like a jewel of the purest water, its bright placid surface making a glorious mirror for them to behold their own stern features in.

It would be unjust to call the Little Kara-kul a lifeless lake. In the course of my topographical labors I many a time disturbed thriving broods of wild duck or wild geese contentedly feeding among the rushes by the shore. On our approach they would fly out into the lake, with legs drooping and necks out-stretched. At night, too, I often heard the wild geese calling to their young, or heard their hoarse honking as they sailed away over the tent in large flocks. Occasionally there were gaps made in one or other of the broods; for we were not averse to vary the deadly monotony of our daily fare.

Most beautiful of all, however, were the atmospheric effects. With a master-hand were painted the most inthralling and gorgeous pictures—scenes so utterly unlike each other that I sometimes fancied myself transported to two or three different parts of the world all within the space of a few minutes. For instance, the sun would rise in a sky of purest blue, the atmosphere being still and warm, Mus-tagh-ata standing out in clear and sharp-cut relief, with the most delicate details of its blue shimmering snow-fields, and every varying tint of its rounded and precipitous altitudes traced in lines of matchless beauty. The dark mountain-sides would be reflected in the ever-changing mirror of the lake, now a light lovely green, now a deep intense blue, while the hush of a perfect Sabbath day brooded over the whole scene. Then, all of a sudden, white clouds, immediately followed by dark ones, would rustle up over the northern horizon. The sky above the Pamirs would put on a steel-gray wintry aspect: in a moment the entire vault of heaven would be packed with clouds. The wind would whistle in sudden gusts, then would blow with unmitigated fury. The lake immediately under the shore became as green as the deep sea, but farther out glowed a dusky violet. From end to end it would be streaked with running lines of white spray; while the waves dashed themselves with headlong violence against the shores, which they have been crumbling down and eating at for thousands of years. But within an hour the storm would be all gone. Then would come a shower of hail; and then a heavy downpour of rain. The wind would die away. The lake would lose its brightness, and become gray from the splashing of the raindrops.

But this spell of bad weather seldom lasted long, and left no traces behind it. Every afternoon, as regular as clock-work, the east wind came piping over the pass of Kara-tash

KENG-SHEVÄR (THE PLACE WHERE THE IKE-BEL-SU ISSUES FROM THE MUS-TAGH RANGE) SHROUDED IN MIST

and down the valley of the Ike-bel-su, wreathing the land-scape in a misty haze. With the exception of our immediate surroundings, every object became lost to sight. The shore faded away in both directions. Right before me sky and water melted together. Not a glimpse of the mountains that overhung the lake met my searching eye. I could easily have imagined I was standing on the brink of the boundless ocean.

On one occasion the mist caught up the artist's brush, and used it with magnificent effects, or rather contrasts. We

were returning from an expedition to the Ike-bel-su. Its valley was filled with murky mist, which surged up the lower
slopes of the Mus-tagh range, darkening every hollow in their
flanks. And so swiftly, so silently, did it boil up and up, that
the mountains speedily vanished from sight, like the image
on an unfixed photographic plate when exposed to the light.
While the lower regions were thus enshrouded in thick gloom,
the towering summits of the Mus-tagh-ata shone out brilliant

MY CARAVAN ON THE MARCH

and vivid, like electric lamps streaming across the billows of
the onrolling mist. The sun sank behind the mountains;
instantly it was twilight. Higher and higher crept the mist
up the mountain-sides. The topmost peaks of the great
mountain, and the snow-fields glancing like silver mail on its
shoulders, were bathed in a scarlet glow, shading away to a
glorious fiery yellow. Less and less grew the sunlit altitudes.
With ill-omened ease and haste the envious shadows mounted up the faces of the precipices. One moment the crowning summit glittered out over the deluge of mist; then paled
—a pyramid faintly, indistinctly outlined against the dark
background of the sky; then, at the end of a few swift-ebb-

(dowry) to her parents. A rich Kirghiz pays as much as ten or twelve jambaus (one jambau equals £9 to £10); a poor one pays a couple of horses or yaks. The girl's parents, therefore, always endeavor to secure her a bai (rich man) for a husband; the young man's a plain and poor daughter-in-law, who will be content with a modest kalim. If the girl be young and pretty, a very large dowry is always asked.

Near the Mus-tagh-ata there lived in 1894 an unusually pretty Kirghiz girl, Nevra Khan, who had suitors from far and near; but her father asked such an unconscionably high kalim, that she had reached her twenty-fifth year without being married. A young Kirghiz, who was head over ears in love with her, begged me to "lend" him the sum demanded; and even the parents of the young people tried to get round me, though naturally without success.

After the contract is made, the betrothal may last an indefinite period; but as soon as the entire kalim is paid, the marriage takes place. A new yurt is pitched, and within it the wedding is celebrated in the presence of as many guests as like to come. Dastarkhan (refreshments) of mutton, rice, and tea are served; then the mollah reads out aloud the duties of the young couple towards each other. Baigas are held. Everybody wears their best khalat (coat). The bride is dressed in all her finery and ornaments. If the man belongs to another aul, the ceremony is performed at the girl's aul, whence the newly married couple are escorted to their future domicile by all the guests.

When a Kirghiz dies, the body is well washed, and dressed in clean white clothes; then, having been wrapped in linen and felts, it is carried with as little delay as possible to the grave. The ground is dug out to the depth of three feet, and at the bottom of the hole, but at the side, another horizontal trench is excavated, and in that the body is laid. Then the outer grave is filled up, and the place covered with a stone; or if the dead man were a bai, his grave is marked by a small dome standing on a rectangular base. For forty days after the interment the grave is visited by the mourners.

KIRGHIZ GIRL FROM TUR-BULUNG

The household goods of a Kirghiz family are not many. When they flit, two or three yaks generally suffice to transport all their belongings. The yurt (uy) itself, with its wooden pole and thick felt covering, the saddles, horse-cloths, "bed-clothes," and loose carpets, are the most bulky. Next come the household utensils, among which the *kazan*, a large iron cooking-pot, is the most important; furthermore, china basins (*chinneh* and *pialeh*), flat wooden dishes (*tabak*), iron or copper cans with handles and lids (*kungan* and *chugun*). A number of other things, such as a loom, a kneading-trough, a corn-sieve, hatchets, sacks for keeping corn and flour in, a cradle, a fiddle, and a guitar, an iron stand for the cooking-pot, pokers, etc., are never wanting in a well-appointed uy. Most of these articles are bought at Kashgar, Yanghi-hissar, or Yarkand, though there are native blacksmiths and carpenters in the Sarik-kol valley. The wood for their yurts is procured from the valleys on the east side of the Mus-tagh-ata, as no trees grow in the Sarik-kol valley.

In every tent there is always a place set apart, the *ash-khaneh* (larder), in which they keep milk and cream in many forms, as well as other kinds of food. The drink chiefly in favor is *ayran* (boiled milk diluted with water, and left to become sour), a particularly refreshing drink in the summer. *Kaimak* is yak's cream of the most delicious description, thick and sweet and yellow, with a flavor of almonds. Ordinary milk is called *sut*. All these various kinds of milk are kept in goat-skin bags.

The Kirghiz live chiefly on yak's milk and mutton. A sheep is slaughtered once or twice a week; and the inhabitants of the aul then enjoy a good square meal. They crowd into the tent, round the fire, where the meat is boiling in the kazan. The portions are distributed among those who are present. Then each pulls out his knife, and eats away till nothing is left but the bare bone; and even that is cracked in order to extract the marrow, which is considered a great dainty. Both before and after the meal the hands are washed, and when it is finished they are carried to the beard, while all cry together "*Allahu akhbar!*" (God is Great!) The five daily prayers of Islam are said punctually by the oldest man of each aul.

In daily life the women drag the heavier load. They pitch and strike the tents, weave carpets and ribbons, wind ropes and yarn, milk the yak-cows and the goats, tend the sheep, the children, and the household. Their flocks are guarded by a number of savage sheep-dogs, which live on what is left over at meal-times.

The men may be said to do nothing. As a rule they sit round the fire all day long, or at most drive the yaks to and from the higher pastures. But they often visit their neighbors to buy or sell or barter their stock. In the winter they generally spend the whole day inside the yurt, sitting round the fire (which is fed with *tesek* or yak's dung) talking, while the storm howls outside and the snow swirls in dense clouds round the yurt.

Thus the Kirghiz passes his life, peacefully and monotonously, one year being exactly like another, with the same occupations, the same recurring migrations. As time passes he grows older He sees his children leave him and make new homes for themselves. His beard grows white, and finally he is carried to the nearest saint's grave, at the foot of the snow-covered mountains, among which he and his forefathers have struggled through an existence which, though scant of joys, has yet been free from serious cares.

For this reason, then, they looked upon my long sojourn among them as an interesting episode. They had never before had an opportunity to see a *Ferenghi* (European) at close quarters, or to observe him going about all his mysterious occupations. They could never understand why I insisted upon visiting every single glacier, why I sketched everything, and actually went the length of hacking pieces of stone off the rocks and filling my boxes with them; for to them they were as commonplace and uninteresting as possible.

Their knowledge of the outer world is very limited. They only know the district they live in, but that they do know extraordinarily well; as also the routes across the Pamirs.

and to the principal towns in the west of East Turkestan. But anything beyond that is a sealed book. They have heard of Russia, England, China, Persia, Kanjut, Kashmir, Tibet, Hindustan, the Great Kara-kul, Lop-nor, and Peking. Their sole knowledge of the busy places of the world is derived from the towns in that part of Asia, or from itinerant merchants; but they seldom pay much heed to what they learn from these sources, for it is mostly matter that is foreign to their own concerns, and the echoes of the peacock " madding crowd " never reach them. To them the world is flat, and girdled by the sea, while the sun circles round it every day. Try how I would to make them comprehend the real facts, they were never able to grasp them; they only answered with imperturbable assurance that at any rate the place in which they themselves lived stood still and never moved.

The old men often told me the story of their lives, and it was always interesting and instructive to listen to, not least for the sake of the language. Among the older Kirghiz, Beg Bulat, of Rang-kul, had had a varied and adventurous life. In the days of Yakub Beg he served for twelve years as a yuz-bashi (chief of a hundred men) in Tagharma. After the death of Yakub Beg, in 1877, the Chinese took Kashgar. Two years later Hakim Khan Tura marched with a thousand men from Margelan to Tash-kurgan, where he was joined by Beg Bulat and his brother, and five hundred Sarik-kol Kirghiz. For an entire week they besieged the Tajik population of Tash-kurgan, but were unable to conquer them. A large Chinese force then entered the mountains for the purpose of quelling the revolt; and the Kirghiz Abdurrahman Dacha was sent by Hakim to Tash-kurgan to make terms of peace, but was killed by the Tajiks. Hakim Khan Tura then led his force to Chakker-aghil, at the opening of the Ghez valley. While waiting there, Kurushi Dacha, Beg Bulat's brother, learned that the Chinese intended to put to death all who had participated in the revolt, unless they gave up Hakim. Kurushi thereupon deserted his leader and went to the Little Kara-kul. He was then ordered by the Chinese to attack Hakim at Muji, and did so. Hakim fled across the Kizil-art

s, and many of his men fell. Beg Bulat continued to
nmand the remnant of the Kirghiz forces. But they, too,
re scattered, and Beg Bulat retired to Rang-kul, while his
)ther was taken prisoner by the Chinese and beheaded in
shgar. Beg Bulat, fearing a similar fate, fled to Ak-baital,
: was followed by fifty Chinese horsemen, who came up
h him at that place and captured him, and took him and
family through Kashgar to Turfan. There he lived in
e for nine years; but the beg of Turfan, who was a Mo-
..ammedan, let him be at large, and allowed him to engage in
ide undisturbed. As he invariably conducted himself well,
· Chinese authorities eventually not only permitted him to
irn to his own country, but, valuing his abilities, offered
the appointment of beg of the eastern Pamirs. But he
tused it, saying that he would not serve a people who had
d his brother. After that the Russians entered the
nirs. At the time of my visit old Beg Bulat was living
Rang-kul in poverty and obscurity.

Thus we used to talk, often till late in the night, while the
blue flames played about the glowing embers of the camp-fire,
dimly lighting the interior of the tent, so that the rugged
features of the bearded men seated round on the carpets
could hardly be distinguished. I do not know whether the
Kirghiz parted from me with regret, for living amid a cold,
niggardly, unyielding climate, the hearts that beat in their
breasts are hard and unsympathetic, and unresponsive to the
warmer feelings. Yet many a friendly "*Hosh !*" (Farewell!)
"*Khoda yoll versun !*" (God prepare the way!), and "*Allahu
akhbar !*" (God is Great!) followed me when I went away;
and they stood a long time on the shore of Little Kara-kul
watching my caravan with wondering eyes; and when I left
their hospitable country for the last time, no doubt many of
them thought within themselves: "Whence cometh he? and
whither goeth he? and what wanted he here?"

A YOUNG WIFE OF THE KARA-TEIT TRIBE OF KIRGHIZ

CHAPTER XXXIV

RETURN TO KASHGAR

ON October 9th we marched to the aul of Tuya-kuyruk (12,740 feet), and the next day continued up the valley of the Ike-bel-su, whose volume was now reduced to 70 or 80 cubic feet in the second, very different from the foaming river we saw during the summer. Upon reaching the enormous and imposing glacier of Kok-sel we struck off to the left, pursuing a zigzag course up the steep slopes on the right side of the valley, which consisted partly of solid gneiss and partly of fragments of rock fallen from the heights above. That evening we reached the aul of Tur-bulung, the inhabitants of which were on the point of changing their quarters to the Little Kara-kul; for the winters are extremely raw and severe at Tur-bulung, and snow-storms of daily occurrence. Wolves, foxes, and bears were common in the same locality.

On the night of October 11th, when we stopped at the aul, there was an unusually high wind, and the Kirghiz continually lighted torches and held them up to the smoke-vent, crying "*Allahu akhbar!*" in order to ward off the wind. Every time an extra violent gust came, they all leaped up and laid hold of the tent, although it was already well secured with ropes and stones. All the same, we managed to make an excursion to the Kara-yilga, where the luxuriant pasture attracted numbers of wild goats and arkharis or wild sheep (*Ovis Poli*). Islam Bai shot one of the latter on a glacier; but unfortunately the animal fell down a crevasse and could not be got up again.

On the 12th we rode across the Merkeh-bel pass, of evil repute. The incline from the west was not particularly steep; but the snow was nearly 16 inches deep. It was a curious pass; the summit broad and dome-shaped, covered with a thin glacier tongue, over which we rode for a mile and a quarter. The adjacent mountains were relatively low; those to the right (the south) entirely sheathed in ice, those to the north being either bare crystalline rocks of a black color or sprinkled with thin patches of snow. The east side, however, was inconceivably steep, consisting of a moraine littered with fairly large fragments of rock and layers of schist with sharp points and edges. There I found it advisable to walk, for the horses continually threatened to come down on their knees. Fortunately, this time we had hired yaks to carry our baggage. By degrees the declivity became less steep, and we got down to the valley of Merkeh without further incident, and encamped in a solitary yurt at an altitude of 11,780 feet.

The following days we travelled at a good speed down towards the plains of East Turkestan. In the glens on the east side it was snowing steadily; and on October 13th there was a high wind into the bargain, so that we rode through driving snow the whole day. The stream that traversed the Merkeh valley, being augmented by a number of tributaries from a series of small side-glens, had excavated a deep channel through the conglomerate terraces, along which we were often obliged to ride

The bottom of the stream was encumbered with large fragments of gneiss and clay-slate. At Sughet (9890 feet), which derives its name from the willows that grow there, the tents were deeply embedded in the snow; but the chief Togda Mohammed Bai had a friendly reception for us.

On October 14th we marched to Chatt, the camp of Mohammed Togda Beg, chief of the Eastern Kirghiz. On the way thither we passed the Kara-tash-yilga, traversed by the stream that comes down from the pass of Kara-tash. The following day's march took us over a secondary pass, Gedyäck-belez (13,040 feet), with a soft rounded summit, composed of slippery yellow clay or fine schistose gravel. Through the adjacent glens floated detached clouds of impenetrable mist.

Our camping-station for the night bore the curious name of Sarik-kiss (the Yellow Maiden).

After leaving, on the 16th, the entrance to the glen of Keng-kol on our right, we were once more in a well-known district, and that evening put up at Ighiz-yar, in the same caravanserai in which we had stayed before. I was very pleased to lay aside my cumbrous, heavy winter clothing, which the mild air now made superfluous. And how good were the fruit and the Kashgar bread and eggs which we had for dinner!

On October 19th I once more took possession of my room at the consulate at Kashgar, delighted to see the pile of newspapers and letters which had accumulated during the course of the summer.

I now settled down at the house of my old friend Consul-General Petrovsky, and was able to enjoy a period of much-needed rest. We spent the long autumn evenings, as before, by the fireside, discussing many an important Asiatic problem. I will not dwell upon my reminiscences of Kashgar, except a couple of incidents which I must mention. My first care was to arrange and label my geological specimens from the Mus-tagh-ata, and to develop the photographs I had taken. After that I wrote a few scientific papers on the work of the summer.

In the beginning of November a breath of air from Europe penetrated to our lonely colony in the far east. Mr. Kobeko, a privy councillor, who was making a tour of inspection through Russian Turkestan, arrived in Kashgar. He was a pleasant, refined, and well-read man, and during the week he stayed with us the days flew past more quickly than usual. I shall never forget the evening of November 6th, the anniversary of the day on which the great Gustavus Adolphus died. We were all sitting round the large drawing-room table, tea-glass in hand, talking politics, and discussing the future of East Turkestan, to the crackling of the fire and the singing of the samovar—when a breathless Cossack courier entered the room without knocking, and going up to Mr. Kobeko handed him a telegram from Gulja, the last station of the Russian telegraph system. It contained news of the death of the Emperor Alexander III. All present rose to their feet, and the Orthodox Russians made the sign of the cross. Deep sorrow was depicted on every countenance, and for a long time there was a dead silence in the room. It had only taken the short space of five days for the sad news to penetrate into the very heart of Asia.

The day after the arrival of the telegram the Dao Tai and Tsen Daloi came to offer their condolences to Consul Petrov-sky. With their many-colored ceremonial costumes, their gongs and drums, their parasols and standards, and with all their pomp and state, they presented a strange contrast to the silent sorrow of the Russians.

The result of the violent changes of climate that I had been exposed to was an attack of fever, which came on in the middle of November, and kept me a prisoner in bed for a month.

Another misfortune overtook me in the Russian bath, to which I went accompanied by two Cossacks and Islam Bai. The bath was heated and everything arranged; but after I had been in a considerable time, the Cossacks imagined that I ought to have had enough of it, and came to see what I was doing. On their entrance they found that I had fainted. Some pipe in the heating apparatus had sprung a leak, and the fumes nearly did for me. The men took me to my room at once, and I gradually came round; but for two days afterwards I had a splitting headache.

Then came Christmas. Christmas! What a host of memories, of regrets, of hopes, lie in that one word! Yes, it was Christmas in Kashgar. The snow fell softly, but evaporated immediately in the arid atmosphere, so that it did not even make the ground white. There was a sound of bells in the streets and market-place; but they were caravan bells and rang all the year round. The stars shone brightly in the sky; but not with the same magic brilliance as those of our northern winter nights. A light twinkled here and there in the windows of the houses; but they were not Christmas candles swinging on the fir branches, only lamps fed with Kanjut oil, as simple as in the time of Christ Himself.

Could there be a more suitable person to pay a visit to on
this holy-tide than the Swedish missionary, Mr. Högberg, who
had come to Kashgar with his family during the summer?
Mr. Macartney, the English agent, and Father Hendricks
went with me, and we took a few small presents for Mr.
Högberg's little girl. The time-worn lessons for the day
were read, and the Christmas psalm was sung to an accompaniment on the harmonium. Then in the darkness of Christmas Eve Father Hendricks and I strolled round to Mr. Macartney's house, where mulled wine and Christmas cheer
awaited us. But shortly before midnight Father Hendricks
went away; nor could we persuade him to stay longer. He
was going home to his lonely cabin in the Hindu caravanserai, and on the stroke of twelve would read the Christmas
mass, alone, alone, always alone!

On January 5th, 1895, Mr. St. George Littledale, with his
undaunted wife, and a relative, Mr. Fletcher, arrived at Kashgar, and I spent many a pleasant hour in their company.
Mr. Littledale was unusually genial, manly, and unassuming
in character, and I esteemed it a great privilege thus to make
the acquaintance of one of the most intrepid and able of living Asiatic travellers. He himself regarded his own travels
with a critical eye, was always modest, and had no pretensions. He said that he travelled simply for pleasure, for
sport, and because the active, changing life was more to his
taste than the gayeties of London. But with the journey he
began in the year 1895 he has written his name indelibly in
the annals of Asiatic exploration, by the side of those of his
distinguished countrymen, Younghusband and Bower.

In the middle of January our English friends left Kashgar
in four large arbas (carts) draped with carpets; and an imposing sight they made as they drove out of Mr. Macartney's
yard. They equipped their large caravan in Cherchen, and
thence crossed Tibet from north to south.

At the same time we heard with dismay of Dutreuil de
Rhins's sad end. He was attacked and murdered in the
summer of the same year at Tam-buddha. The news was
brought by four of his men, who had returned to Kashgar.

Then came the Russian Christmas, twelve days after ours, and the consulate became busy and animated again. Cossack waits woke me up with plaintive songs on Christmas morning, and in the consul's house there were great festivities.

It was a great pleasure to me, on my return to Kashgar, to meet a fellow-countryman in the person of the missionary, Mr. Högberg, who had come there with his wife and little girl, a Swedish lady missionary, and a converted Persian, one Mirza Joseph. In the first place, coming there at all with two ladies had been an imprudence; for the Mohammedans could not be brought to believe other than that Mr. Högberg had two wives. But when, later on, Mirza Joseph married the Swedish lady missionary, the prospects of the mission in that town were destroyed for many a year to come; for in the eyes of the people of Kashgar Mirza Joseph was still a Mohammedan, and such, according to the Koran, are forbidden to choose their wives from among an unbelieving people. I gladly pass over the construction put upon this marriage and the unpleasantness it caused, but to many in Kashgar it afforded a painful illustration of the way in which missionary work is often mismanaged, and how lightly missionaries take the grave responsibilities which they have voluntarily incurred.

When Mr. Högberg found that it would be dangerous to begin an active propaganda at once, he wisely restricted his energies to the manufacture of various common household articles, such as the people of Kashgar would find useful, and such as they made themselves in a very primitive fashion. For instance, he constructed a capital machine for the treatment of raw silk, to say nothing of spinning-wheels, bellows, etc.—all extremely well made and a source of admiration and astonishment to the natives.

It was always a pleasure to meet him and his wife; for, like all the other missionaries with whom I have come in contact, they were kind and hospitable people, and looked at the future from the bright side. One cannot but respect people who labor for their faith in the light of honest conviction, despite the errors of judgment they may fall into.

CHAPTER XXXV

TO MARAL-BASHI

At eleven o'clock on the morning of February 17th, 1895, I, together with Islam Bai, the missionary Johannes, and Hashim Akhun, set off to travel eastward to Maral-bashi.

Our caravan consisted of two large arbas or arabas on high iron-rimmed wheels, each drawn by four horses. The straw roof of the first, in which I drove with Johannes, was lined on the inside with a kighiz (felt carpet), and the opening at the back was also closed with felts, to keep out the dust as much as possible. The bottom of the arba was covered with felts, cushions, and furs, to make a soft, comfortable seat; but over the bad roads the vehicle jolted to such an extent that we might as well have been on a rough sea, and the noise it made was deafening. The owner of the vehicles accompanied us; and each team had its own driver, with a long whip, who sometimes walked by the side, sometimes sat on one of the shafts, and whistled. In the other arba were Islam and Hashim, together with all my baggage; and our two dogs, Yolldash and Hamrah, were tied under my cart. The two arbas creaked and groaned along the highway, by the side of the west wall of the town, till we came to Kum-därvaseh (the Sand Gate), whence it was nearly two hours to Yanghi-shahr, the Chinese quarter of Kashgar. There we had a ridiculous adventure.

A Chinese soldier rushed out on us, stopped the horses, and declared that Hamrah was his dog. A large crowd quickly gathered round the carts. I gave orders to drive on. But the man shouted and gesticulated, and finally threw himself on the ground under the wheels, declaring that the dog was his, and demanding that he should be given up to

him. To pacify the fellow, I agreed that Hamrah should
be let loose and kept back. If he then followed the Chinaman, the dog was his; but if he followed us, he was ours.
No sooner was the dog untied, than he set off as fast as his
legs could carry him along the road, and disappeared in a
cloud of dust. The valorous Chinaman looked very much
crestfallen, and slunk away amid roars of laughter from the
crowd.

The day was dull and cold and disagreeable; the sky
gloomy; the air still, but filled with a thick dust-haze, which
obscured the view. A dense cloud of dust, caused by the
great amount of traffic which passed up and down, hung in
the willows that lined the road.

At this season of the year the Kizil-su had hardly any current; what little there was was frozen under the double
bridge. After passing it we turned to the east, and thus had
the river on our left. It was nine o'clock at night when we
reached the village of Yaman-yar (the Miserable Place), having driven the last two or three hours in pitch darkness.
We ourselves turned in in a rest-house, but the two *arabakeshes* (arba drivers) slept each in his own vehicle, so as to
protect my baggage against thieves.

On February 18th we drove through a number of small
villages as far as Faizabad (the Abode of Blessedness), the
chief town on the road between Maral-bashi and Kashgar.
It happened to be bazaar-day, and the narrow streets were
thronged with an unusually busy crowd, resplendent in color.
The inhabitants of the neighboring villages resort to the
place once a week to lay in a supply of provisions. On the
way thither we met or overtook numbers of wayfarers, some
on foot, some on horseback, conveying to market various
kinds of country produce, such as sheep, goats, poultry, fruit,
hay, fuel, wooden household utensils, etc. The long bazaar
echoed with the shouting and din of the multitude, as they
pushed their way up and down it, squabbling with the stall-
keepers, while the vendors vociferously cried up their wares.
Every now and again we met women, in large round caps
and white veils, Chinamen dressed from top to toe in blue,

donkey caravans slowly forcing their way through the throng.
The place was as lively as an ant-heap.

At each end of the bazaar there was a gate closed with
wooden doors; but the town was unwalled. Counting the
outlying farms, the place numbered between 700 and 800
houses or families. The greater part of the population were
Sarts (Jagatai Turks); though Dungans were also numerous,
and there were a few Chinese colonists. The town produced
rice, cotton, wheat, and other cereals, melons, apples, pears,
grapes, cucumbers, and various species of vegetables.

February 19th. After leaving Faizabad we entered a dead
level plain, grayish yellow, and of a monotonously barren appearance, covered with dry, finely powdered dust, which blew
up at the slightest breath of wind. The dust penetrated
everywhere, searching into our furs, into everything we had
inside the cart, and collected in thick layers on the roof. We
covered the cart with the tent-felts, to try and protect ourselves a little, letting the folds hang down in front as far as
was possible without shutting out the view. The dust was
so thick and deep that it was like driving over a vast feather-
bed, and the wheels of the arbas were almost sucked down
into it. Our progress, heavily laden as we were, was necessarily very slow. When walking, the whole foot sank into
the dust at every step, and the track you left behind you was
nothing more than a series of " caved in " dimples. The unfortunate horses strained at their traces with all their might,
till the sweat ran down their sides; they, too, were smothered
with dust, and were all of the same dirty-gray color. Three
of them were harnessed side by side in front and pulled by
means of long traces; the fourth was between the shafts.
The shaft-horse balanced the cart, which had to be properly
packed, so as not to press upon him with too great a strain.
If he stumbled, we might expect a shaking.

Shortly after noon we rested the horses for four hours at
the caravanserai of Yanghi-abad (the New Town). In the
court-yard there were a number of other arbas, loaded with
fuel from the nearest *yangal* (forest). Then we drove the
whole night, from five in the evening to five next morning,

through the pitchy darkness. The road was wretched in the extreme; the arbas lurched and swayed miserably. But, being softly bedded, we were soon rocked to sleep in our cushions, furs, and felts.

February 20th. During the night we managed to lose ourselves, for the arabakeshes seized the opportunity to take an occasional nap. After a good deal of hunting about, in the course of which we were overturned, we eventually got back into the right track. At the village of Kara-yulgun (the Black Tamarisk) we crossed the Kashgar-daria by a wooden bridge. Soon after that we passed through the village of Yaz-bulak (the Summer Spring), which derives its name from the fact that in summer the river overflows its banks and inundates large expanses of the low, flat country on each side of it. Even at that season of the year there were sheets of flood-water still remaining, although frozen over, and in them grew an abundance of kamish (reeds). During the warm season of the year the great road makes a considerable detour to avoid these inundated parts. About five o'clock we arrived at a place of this kind, where a frozen branch of the river stretched right across the road. We were going at full speed, till down went the leaders on the slippery ice. There was a tremendous crackling and splintering. The ice broke, and the wheels of the arba went through to the axle. There it stuck, as if fixed in a vice. All the horses were taken out and harnessed to the back of the vehicle; but it cost us an hour's hard tugging and hauling before we succeeded in righting the cart. After that we tried another place. My arba got over without mishap; but one wheel of the second cut like a sharp knife into the ice, making it hum and whine like a steam-saw. We were obliged to unload the baggage and carry it across. As the weather was cold and disagreeable, Islam Bai made me a huge fire on the bank, while the others were working away to get the arba across. At half past one in the morning we reached the village of Ordeklik (the Dutch Village), and there baited a while.

February 21st. Just beyond the station we entered a thin

poplar forest, which, however, gradually became thicker. The road was in some places rather deeply trenched in the loess, and often ran between low conical hills, crowned with tamarisk and other bushes. The court-yard of the rest-house of Tungan-masar (the Grave of the Dungan Saint) was surrounded by cart-sheds on piles, with a roof made of twigs and branches. The saint's grave was indicated merely by a pole hung with tughs or offerings of rags. We encamped for the night at Kara-kurchin, a good way from the river.

February 22d. We drove the whole day through a forest, which was said to be the haunt of tigers, wolves, foxes, deer, antelopes, and hares. The station of Chyrgeh was rather more than four miles from the Kashgar-daria.

These station-houses, with their stacks of hay and fuel, their sheds and carts, were often very picturesque and full of life — cattle, sheep, cats, dogs, and poultry. Eggs, milk, and bread were obtainable everywhere. The traffic was mostly carried on by means of donkey caravans, conveying cotton, tea, carpets, hides, etc., between Kashgar and Ak-su.

The distance between the two places is about 340 miles, and is divided into eighteen *örtäng* (*i.e.*, stages), each a day's march for an arba or a caravan. The Chinese mails, on the other hand, are carried in three and a half days, especially if they contain documents of importance. At every station there is a Chinese post-superintendent and three Mohammedan assistants, one of whom acts as servant to the Chinese postmaster, while the other two carry the mails. The mail-bags are only taken to the next station, whence they are immediately conveyed another stage by another man on horseback. Every station keeps ten horses, and the mails are carried quickly and punctually. Since the Chinese Government, at the suggestion of the British Government, introduced telegraphic communication, the old postal service no longer possesses the importance it used to have, particularly between Kashgar and Ak-su, and from thence to Kara-shahr, Urumchi, Khami, Su-chow (Su-chau), and Liang-chow-fu. It was strange to see telegraph-posts so far in the interior of

y were put in as straight a line as possible and
llous care. When the Chinese were working at
ey were accompanied by an army of Sarts, with ar-
) ovided them with victuals and tools.

23d. The forest ceased some distance before
;aral-bashi. From the point where it did cease
. was bad, and the country bare and uninteresting.
ssed the Kashgar-daria a second time, at a spot where
as dry, by a small wooden bridge, and drove past the
ese fort of Maral-bashi, with its battlemented walls of
made bricks and small towers at the corners. It was
to have a garrison of 300 men. The chief bazaar of the
. which ran from west to east, was very long, very
;ht, and very dirty, and was lined with the shops of the
se and Sarts. Off it opened the gates of the caravan-
. We were allowed a couple of rooms for ourselves
ur paraphernalia in a miserable hovel.

ruary 24th. Maral-bashi, together with the neighbor-
shlaks, was said to amount to a thousand households.
town is also called Dolon, and in certain parts of East
Turkestan—for instance, in Yarkand—this name is the only
one in use. The word *dolon* signifies " a wild wooded tract,
without villages," and is used here in contrast with Kashgar
and Ak-su. The inhabitants, who are proud of being called
Dolons, have the same language, customs, and religion as the
rest of the population of East Turkestan, but seem to be
somewhat differentiated from them, in that they approach
more nearly to the pure Uigur type.

I took a walk through the little town, which is not of
much importance, though, like Faizabad, it has two small
gates, here also situated at each end of the bazaar, and called
Kashgar-därvaseh and Ak-su-därvaseh (the Kashgar gate and
the Ak-su gate). There were two principal mosques, called
Dolon and Mussafir, with simple façades of gray clay, and
wooded balconies inside the court-yard. The former was
situated near the Ak-su-därvaseh, and outside of it there was
a burial-ground (*gabristan*). Here we came upon the Kashgar-daria, containing a little water almost stagnant ; and from

it ran ariks (irrigation canals), which were used for driving
mills situated near the banks.

We went to look at one of these mills; it was simply a
thatched shed resting on piles. The corn was ground in a
corner of the shed between horizontal millstones, brought
from Kashgar at the cost of 100 tengeh (22s. 6d.) each. They
can be used for about five years before being worn out. Just
at that time maize (*konak*) and wheat (*bogdai*) were being
ground. The miller's perquisite was one-sixteenth of the
flour ground, and he could grind from 32 to 40 chärecks
(= 16 jings or 24 lbs. avoirdupois) in a day. In another place
rice was being husked. Raw rice before being husked (paddy)
is called *shall;* whereas pure white rice, freed from its awns,
is called *grytch.* The husking-mill consisted of a water-wheel
running on a horizontal crank and driving a couple of wooden
hammers, which fitted into two hollow slanting grooves, in
which the raw rice, or paddy, was poured. The rice was
freed from its husks and awns by repeated beatings of the
hammers, the refuse being afterwards sifted away. Every
sackful of rice was put three times through the mill. For
this the miller got a tithe of the husked rice, and he could
finish 15 chärecks in the day. As a chäreck of rice costs
4 tengeh in Maral-bashi, the man thus earned 6 tengeh (1s.
3d.) a day. Large quantities of rice, maize, and wheat are
grown in the neighborhood.

In the morning a Chinese official and four begs came to
welcome me in the name of the amban (governor of the town).
The begs were extremely civil and communicative, and considered that my plan of crossing the Takla-makan Desert was
feasible. They told me that there once existed a large town
called Takla-makan in the desert midway between the Yarkand-daria and the Khotan-daria, but for ages it had been
buried in the sand. The whole of the desert was now known
by this name, although it was sometimes shortened to Takan.
They reported further that the interior of the desert was
under the ban of *telesmat* (an Arabic word, meaning "witchcraft," "supernatural powers"); and that there were towers
and walls and houses, and heaps of gold tacks and silver

jambaus (tack and jambau being Chinese coins). If a man
went there with a caravan and loaded his camels with gold,
he would never get out of the desert again, but be kept there
by the spirits.   In that case there was only one way by which
he could save his life, and that was by throwing away the
treasure.   The begs thought that if I followed the Masar-tagh
as far as I possibly could, and took a supply of water with me,
it would be possible to cross the desert.   But under no circumstances could horses cross it; they would certainly die.

CHAPTER XXXVI

AN EXCURSION TO THE MASAR-TAGH

FEBRUARY 25TH. From Maral-bashi I made an excursion
to the Masar-tagh, a mountain-range a day's journey to the
east of the town. Only one driver, Islam Bai, and Yolldash
were of the party, and the lightly laden arba carried us swiftly
along the road. After a couple of hours' driving the mountain
became visible through the dust-haze, as a somewhat darker
background, with a serrated crest. We turned off to the
right from the high-road to Ak-su and struck across a hard,
barren steppe with thinly scattered tussocks of grass. Then
we passed between two spurs of the mountain. The one on
the right, which was larger than the other, was a wild, rugged
highland region, exhibiting proofs of severe weathering and
of the erosive power of the wind. Its rock was a species of
light-green crystalline schist. At the base of the mountains
there was sufficient grass for a few small kishlaks (winter
pasture).

Not far from the northeast foot of the mountain stood the
Ullug-masar (the Great Tomb), surrounded by a gray wall of
sun-dried bricks. The first place we entered was a large
square court-yard, in which a ring of long sticks were thrust
into the ground round a bush. Both sticks and bush were
hung with flags and pennons, some white with red edges,
others entirely red or blue; others again were three-tongued,
with vandyked edges, and so on. Thence a door led into a
khanekah, or prayer-house, the floor of which was covered
with carpets. At the far end there was an open wood-work
screen, and behind it the tomb of the saint, marked by an
ordinary tombstone, in a square, dark room decorated with
flags, tughs (rags), deers' antlers, and the horns of wild sheep.

The shrine, together with its *gumbez* (dome), was built of kiln-burnt bricks, and was visited every Friday by pilgrims from the neighborhood. In the outer court there was an *ashbazkhaneh*, or kitchen, where they cook their food.

We took up our quarters in a hospitable house in the kishlak of Masar-alldi (in front of the Saint's Tomb), and were at once visited by the dignitaries of the place. I got a good deal of valuable information out of them. For instance, they told me that in that part of its course the Yarkand-daria was divided into two arms, and went on to describe three very large lakes situated in the neighborhood, which not only increased in size when the river was in flood, but also abounded in fish. I was especially interested to learn that the Masar-tagh continued in a southeasterly direction through the desert as far as the Khotan-daria, though the information seemed, on the whole, to be doubtful, as none of the men had themselves seen how far the mountains extended into the desert.

Some of them called the desert Dekken-dekka, because a thousand and one towns are said to be buried under its wastes of sand. Moreover, vast stores of silver and gold might be found in them. It was possible to reach them with camels; and probably water would be found in the depressions.

February 26th. It was now my object to obtain a general idea of the Masar-tagh. Accordingly we took a guide and drove along their eastern foot in the arba, having on our left a marsh shut in by barren sand-hills. After a three hours' drive we reached the Kodai-daria (the Swan River), the northern branch of the Yarkand-daria, a good hundred and twenty yards broad, and covered with soft ice, which bore men on foot but broke under the weight of the arba. The boat which the Dolons used when the river was high was frozen fast in the ice. In summer, when the river is in flood, enormous volumes of water flow through both branches, causing them to overflow and unite into a lake-like expansion, while at the same time considerable stretches of the woods on the right bank of the river become half inundated.

In the beginning of April a large number of Dolons resort thither with their flocks, and there spend half the year in the woods, dwelling in reed huts erected in situations where they are safe from inundation. These summer camps, some of which still remained *in situ*, are called *yeyliks*. Thus the Dolons may be said to be semi-nomads.

When I could get no farther with the arba, I mounted a horse, and taking one man with me, rode over the Masar-tagh by a very difficult pass, and then proceeded along the western foot of the mountain, till I came to the reedy Shor-kul (Salt Lake), which, however, contained perfectly fresh water and swarmed with wild geese. The mountain was built of a species of coarse-grained eruptive rock, encumbered all along its base with fallen fragments of stone, which were polished and carved by the wind into grotesque, saucer-like hollows, overtopped by rounded masses poised on narrow stalks or pedestals. The Shor-kul, which lay parallel to the left bank of the Yarkand-daria, was a typical fluvial lagoon. It owed its origin to the gradual deposit of sediment in the bed of the river, lifting the current above its banks until it overflowed on to the lower lying country on each side.

We returned to camp by way of the Ullug-masar. The Masar-tagh we found consists of crystalline schist, porphyry, and a species of rock resembling sienite. It stands like a ruin in the angle between the Kashgar-daria and the Yarkand-daria, and is itself looked upon as a masar or saint's tomb.

February 27th. We now returned, in a north-northeast direction, to the great Ak-su road, which we struck at Charbagh (the Four Gardens). Once more we crossed the Kashgar-daria, or rather the numerous branches into which it was there divided, each spanned by a small wooden bridge. Soon after that the hill of Akhur-masar-tagh loomed out through the dust-laden atmosphere, one of its projecting spurs crowned with the masar Hazrett-Ali. There had been some wind in the morning from the east; but towards mid-day it came on to blow rather strongly, enveloping everything in an impenetrable dust-haze, while clouds of dust hung along the road in

the track of our arbas.   Every now and then we caught a
glimpse of trees and bushes, of houses and villages, looking
as though they were covered with dirty water.   There were
but few travellers on the road in such weather.

Mount Tumshuk, which sent out four spurs towards the
north, now came into view.   On its steep slopes, built up like
the seats in an amphitheatre, but clinging to the naked rock
like swallows' nests, were a number of ruined houses and
walls, ascending as high as 60 to 80 feet above the level
ground.   Two different periods of architecture were plainly
distinguishable.   The houses of the older period were built
of burned bricks, while those of the later period were constructed of sun-dried clay.   On the level ground, at the foot
of the mountain, there were also a great many ruins.   All
these are the remains of an old city, which was no doubt protected by a citadel crowning the mountain behind.   The
region is now sterile and uninhabited; changes in the channel of the Kashgar-daria having in all probability led to the
desertion of the town.

February 28th.   One hour northwest of the station Tumshuk lay another collection of ruins known as Eski-shahr (the
Old City).   These, too, I visited.   The best-preserved building
was a square structure, each of its sides ten yards long, built
true to the four cardinal points, and with a doorway to the
east.   It was constructed of hard-burned bricks, and had probably been a mosque.   The corners in the interior were decorated with friezes in relief.   The doorway, too, was embellished with ornamental brick-work, and perhaps in its day had
been covered with tiles.

There was a hill in the vicinity, from which two parallel
ridges projected towards the northwest; there we discovered
the ruins of former stone walls.   The style of architecture
was Mohammedan; accordingly these archæological remains
could not date back more than 1150 years.

The storm still continued.   About mid-day the sun was
darkened, as when a thunder-storm threatens; sand and dust
whirled along the ground, and rose in spinning columns into
the air.   Thinking discretion the better part of valor, we

hastened to return to the rest-house at Char-bagh, and a disagreeable drive it was. Every breath we inhaled was charged
with choking dust; even the horses in front of the arba disappeared from view every now and then, so that, when we
reached our destination, we were absolutely smothered with
dust.

March 1st. The storm subsided, and we had good weather
for the return journey to Maral-bashi, where to my delight I
found letters awaiting me from home. The post-jighit
(courier) who brought them was a capable fellow, an old Sart
from Osh in Fergana, whom I had seen before on the Murghab. I took him for the time being into my service.

An old man of eighty, who heard that we were going to
try and cross the Takla-makan Desert, came to my house,
and told me that in his youth he had known a man who,
while going from Khotan to Ak-su, lost his way in the desert, and came to an ancient city, where he found innumerable
pairs of Chinese shoes in the houses; but directly he touched
them they crumbled to dust. Another man started out into
the desert from Aksak-maral, and by pure chance stumbled
upon a town, amid the ruins of which he unearthed a quantity
of gold and silver *jambaus* (Chinese coins). He filled his
pockets with them, as well as a sack he had with him. As
he was going off with his booty a pack of wild-cats rushed
out upon him and frightened him so much that he threw everything away and took to flight; when, sometime afterwards,
he plucked up courage to venture his luck a second time, he
was unable to find the place again. The mysterious town
was completely swallowed up in the sand.

A mollah from Khotan was more successful. He had fall-
en into debt, and went into the desert to die. But instead of
dying he discovered a treasure of gold and silver, and was
now an exceedingly rich man. The number of those who
had gone into the desert with the same design, and never returned, was legion. The old man solemnly assured me that
the evil spirits must be exorcised before the hidden treasure
could be sought for with any likelihood of success. The
spirits bewitch the unhappy beings who venture thither, so

that they become confused and bewildered, and without knowing what they are doing they go round and round in a circle,
retracing their own footsteps, and go and go until they fall
down from sheer exhaustion, and die of thirst.

There is a tribe of ne'er-do-weels hanging about the places
round the outskirts of the desert, who firmly believe that
sooner or later they will discover the hidden treasures which

A DERVISH FROM EAST TURKESTAN

lie buried among its sands. These gold-seekers are always
looked at askance by their neighbors, and should be avoided.
They will not work; but live on the hope of making their
fortune at a single stroke. They are parasites, a burden
upon their neighbors, who in their "spare time" occupy
themselves with thieving and robbery. For, needless to say,
they never find any hidden treasure.

But whence do all these legends come? How explain all
these confirmatory accounts of buried cities, and these vary-

ing traditions of the great city of former times, Takla-makan, which was swallowed up in the sand? Is it merely by accident that these legends fly from mouth to mouth in Khotan and Yarkand, Maral-bashi and Ak-su? Is it merely by accident that this ancient city is always known by the same name? Is it merely for the sake of making themselves interesting that the natives describe these deserted houses in detail, which they say they have seen, and where, they say, in former times there were great forests, the home of the musk-deer and other big game? No, it *cannot* be by chance; these legends *must* have a foundation and a cause. Deep under them there must verily be some reality for them to rest on; they ought not to be scorned, they ought not to be despised and neglected.

To these fabulous, these adventurous tales I gave the eager ear of a child. Every day added to the allurements of the perilous journey I contemplated. I was fascinated by all these romantic legends. I became blind to danger. I had fallen under the spell of the weird witchery of the desert. Even the sand-storms, those terrible scourges of Central Asia, which have their cradle in the heart of that sand-heated furnace — even they were in my eyes beautiful, even they enchanted me. Over there, on the verge of the horizon, were the noble, rounded forms of the sand - dunes, which I never grew tired of watching; and beyond them, amid the grave-like silence, stretched the unknown, enchanted land, of whose existence not even the oldest records make mention, the land that I was going to be the first to tread.

March 2d. Having paid and settled up, we left Maral-bashi, and drove southwest towards the village of Khamal (the Wind), situated on the left bank of the Yarkand-daria. The road led across a slightly broken steppe country, with scanty herbage, tussocks of grass, and bushes. Khamal was inhabited by thirty families, who cultivated wheat and maize; their fields being irrigated by an *arik* (irrigation canal) led from the river. During the summer, when the river is in flood, it overflows and inundates wide tracts along the banks. The spring floods, caused by the melting of the winter ice,

I.—29

likewise bring down considerable quantities of water, as we witnessed every day.

March 3d. Through jungle and reeds, through poplar groves, across small belts of sand, and through marshes, where the ice was just on the point of breaking up, our creaking carts ploughed their way along the western bank of the Yarkand-daria. Wild boar abound in the jungle, and do much damage to the crops in the villages around. To prevent this the natives put up sheds here and there about the fields; and there they live and keep watch when harvest time is approaching.

The amban (Chinese governor) of Maral-bashi had given orders beforehand to the *on-bashis* (chiefs over ten men) of the various villages that they should receive me in a fitting manner; and as a matter of fact his words were carried out to the letter. At every place we stopped at we found rooms ready prepared, and everything we needed in the way of food for ourselves and for our animals was provided for us.

Aksak-maral (the Lame Deer), where we made our next stop, consisted of thirty houses, most of them occupied by Dolons, who reared cattle and sheep, and grew wheat and maize. The winters there are cold, but the snowfall is inconsiderable. The springs are windy. The small amount of rain which falls generally comes in the autumn, often to the detriment of the crops.

During the night, when the air was still and cold, and the currents set up by the active radiation of the daytime ceased to rise, the atmosphere generally cleared. So it did to-day. During the morning and afternoon the sky was an ashen gray; but in the evening the moon and stars shone fairly bright in the zenith, although near the horizon they were swallowed up in the dust-haze. In the morning again the blue sky was only visible at the zenith, but gradually merged into gray towards the horizon.

March 4th. Our day's march took us across a very extensive marsh, through which the Chinese authorities had built a road some seven years previously. As it was built to withstand the encroachment of the floods, it was constructed of piles, stakes, fascines, and earth. It wound through the marsh like a narrow ribbon; and in certain places was carried over bridges, so as not to check the free flow of the water. In spite of this, however, the road is frequently inundated during the months of June, July, and August, compelling travellers to go all the way round by Kashgar. The marsh is in reality a low-lying lagoon, and is said to have existed from time immemorial. It is called Cheraylik-togaktasi-köll (the Fair Poplar Lake).

Ala-ayghir (the Dappled Mare) was the name of the next station, a kishlak of twenty-five Dolon families. The same conditions of life and climate obtained there as in the foregoing villages. There, too, east winds prevail during the spring. Between Maral-bashi and Yarkand there was Chinese postal communication, as well as in general a very lively traffic, carried on chiefly by means of arbas (carts) and donkey caravans. Camels are very seldom used.

Ala-ayghir was situated rather more than half a mile from the Yarkand-daria; but when the river rises in the summer, the water reaches the village. Two years ago even the winter shore-line ran just below the village; but I was told that, more particularly during the last few years, the river has shown a tendency to shift its channel somewhat to the east.

March 5th. We drove ten hours to-day, often over heavy roads, soaked in water, so that the wheels of the arbas cut deeply into the sandy mud. We passed three villages; and at the fourth, Meynet, we turned in at an unusually comfortable caravanserai. On the wall was posted a large yellow placard, in Chinese and Turki characters, conveying the following paternal announcement: "Whereas I (the Emperor of China) have heard that certain begs have imposed unlawful taxes on my people, and have furthermore monopolized their rights of fishing, it is my will and desire that all such infringements be forthwith reported to the nearest Dao Tai, and if the latter will not listen to and remedy the same, the people shall address themselves direct to me.—Kwang Tsü." Poor Kwang Tsü! He has never even heard of the village of Meynet, and what cares he for the fishing in the Yarkand-

Meynet boasts of fifteen Dolon households. The
:r-forest was at that point only a few miles broad,
in thinned and died away in the desert. Wolves
ommon, and preyed upon the flocks. On the other
e have been no tigers for many years, except that
)f years ago a single tiger showed himself at Ala-

rch 6th. The first few miles ran through luxuriant
r woods, until we came to the river. It was there di-
d into two principal branches and many smaller ones,
sheeted with soft ice, except that there was a belt of open
r close under the banks.

ir stopping-place for the day was Lailik (the Dirty Clay-
lace), the last village in this direction subject to the
in of Maral-bashi. On the south it adjoined the Yar-
district. Its population consisted of fifteen Dolon fami-
Fishing was carried on in the river, the maximum
t of which at the season of high flood was said to ap-
mate the added statures of five men. The velocity of
.... current was pretty considerable, though not so swift as
the pace of a mounted man. It takes a man on horseback
four days to reach Maral-bashi, whereas the river wants as
much as ten days to do the distance.

March 7th. Lailik was for some time our headquarters,
as considerable preparations had to be made for our expedition across the desert. The most important difficulty was
the procuring of camels. I had been rather misled by the
merchants in Kashgar, who told me that Maral-bashi was the
best place to get good camels. We hardly ever saw a camel
there. I had no resource except to try and procure some
from Kashgar. This mission I intrusted to Mohammed Yakub, who, in any case, had to go there to post letters and
bring others back. A fairly good camel cost 500 tengeh
(£5 15s.) in Yarkand; but in Kashgar only 400 (£4 12s.).
Yakub took with him letters to Consul Petrovsky, and to the
aksakal, asking them to assist him in the transactions, and
within ten days he was to be back again, bringing with him
eight fine camels and two men.

Our arabakeshes were now dismissed, being paid 200 tengehs (£2 6s.) for the journey from Maral-bashi. They thought of going to Yarkand to try to get work there, and meant to fill their two arbas with firewood from the last patch of forest along the road. A donkey-load of firewood was worth three tengeh (8d.) in Yarkand, and an arba would hold ten such loads, so that the men hoped to make an extra sixty tengeh (13s. 9d.) by the return journey.

Islam Bai was despatched to Yarkand on horseback to buy several things that were required for our desert expedition—for example, iron tanks for water, bread, rice, ropes, and a number of tools, such as spades and hatchets. I also instructed him to bring a supply of sesame oil (*yagh*), and the chaff from the crushed seeds of the same plant (*kynchyr*), etc. The oil was intended to feed the camels on in the desert. A *jing* (not quite one pint) of oil will sustain a camel for a month without other food; though it is always a great advantage to find supplies of herbage during the march, so that the animals may to some extent freshen up and recover from their exertions. In March and April they cannot well go longer than three days without water; but in the winter, and on level ground, they can last out six or seven days if necessary.

My party had vanished like chaff before the wind. The missionary Johannes was the only one now left.

March 8th. I walked through the young forest as far as the river in order to take some observations; and found a ferry-boat, which was punted across in seventy seconds, and which could carry seven horses, six donkeys, and twenty men at once.

The two banks were very dissimilar. The left bank was low, flat, and bare, with many sand-banks. The right bank was worn perpendicularly by the current, which ran immediately underneath it; and was luxuriantly wooded with poplars and tamarisks, whose roots stuck out of the fine alluvial soil of which it was composed. The river thus showed a marked tendency to press against the right bank, and eat it away. But the current meandered so much that in other places it was the left bank which was eroded, although on the whole to a much less extent than the right bank.

The forest on the right bank was six feet above the level of the stream; nevertheless it is overflowed in July. The breadth of the river was 200 feet, the maximum depth six feet three inches, velocity of the current two feet eight inches in the second, and its volume 3060 cubic feet in the second—a volume which must be inconsiderable when compared with the masses of water which in the height of summer pour down towards Lop-nor. The temperature was 46.9° Fahr. (8.3° C.), and there was no ice anywhere. The water was, however, only transparent to a depth of barely two inches.

CHAPTER XXXVII

THE SHRINE OF ORDAN PADSHAH

MARCH 9TH. With the view of employing profitably the time while my men were away, I decided to visit the shrine of Ordan Padshah in the desert, two days' journey west of Lailik. I got hold of a man who knew the way; and at eight in the morning we were in the saddle, riding at a smart pace west-nor'west, first through forest, which gradually passed over into brushwood, then across steppe-land, which in its turn gave place to the desert. The sand, however, was not deep, nor the sand-dunes high; but the latter had their steep slopes facing westward, indicating the prevalence of easterly winds at that season of the year.

It was an interesting excursion; for the region had never before been visited by a European. After leaving the large village of Mogal (Mongol) on our right, we came to Terem, where the beg placed his house at my disposal. I required little room, however, for I had nothing with me beyond the barest necessaries, and only had two horses.

The villages of Terem and Mogal consisted of 200 households each, and were governed by a beg and eight on-bashis; though a Chinese tax-collector also lived there. The word Terem means a "cultivated place," and the inhabitants told me that in point of fact Terem was in former times famous for its good harvests and abundant water-supply. People came thither from all parts to buy corn. The change which has taken place must unquestionably be attributed to the alteration in the course of the river. The place now gets its water-supply from the great irrigation canal of Khan-arik, which issues like a main artery from the Ghez-daria, and, passing through the villages of Tazgun and Khan-arik, stretches its last net-work of arterioles as far as Terem. But the supply is insufficient, irregular, and uncertain, and consequently the harvest often fails.

In the case of the Khan-arik there exist special regulations, made by the Chinese authorities, by which each village is only allowed the use of the water for a certain time. Terem had now been furnished with water for three months past; but in twelve days' time the supply would be cut off, and for four whole months not a drop would reach it from the irrigation system. The inhabitants would be obliged to content themselves with what their wells would yield. Late in the summer they would again have the use of the life-giving waters for the space of thirty-four days.

On March 10th we left Terem, and rode in a westerly direction through steppe, desert, and marsh. Here I made the important discovery of four ancient river-beds, now, however, dried up, but still very plainly marked, each from one hundred to a hundred and ten yards broad, and running towards the north-northeast. They could not possibly be anything but deserted channels of the Yarkand-daria. In Bai-khan-köll (the Rich Khan's Lake), a salt and shallow sheet of water, with marshy shores overgrown with kamish (reeds), we nearly stuck fast altogether. The lake is largest in winter, when it becomes frozen; but in summer the water evaporates almost entirely, despite the fact that the lake receives the overflow of the ariks of the Yanghi-hissar. In the district of Kizil-ji we crossed by a bridge another prolongation of the ariks of the Yanghi-hissar. In that neighborhood there was a saint's tomb called Kizil-ji-khanem, an interesting fact, for the name occurs in the map of Edrisi, the famous Arab geographer of the twelfth century.

At the point where the desert proper began, and where the sand-dunes were about twenty-five feet high, stood the insignificant village of Lengher (the Rest-Station). There a dervish resides during the great annual religious festivals, to take charge of the pilgrims' horses, which are left to graze on the grass and kamish which abound in the neighborhood. He also sells maize to the pilgrims, and supplies the shrine with fuel. Beyond this place the sand-dunes were fairly continuous; but as they ran south-southwest to north-north-east, and we were riding south-southwest, we were generally able to take advantage of the intervening hollows, where the soil was hard clay.

An hour's ride short of the shrine we caught up a party of forty-five pilgrims—men, women, and children—who were on their way thither from Lengher to pray at the tomb of the saint. Fifteen of the men carried tughs—*i.e.*, long sticks with white and colored pennons fluttering from the ends. At the head of the procession rode a flute-player, and on each side of him was a man banging away at a drum as hard as hands and arms could move. Every now and then the whole concourse shouted "Allah!" at the full pitch of their voices. When they drew near to the shrine they greeted the sheikh who had charge of it with wild howls of "Allah! Allah!" while the standard-bearers performed a religious dance.

It was dusk when we reached the khanekah (prayer-house), adjoining the shrine, and standing in a village of twenty-five households. Most of the people only sojourn there for a short time; but four families remain the whole year round to take care of the saint's tomb. The principal sheikh, who also has control over the Hazrett Begım's tomb, was for the time being absent at Yanghi-hissar. He constantly travels backward and forward between the two shrines, spending some time at each, and for this reason has a wife at each. One of the resident custodians informed me that every winter 10,000 to 12,000 pilgrims visit the shrine of Ordan Padshah; but in the summer there are usually not more than 5000, as at that season of the year the heat and scarcity of water render travelling irksome. The pilgrims who came from Lengher at the same time we did brought with them two sacks of maize as an offering, and placed them in a bronze vessel in the prayer-house. Then they made a thorough good meal off it, in which they were joined by the custodians of the shrine. The tribute was, however, a prayer for a fruitful year.

There were eight houses in the village, standing in two

rows, with a street running east to west between them. To
the north two or three more houses were half buried in the
sand-dunes, which were threatening the village itself.

I was assigned an exceptionally comfortable room in the
upper story of the guest - house, with latticed windows, looking out upon the dreary desert on the south. In spite of the
hideous din that was kept up in the street below all night
long, by the pilgrims marching in procession backward and
forward, playing flutes, singing, beating drums, and waving
flags, I slept soundly till morning. When I awoke I found a
furious sand-storm blowing, and clouds of dust whirling in
through the latticed window and dancing in giddy eddies
round the room.

March 11th was devoted to making a nearer acquaintance
with this curious place of pilgrimage, which has only been
visited once before by a European—namely, by Major Bellew,
in April, 1874. He reached it from the west, I approached it
from the east; our investigations, therefore, supplement each
other.

In addition to the principal sheikh, the permanent person-
nel of the shrine consisted of an imam or reader of prayers,
a *mutevelleh* or steward of the shrine properties, and twenty
sufchs or men-servants. All these are fed and maintained
at the exclusive expense of the pilgrims. These, according
to their circumstances, bring horses, sheep, cows, poultry,
eggs, seed-corn, fruit, khalats (coats), and other useful articles.
With the exception of the live-stock, everything goes into the
largest of the metal vessels set apart for receiving the pilgrims'
offerings. Of these there were five, all built into a brick fire-
place, in the walls of the *kazan-khaneh*, or "caldron-house."
The Altyn-dash, or Gold Stone, as the largest of the five vessels is called, was about five feet in diameter, and was made
of bronze; it is said to date back eight hundred years, from
the time of Ordan Padshah himself. Next came a handsome
copper vessel, 3 feet 4 inches in diameter, a present to the
shrine by Yakub Beg of Kashgar, who himself made three
pilgrimages to the place. The other three were smaller and
of various sizes. When there is a great influx of pilgrims,

the custodians of the shrine make *ash* or pillau (mutton with rice and spices) in the biggest vessel for everybody at once. At other times the smaller vessels are used. according to the number of the pilgrims. The "caldron-house" was built two years ago. The old one is now half buried in a sand-dune, which already threatens to enclose the new structure within the horns of its hollow crescent. The winds which determine the movement of the sand-dunes in this region blow from the northwest.

On the windward side of the nearest sand-dune was a half-buried grave-mound decorated with tughs. It contained the dust of Shah Yakub Sheikh, and was said to be 710 years old. According to the direction in which the dunes are at present moving, the tomb will soon be entirely exposed again. The maximum breadth of the sand-dune was nearly 400 feet, and its height about 16 feet, so that it overtopped the roofs of the houses. The little village stands in the clay hollow between the leeward side of this sand-dune and its nearest neighbor on the southeast, on a space some 170 yards broad. In violent storms the sand is blown right across from the one dune to the other.

The khanekah, or prayer-house, contained an oratory, and a balcony, with an eastern aspect, supported by sixteen pillars. Immediately north of the village the fresh-water spring, Chevätt-khanem, bubbled up out of the ground, filling a round pool surrounded by a wooden railing. The water was tolerably clear. considering that the sand was only cleaned out once a year; but it issues so slowly that it is insufficient on festival days. On such occasions the pilgrims have to fall back upon another spring, Cheshmeh (a Persian word meaning "a spring"), which yields saltish water, and is ten minutes farther away.

At a distance of twenty minutes towards the northwest stood the saint's masar or tomb, a truly extraordinary structure. It was composed of a sheaf of two or three thousand tughs, each with a pennon attached, stacked up in the shape of an Eifel tower. Standing forty feet high, on the top of a sand-dune, it was visible to a great distance. An attempt has

m le to render the dune stationary by planting sheaves
     (reeds) in the sand round the masar; and the expe-
t has been to some extent successful, for the portion of
sand-dune upon which the masar stands projects so far
ards the northwest — *i.e.,* to windward — that it is now
eatened by the dune which comes next on that side.

e sand-storm raged with undiminished violence, so that
hundreds and hundreds of pennons flapped and fluttered
ously, with an endless series of small reports.   These
is are brought there year after year by the pilgrims, so
the curious sheaf goes on increasing in size.   To prevent
whole structure from being blown over, the sticks are
red at the top by a couple of square wooden cross-pieces.
number of smaller bundles of tughs form a fence, thirty
s square, all round the tomb.

he imam told me something of the story of Ordan Pad-
. His real name was Sultan Ali Arslan Khan; and
: hundred years ago he was at enmity with the tribe of
arashid-Noktarashid, among whom he was endeavoring
propagate Islam.   In the midst of the strife he was overtaken by a kara-buran, or black sand-storm, from Kharesm
(Khiva), which buried him and the whole of his army.   Hence
to this day he plays an important part in the martyrology of
East Turkestan.

In the afternoon we rode through the villages of Dost-
bulak (the Friend's Spring), Khorasan, and Psänn due north
to Achick (Bitter), the yuz-bashi of which received me in a
friendly spirit, telling me a good deal about the climate and
the roads in the vicinity.

March 12th.   Having an eight hours' ride to Terem, we
started early, and rode through a strong nor'westerly gale.
The district between the two places was chiefly of a marshy,
steppe-like character, with occasional thickets of tamarisk,
thistles, and tussocks of grass; which, when they get thoroughly dry, are often uprooted, curled into balls by the wind,
and so swept along the ground.   The surface was covered
with fine loose dust, which was driven up like smoke before
the gale.   We often rode through swamps of stagnant arik

water, and were sometimes constrained to make détours to avoid the more sodden places. In so doing we managed to lose our way several times, but were put right by shepherds, who with the help of their dogs were guarding their flocks of goats and sheep.

Not a glint of the sun was discernible. The sky was a ruddy yellow, sometimes turning to murky gray. When we eventually reached Terem, by way of Kötteklik (the Dead Forest), both horses and riders were smothered in ash-gray dust.

March 13th. The gale still continued unabated. To-day, however, the wind veered round to the north and northeast. It was thus a three days' storm, what the natives call a *sarik-buran* (yellow storm), because it just tinges the sky yellow.

From Terem we rode southeast to the village of Terek-lengher (the Poplar Rest-house), on the Yarkand-daria. It was nine hours' smart riding through a country known by the name of *ala-kum—i.e.,* alternating steppe and sandy desert. In the vicinity of the river we crossed a bridge spanning the Khandi-arik, an important irrigation canal, which takes its rise a day's journey above Yarkand, and supplies a great number of villages with water. Nine years ago it was repaired by command of the Chinese, a task which is said to have given employment to eleven thousand men. This vast undertaking seems to have been considerably simplified in the first instance by the utilization for long distances of a former bed of the Yarkand-daria. Between the canal and the river several former river levels were clearly distinguishable. The villagers declared that at one time the river flowed close past their village, although it was now situated two miles from it. They expressed themselves as well satisfied with this caprice of nature, for it had allowed them to extend their fields over the alluvial soil of the former river-bed.

March 14th. The wind subsided a little to-day, and shifted right round to the east. I noticed that the storms often began in the west, and later veered round by way of north to the east. We kept along the river in a northeasterly direction till we reached Lailik. For some distance the river-bank was very much eroded, rising like a vertical wall to the height of 13 feet, and

disclosing a horizontal stratum of fine yellow soil, sand and
alluvium, riddled by numberless roots, which sometimes hung
swaying over the water. The first half of the journey took
us through a series of villages; then the country was barren
until we reached the woods near Lailik, where we arrived
just after mid-day, and found everything in good order under
Johannes' care.

CHAPTER XXXVIII

ON THE THRESHOLD OF THE DESERT

MARCH 15TH. This day marked the beginning of a long period of waiting, extremely trying to my patience. Day after day went by, but no camels arrived. I would gladly pass over these twenty-five days altogether, but find in my note-book certain incidents and facts that are not without interest. I made it my business to gather all the information I could about the desert that stretched to the east. For instance, to-day I heard of two men who, a few years ago, started from the village of Yantak, on the right bank of the Yarkand-daria, taking with them provisions for twelve days. After three days they reached a disused river-bed, deep and stony, with a wooden bridge across it, but so dilapidated that it would not bear them to walk on it. They thought at first of following up the course of the river; but as they found no water in that direction they retraced their steps, and went down stream, and there discovered quantities of nephrite or jade. After another seven days they reached the mountain of Masar - tagh, where they found kamish and obtained water by digging.

Shahr-i-katak, as a rule curtailed to Ktak, is another legendary town which haunts the same part of the great Asiatic desert. Its reputed situation varies a good deal. At Lailik I was told it lay five potais (twelve and a half miles) west of the village, and that many years ago a man found the ruins there; but when it was searched for afterwards, it could not be found. The people say that none but Allah can lead a man thither. No matter how perseveringly he may search himself, he will never find the place unless God wills he should. I heard also that twelve men were just about to set out from Yarkand into the desert in quest of gold. They generally choose the spring for these expeditions, as they say that the sand-storms are then more likely to expose the gold. A month previously a man had gone into the desert, and had not returned. At Yarkand the people believe that the traveller through the desert often hears voices calling him by name, but that if he follows them he goes astray and dies of thirst. It is interesting to compare this with what Marco Polo has to say of the great Lop desert: " But there is a marvellous thing related of this desert, which is, that when travellers are on the move by night, and one of them chances to lag behind, or to fall asleep, or the like, when he tries to gain his company again he will hear spirits talking, and will suppose them to be his comrades. Sometimes the spirits will call him by name, and thus shall a traveller ofttimes be led astray, so that he never finds his party. And in this way many have perished."*

To-day Islam Bai returned from Yarkand, bringing with him four *chelleks* (iron tanks) for water, six *tulums* (goat-skins for water), sesame oil and seed-husks for the camels, petroleum, bread, *talkan* (toasted flour), *gauman* (macaroni), honey, sacks, spades, whips, bridle-bits, bowls, cups, and divers other requisites.

March 18th. During these days I had frequent opportunity of observing how closely the radiation was dependent upon the amount of dust with which the atmosphere was charged. When the atmosphere was nearly clear, the radiation went up to $114.8°$ Fahr. ($46°$ C.); but after a violent buran it sank to $69°$ Fahr. ($20.6°$ C.). This was on March 16th; after that the air gradually cleared, so that the radiation on March 17th went up to $81.7°$ Fahr. ($27.6°$ C.), and the following day it was $97.9°$ Fahr. ($36.6°$ C.). Concurrently with this the minimum temperature during the night sank after the buran had ceased, while the atmosphere gradually cleared. For example, before the buran the minimum thermometer read $21.2°$ Fahr. ($-6°$ C.); during the last day of the buran it

* From Yule's *The Book of Ser Marco Polo*, I. p. 203 (1874).

rose to 31.3° Fahr. (−0.4° C.), but again fell to 28.4°
Fahr. (−2° C.), and yesterday to 25.7° Fahr. (−3.5° C.).
In other words, the radiation increased in proportion as
the dust dropped back to the earth and was blown away.
In the same way the temperature of the air rose in
the shade at mid-day in proportion as the atmosphere
cleared; thus on March 16th, 17th, and 18th respectively I
got readings of 41.7° Fahr. (5.4° C.), 45.3° Fahr. (7.4° C.), and
51.8° Fahr. (11° C.). The quantity of dust with which the
atmosphere was charged thus exercised considerable influence upon the readings of the meteorological instruments.

On March 19th we moved over to the large village of
Merket, on the right bank of the Yarkand-daria, whence the
caravan was to make its start for the desert. In the morning
a number of the inhabitants of Merket came to escort us to
their village. The beg, Mehemmed Niaz Beg, arrived with
a present of chickens, eggs, and dastarkhan (light refreshments). He was a tall man, with a thin white beard, and
looked energetic and severe. Transport horses were employed to carry over our baggage, and after the on-bashi of
Lailik and his pretty wife, who had both been very kind and
hospitable during my stay in their house, had been well rewarded with money and cloth, we marched down to the ferry,
which conveyed us and our large caravan across in four trips.
The ice had evidently ceased to melt farther to the south, for
the river had fallen eleven inches since March 8th; and from
this time onward it would continue to sink until the summer
floods came down from the mountains.

After a quarter of an hour's ride in a southeasterly direction we passed the village of Anghetlik, which received its
irrigation water from an eastern branch of the Yarkand-daria.
At the end of an hour we reached the village of Chamgurluk,
and after another three-quarters of an hour were in Merket.
The beg placed his own house at my disposal, and I was soon
installed in a large and pleasant room covered with carpets
and with niches in the walls.

Counting in the surrounding kishlaks (winter villages)
Merket numbered a thousand dwellings, of which 250 were

in the immediate vicinity of the bazaar. The village of Yantak, a short distance farther north, had 300 houses. Yantak, together with Anghetlik and Chamgurluk, constitute a *beklik* or *beglik* (administrative division under a beg), while Merket has its own beg. In the latter place dwelt two tax-collectors, two Chinese merchants, and four Hindu moneylenders from Shikarpur. It was a fruitful region, producing wheat, maize, barley, beans, turnips, cucumbers, melons, beetroot, grapes, apricots, peaches, mulberries, apples, pears, and cotton. In good years the crops are so plentiful that large quantities of seed-corn are exported to Kashgar and Yarkand, but in bad years the reverse is the case, and grain is imported from Yarkand.

Although Merket is so close to the banks of the Yarkand-daria, it does not derive its irrigation water from it, but from the Tisnab-daria, the river of Kargalik, which flows parallel with the Yarkand-daria. When the current is low this river does not reach farther than Yantak, but at other times it advances a considerable distance farther north, and forms two small lakes, which, however, are dry at all other seasons. Its right bank, too, is bordered by a belt of forest, but not more than twelve and a half miles broad at the outside. The winters are cold, though the fall of snow is small, and the snow melts directly; the summers, on the contrary, are hot. The rainfall is distributed equally over the whole of the warm season, and sometimes is so heavy that it destroys the flat roofs of the houses. Northeasterly winds prevail, and the storms last from two to four days, loading the atmosphere with dust and occasioning a "rain" of dust, which settles on the vegetation in the form of a thick grayish-yellow down.

Strange to say, Merket has never before been visited by any European. The name appears for the first time, though in the form Meket, in General Pievtsoff's account of his travels; but he could not visit it while the Yarkand-daria was in flood. The Chinese, however, have long known the place, for it is mentioned under the name of Mai-ghe-teh in the *Si-yi-shuy-dao-tsi*, a work published in 1823. According to Chinese transcription, Yantak, or Yantaklik, becomes

Yan-va-li-ke, and Tisnab becomes Tin-tsa-bu. The author of the work in question states that this river unites with the Yarkand-daria, and that certainly would be the case if the water were not employed for irrigation, and did not become dissipated in the small lakes already mentioned. His description, however, may have been correct enough eighty years ago.

In Merket, too, there were some of the loafing gold-seekers I have mentioned. One man told me that, along with some

ENTRANCE TO A BAZAAR IN A CENTRAL ASIAN VILLAGE

companions, he had travelled for twenty days on foot through the desert, carrying with them supplies of food and water on donkeys. After going seven days east-northeast by the side of gigantic sand-dunes, they reached a long, straggling mountain. They had occasionally seen a few tamarisks, and in some places had obtained water after digging. My informant, besides many others, was in the habit of going out every year into the desert to look for gold, but as yet had found nothing. They called the desert Takla-makan; and the general consensus of opinion was that, given strong camels, we ought to be able to cross right over it to the Khotan-daria.

In the evening I held a levee. Niaz Beg and the on-bashi of Anghetlik, Togda Khodia, each presented me with a sheep, while the Hindus gave me a goodly supply of potatoes and butter, both exceedingly welcome. Afterwards we were entertained for a long time with the music of a *setar* (zither) and a *ghalin* (small harp), which, played in a slow time, sounded very well together, although the music was rather melancholy.

March 20th. Togda Khodia was a thorough gentleman. He often came to see me, and would sit talking in my room by the hour together. When I began to grow impatient at receiving no news of the camels, he always exhorted me to patience, saying with unruffled composure, and with a conviction which allowed of no demur, "*Kelladi! Kelladi!*" (They will come! They will come!) But nothing was heard of them; and precious time was being wasted. I felt that we were heaping glowing coals on our heads, for spring was upon us, and during the hot season of the year the desert is simply a furnace.

Meanwhile Togda Khodia gave me much valuable information. To-day, for example, he told me that the inhabitants of Merket are Dolons, and that in their own opinion they are in nowise different from the people of Kashgar. They possess a few slight dialectical differences of speech, that is all. But Togda Khodia himself considered them very different from their neighbors. Their natures were hard and cold, and they were so unforgiving that trifling disputes would linger on for years.

The observances of Islam were jealously kept at Merket. On the last bazaar-day, in the middle of the fast, a man ate before the sun set. He was immediately seized, flogged, and with his hands tied behind his back was led in a rope through the bazaar, from every corner of which the following questions and answers were re-echoed as the offender passed:

" Did you eat?"

" Yes."

" Do you mean to do it again?"

" Never."

It is also customary to blacken the culprit's face before he makes his penitential promenade through the bazaar.

On March 21st I visited the bazaar. It was very spacious, and every trade and calling had a special alley allotted to it. Nevertheless, there was no trading done except once a week—namely, on the bazaar-day, when stalls and wares are brought out of the houses and arranged on platforms built in front of them. At the time of my visit there were a number of women sitting on the platforms sewing. The women were always unveiled, generally bareheaded, and wore their thick black hair in two long plaits. Sometimes, however, their heads were covered with a small round coif or calotte. A particularly popular occupation with them seemed to be the extermination of certain undesirable parasites, and it was a by no means rare thing to see one woman with her head resting in her neighbor's lap.

Immediately outside the village there was a sand-dune 25 to 30 feet in height, running south-southwest to north-northeast as regularly constructed as though it had been built of set purpose. Its summit, which was crowned by the masar (tomb) of Chimdereh Khan, commanded a fine view over the village, with its flat-roofed houses surrounding small square court-yards.

At last, on March 22d, Mohammed Yakub came back from Kashgar, bringing a bulky mail-bag, but no camels! I was thus left precisely where I had been at the beginning of the month. Now I fell back upon my excellent Islam Bai, and on the next day sent him off to Yarkand post-haste with peremptory orders not to come back again without camels. Happily I had my meteorological and astronomical observations, to say nothing of the letters I had just received and of old Togda Khodia, to help me pass the time. I did not find Johannes, the missionary, much of a resource. He was one of those morbidly religious people who imagine that true Christianity is incompatible with a sober joy in life, as well as with good spirits. This was no doubt partly due to his being a converted Mohammedan: such proselytes are often ten times worse than their teachers. However, he was good-natured and helpful, though he always seemed to be depressed and in dull spirits.

A few days afterwards I fell a victim to a very bad and painful sore throat, known by the name of *gorkak*, very prevalent thereabouts. After I had tried the beg's prescription, which was to gargle my throat with warm milk, but to no purpose, he proposed that I should give the *peri-bakshis* or spirit-exorcisers a trial. I told him that I did not believe in such nonsense; but that the peri-bakshis were welcome all the same.

After dark, when there was no light in the room save what came from the glowing coals on the hearth, the peri-bakshis were introduced—three big, bearded men, in long white *chapaus* (cloaks). Each carried a drum (*doff*) of extremely tightly stretched calf-skin, and on these they proceeded to perform by tapping them with their fingers, beating them with the flat of the hand, and thumping them with their fists. The drums gave out such a volume of sound that it might have been heard at Lailik, six or seven miles off. The performers beat the instruments at an incredible speed, and all three in exactly the same time. After tapping the drums with their finger-tips for some time, all three would give a bang at one and the same moment, and then follow it up with half a dozen hollow whacks with their fists. Then the finger tapping would begin again, and the whole process be repeated without a moment's cessation. Sometimes they sat still; sometimes they were so carried away by their peculiar music that they got up and danced; and sometimes again they tossed their drums into the air and caught them with a bang. At every round, which lasted five minutes, the beating recurred in a certain order, which explained the fact that all three were able to keep time so well together. The full measure of rounds for putting evil spirits to flight is nine; and once the exorcisers have begun, it is impossible to stop them until the "full tale of bricks is told!"

The peri-bakshis are called in mostly at births and by sick

women; for the women are much more superstitious than
the men. The exorcisers enter the sick-room, and gaze attentively into the flame of the oil-lamp, where they say they
can see that the woman is possessed of an evil spirit. Then
the drums begin at once, while the invalid's friends and acquaintances gather inside and outside the room. But the
performance does not end there. When the last thundering
roll of the drum has died away, the assembly withdraws, and
the peri-bakshi, and the sick woman are left alone in the room
together. In the middle of the floor the sorcerer drives a
rod with great force, having a rope tied to the top of it, while
its other end is fastened to the ceiling. The woman pulls
and tugs at the rope until she succeeds in getting it loose,
while the peri - bakshi bangs at his drum. The moment the
rope breaks loose from the roof, the spirit departs from the
woman.

The hunting falcon, too, is credited with similar powers of
exorcism, and is therefore called *ghush-bakshi* (the falcon ex-
orciser). The peris or evil spirits are supposed to fear her
greatly. During the pangs of childbirth the woman sees
evil spirits flitting about the room, though they are invisible
to other people. The falcon, however, sees them, and is let
loose in the room to chase them out. It is very evident that
the falcon, the drums, and the rope and stick all tend to
the same end—namely, to distract the woman's attention to
a certain extent, and so make her forget herself.

March 26th. Niaz Beg administered justice at his own
house every day. His usual seat was beside one of the columns which supported the roof of the veranda, and so long
as the proceedings lasted he assumed a very severe expression of countenance. On the platform by his side sat his
mirza or secretary, who entered the proceedings in a proto-
col. Round about him stood his men and the officers of the
law, and before him the culprit.

To-day there was a very curious case. A man had five
wives. The fifth, a handsome, stalwart young woman, had
run away to Kashgar with another man. The beg had given
information to the authorities there, and they found the wom-

. sent her back to Merket, where she was now to an-
her transgressions. After she had been convicted
:hfulness, the beg gave her a slap on either cheek,
.... began to weep. The only thing she had to say in
own defence was that life with the other four wives was
gether unbearable. She had a knife on her person, and
n the beg asked her what she was going to do with it,
answered that she meant to kill herself if she were com-
d to return to her husband. Her punishment was that
a time she should go and dwell with the mollahs, till she
l be in a better frame of mind, and then should quietly
a home to her husband.

.cer that another young woman was brought forward, her
bleeding and lacerated, and followed by her mother and
husband. She also had left her husband; but in this
the man had taken the law into his own hands, and had
kicked and mishandled her. Several witnesses con-
l the statement that he had made use of a razor; this,
er, the defendant denied. To make him confess, the
gave orders for his hands to be tied behind his back, and
then had him strung up to the branch of a tree. He did not
hang there long before the device produced the desired
effect. The man was taken down, and forty strokes of the
rod were administered on that part of the body which seems
to have been providentially provided for castigation. Meanwhile he declared that his wife had beaten him on the back.
Forthwith he was stripped; but as no marks were visible, a
second whipping was the result.

In these distant regions the sense of justice is somewhat
elastic. If the accused has a well-lined purse he gets off
scot-free, and in any case the beg receives certain tengeh
for his trouble. If the plaintiff is not satisfied with the ver-
dict, he can appeal to a higher authority — the nearest Chinese mandarin—and to him the beg must answer in his turn.
The Chinese administration is admirable. One prudent feature in it is that they allow the natives to retain the same
system of local self-government which obtained in the time
of Yakub Beg of Kashgar.

Cases of conjugal infidelity are not on the whole uncommon, nor are they punished with particular severity. As a rule, the woman has her face blacked, is placed backward on a male ass, and with her hands tied behind her is taken through the streets and bazaar of the village. Monogamy is the rule; it is very seldom that a man has four or five wives. If a woman marries a Chinaman or a European she is considered impure; and when she dies is not interred in the general burial-ground of the place, because she has consorted with "one who eats swine's flesh," so that her body would pollute the graves of the faithful.

With regard to *kalim*, or the dower of a bride, the customs of these people are much the same as those of the Kirghiz. The kalim is paid to the bride's parents, and varies according to the man's circumstances and means. A bai, or rich man, gives as much as two jambaus (£9 to £10 each). As a rule everything is paid in kind; but the bride's trousseau is compulsory kalim. A poor man offers merely a measure of food and clothes. The amount depends entirely upon the demands of the parents; but beauty and physical charms are of less importance than among the Kirghiz. If a young couple cannot obtain the consent of their parents, it is not unusual for them to run away. They generally come back, however, after a few months, and invite the old people to a feast, when all misunderstandings are cleared up.

On another occasion the beg gave judgment on two men who had been gambling. One of them had a deep gash in his ear, and the whole of his face and chest were covered with blood. He had lost seven tengeh (1s. 6d.), and promised to procure the money in the bazaar. The winner, however, demanded his winnings on the spot, whereupon the loser drew his knife and slashed himself on the ear, crying, " You shall have that instead of your money." The beg ordered the winner to be publicly whipped. The other man was to be whipped as soon as his hurt was cured. The winnings, needless to say, found their way into the beg's pocket.

CHAPTER XXXIX

THE START FROM MERKET

.ᴀᴍ and Yakub came back on April 8th. After a great
of haggling and trouble, they had succeeded in getting
rgalik eight splendid male camels for a trifle over £6
apiece. It had somehow got wind among the inhabi-
that we absolutely *must* have camels for our desert
ey; and in consequence they put up their prices to
e or three times what they usually were. A further
ilty arose out of the fact that the only animals which
serve our purpose must be such as were accustomed
level plains, and to travelling in desert regions—
ls which were used to moving over sand and could
e heat and other privations. These qualities were of
much more consequence than the appearance of the beasts,
and their condition of flesh.

During the morning we christened the camels, and measured their girths between the humps, with the view of ascertaining how they would compare in that respect at the end
of the journey. Here are the names and measurements of
the several animals:

Name	Age	Girth
Ak-tuya (The White Camel)	8	7ft. 9in.
Boghra (The Male)	4	7ft. 8¼in.
Nähr (The Tall)	2	7ft. 4½in.
Babai (The Old)	15	7ft. 5½in.
Chong-kara (The Big Black)	3	7ft. 3½in.
Kityick-kara (The Little Black)	2	7ft. 3in.
Chong-sarik (The Big Yellow)	2	7ft. 6¼in.
Kityick-sarik (The Little Yellow)	1½	7ft.

How little we foresaw that only one camel—namely, Chong-kara—would survive the journey! Ak-tuya, a handsome white camel, which led the string, with a big copper bell provided with a heavy iron-tongue, did get to the other side of the desert; but he died soon afterwards from the fatigues of the march. Boghra was an exceptionally well-proportioned animal, patient and good-tempered; I chose him to ride upon. Nähr was a vicious beast, always trying to bite and kick the moment anybody went near him. Babai, the oldest in the troop, and of a gray color, was the first to succumb. The other three were young, lively things; having had a long rest, they were always ready to march, and took real pleasure in being on the move.

They chanced to be just "moulting" when they arrived. Every day big shaggy cots of their thick, warm winter hair

A CAMEL'S HEAD

fell off, so that they had a patched, shabby appearance so long as the process of shedding lasted. Each camel was provided with a good soft pack-saddle, stuffed with hay and straw. Islam brought also a whole armful of *arkhans* (ropes of camel's hair) to tie on the baggage with, and three large camel-bells.

The animals were tethered in a large court-yard immediately opposite Niaz Beg's house, and were given their fill of good hay, a luxury they enjoyed for the last time. It was very pleasant to stand and watch my own splendid camels crouched on the ground, eagerly munching the fragrant hay, and see how their big brown eyes shone with placid enjoyment. Our two dogs—Yolldash and Hamrah—were, however, of a different opinion. The former in particular could not tolerate the camels. He barked at them till he was hoarse; and was visibly well pleased with himself when he could get near enough to snatch a tuft of hair out of one or the other of them.

Islam Bai had further engaged two trustworthy men in Yarkand. One, Mohammed Shah, was a graybeard of fifty-five. He was accustomed to looking after camels, and was the only person who could go near the refractory Nähr without being bitten. Although he had left wife and children behind in Yarkand, the desert had no terrors for him. He was a capital fellow, as honest as the day. I can see him now as plainly as though it were only yesterday we parted. His philosophic serenity never deserted him. When the clouds of misfortune gathered thick round our ill-fated caravan, his good humor never failed; there was always a smile on his face. Even when he lay in the delirium of death, a gleam of triumphant serenity shone in his eyes, and the light of an inward peace spread over his withered, copper - brown countenance.

The second man, who was to help in the management of the camels, was Kasim Akhun, a native of Ak - su, but at that time an inhabitant of Yarkand, forty-eight years of age, unmarried, and a caravan-leader by profession. Of medium height and strongly built, with a black beard, he was of a serious disposition, and never laughed, though always friendly and pleasant; but he had very often to be reminded of his duties.

A CAMEL IN WINTER DRESS

We wanted yet another man. Him Niaz Beg found for us in another Kasim Akhun from Yanghi-hissar. He was of the same age as Mohammed Shah, and every spring, for six years past, had gone a ten to fourteen days' journey into the desert in quest of gold, taking his food on the back of an ass, but not venturing farther in than he was able to get water by digging. During our journey, in order to distinguish him from the other Kasim, we called him sometimes Yollchi (the pointer out of the road), sometimes Kumchi (the man of the desert). A few years previously he had flitted to Merket, and now left wife and grown-up children there behind him. His subsequent fate was in part of his own causing. He was brutal and of a violent temper; and the other men, whom he attempted to tyrannize over, soon came to hate him. He conceived that his experience of the desert warranted him in assuming a domineering tone; and he entertained an especial grudge against Islam Bai, because Islam was appointed kara-van-bashi, or caravan-leader, and the other three men were bidden obey him. Some of the inhabitants of Merket warned us against this man, telling us that he had been more than once punished for theft; but the warning came too late. When I engaged him I thought we had lighted upon a treas-ure-trove, for he was the only man in the place who knew anything of the desert.

Our menagerie of live-stock also embraced three sheep, which we intended to kill one after the other, half a score hens and a cock, which woke us up in the morning. These last travelled in a basket perched on the top of a camel's-load of baggage. The first few days the hens laid two or three eggs; but as soon as the water began to fail, they stopped laying. The cock was an eccentric animal; he entertained a rooted objection to riding on a camel's back. Every now and again he used to wriggle through the covering of the basket; and, after balancing himself a while on his elevated perch, flew down to the ground with a noisy cackle. Every time we pitched camp the poultry were let out for a run. They imparted a little life to the otherwise desolate surround-ings; and a few handfuls of corn were thrown down among the sand, to keep them employed and in motion.

On April 9th we made our final preparations; we packed

the two or three bags of bread which had been ordered beforehand, and filled the four iron tanks with fresh water from
the river. They held 17½, 19, 19, and 27 gallons respectively; add to this 17½ gallons in a goat-skin, and we get a total
of 100 gallons, amply sufficient for a 25 days' march. - The
tanks, which were oblong in shape, were specially made for
conveying honey from India to Yarkand, being surrounded
by a wooden grating to protect the thin iron plates against
damage from knocks. Grass and weeds were packed in between the tank and the grating to prevent the sun's rays from
beating directly upon the iron.

A few words about the plan of my journey. Przhevalsky,
and Carey and Dalgleish, were the first Europeans who ever
saw (1885) the mountains of Masar-tagh on the left bank of
the Khotan-daria. The first mentioned wrote in this connection: " After three short day's marches (from Tavek-kel) we
arrived at that part of the Khotan-daria where the Masar-
tagh chain overlooks its left bank. The eastern portion of
the range does not exceed 1¼ miles in breadth, and rises to a
height of some 500 feet above the surrounding country. It
consists of two parallel ridges strikingly dissimilar. The southern ridge is composed of red argillaceous slates, interspersed
with numerous beds of gypsum. The other, or northern
ridge, is a homogeneous mass of white alabaster. Flints are
obtained from the Masar-tagh at a distance of 16 miles from
the Khotan-daria, and taken to Khotan to be sold. Beyond
that point we lost sight of the mountains, which became
blended with the sandy desert. But they bent round towards the northwest, and, increasing in height in the middle,
stretched, the natives told me, as far as the fortified post of
Maral-bashi on the river of Kashgar. Of vegetation there
was not a trace. The slopes of the mountains were buried
in drift-sand half way up from the foot."

Relying upon the data thus given him by the natives,
Przhevalsky indicated on his map a chain of mountains
stretching at an oblique angle across the desert. His mistake was natural enough; for he was told that at Maral-bashi,
too, there is a mountain known by the name of Masar-tagh;

and what more natural than to suppose that it was simply the continuation of the Masar-tagh of the Khotan-daria? Carey was more cautious. His map shows only so much of the range as he was able to see from the river.

I reasoned, therefore, that if from Merket we steered our course eastward, or rather towards the east-northeast, we were bound, sooner or later, to come in contact with the Masar-tagh; and, like the natives, I was convinced that we should find a lee side to the range, where the drift-sand would not be blown together, but we should be able to make long, easy day's marches on firm ground, and possibly might even discover springs and vegetation, and perchance light upon traces of an ancient civilization. On the maps which I had at hand the distance through the desert, as the crow flies, measured 180 miles; and if we did only 12 miles a day the entire journey ought not to take us more than fifteen days. Our supply of water was therefore, by every calculation, more than sufficient. I was quite satisfied with my estimate, and thought we had an easy task before us. As an actual fact the journey took 26 days, or nearly twice as long as I anticipated.

April 10th. Long before sunrise the court-yard was all alive. Our various boxes, bales, and other impedimenta were carried out and weighed so that the camel's burdens might be suitably adjusted, and the several packages properly roped. These preliminaries over, they were placed along the ground two by two, at such distances apart that a camel could just get between them, and be made to kneel down while his load was fastened to his pack-saddle. After he got up on his feet, a big rope was lashed criss-cross right round the whole, and fastened to the horizontal bars in the framework of the pack saddle. We took with us an extensive equipment, provisions for several months, particularly rice and bread, preserved foods, sugar, tea, vegetables, flour, and so forth. In addition, we had a large supply of winter clothing, felts, and carpets; for, after leaving the Khotan-daria, I intended making for Tibet. Then I had my scientific instruments, photographic apparatus, with close upon a thousand plates, some books, a year's issue of a Swedish journal, of which I purposed reading one num-

I—21

ber every evening, a cooking-stove with its appurtenances,
metal utensils, crockery, three rifles, six revolvers, a supply of
ammunition packed in two heavy boxes, together with a multitude of other things. Add to all this water supplies for 25
days, and it will be clear that each camel had a pretty heavy
load to carry.

While the animals were being loaded, I measured my first
base-line of 400 meters (close upon a quarter of a mile).
Boghra walked it in five and a half minutes. This was a
daily recurring task, for the contours of the ground varied a
good deal; and the depth of the sand made a very appreciable
difference in the time the camels took to do the same distance.

The 10th of April, 1895, was a great day in the annals of
Merket. The court-yard, every alley, every house-roof in the
neighborhood, was crowded with people, all anxious to see us
off. "They will never come back again—never!" we heard
them cry one to another. "The camels are too heavily laden;
they will never get through the deep sand." These croakings
did not disturb me in the least. The ground burned under
my feet to get off. And we had an antidote to their ill-
omened prophecies in the action of the Hindus, who, just as
I put my camel in motion, flung a few handfuls of *da-tien*
(Chinese bronze money with a square hole in the middle)
over my head, crying, "Good-luck go with you!"

The camels were tied together in two strings of four each.
A piece of stick was thrust through the cartilage of the
animal's nose. A rope, fastened to one end of the stick,
was loosely knotted to the tail of the camel in front in such
wise that if the second camel fell the knot would come undone
of itself.

The other end of the piece of stick terminated in a knob,
which prevented it from slipping out of the animal's nose.
The four young camels went in the first string. After them
followed Boghra, with me on his back, and behind him Babai,
Ak-tuya, and Nähr. Mohammed Shah never left hold of
Boghra's bridle, so that I had no need to trouble myself in
the least about my camel, but gave my attention wholly and
undivided to my compass and watch, by which I steered our

course and measured the length of our day's march, and to
the observation of the country we were travelling through.
Islam Bai had shown much ingenuity in arranging my load
for me. It consisted of the two boxes which held my most
delicate instruments, and such things as I generally needed
when we encamped for the night.   On the top of the boxes
and between the camel's hump he spread pelts, carpets, and
cushions, so that with one leg on each side of the front hump
I rode as comfortably as though I were sitting in an easy-
chair.   When all was quite ready I said good-bye to Niaz
Beg, whom I rewarded handsomely, as well as to the missionary Johannes and Hashim.   The former had already said
at Lailik that he did not really mean to go with me through
Takla-makan.   Now, when he saw the caravan ready to start,
his courage completely failed him, and for the second time
he deserted me in the moment when danger had really to be
faced. I despised the fellow. Notwithstanding his pretended
piety, he utterly lacked the courage which makes a man place
all his reliance upon God.   What a strange contrast to Islam
Bai, the Mohammedan, the beau-ideal of a good and faithful
servant, who throughout the days and months that followed
never once hesitated to follow his master, no matter where I
went, even when I rushed into dangers which prudence should
properly have guarded me against!

Spring had come.   Signs of the change manifested themselves more and more every day.   The temperature rose
slowly but steadily, the minimum remaining permanently
above freezing-point.   The sun began to have some power.
The spring breezes murmured in our ears.   The fields were
being sown with corn, the rice-grounds put under water.
The air was alive with the flittings and buzzings of flies and
other insects.   It was with this beautiful Asiatic spring-time
all about us—the season of perennial hope—that we set out
on our journey to the country where all things are gripped in
the deathly embrace of a thousand years' torpor, where every
sand-dune is a grave—a country whose climate is such that,
compared with it, the sternest winter would be a smiling spring.

On through the narrow lanes of the town, crowded with

people, strode the long string of camels, with a grave and majestic mien, holding their heads high. It was a solemn moment. Every spectator was impressed. A dead silence reigned throughout the crowd. When my mind goes back to that moment I am involuntarily reminded of a funeral procession. I can hear the dull, monotonous clang of the caravan-bells still ringing in my ears; and of a truth their slow, mournful cadences were the virtual passing-bell of most of us who set forth on that eventful day for the sand-wastes of the terrible desert. A sad and peaceful grave amid the eternal ocean of sand—such was to be their melancholy end!

The environs of the town were level, the town itself scattered about among the old *tograks* (poplars), fields, groves, orchards, and irrigation canals. For half an hour or so we marched on quietly through these pleasant surroundings; then all of a sudden there arose a fearful uproar. The two youngest camels, being full of spirit, broke loose from their halters, shook off their loads, and, frisky as two playful puppies, began to race round the fields till the dust rose in clouds behind them. One had been loaded with a couple of water-tanks. Upon being thrown off, one tank sprang a leak, but, luckily, near the top corner, so that but little real damage was done. The runaways were soon caught and their burdens lashed on again. After that each was led separately, for we had plenty of help, fully a hundred mounted men accompanying us to the outskirts of the village. An hour later two other camels broke loose. Several things were chafed and bruised, and the ammunition-box was trailed on the ground. Mohammed Shah said that "camels always get refractory after a spell of rest. They wanted to stretch their limbs; but a few days' steady tramping would make them as quiet as lambs." After that, as a precaution, each camel was led by a single man.

But even then, as so often happens during the first day or two after starting on an expedition, we had several unforeseen hinderances to contend against. For example, the left-hand side of a camel's load would be heavier than that on the right-hand, and so had to be adjusted; or a bag of rice was on the point of slipping off, and had to be tied faster; and so on.

CHAPTER XL

SKIRTING THE DESERT

THE second day's march passed off more quietly, and in a much more orderly manner. Profiting from our first day's experiences, we weighed and distributed the packages more successfully, and loaded our most precious possessions—first among them the water—on the quietest camels. I myself sat perched at a pretty good height above the ground, and had a splendid view in every direction. At first the motion made me feel somewhat giddy; but I soon became accustomed to the monotonous and unceasing jolting backward and forward, combined with the peculiar swaying motion from side to side, and suffered no ill effects from it whatever. But I can readily believe it would be very disagreeable to anybody subject to sea-sickness.

Having left behind us the last house and field belonging to Merket, we struck into a level steppe (*däsht*), where thickets and tangled bushes grew pretty well everywhere, and there were even clumps of poplars in a few places. The wind blew in gusts from the west-northwest, and grayish-yellow "sand-spouts" drifted eastward at a great altitude, their upper ends slightly bent over in the direction of the wind. The surface of the ground was partly covered with fine, soft dust, partly with deposits of salt; but we soon passed into a region of nothing but sand, blown up into small low dunes or ridges. However, it proved to be only a narrow belt, for on the other side we once more came upon plenteous plant-life, chiefly kamish (reeds) and poplars; and there on the brink of the ravine we pitched our camp for the night.

Half an hour later the loads were all off the camels, and the animals themselves were tied together in a ring to prevent them from lying down and getting stiff-legged. After standing a couple of hours, they were let loose to browse upon the thickets of reeds. Our camp, with its many packages and animals, made a very picturesque appearance; and it gave me a feeling of deep satisfaction to think that all those things were mine. My tent, a neat Indian officer's tent which Mr. Macartney had given me, was pitched underneath a poplar-tree. Within it young Lieutenant Davison had died during his journey across the Pamirs to Kashgar. But it had been well disinfected, and I was not superstitious. The ground inside was covered with variegated carpet, and all round its sides were ranged my boxes, instrument-cases, photographic camera, and my plain, simple bedstead. The other boxes and packages, together with the water-tanks, were left outside in the open air. My men kindled a fire, and crouched around it to prepare dinner—rice pudding and eggs, for of these last we had brought a good supply. The sheep were turned out to graze, and the poultry made themselves quite at home among the scraps from the cooking-pot. The dogs, having swallowed the pieces of meat that were thrown to them, began to chase one another over the sand-dunes. In a word, we made quite a rural picture.

As soon as the camp was settled, my first care was to examine the ravine which had stopped us. It ran from north to south, and had undoubtedly been formed by a branch of the Tisnab-daria, but was now dry. It was 20 feet wide and 5 feet deep; and when I bade the men dig a hole in the bottom, the water began to trickle up as soon as they got 3 feet 6 inches down. The temperature of the water was 49.8° Fahr. (9.9° C.), while that of the air at the same time—viz., two o'clock in the afternoon—was 76.6° Fahr. (24.8° C.). Although tasting bitter and nauseous, it was greedily drunk by both dogs and sheep. The camels were not allowed any water until nearly an hour before the start next morning.

From the very outset we were obliged to exercise the most rigid economy with our supplies of fresh water; and therefore used the water from the ravine for boiling our eggs in, for washing the dishes, and for personal ablutions. Mohammed Yakub, who had followed us all the way to camp, brought us the very welcome present of a couple of copper vessels, filled with fresh river-water; so that every member of the caravan was able to quench his thirst to the full without our having to open the water-tanks.

It had been a warm day; but no sooner did the sun set than we felt it cool, and put on our extra coats. In the evening it was a dead calm. The tent flap was thrown back, but the flame from the candle never quivered. Our " Desert Man " gave us a taste of his knowledge. He advised us at first to keep for some days to the right bank of the Yarkand-daria, till we came to a mountain called Chackmak, and to a large lake, which was connected with a river that flowed to the north. To reach that place would take us eighteen days, and from there one day more would bring us to the Masar-tagh, the loftiest mountain in all that region. From the Masar-tagh to the Khotan-daria on the east was no great distance. North of Mount Chackmak there was a track which the gold-seekers were accustomed to use, and which led to a *yagatch-nishan* or sign-post. Beyond that mark the desert was known by the name of Kirk-kishlak or the Forty Towns, because of the numerous ruins of ancient cities which it contained.

April 11th. After a quiet and refreshing night's sleep I awoke before sunrise, and found the weather the reverse of agreeable. A violent nor'easter whistled through the camp, and the air was thick with dust, so that, except in the immediate vicinity of the tent, the whole landscape was shrouded in a uniform gray haze.

Unloading the baggage and putting up the tent took next to no time at all; but to get everything loaded up again, and all started, required a good two hours, although that included the preparations for breakfast. The camels objected to be loaded; but afterwards, during the remainder of the march, behaved very well. All vegetation gradually ceased, and we lost ourselves in a labyrinth of sand-dunes, 15 to 20 feet high, and of irregular formation, though they had for the most part a north-south strike. We tried to skirt round them as

much as possible; still there were a few difficult ridges which
we were compelled to go over. On one or other of these
the camels which carried the water fell; luckily it was only
the fore legs which gave way in each case. But we could not
get the animals up until after we had taken off their loads:
and then we had to pack them on again. The camels were
very clever at sliding down the sandy slopes, making use of
their hind legs as a brake in doing so. In the middle of the
day we got entangled in sand-dunes so high that we were
obliged to make a long détour to the north to get out of
them. Yollchi asserted that it was no use going east, for
we should only be forced to turn back, there being nothing in that direction but *chong-kum* (big sand). Our route
that day was a sinuous line along the edge of the "big sand."
The dunes dropped again to only 10 feet in height, and occasionally we travelled over soft dust, with a tolerably level
surface. And not a few times we rode into a kind of *cul-de-
sac* between the horns of the crescent-shaped dunes, and were
compelled to turn back. Every now and again we passed a
few solitary poplars and shrivelled reeds, at which the camels
snatched as they rolled on past them.

The nor'easter blew all day long; the sky was clouded
and gray; and it was raw and cold. We halted at dusk, after doing about 13¼ miles, pitched our camp on the top of a
hard, level dune, where we had comfortably dry ground under our feet. Close by were some withered poplars, from
which we obtained fuel for our fire, and clumps of reeds,
which furnished fodder for the camels. These last were
warm after their long tramp, and were led about for a time
to cool, to prevent them from taking cold.

We found a spot between two dunes where the sand was
already damp. There we dug our well, and came upon water
at a depth of 2½ feet: its temperature was 49.1° Fahr. (9.5°
C.), and it had the same brackish flavor as the water in the
ravine the day before.

April 12th. We travelled nearly fifteen miles, still along
the edge of the great sandy desert, which sent out promontories to the north. Several of these we were obliged to

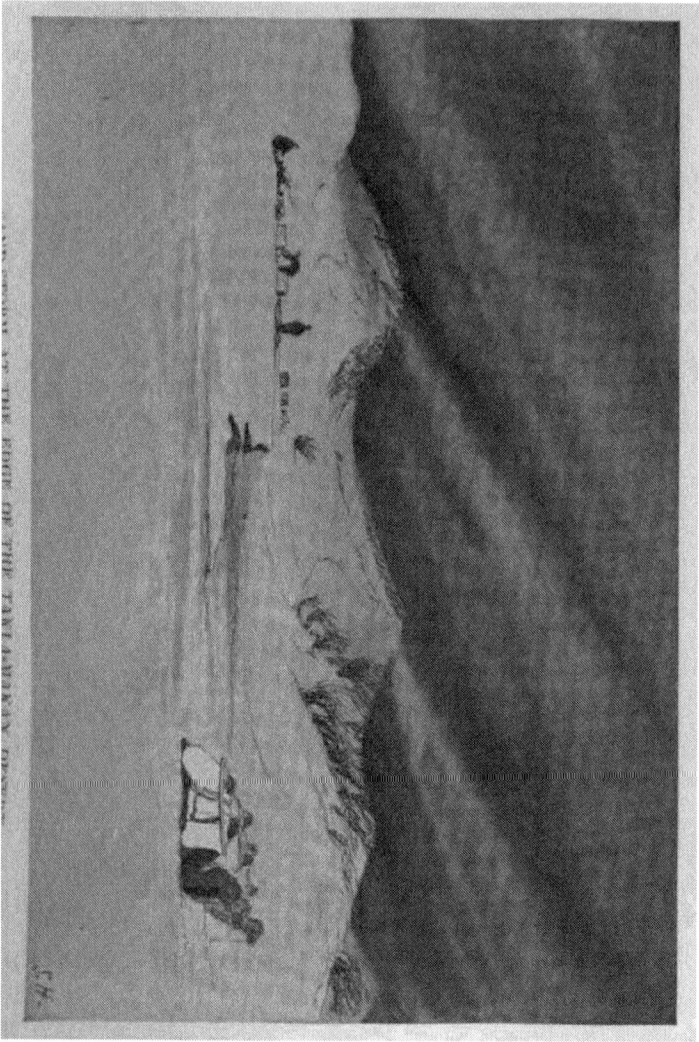

AT THE EDGE OF THE TARLAWAN DESERT

cross over. In other respects barren desert alternated with narrow belts of steppe, upon which grew scanty tussocks of grass, withered and hard as glass, and which snapped off with a crackling sound at the least touch. The easiest ground to travel over was firm, level sand; but in several places the earth was covered with a coating of dust, in which every footmark of the flat-footed camels was sharply outlined. The dust was as soft as wool, and in two or three places so deep that the animals dropped in it up to the knees. Sometimes a thin crust of salt, which crunched under the camels' hoofs, was spread over the horizontal portions of the sand. Solemnly and slowly the ungainly beasts strode on one after the other, stretching down their long necks to pluck the tussocks of grass which grew within their reach, as though they had a premonition of the hard times in store for them.

At camp No. III. two of the men as usual dug a well; but could not get down lower than six feet. Still there was no water. We then left the well to itself for a couple of hours, and the water percolated through and gathered in a little pool at the bottom of the hole. The dogs and poultry were always deeply interested spectators of the digging. They knew perfectly well what it was for, and were always fearfully thirsty. So far all was going well: our precious stores were as yet untouched. The stock of camel's provender was likewise undiminished, the animals having to content themselves with kamish (reeds) and brackish water. The dogs were fed on bread, the poultry on corn and egg-shells. The first day the hens laid three eggs, the second day two, the third one. However, we had a good supply without that, packed away in chaff in a basket.

During the course of the day we came across the track of herds of antelopes going towards the southeast. Yollchi told us there was a large lake in that direction called Yeshil-kul (the Green Lake). But neither he nor any other person known to him had ever seen it; he had only heard speak of it, so that the information must be accepted for what it is worth. He added that it was fed by natural springs, for no stream ran into it. It is, however, remarkable that the older maps show a lake of that name; but it is given a different situation—namely, south-southwest from our camp No. III.

April 13th. By the morning there were seven inches of water in the bottom of the well. All day long, during our march of 12½ miles, we travelled continuously among the dunes. They were all crescent-shaped, with their convex side towards the east, and the horns or wings and the steep side looking towards the west or southwest; proving that in this season of the year the prevailing winds blew from the north and northeast.

Poplar-trees were common everywhere throughout this march. On some of them the leaf-buds were already beginning to burst; and the fresh green tufts made the horses' mouths water. In most cases the dunes seemed to avoid the poplars, but formed a circular wall round them, leaving the trees in the middle of the hollow. There, too, finding shelter from the wind, dried branches and withered leaves lay in thick heaps.

It was a warm day. The dogs hunted vainly for game, eagerly running towards every little depression which looked at all like the places in which we dug our desert wells. For lack of better protection from the sun, they lay down in the shade of every poplar we passed, having first scratched away the top layer of hot sand, till they came to the stratum that still retained some of the coolness of the night.

Islam Bai rode on the first camel, which was also led by Yollchi, our guide. But as Islam commanded the better view, he often corrected Yollchi, and suggested taking other directions. That gave umbrage to the ill-natured "Desert Man"; so that two or three times he flung down the rope, threw himself on the sand, and challenged Islam to guide the caravan himself. When we came to camp, a violent quarrel broke out between the two men. Yollchi came to my tent, and said that if he was to be interfered with by Islam he had better go back; and he also accused Islam of being close-fisted with the bread. He was considerably taken aback when I quietly remarked, "Yes, he had better go back;" but added that "before he did so he must repay me

MAROONED IN A SANDSTORM

the 100 tengeh (22s. 6d.) which he had received in advance as his first month's wages." That brought him to his senses, and in the most earnest tones he begged to be allowed to remain with me. I allowed him to do so; but on the distinct understanding that henceforward he was to obey Islam. I had my misgivings, however, that when we came to face the loneliness and monotony of life in the desert, the differences between the two men would break out again. But there were no more quarrels. Although Yollchi nourished a growing spite against Islam, he wisely held his tongue. He always kept himself to himself, never talked to the other men, and slept apart, a little distance from the rest; nor did he ever go near the camp-fire until after Islam and his comrades had gone to bed. Were they right, I wonder, in suggesting that Yollchi purposely led us in the wrong direction? If so, he paid the penalty; for he died of thirst in the desert.

At the depth of about 3¾ feet we came upon water, with a temperature of 50.7° Fahr. (10.4° C.). The dogs were so thirsty that they tried to fling themselves in the hole, and we were obliged to tie them up to prevent them from doing so.

April 14th, Easter Day, we only travelled 11½ miles. In one place the dunes on their sheltered side were a steel-gray color. Upon examination I found that they were coated with a thin crust of mica. I also made the discovery that the green poplars only grew among the dunes. Where the dunes came to an end, there the poplars ceased also. Possibly the trees or their roots help in the formation of the dunes.

We then came to a belt of desert absolutely barren, the ground being a hard, level plain of a variety of brown colors, crossed by low dunes of yellow sand that looked like logs of wood lying on the earth. Many small pebbles were scattered over the plain. During this day's march we came across the first traces of the wild camel; at least, Yollchi said it was a wild camel, but I was not at all sure of it. Farther on the camel-tracks became numerous. But, on the other side of the argument, it was not very likely that tame camels would have run away into the desert by themselves. We also observed

the droppings and footmarks of horses; and Yollchi swore
that the wild horse ranged that part of the desert. On the
top of one of these dunes I halted a moment in order to observe through my field-glass a troop of animals grazing on a
bed of reeds a long way off towards the north. But before I
could make out whether they were horses or antelopes they
disappeared, going off northward. The dry gray clay was
built up into small terraces and ridges, so strangely like the
gray clay houses in the towns that I could not rest until I
went and examined them at close quarters.

That day the dogs were very restless, and several times
went off a long way from the caravan. Once they were absent a quarter of an hour, and when they came back they
were wet underneath. Evidently they had discovered water
somewhere. After going about 11½ miles we stumbled by
chance upon a pool. I bade Kasim try what it tasted like.
"Sweet as honey," he replied, after swallowing a good mouthful. The consequence was that we pitched the tent and
made our camp by the side of the pool. Men, dogs, sheep,
poultry—all hastened to quench their thirst; and, as the day
was hot, we were all properly thirsty. The water was as
clear as crystal and perfectly sweet, and bubbled up out of a
spring, afterwards running into a hollow of the ground some
eighty or ninety yards long by about four wide; so that the
water stood at about the same general level below the surface
that it did in the wells we had dug. All the same, it was
not more than four feet down. The temperature was 71.4°
Fahr. (21.9° C.) at five o'clock in the afternoon; at the same
hour the temperature of the air was 77.9° Fahr. (25.5° C.).
Water-spiders and beetles were very numerous. The latter
hummed about over the plain, and off went the hens in chase
of them. The first of the sheep was slaughtered here with the
usual ceremonies; and the dogs got a good meal out of the
blood and offal. In a word, considering it was the desert,
the place was quite idyllic. The sun disappeared from sight
in the dust-haze while still twenty degrees above the horizon; thereupon the heat decreased with marvellous rapidity.
By nine o'clock at night the temperature of the spring-water

had fallen to 59.4° Fahr. (15.2° C.), proving that its temperature varied directly with the temperature of the air.

This pleasant camping-ground tempted us to give up a day to rest, which was equally welcome to us human beings as to the animals. We all enjoyed a good long sleep, and spent the next day in putting several things in order: the water-tanks were filled up, clothes were washed, saddles and straps mended. The day turned out hot, the sand becoming heated to 112.3° Fahr. (44.6° C.). But two or three whirlwinds came up out of the north-northeast, and cooled the air splendidly; while without any reproach of conscience we could drink as much water as ever we liked. As for the camels and dogs, they drank so much that you could actually see their skins swelling out. The rest also suited the hens: they managed to lay four eggs. During the night the dogs barked incessantly, and kept running back along the route by which we had come, and on which we had seen the tracks of the wild camels. No doubt the denizens of the desert were accustomed to frequent the springs during the night; but finding us in possession of the place they kept themselves at a safe distance for that night.

On April 16th we did 16¾ miles, through a country where sand-dunes fifteen or sixteen feet high alternated with steppes of withered reeds, which "crunched" under the camels' feet and sent up little clouds of dust when trodden upon. Tamarisks and poplars occurred in sporadic clumps. We passed two pools of water, like the one we left in the morning. All three lay along the same line, stretching east-northeast; in all probability they mark the course of a former affluent of the Yarkand-daria.

We put out farther and farther into the unknown ocean of sandy desert. Not a sign of life to be seen; not a sound to be heard, except the monotonous ding-dong of the bells tinkling in time to the soft tramping of the camels. Every now and again we made a short halt, whenever, in fact, we were at all uncertain of the course we ought to steer—opportunities which the men seized upon to eat their simple breakfast, consisting of a few handfuls of *talkan* (toasted flour)

I.—32

steeped in water, which they supped out of wooden bowls. The water in the tanks became tepid during the course of the day. For my own part, I always missed our breakfast, and contented myself with two meals a day.

April 17th. To-day there was a fresh westerly breeze; but the sky remained perfectly clear. On several occasions I noticed that the dust-storms were only raised by the easterly and northeasterly winds; while no matter how strongly it blew from the west, the sky always remained pure and clear.

Before we had gone very far we perceived in the north a tolerably high mountain, like a cloud or slight thickening of the atmosphere, fringing the horizon. Hour after hour we rode towards it; but the mountain grew no plainer to the eye, nor did we seem to approach any nearer to it. The dunes reached sixteen feet in height, and were often very difficult to get over. Between them the reed steppes became more frequent and the reeds ranker in growth. A few hares leaped out from among them as the caravan drew near. This day, too, we passed some small pools; but they were surrounded by saline incrustations, and the water in them was brackish. Away towards the east-northeast a former river had cut its sinuous way through the desert; the channel, which was half choked with sand, and contained only a few disconnected pools of water, was forty-five yards wide and six and a half feet deep. Another river-bed, quite dry, was twenty-two yards wide. In the north there were a few dark flocculent clouds, like smoke drifting up from the ground. Yollchi's explanation was as follows: The mountains we saw were the southeastern continuation of Masar-tagh, stretching down to the right or southern bank of the Yarkand-daria. The two dried up river-beds had been afflu-ents of the Yarkand-daria, which used to receive a portion of their waters during the height of the summer. The clouds we saw in the north were columns of steam or evaporation from the Yarkand-daria, reflected against the pure blue sky. In all these explanations he was unquestionably right; at a later period I was able to test two or three of his statements, and found things to be exactly as he had said.

For a whole hour we travelled between two parallel ridges of sand, which stretched north by fifteen degrees east. The one on our right was more than thirty feet high, and both had rounded outlines. The level steppe between them was overgrown with exuberant thistles and poplars. We crossed the ridge on our right, and then passed along a second valley running parallel to the first. At the end of seventeen and a half miles we pitched camp No. VII. under the shade of a couple of leafy poplars. We had no need to dig for water; there were several indications that a lake or running stream could not be far off. North of us was a thick forest of poplars. Mosquitoes, flies, and moths were abundant. At night the last-mentioned fluttered round my candle in hundreds.

CHAPTER XLI

AN EARTHLY PARADISE

APRIL 18TH. The new day dawned with a fresh nor'easter blowing. The tent threatened to go over, although we had anchored it during the night. The sky preserved its uniform gray tint, and the mid-day heat remained absent. We decided to march straight for the highest point of the mountains ahead, being persuaded we could reach it before evening. But it was not to be—we lost our way in the poplar wood, and the mountains disappeared from view in the dust-laden atmosphere.

The sand-dunes were all round us, branching away irregularly in every direction, and growing all over them was a large forest of poplars. The ground was littered with heaps of withered leaves, dried tree-trunks, branches, and sticks. Of the desert there was not a trace. In and out among the trees we wound a hundred, a thousand times; and it was as much as I could do to see for the branches I was riding under. We came to an extensive marsh, around which the poplars were already wearing their full mantles of spring-time greenery. To our amazement we perceived traces of human beings and of horses, as well as ashes and charred wood, showing that a fire had been lighted. It was clear we had reached the districts to which the Dolons are accustomed to drive their flocks to graze in the spring, and from which the inhabitants of Maral-bashi fetch their fuel.

Our path was soon stopped by several long narrow creeks running out from the marsh. But we were obliged to cross them; so one of the men went into them barefooted and sounded their depth. The bottom consisted of hard clay, strong enough to bear the camels. Advancing a short distance farther, we found the marsh terminated in a long lake extending towards the north. We skirted its eastern side, keeping along the flanks of the tolerably high sand-dunes which sloped down to the edge of the pure blue water. The forest was still dense, in many places so tangled with thickets that we were compelled to make détours so as to get out into more open ground. But, as I said, for the most part we kept close to the shore of the lake, getting many a picturesque glimpse of it through the trees. The fresh green of the leaves contrasted strikingly with the deep blue water, and both against the gray haze in the background.

The lake, which was nearly a couple of miles wide in its widest part, although it narrowed greatly towards its northern and southern extremities, has no doubt been formed by a branch of the Yarkand-daria, and fills during the season of the summer overflows. In the winter a large portion of the water remains, freezes, thaws again in the spring, and dwindles on till the summer brings it the usual increase. On the edge of the dunes I observed a higher shore-line, indicating that in the previous summer the level of the lake had been half a yard higher than it was at the time of our visit.

At length we left the lake on our left, and soon became lost in a tangle of reed-beds of unprecedented thickness and the height of a man. As the camels forced their way onward among the dry, brittle reed-stalks, there was quite an orchestra of crackling, rustling sounds. Only we who were riding had a free outlook.

The reed-beds passed, we plunged into another forest, so thick that, after one or two narrow escapes of being swept off my camel by the branches, I was obliged to get down and go on foot. In a part of the forest where all the trees, although young, were dead, we literally stuck fast. The men were forced to get out their axes and hew a path. This occasioned a great loss of time; but after considerable labor we managed to struggle out once more on to the level steppe. There, on the summit of an isolated dune, whose horns pointed to the south and southwest, we pitched our camp.

With the idea of making our presence known, in case there

was anybody in the vicinity who could give us a little topographical information, we set fire to a dry poplar thicket at the foot of the sand-dune. The flames shot out their ruddy reflection to a long distance, but never a human being showed himself. We were all tired after our toilsome day's march of sixteen miles, and went early to bed. The camels, however, were best off; every day they got full rations of both water and food.

April 19th. When the tent was struck we found a scorpion under the carpet, an inch and a half long. Upon being disturbed he made violent efforts to use his tail. We were all tired with our exertions of the day before, and it was after nine o'clock when we got started. The little mountain-chain towards which we were now steering our course loomed up on the east and ran towards the southeast, where it became lower, and finally was lost in the haze. There was another mountain in the north. According to the itinerary I had mapped out for our journey, the latter ought to be the Masar-alldi. Between the two ranges winds the Yarkand-daria; but we were unable to see the river.

This day we covered only 7¾ miles, for although our route lay across a steppe, the steppe was excessively cut up by ravines and marshes. But the mountain became gradually more and more distinct. Its weathered, rugged outlines were easy to make out. The sand-dunes climbed up its northern slopes to a pretty considerable height. Along their foot was a chain of small fresh-water lakes, separated from one another by low isthmuses. A channel entering into the largest of the group revealed the fact that they drew their supplies of water from the river. During the summer they no doubt shrink together and form only a single lake. Keeping between the lakes and the mountain, we steered at first towards the east; afterwards, in order to get round a spur of the range, we altered our course towards the northeast. We pitched our camp on the shore of the lake under the shade of some leafy poplars. The mountain appeared to stand quite alone, unconnected with any other and without continuation in any direction.

Our second sheep was killed, and the dogs, which for several days had been without meat, being fed on bread alone, were given a good meal. A hawk began to hover above the poultry, but was frightened off by a rifle-shot, which missed it.

April 20th. Our camp was so pleasantly situated that we could not resist the temptation to indulge ourselves with another day's rest. It turned out a broiling hot day, despite a fresh breeze from the northeast all night and all the morning. The radiation rose to 146.3° Fahr. (63.5° C.), and at two o'clock in the afternoon the sand was heated to 126.9° Fahr. (52.7° C.). We had an incessant craving for drink, and flew to water at least every half-hour. We had hard work to keep the water in the iron tanks even tolerably cool, but we did what we could by wrapping a damp cloth round them and hanging them on a bough in the shade, where they could catch the breeze.

Islam Bai went out in quest of wild geese. He shot a couple, but they fell into the lake and he was unable to get them. The other men spent the day sleeping. For my own part, I walked to the top of the nearest hill and discovered a vein of porphyry piercing the same species of rocks that I had observed in the mountain system of the Masar-alldi. I had a magnificent view. In the west-southwest the two limpid sheets of water which we had passed the day before reflected their environing mountains, with their sand-coated sides, as in a mirror. Mount Masar-alldi lay northwest of us, and between it and our camp, and stretching round to the northeast, was a steppe of moist, luxuriant grass, thickly studded with glittering pools and marshes. In the east, too, I saw a mountain-crest, and in the south a maze of small weathered peaks belonging to the same system which overhung our camp. The poplar groves and reed-beds on the north tinted the steppe green and gold; the mountains were softened into violet shades; the sheets of water glanced dark-blue.

While I sat admiring the scene from the top of the hill in the cool of the afternoon, the wind gradually died away, the sun set, steppe and lakes became enveloped in a light mist, stillness and peace reigned over the scene. The only sounds my ear could catch were the gentle hum of the [...] and midges, the croaking of a frog or two in the [...] distant scream of a wild goose, and every now and [...] tinkle of the camels' bells among the reeds. It was [...] spot. I enjoyed its soothing beauty to the full. [...] ent from the days which followed! How often [...] next two weeks did my mind fly back to that idyll[...] to an earthly paradise!

But in those regions the twilight is very sh[...] hastened to get back to camp. The men were [...] asleep, except Islam Bai, who was busy getting [...] ready—mutton broth, fried potatoes, and tea. The [...] eter read 68° Fahr. (20° C.), but during the nigh[...] 50.7° Fahr. (10.4° C.), and I felt it actually cold. [...] lakes we again came upon traces of human bei[...] were one or two deserted reed huts on the sho[...] day, April 21st, when we continued our journey [...] lakes and the mountain, we came, on the other side [...] high dunes, upon the wheel tracks of arbas (high wooden carts) going through a poplar wood. The discovery vastly surprised us all. My men at once set them down as marking the road which they had heard speak of as following the left bank of the Khotan-daria. But I surmised it was some hitherto unknown track, which skirted the base of the Masar-tagh as far as the stream just mentioned. To clear up the mystery we resolved to follow the trail as far as it went, no matter where it led us to; but we had only advanced a little way when the wheel-tracks disappeared and the path came to an end. Shortly afterwards the poplar wood came to an end also.

After that we continued to move towards the southeast, keeping between the mountains which overhung our last camping-place and an isolated ridge which lay to the east. Our route lay across a hard level steppe, thinly overgrown with grass, where travelling was unusually easy. The camels marched in regular time, and their bells tinkled in strict

accord with their paces. At the foot of the eastern ridge
there was another lake, and to our amazement we perceived
three horses grazing on its banks. It was now plain there
were people in the neighborhood. Who were they? How
were we to find them? I told off two of my men to follow
a fresh trail, which led between the sand-dunes and up the
slopes of the mountain in the west. Ere long they returned,
bringing with them a man from Maral-bashi, who occasionally
came to that spot to fetch salt, of which, he said, there was a
large deposit in the mountain. I saw some of what he had
gathered. It appeared to be of excellent quality. He took
it to Maral-bashi, where he said he made a first-rate price of
it in the bazaars. When I asked him in which direction the
town lay, he pointed towards the northwest, and told me it was
two short days' journey to it. The mountain we had seen in
that quarter was, as we supposed, the system of the Masar-
alldi. About the country to the southeast, and the distances
to the Khotan-daria, he knew nothing; he was only able to
add that he had heard there was nothing but sand to the
south, with not a single drop of water anywhere, and he knew
that the desert was called Takla-makan.

We said adieu to the lonely salt-gatherer, and continued
south-southeast across the hard, barren, trackless plain. As
we advanced, the mountain on our right gradually decreased
in height until it merged in a sand-ridge, which eventually
became lost in the desert. This mountain, therefore, had no
continuation. We could only surmise that it was the eastern range which was connected with the Masar-tagh that
Przhevalsky marked on his map as terminating near the
Khotan-daria.

The ground we were now travelling over consisted of
hard, dry clay, cracked in thousands of directions, plainly
proving that it was under water during the summer. We
kept close to the shore of the lake all along until it began to
narrow, and we were compelled to make détours round the
marshes which extended some distance from it. From the
southern end of the lake several long, narrow creeks stretched
out like fingers into the gradually rising ground. It is worthy

of remark that all these desert lakes were situated at the foot of the mountains.

At length we reached the eastern shore of the lake by a long roundabout way, and there pitched our camp. Believing that this was the last place in which we were likely to obtain fresh water, we gave up the following day, April 22d, to rest. The camels and sheep were given their last good meal off the reeds which grew beside the lake. I climbed to the top of the mountain, and therefrom gained a commanding view of the surrounding country. The mountain itself jutted out in a southeasterly direction like a cape into the desert ocean, and only showed one solitary peak of no great altitude. Except for the range on which I stood, there was not a glimpse of a hill to be seen. We had reached the southeastern extremity of the Masar-tagh of Maral-bashi; consequently it had no connection with the Masar-tagh of the Khotan-daria. To the southeast, south, and southwest, as far as eye could reach, there was nothing but the dreary desert ocean! The horizon on that side was a straight line. When, during the days that followed, we went on and on towards the east-southeast and east without discerning a single trace of a mountain-chain, I could not help thinking that the continuation of the Masar-tagh of Maral-bashi would crop out again farther on in the desert, and that we had left it on our right; and yet, again, that was hardly likely

Before the day came to an end, we took counsel together. Yollchi assured me that the Khotan-daria was only four days distant to the east. The best Russian maps I had made the distance about 78 miles, and at the rate of about 12½ miles a day we should reach the river in six days; but at two days' march from its bank we ought to be able to get water by digging, as we had done near the Yarkand-daria. However, I bade the men take sufficient water to last ten days—that is, to fill the tanks half full, so as not to overstrain the camels in the deep sand. With such a margin I felt perfectly safe against all risks; indeed there would be a sufficient supply to water the camels twice during the six days. Yollchi and Kasim were told off to fill the tanks. They were at it a long spell in the evening, and all the time I heard the precious fluid pouring into the iron vessels. All the loads were got ready that night, so that we might start early in the morning.

CHAPTER XLII

IN THE BAN OF THE DESERT

APRIL 23D. It proved to be a warm day; but the camels had profited from their rest, and we did 17 miles before halting. At first our route lay across the thinly grassed dusty steppe, which stretched away southeastward from the lake, and was dotted all over with small mounds and terraces of clay, that bore a striking resemblance to houses. After we had gone about an hour and a half, the sand began to take the form of low furrowed ridges. Then ten minutes farther on and we were in the midst of a regular chaos of sand-dunes, all linked together, running without break one into another. Their prevailing direction was from northeast to southwest, and their steeper faces all fronted towards the south, southwest, and west. They were 20 to 25 feet high, and often extremely difficult to get over. My men called them *yaman-kum* (hateful sand), *chong-kum* (big sand), and *ighiz-kum* (high sand); to their crests or summits they gave the name of *beles* (pass). Already we perceived several peculiar sand formations. When two systems of sea-waves clash together, they mount on the top of one another up to double their original height. In like manner some of these gigantic sand-waves were piled up in pyramidal masses overtopping the level of the rest. This was where two separate dunes were driven one across the other by the ever-varying winds.

Right across our path, running from north-northeast to south-southwest, was a ridge of gigantic dunes, exceeding in altitude all others we could see; they were probably formed over uneven ground. It was wonderful to see with what surety of foot the camels clambered up the steep inclines, which the men only climbed with the utmost exertion, slip-

ping back at every step they took.   The ridge rose to relatively but an inconsiderable height above the general level;
all the same, it afforded a wide view.   Why did I not pale
with horror when my gaze swept eastward over that unending ocean of fine yellow sand, and its gigantic billows peeping up one behind the other for miles upon miles?   I can
only suggest, it was because I believed that the star of my
fortunes, which had always shone so clear above my head,
would not become extinct now.   On the contrary, to my
eyes the desert ocean was invested with a fascinating beauty.
Its silence, its unbroken stillness, exercised a magic charm
over me.   It was a grand, a majestic sight.   The wizard
power of the *desiderium incogniti* was drawing me on with
an irresistible spell to enter the castle of the desert king,
where I was to unseal the revelations of bygone centuries,
and discover the buried treasures of old-world legend and
story.   My motto was " Win or lose."   I knew nothing of
hesitation, nothing of fear.   "Onward! Onward!" whispered
the desert wind.   "Onward! Onward!" vibrated the camels'
bells.   A thousand times a thousand steps to reach my object; yet accursed be the first step I take backward!

The dunes increased rapidly in height, the maximum being
some 60 to 70 feet.   It was terrible work getting over them.
The camels slid cleverly down the steep slopes.   Only one
of them fell, one of the two that carried the water-tanks, and
had to be unloaded and reloaded.   Sometimes, when our
path was stopped by abrupt declivities, we were obliged to
stand still, while the men dug out and trampled down a path
for the animals.   By this the dunes had increased to a height
of 80 to 100 feet.   When I stood at the base of one of them,
and looked up at the caravan creeping along its brink, I
thought how little it looked.   As far as possible we kept to
the same curving line of summits, so as to escape going up
and down more than we could help.   As a consequence of
this, our track was very zigzag.   We took all the advantage
we could of the softer, rounded summits, going from the one
to the other; nevertheless we were very often obliged to go
down a steep slope which we found it impossible to get

I.—33

round. When, after some little hesitation, the camels began to slide down the loose sand, every man's utmost watchfulness was needed, for the sand poured down after them in a torrent, covering them to the knees.

We missed the small patches of hard clay soil of which we had passed so many during the first few days of our desert journey. We were now entirely among the sand. The last of the tamarisks, which still defied the visitation of death, was left behind. There was not a blade, not a leaf, to be seen; nothing but sand, sand, sand—fine yellow sand—whole mountains of it, stretching over boundless spaces, as far as the eye, with the field-glass to help it, was able to reach. No bird gave animation to the expanses of the sky. All traces of gazelle and deer had long since ceased. Even the very last promontory of the Masar-tagh had vanished from sight in the dust-haze that obscured the atmosphere.

The poor dogs! How they suffered from the heat, in their thick hairy coats! Hamrah in particular whined and howled, and lagged behind time after time. We spent a whole hour vainly looking for a suitable camping-ground, and at last, about dusk, found a very small patch of hard clay, where the last two tamarisks grew. Both trees were instantly peeled by the camels. Other green food there was of course none. We gave the animals oil and sesamum husks. We set about digging a well; but, as the sand still remained dry at a depth of 2¼ feet, we abandoned the attempt. Then we missed Hamrah. We whistled; we shouted. The dog did not appear; nor did we ever see him again. Half-way from our last camp Mohammed Shah saw him scratch up the sand underneath one of the very last tamarisks we passed, and then lie down in it. The men believed the dog had died of sunstroke. With greater probability the sagacious animal had grown tired of running through the sand, had scented out that there was nothing but the terrible desert before us, and wisely judged that evil was in store for him if he followed us. Having, therefore, turned the matter well over in his mind, he made his choice, and turned back to the last lake we had left; then, having drunk and cooled his coat with a good bath, he would no doubt make his way to Maral-bashi, although to get there he would have to swim over the Yarkand-daria. When I got back to Kashgar I made inquiries after the dog; but I could learn nothing of him. Yolldash stuck to us faithfully; but, poor beast! his fidelity cost him his life.

A strange and inexplicable feeling came over me when I encamped for the first time in the dreariest desert there is on the face of the earth. The men spoke but little; not one of them laughed. An unwonted silence reigned around the little fire of tamarisk roots. We tethered the camels for the night close to our sleeping-place, to prevent them breaking loose and going back to the lake, where they had their last good browse. A death-like silence held us all under its spell; even the camels' bells were frequently silent. The only sound to be heard was the heavy, long-drawn, measured breathing of the camels. Two or three stray moths fluttered around my candle inside the tent; but no doubt they had travelled with our caravan.

April 24th. I was awakened at half-past three in the morning by a hurricane-like wind from the west. Clouds of sand were swept into the tent. The storm whistled and rattled among the tent-ropes and tent-pegs, and the tent itself shook to such an extent that I expected every moment it would be blown away. The wind struck us from every quarter, for our camp was pitched in a sort of hollow, surrounded on all sides by dunes of drift-sand. There was one gigantic ridge on the north of us, another on the east, and yet another on the west, this last inclining one degree to the south. The surface of the dunes was corrugated all over, the lines of corrugation running from north to south. On the south there was a fourth dune, lying almost parallel to the third, and with an inclination of ten degrees towards the north. The steep faces of the sand-ridges in that part of the desert were turned towards the south and the west, the flatter, easier declivities towards the east and the north—an arrangement which was the exact contrary of what we should have preferred.

Notwithstanding the violent gale, the sky was perfectly

clear. But then the wind came from the west; while it is
only the easterly winds which bring the dust-storms. It
turned out a hot day, although the air was somewhat cooled
by the wind. Clouds and columns of sand whirled in a mad
dance across the desert, so that every now and again we became entirely swallowed up in them. But, as they seldom
exceeded a dozen feet in height, the zenith retained all the
while its fresh blue color, and the sun's rays beat down upon
us with undiminished fierceness. The horizon was veiled in
an unbroken yellowish-red haze. The fine drift-sand penetrated everywhere—into mouth, nose, ears; even our clothes
became impregnated with it, so that we experienced a disagreeable grittiness of the skin, to which, however, we soon
grew accustomed. The haze on the horizon was very embarrassing; for we often found it difficult to decide which
way to go. It would have suited us very much better had
things been reversed—namely, the zenith been clouded, but
the horizon clear. Meanwhile the top of every dune afforded
us an opportunity to observe how the drift-sand stood over
like a plume or inverted tassel on the brink that faced the
direction of the wind; how one moment the minute grains
of sand were whirling round and round in a frenzied dance
on the windward side of the dune, then the next moment
quietly settled down on the lee side in fine crumpled folds,
as though some mighty master-hand were weaving them
together after a tastefully designed pattern. But when our
heads rose up to the same level as the sand-storm, which
came whistling between the summits of the dunes, the effect
absolutely baffles description. We shut our eyes and mouths
tight; we lowered our heads against the fierce blast, which
shrieked and moaned about our ears. But, the whirlwind
passed, we stood still and literally shook the dust off our
clothes by the pound. I had brought with me a good stock
of snow-spectacles, with a fine mesh-work of black wire across
them; these now proved invaluable, although the fine sand
partly forced itself in between the tiny meshes.

There was, however, one advantage attending a westerly
gale. It tended to level down the abrupt faces of the sand-

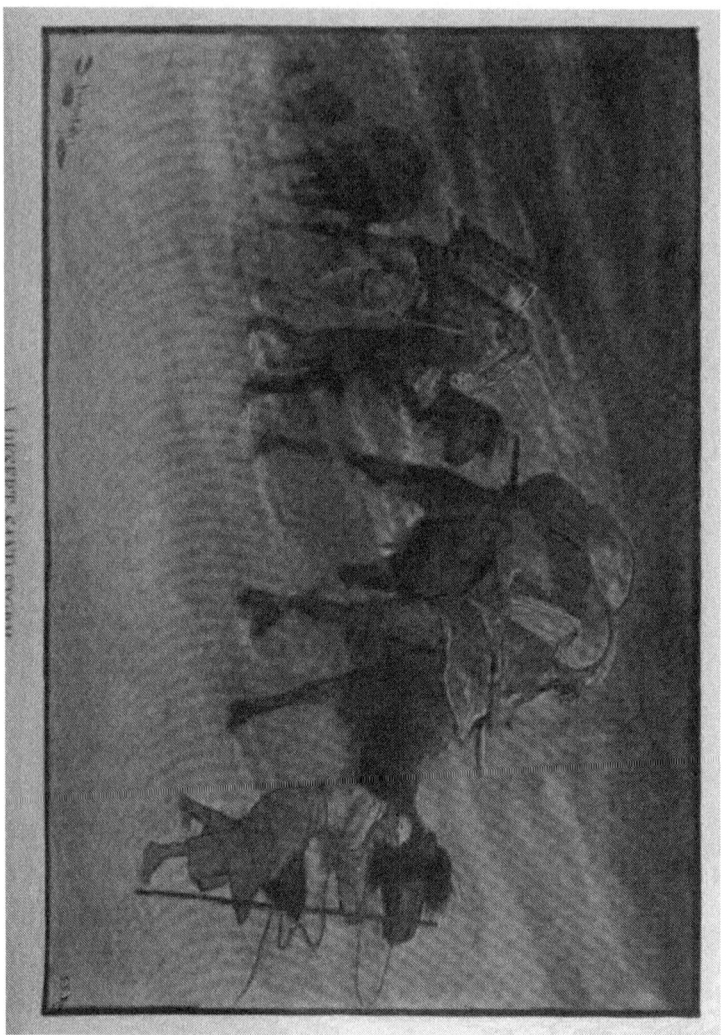

DESERT CARAVAN

dunes, and hurl them over on to the eastern sides. And yet what can one hurricane effect as against the labor of centuries?

My men set out in the morning full of hope that before evening we should reach a part of the desert where the dunes were lower, and where we should be able to find water, and, maybe, pasture for the camels, and fuel for a fire as well. But no such thing. The sand-hills grew higher and higher, and we drifted farther and farther into the unknown terrors of the desert. Only once during the day did the dunes become really lower—namely, forty to fifty feet. In that solitary spot we caught a glimpse of a few patches of bare level soil, partly clay, partly sheeted with saline incrustations.

At first it had been my intention to keep steadily on towards the southeast, in order to find out how far it was before the Masar-tagh cropped up again out of the sand of the Takla-makan Desert. But we saw no glimpse of a mountain, and so gradually bent our course round to the east, under the belief that that was the shortest way to the Khotan-daria. Islam Bai was our pilot now, and excellently well he did the work. He went on a good distance ahead, picking out the easiest path, and holding the compass in his hand all the time. Down he went behind a dune, and became lost to sight; but he soon reappeared on the crest of the next ridge, then down again; and so it went on, time after time. The caravan followed slowly in his footsteps. Our line of march thus formed an undulating curve, winding across the troughs of the desert waves, and over the saddles of the dunes—*i.e.*, the lower transverse ridges which connected the loftier crests— and thus afforded relatively easy passages from one depression to another. But when Islam stopped, and stepped aside up a pyramidal peak, and putting his hand to his brow to shade his eyes, gazed fixedly eastward, I confess I did not feel very comfortable. The action would bear only one interpretation : the road was growing still more difficult. Sometimes he came back quite discouraged, crying "*Hetch yoll yock*" (Perfectly impassable), "*Her taraf yaman kum*" (Hateful sand everywhere), or simply "*Kum-tagh*" (Mountains of sand).   When that happened, we were forced to make a wide détour to the north or south, so as to get past the hinderances which blocked the direct line of advance.

All the men walked barefooted, the perspiration rolling off them, all alike silent, weary, and downcast at finding their hopes of easier sand so bitterly and so constantly deceived. Time after time they stopped to drink; but the water itself was hot, its temperature being 86° Fahr. (30° C.); for it was incessantly washed backward and forward against the heated sides of the iron tanks, which we were no longer able to shade with bundles of reeds, for the camels had eaten them all up to the last stalk.   Anyway, we all drank excessive quantities of water, in order to increase the transpiration, for the wind struck cool upon our skin.

The caravan crept slowly on at a snail's pace.   We always took a general look-round from the top of each outstanding eminence; but towards every point of the compass it was always the same monotonous, discouraging outlook — one sand-ridge peeping up behind another—a billowy ocean without a shore, actual mountain-chains of nothing but fine, yellow sand.   The camels still continued to climb up and slide down the slopes with the same marvellous surety of foot; nevertheless, we were often obliged to make a path for them. These difficult places, which the men called *davan-kum* (sand-pass), generally discouraged us all a little; but whenever we were favored with a good piece of level ground (*darah*) between the dunes, we quickly recovered our spirits and pushed on with fresh vigor, the men crying "*Khoda kalesa*" (God grant it!), "*Inshallah*" (With God's will!), and "*Bismillah*" (In God's name!).   But after advancing a little way a fresh ridge would face us, and fresh crests would tower up ahead as far as the eye could reach.

On the top of a commanding dune we made a long halt, for the purpose of reconnoitring and of quenching our thirst. Occasionally poor Yolldash and the sheep, which were dying of thirst, were given their fill.   Yolldash was wild the moment he heard the sound of water.   Every time anybody went to the water-tank, he came running up wagging his tail.

The last survivor of the sheep followed us with the patience and fidelity of a dog. The men grew so fond of the creature that they said they would rather perish of hunger than kill it.

But the camels were visibly tiring. Heavy falls grew more and more frequent. When they fell on a steep incline, they were unable to get up without help. One of the beasts, which came down near the summit of a ridge, we were obliged to free entirely from his burden, saddle and all; and then, all putting our shoulders to him, we rolled him seventy feet down the slope into a hollow between two sand-dunes. It was only then that he was able to recover his feet.

After going eight miles, we had had enough of it for that day; and camped on a small patch of bare ground, so hard that we did not even attempt to dig a well. Every trace of organic life had now absolutely ceased. No moths came fluttering round my candle at night. Not a single yellow leaf came dancing down the wind to break the deadly uniformity. As soon as our duties were finished, we sat down and discussed the doings of the day, and what should be done on the morrow. It was truly touching to hear Islam Bai doing his best to keep up the courage of the others. He told them about our former journeys, about the masses of snow we encountered in the Alaï valley, " which were much worse than the sand," about the glaciers of Mus-tagh-ata, and our several ascents of the great mountain.

CHAPTER XLIII

THE CAMELS BREAK DOWN

RIL 25TH. As a consequence of the limpid purity of the
phere, the minimu— thermometer sank to an unusually
not more than a couple of degrees above freezing·
and in the morning a nor'wester was blowing and the
ras again thick with dust. All day long, therefore, the
rature remained more than ordinarily low; we had no
ds for complaining of the heat, even at noon. Under
ear night sky radiation had been very active; then came
l of dust, shielding the earth like an umbrella, so that
un's rays were a long time in warming the ground.
while the air grew so thick that we had difficulty in
...ug beyond the next dune or so.

The terraced patches of clay and silt, which lay embedded
between the sand-dunes, and on which we preferred if possible to encamp, were formations of a remarkable character.
They consisted of a series of horizontal flakes of clay, brittle,
friable, and saline, and crumbled to pieces at the least touch.
The several flakes did not lie at the same level, but generally rose layer above layer like a series of steps. There was
not a trace of sand in them, nor of vegetable matter either.
They were pure alluvial clays; of that there could not exist
a doubt. Probably they were the last surviving fragments of
the bed of the great Central Asian Mediterranean, which has
dried up in the course of countless centuries, and the differ·
ent terraces possibly indicated different sea-levels. As a rule
none of these patches of clay was bigger than the deck of a
brig; and the sand-dunes, in their restless onward movement,
keep pouring over them and covering them up.

When morning came I made a most unwelcome discovery·

I had noticed the day before how the water washed very noisily to and fro in the water-tanks, and I looked into them to ascertain the cause. They contained only *water enough to last two days!* I asked the men why they had not obeyed my instructions, and put in sufficient water to last ten days. They answered that Yollchi was responsible for the quantity of water brought. When I reproached Yollchi he answered, " We might be perfectly easy; for it was merely a four days' journey from the last of the desert lakes to the place where we could get water by digging for it." This statement agreed with the maps I had. Consequently I relied upon the man, all the more since his information hitherto had invariably turned out to be correct. We were all without exception convinced that we were every bit as near to water by going east as by going west; consequently nobody said a word about going back to the last of the desert lakes. And yet what suffering, what loss, what sorrow would have been spared both to ourselves and to others, who were anxious about our fate, if we had retraced our steps to that little desert lake! However, we all agreed to watch over the water we had, and husband it like gold. Privately, I instructed Islam Bai not to let the two water-tanks out of his sight for a single moment. From that morning the camels never got a drop more water to drink.

Thanks to the dust-haze, the air remained beautifully cool. The crests of the dunes gleamed out of the gloom like fantastic ghosts, yellow dolphins with arched backs, mocking us for our audacity in daring to defy them. The thick atmosphere embarrassed us considerably in judging of distance and perspective. We were often brought up suddenly at the bottom of a dune, which, owing to its blurred outlines, we still imagined to be a good way ahead of us.

In front of us extended an endless world of ridges and hummocks of sand. The greater portion of the dunes stretched from north to south; the highest ones extended from east to west. The horizontal terraces of clay, which were at least evidence that the ocean of sand was not quite without a bottom, and which buoyed us up with the hope that we should ultimately get beyond the sweep of its sand-waves, had now entirely ceased. Everything was completely buried under sand; the dunes were sand; every hollow between them was sand. It was plain we were entangled in the very worst part of all the desert; and I became painfully conscious of the seriousness of our position.

I travelled all that day on foot, partly to spare my excellent camel Boghra, partly to encourage my men. The camel Babai kept stopping every minute. Time after time the cord that he was led by broke, and his nose became sore and tender. At last he lay down on the sand, and refused to exert himself any further. We took off his load. Then he got up. We fastened his load on again as he stood. But he walked slower and slower, stopped oftener and oftener, and had to be led all the time by one of the men. Finally we relieved him of his burden and divided it among the other camels, and left him to make his way alone in the wake of the caravan. It was a terrible sight to see "the ship of the desert," man's only hope on that endless sea, become a wreck. We gazed and gazed impatiently eastward, seeking some abatement of the difficulties of the road; but we gazed in vain. There was nothing but mountains of sand as far as the eye could pierce. All of a sudden a gadfly came buzzing among the camels. Instantly our hopes rose to fever point: we believed we were nearing "land." Yet in all probability it was merely a deceiver, which we had not observed before —a straggler which had quietly lain hidden in the hairy hide of one of the camels.

Babai delayed us continually; at last we decided to halt for an hour, so as to afford him an opportunity to rest. We gave him a few pints of water and a few handfuls of hay out of his own pack-saddle; he devoured them voraciously. When his saddle was taken off, we perceived he had an open sore on his back, where a rough piece of the saddle had chafed his unhealthy yellowish flesh. His legs trembled; his tongue was white. It was painful to see the poor creature. Leaving Mohammed Shah to look after him, the rest of us went on. For a long time we heard the sick animal crying after us.

The highest dunes now rose 150 to 200 feet above their bases. Farther on again they sank to 100 to 120 feet.

"*Karga! karga!*" cried Islam Bai, as he pointed to a raven, which circled two or three times round the caravan, hopped about on the summit of a dune, and finally disappeared. This incident awakened universal joy. We looked upon it as an indication that the Khotan-daria was not far off. The raven was hardly likely to have sought the depths of the desert for the mere pleasure of the thing.

After we had gone 12½ miles, Chong-kara, the big black camel, refused to go farther. This obliged us to make camp No. XIII. We gave the camels what was left of Babai's saddle to eat; for we had a good reserve supply in the saddles of the other seven, which were all stuffed with hay and straw.

My dinners grew gradually simpler, till at last I was forced to content myself with tea, bread, and tinned foods. The men lived on tea, bread, and talkan (toasted flour). Our fuel had pretty well run out. The small supply we had started with was all done, and we had no resource left but to sacrifice some of the less valuable packing-cases. In the evening we again took counsel together. We considered that, at the most, we had only three days to the Khotan-daria, but hoped before then to come to a belt of poplars, where we should be able to obtain water by digging for it. A couple of gnats came and kept me company in the tent. The question was, had they travelled with us or had they been blown to that spot by the wind from some wood in the vicinity?

April 26th. At daybreak, while the men were occupied with getting the tent down and preparing the caravan for a start, I set off alone, on foot, to try and find a passage eastward. From that point I travelled on foot all the way to the Khotan-daria; consequently I was no longer able to calculate the distance from the camel's paces. Instead of that, I adopted the device of counting my own, an occupation which greatly interested me. Every hundred paces I went was so much space won towards "land"; and with every thousand my hopes of safety rose a degree.

Meanwhile, with my compass in one hand and my field-glass in the other, I hastened eastward, due eastward; for there ran the river of safety. The camp, the camels were soon lost to sight behind the summits of the sand-hills. My only companion was a solitary fly, which I regarded with unusually friendly eyes. Otherwise I was alone, absolutely alone, in the midst of a death-like silence, with a sea of yellow sand-dunes before me, rolling away in fainter and fainter billows right away to the horizon. Deeper Sabbath peace never brooded over any graveyard than that which environed me. The only thing wanting to convert the simile into actual fact was the headstones to the graves.

I soon fancied the dunes were not so high as usual. I tried to maintain the same level, as far as possible, by keeping to their crests and circling round the highest points. I knew the poor camels would have many a toilsome, many a weary step to take in my wake. A bewildering chaos of ridges, lying northeast to southwest, and east to west, were flung across one another in the strangest fashion. Our position was desperate. The dunes burst up to heights of 140 to 150 feet. As I looked down from the top of one of these giant waves, the depression at my feet, on the sheltered side of the dune, looked a long way below me, at a giddy depth. We were being slowly but surely killed by these terrible ridges of sand. They impeded our advance; yet over them we must. There was no help for it, no evading them. Over them we must—a funeral procession, marching to the doleful clang of the camels' bells.

The steeper faces were now turned towards the east and southeast. Evidently the northwest wind had prevailed in this quarter during the past few days. A good crisp breeze was cutting across from that direction even then. On its wings rode every now and again a few small tufts of some species of white vegetable down. Over one of the ridges rolled a handful of dry and withered thistles, closely matted together. Unfortunately, these scant tokens of organic life were wafted thither by the northwest wind. In all probability they had travelled a route coincident or parallel with ours.

Noon came, and I was near fainting from fatigue and thirst. The sun glowed like a furnace above my head. I was dead beat; I *could* not go another step. Then my friend the fly swung round to the other side of me and buzzed such a lively tune that he roused me up. "Just a little bit farther," he buzzed in my ear. "Come, drag yourself on to the summit of the next dune. Tramp off another thousand paces before you give in. You will be all the nearer to the Khotandaria—all the nearer to the flood of fresh water which rolls down to Lop-nor—all the nearer to the dancing waves of the river, which sing a song of life and spring, and of the spring of life." I tramped off the thousand paces. Then I dropped on the top of a dune, rolled over on my back, and pulled my white cap over my face. O, burning sun! hasten, hasten westward; melt the ice-fields of the "Father of the Ice Mountains;" give me but one cup of the cold crystal streams which pour from his steel-blue glaciers and foam down his mighty flanks!

I had walked eight miles. It was delightful to rest; and there was a stir of air on the dune top. I fell into a kind of torpor; I forgot the gravity of our situation. I dreamed I was lying on a patch of cool emerald-green grass, underneath a leafy silver poplar, and a gentle breeze was whispering through its trembling leaves. I heard the wavelets beating their melancholy cadences against the shore of a lake, which washed the very roots of the poplar. A bird was singing in the tree-top—singing a song of mystic meaning which I did not understand. A beautiful dream! How gladly would I have continued to steep my soul in its false illusions! But alas! alas! the hollow clang of the funeral bells again woke me up to the grim realities of that evil desert. I sat up. My head was heavy as lead; my eyes were blinded by the glittering reflections of the eternal yellow sand.

Up staggered the camels, their eyes dull and lustreless, like the dying gleams of the setting sun. It was a look of resignation, a look of indifference; all desire for food had gone out of it. Their breathing was labored and slow; their breath more disagreeable than usual. There were only six of them, led by Islam Bai and Kasim. The other two men had remained behind with Babai and Chong-kara. Even at the beginning of the day Chong-kara's legs had failed him. "They would come on to camp," said Islam, "as quickly as they were able."

After that the desert showed us another of its features. Every now and again we stumbled into level pools of inconceivably fine dust lying embedded between the dunes. We sank into them up to the knees as though we trod on soft mud. Accordingly, after that we kept a vigilant lookout for these treacherous spots. In other places the sand was covered with a thin sprinkling of minute particles of flints with sharp edges. They appeared to exercise much the same sort of influence upon the sand-dunes that oil does upon the waves of the sea. Where they were present the dunes were flattened down, rounded off, and lost their delicate rippled surface.

Between two of the sand-dunes we made a strangely unexpected discovery—namely, a portion of the skeleton of a donkey, or, as the men asserted, of a wild horse. There was nothing but the leg bones, which were white as chalk, and so brittle that a mere touch caused them to crumble to pieces like ashes. The best preserved parts were the hoofs. They were too large to be those of a donkey, too small to have belonged to a tame horse. What was the creature doing out here in the desert? How long had the bones lain there? To these questions the obdurate desert sand returned no answer. For my part, I fail to see why those bones may not have lain where we found them for thousands of years. I ascertained subsequently from several instances that the dry, fine desert sand unquestionably does possess the property of preserving organic matter for a very long period of time. Perhaps the skeleton had lain buried beneath the sand for centuries, and had only quite recently been exposed through the drifting away of the superincumbent dunes.

We were all completely done up through weariness and the cravings of thirst. We were unable to drag ourselves on more than another mile and a half, and then halted on a patch of hard level clay. There, too, we lighted upon a number of curious objects—namely, small, brittle, white snail-shells, tiny pebbles, which some time or other had been rolled and polished by water, amorphous pieces of flint, a fragment of a mussel-shell, and a large quantity of pipe-like formations of lime-stone, as though lime had been moulded round the stalks of reeds.

It was evening when Yollchi and Mohammed Shah strug-gled into camp, tired and thirsty, supporting their steps on their hand-staves. They came alone. The two camels re-fused to go any farther, and so they had left them to their fate. As soon as it turned a little cooler I sent a man to fetch them. He found that they had picked up a bit, and towards midnight brought them in.

Our spirits all revived that evening. Looking to the east with my field-glass, I thought the dunes were much lower, 40 to 50 feet at the most. To-morrow we should be through the high sand-ridges: we should perhaps be able to encamp in the woods of the Khotan-daria! A glorious thought! It put life into us all.

From this point I did without the tent. It was necessary to husband our strength for more essential exertions. We all slept comrade-like under the open sky. Yollchi, however, held aloof from us, and never spoke unless he was spoken to first. There was a traitorous look in his eye; we felt more comfortable when he was out of our sight. The word that was oftenest heard during the day was "Yaman" (Bad; things look bad). But after a while something of the grim humor of despair began to creep over us. We passed some flakes of stone. One of the men advised another to look for gold. But no matter how the day went, our spirits invariably rose as we drew near to the next camping-place. Besides, what was the use of worrying ourselves about the morrow; only let us rest after the toils and fatigues of *that* day, and re-cover from *its* deceptive hopes! After the heat of the day the coolness of the night was always welcome.

In the evening, about six o'clock, a bright idea occurred to me. Why not try to dig a well? Islam Bai and Kasim were instantly all eagerness. While the former made haste to get

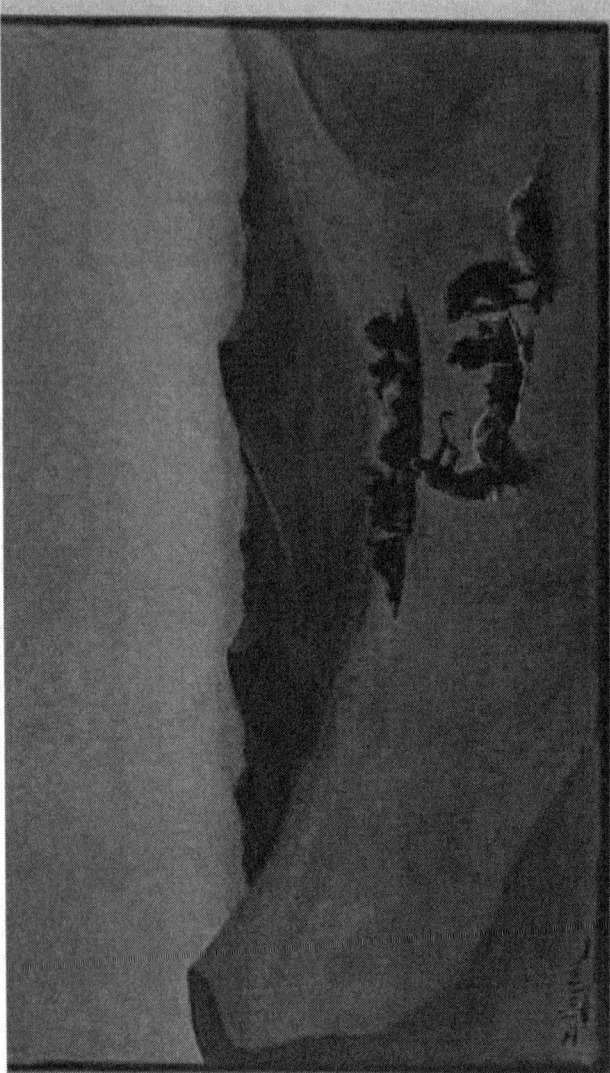

DIGGING THE DECEITFUL WELL

my "dinner" ready the latter set to work to dig. He rolled
up his sleeves, spat in his hands, and laid hold upon the *he-
men*, a sharp-pointed Sart spade, the blade of which was set
on at right angles to the shaft. The dry clay crackled, and
Kasim sang as he dug. After the other two men came into
camp, all three took their turns in digging. In answer to my
question whether there was water there, Yollchi smiled scorn-
fully, and said: " Oh yes, there was plenty of water, if we dug
down thirty *gulatsh* (fathoms)!" Kasim got down about a
yard. The clay was mixed with sand and it was *moist!*
Yollchi was put to shame, and worked with double zeal.
The hopes of all of us revived. I hurried through my simple meal, and with Islam hastened to the well. And at it we
went, all five of us, as hard as we could work. The hole grew
deeper. The man digging could not be seen from the level
ground; nor was he able to throw the sand to the surface. A
rope was tied to the handle of a bucket, and by that means
the loose sand was drawn up to the top. A third man emptied the bucket. Gradually a circular mound rose round the
opening, until I set to work and shovelled it away to make
room. We began work at six o'clock. At that hour the
temperature of the air was 83.5° Fahr. (28.6° C.); of the surface of the earth 80.2° Fahr. (26.8° C.). At a depth of 3½ feet
the argillaceous sand showed 61.9° Fahr. (16.6° C.), and at
five feet 54.3° Fahr. (12.4° C.).

The material we dug through was clayey sand of a grayish
yellow color, and contained in places reddish brown husks,
the relics of some species of decayed vegetation. Of stones
there was not a trace.

It was pleasant and refreshing to lie on the cool sand.
The water in the iron tanks was 84.9° Fahr. (29.4° C.) warm.
A tinful was embedded in the sand that was thrown out of
the well, and it speedily became cool enough to quench our
thirst.

Slowly and gradually the sand grew moister. It was evident there was water, although Yollchi believed it was a long
way down to it. When we got down about 6½ feet, the sand
was so moist that we could squeeze it into balls, and by so

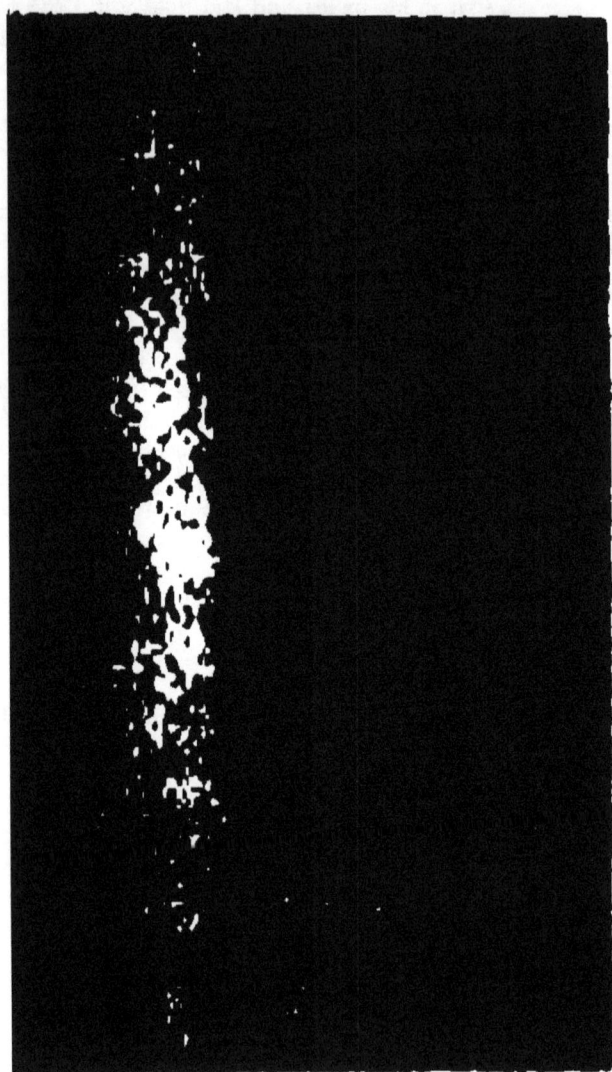

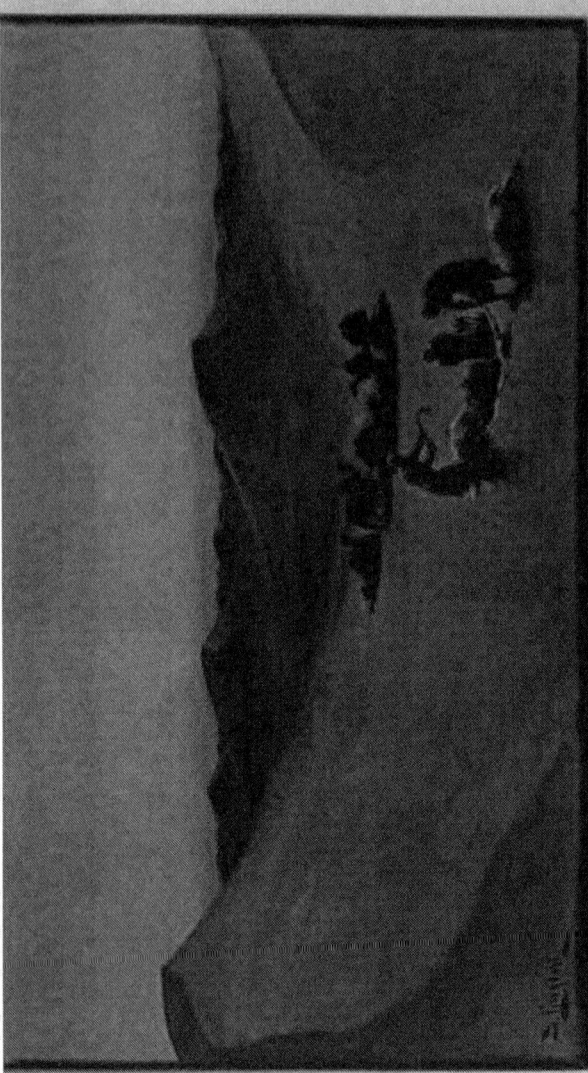

DIGGING THE DECEITFUL WELL

doing made our hands moist. And how pleasant it was to cool our heated cheeks against it. In this way a couple of hours passed. The men had grown tired. Their breasts and shoulders, which were bare, dripped with perspiration. They kept stopping to rest oftener and oftener, and every now and again swallowed a mouthful of water. Nor did our conscience reproach us for the extravagance; for were we not going to fill our empty tanks at the well we were digging?

In the mean time, it had grown pitch-dark, and the work went on by the light of a couple of candle-ends stuck in niches in the sides of the well. Their own instinct brought all the animals round the mouth of the hole. The camels, waiting impatiently, stretched their long necks over it and sniffed at the cool wet sand. Yolldash came and squatted down on it with his legs out-stretched before him. Every now and then the hens, too, came and took a peep at what was going forward.

Inch after inch we forced our way down, working with the energy of despair for life—dear life. The hope of deliverance gave us new strength. We were resolved not to be beaten; we would dig on all the next day before we would give in. We *would* find water.

We were all standing in a ring round the gaping hole we had made in the ground, talking about it, and watching Kasim, who, half-naked as he was, looked strange and eerie in the dimly lighted cavity at our feet, when all at once he stopped, letting the spade drop out of his hands. Then, with a half-smothered groan, he fell to the ground.

"What is the matter? what has happened?" we asked, one and all stupefied with amazement.

"*Kurruk kum!*" (The sand is *dry!*) came a voice as if from the grave.

A couple of spade-strokes convinced us that the man was right: the sand had become as dry as tinder. The deceptive moisture was possibly due to a fall of snow during the winter, or to a shower of rain. But we did not know that; and the sand-dunes do not betray their secrets. We got down as far as 10½ feet; and there the temperature was 52.2° Fahr.

This unwelcome discovery made, we became instantly conscious of our weariness, and realized how much of our precious strength we had wasted during the three hours we had toiled in vain. We literally collapsed, became unnerved, lost all our energy. A deep and bitter gloom darkened every face. We shunned one another's glances. We staggered away each to his sleeping-place, seeking oblivion of our despair in a long and heavy sleep. Before I lay down I had a private conversation with Islam Bai. We did not conceal our apprehensions from each another. We recognized the extreme gravity of our position, and pledged each other to keep up our own and the other men's courage to the utmost extremity. According to my maps, we could not be very far from the Khotan-daria; nevertheless, it was as well to be prepared for the worst. Before lying down, I took the opportunity of the other men being asleep to examine the contents of the last of the tanks. It contained sufficient water to last one day. We should have to watch over it as if it were gold. In fact, if we could have bought one more day's supply of water with all the money we had, we should not have hesitated about it a moment. We resolved to measure out the last precious portions drop by drop. It *must* be made to last three days: that could be done if we confined ourselves to two cups a day to each man. For three days the camels had not tasted a drop, nor did they get a drop more. Yolldash and the sheep got a bowlful each once a day, and on that they managed very well. Then we two also sought rest, leaving the patient, docile camels standing in a circle round the mocking well, waiting in vain for what they could not get.

CHAPTER XLIV

NO WATER LEFT

At sunrise of April 27th we did all we could do to preserve the camels' strength. We took out the hay stuffing of one of the saddles and gave it to them; they devoured it greedily. Then they looked about for water; but we could only moisten their lips. After the hay they got a sackful of old bread and some oil. To relieve their burdens a little we left behind us my tent-bed, a carpet, and several other articles of minor importance.

As soon as I had swallowed my tea I hastened on in advance. I was consumed with impatience to get on, for the dunes were lower than usual, not more than thirty-five feet in height. All the same, I observed that the brown substratum, which every now and again peeped out from underneath the sand in the hollows between the dunes, was slightly uneven in contour; so that the lower elevation of the dunes may have been due to inequalities in the natural surface of the earth, and to the top of the higher parts being less deeply buried in sand. Consequently I did not deceive myself. An hour later I was again entangled in a maze of lofty sand-dunes, quite as difficult to cross and equally boundless as heretofore. The larger agglomerations of dunes stretched from east to west; while the secondary or transverse dunes lay from north to south or from northeast to southwest. The steep slopes were now turned towards the east and towards the south. But not a sign of life, not a single tamarisk to break the straight line of the horizon, nothing to indicate the approximate presence of "land." My senses reeled as I gazed across that desolate ocean of sand in the depths of which we had hopelessly lost ourselves. Again and again, from the top of every

sand-ridge I came to, I swept the horizon with my field-
glass, hoping to discern in the east the dim dark line of the
woods of the Khotan-daria. But all in vain.

Going down the side of one of the dunes, my eye fell upon
a small object resembling a root. I stooped down to pick it
up, when suddenly it darted away and disappeared in a little
hole on the edge of the dune. It was a lizard, of the same
yellow color as the sand. How did the creature live? Did
it eat nothing? Did it never want a drop of water to drink?

It turned out a splendid day. The sky was flecked with
light feathery clouds; the heat was not at all oppressive; radiation was less active than usual. At the end of three and
a half hours I was overtaken by the caravan, which continued to go well all day long. But when they came up, Mohammed Shah and the two sick camels were already missing.
"They were coming on slowly after them," said the other
men. High up in the sky we perceived two wild geese,
scudding away to the northwest. This again revived our
hopes; for we conjectured that they came from the Khotan-
daria, and were making for the little desert lake that lay at
the foot of the mountains we had passed. And yet, after all,
we were only trying to deceive ourselves; for wild geese only
fly at such a great height when they are migrating from place
to place, and when they are doing that, what signifies to
them the crossing of a desert some 200 miles broad?

I got up on Boghra's back for a while, and he received the
accession to his burden without murmuring. As soon as I
was mounted I felt myself terribly tired; yet when I noticed
how the animal's knees tottered at every step he took, I got
down again and walked.

That day the sand-hills were the highest of any we had
yet crossed—fully 200 feet high. The way I estimated their
height was this. I stationed myself a little way off a dune
along the top of which the caravan was moving. I knew by
previous measurement the exact height of one of the camels.
On a pencil I marked notches at equal distances apart, each
space representing the height of the camel. Then, holding
the pencil up to my eye, I measured how many notched

spaces were required to cover the height of the dune; in other words, I measured how many camel's heights it was. Apart from that my eye alone told me that the camel was an extremely small object as compared with the dune, which was more like a high hill. It will readily be understood that over gigantic billows of sand like this we could not advance very rapidly. We were compelled to make many a détour, involving great loss of time, in order to avoid them; in fact, we were sometimes compelled to travel for a time in the exactly opposite direction from that in which we wanted to go.

Yolldash kept close to the water-tanks, in which he could hear the last few drops of the precious fluid splashing against the sides, and whined and howled every time he heard a splash. Whenever we stopped, uncertain which way to turn, he yelped, and sniffed at the tanks, and scratched in the sand, as if to remind us that we ought to dig a well, and to let us know that he wanted water. When I lay down to rest the dog would come and crouch in front of me, and look me straight in the eyes, as if to ask me whether there really was no hope. I patted him, and spoke soothingly to him, and pointed towards the east, trying to make him understand that there was water there. At that he would prick his ears, jump up, and run in that direction; but he soon came back again, downcast and disappointed.

After some trouble Islam Bai and I climbed to the top of a pyramidal dune, and took a long and searching reconnaissance of the country ahead through my field-glass. But there was no abatement of the billows of sand, no gap in the dunes towards which we could steer our course. Everywhere the same curdled sea of giant sand-waves. No matter which way we looked, we were surrounded by the same desolate, lifeless landscape. As the result of our deliberations we resolved to keep pushing on as long as the six camels were able to walk, and until a really serious crisis confronted us. That crisis occurred at six o'clock that same evening, on the slope of a dune looking towards the north, where we made camp No. XV., a camp shut in on every side by " ugly " country.

Shortly after reaching camp we were joined by Mohammed Shah. He said that even at the beginning of the day's march the camels refused to move, and he had, therefore, abandoned them to their fate. One of the two carried a couple of empty water-tanks, and the other had bread. If I had been there when they stopped I should have had them shot; for the old man said that at the most they could not last longer than two days. But he believed they might be saved, if we could find water before night. As it was, just then, they were abandoned for lost, and would have to wait in patience for a painful death. God grant it came speedily!

Mohammed Shah's report made an extremely painful impression upon me. I was to blame for the loss of the innocent lives. It was I who was answerable for every moment of agony, every pang of pain, which the men and animals of my caravan suffered. I was not present, it is true, when the first camels were delivered up to the power of the evil desert. But in imagination I saw the action vividly. It weighed upon my conscience like a nightmare, keeping me awake at night. I saw Babai lie down when Mohammed Shah left him. The other camel remained standing, although his legs trembled under him, and, with expanded nostrils and shining eyes, followed the departing caravan with a wistful and reproachful look. But the caravan soon passed out of sight. Then I imagined him slowly turning his head towards his companion, and thereafter crouching down beside him. Then they both stretched out their necks along the sand, half closed their eyes, and lay motionless, breathing heavily through their expanded nostrils. Their weariness increased; they rolled over on their sides with legs out-stretched. Their blood coursed slower and slower, thicker and thicker, through their veins; the rigid torpors of death gradually stiffened their limbs. The pauses between their breathings became longer and longer, until at last the end came. In all probability Babai would die first, for he was the weaker. But how long did that death-struggle last? We shall never know. My blood curdled with horror as the thought flashed across my mind that perhaps they might live some days, and be buried

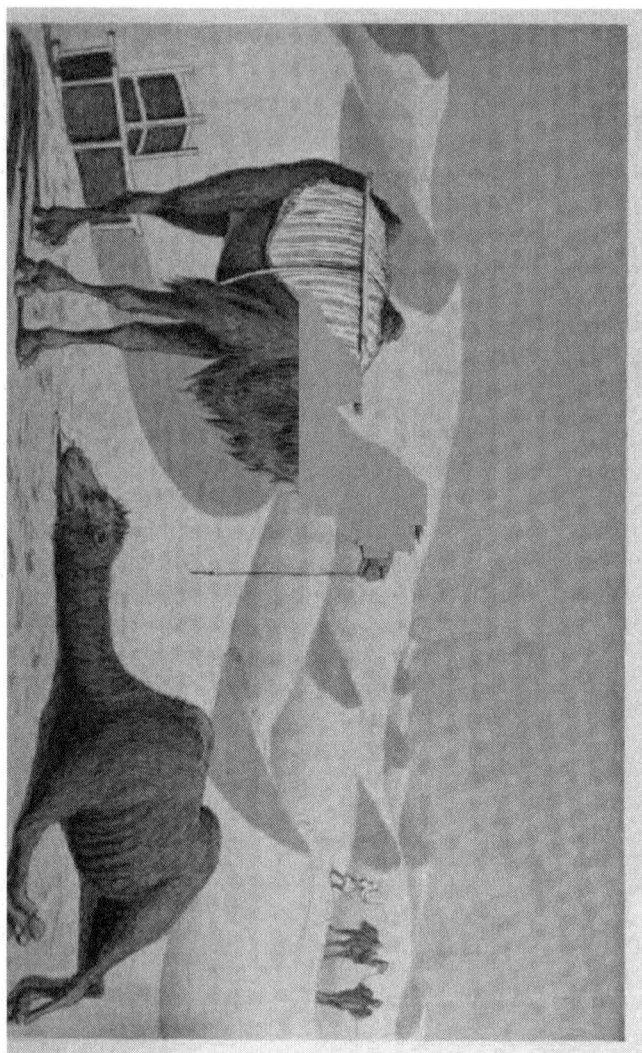

alive by the sand-storms. Ah well! they are now sleeping their century-long sleep under the moving billows of the remorseless and interminable desert.

Later on in the afternoon we perceived that the western sky was full of thick steel-blue clouds, heavily charged with rain. They were the symbols of water and of life. *We* were surrounded by aridity and death. They widened out; they drove closer together. The sight of them fairly fascinated us. We could not take our eyes off them. Our hopes of rain grew stronger from moment to moment. We set out two of the empty water-tanks. We spread out the tent-covering on the ground, with one man at each corner, ready to hold it up. We waited and waited. But the clouds slowly drew over to the south, vouchsafing us not a drop.

Islam Bai baked bread for me for the last time. Mohammed Shah declared that we had fallen under the spell of *telesmat—i.e.,* witchcraft —and should never find our way out of the desert. With superb calmness, as if stating a mere matter of course, Islam Bai remarked that the camels would fall one after the other, and then it would be our turn. It was simply the inevitable course of events. I answered, I was convinced we should *not* die in the desert. Yollchi mocked at my compass—my *keblah-nameh* (the shower of the direction to Mekka)—and swore it was it which was deceiving us, by leading us round in a circle. No matter how many days we travelled, he said, the result would be just the same. The best thing we could do was not to exert ourselves unnecessarily: we were bound to die of thirst at the end of a few days. I assured him that the compass was a perfectly trustworthy guide, and had led us due east all the time; he had only to note the rise and setting of the sun to convince himself of the fact. His reply was that the dust-haze, together with telesmat (witchcraft), affected even the sun, so that it was no longer to be trusted to.

On April 28th we were awakened by an unusually violent hurricane of wind out of the north-northeast, which enveloped the camp in blinding clouds of sand. Up over the dunes dashed the whirling columns of sand, down they plunged on the lee side, and careered away one after the other in a frenzied dance. I tossed a handful of pieces of paper on the wind, and watched how they dropped to the ground directly they got to the sheltered side of the dunes, and there remained. The atmosphere was choked with dust and sand; it was so thick that we were unable to see the summits of even the nearest dunes. We could not possibly have steered our course by the sun that day. There was not the faintest glimmer of light in the sky to indicate his position. This was the worst storm we had experienced throughout the whole of our journey through the desert, one of those terrible kara-burans or "black storms," which convert day into night.

We slept the previous night under the open sky. The night being cool, I lay down wrapped in my furs, with a *bashlik* (hood) pulled round my head. In the morning, when I awoke, I was literally buried in sand. A thick sheet of fine yellow sand covered my neck and breast. Fine yellow sand had penetrated through every opening in my clothing. When I stood up it slipped down inside my shirt next my skin, so that I had to take off my clothes and shake them. My furs were indistinguishable from the surface of the dune. Every object about the camp was in a precisely similar plight, half smothered in sand. It cost us a great deal of trouble to fish them all out with our hand-staves.

The going that day was fearful. We could not get a glimpse of our surroundings; we did not know which way to go. But the air was cool, and that and the gale made us forget the cravings of thirst.

That day I was unable, of course, to go on in advance; my footsteps would have been obliterated almost instantly. All we could do was to stick close together, men and animals in a clump. If you once get separated from your companions in such a storm as that, it is utterly impossible to make yourself heard by shouting, or even by rifle shots. The deafening roar of the hurricane overpowers every other sound. If you do get separated from them you are bound to wander astray, and so become irretrievably lost. All that I could see was the camel immediately in front of me. Everything else

was swallowed up in the thick, impenetrable haze. Nor can you hear anything except the peculiar whining and moaning made by the millions upon millions of grains of sand as they whiz without cessation past your ears. Perhaps it was this eerie sound which worked upon the imagination of Marco Polo, and led him, when speaking of the Great Desert, to write thus: " Even in the daytime one hears those spirits talk. And sometimes you shall hear the sound of a variety of musical instruments, and still more commonly the sound of drums. Hence in making this journey 'tis customary for travellers to keep close together. All the animals, too, have bells at their necks, so that they cannot easily get astray. And at sleeping time a signal is put up to show the direction of the next march."*

We had a hard and trying march. Through the greater part of the middle of the day it was as dark as pitch; at other times we were environed by a dim, murky light, half yellow, half gray. Several times when the sand-blast met us full in the teeth we were nearly suffocated. In fact, when the more violent gusts struck us we crouched down with our faces on the ground, or pressed them against the sheltered side of a camel. Even the camels turned their backs to the wind and stretched out their necks flat along the ground.

The sand-hills grew no lower, but towered up in front of us as high as ever they did. No sooner had we surmounted one summit than we saw another looming out of the haze ahead of us. During the course of the day one of the younger camels gave up. It was easy to see the animals were exhausted. They staggered, their legs trembled, a dull, glassy look was in their eyes, their lower lip hung limply, their nostrils were expanded. We were in the act of laboriously surmounting the summit of a dune, where the storm seemed to rage with tenfold fury, when Yollchi, who was leading the dying camel last of all in the order of march, came hurrying forward alone. He was afraid to lose sight

* From H. Yule's *The Book of Ser Marco Polo the Venetian*. London, 1874-5, vol. i. p. 203.

I.—35

of us, lest he should not find us again. The camel had not been able to get over the last crest, he said, but had fallen close to the top and rolled over on his side, and would not get up. I commanded the caravan to halt, and sent back two of the other men to see if they could not somehow persuade the camel to rise and follow us. They disappeared in the dust-haze, but soon came back, saying that the trail was already obliterated, and they had not dared to go too far from the caravan.

Thus we lost our third camel, which, like the other two, was abandoned to a painful death in the desert. We gradually became hardened to these affecting losses. Our only concern now was to save our own lives. When people fall into such desperate straits as we were in, their feelings get blunted, and they grow indifferent to the sufferings of others. Every morning when we started I used silently to question myself, Whose turn will it be next to start on the long, dark journey that hath no end?

At six o'clock in the evening we stopped, having travelled 12¼ miles during the day. After carefully considering our situation we agreed to abandon everything that was not absolutely necessary. I and Islam Bai went through our stores *seriatim*. We unpacked the cases of sugar, flour, honey, rice, potatoes, and other vegetables, macaroni, and two or three hundred tins of preserved foods. The greater part of these things, together with several furs and felts, cushions, books, a big bundle of journals, the cooking-stove, and petroleum-cask were stowed away in boxes and covered up with carpets, and left in a hollow between two dunes. On the summit of the next dune, which was visible for a long distance, we planted a staff, and fastened to it a number of a Swedish journal, so as to make a flag. It was our intention, if we found water, to come back and fetch the things we left. Consequently, during the course of the evening we made a score of laths out of the lid of a packing-case, and tied a number of the same journal round each. These little flags we purposed to stick in the tops of the highest dunes we crossed during the succeeding days, so that, like buoys in an unfa-

miliar fairway, they might serve to guide us to camp No.
XVII., where we left our stores.

I picked out all the tinned provisions which contained
anything of a liquid nature, such as mushrooms, lobsters, and
sardines. My men, having convinced themselves that the
tins contained no pork or bacon, ate up their contents with
great delight. What they did not eat were used next day.
The remainder of the water, scarcely 3½ pints, was put into
two *kungans* (iron pitchers). We took with us the last two
tanks, in case we should discover water. The camels had
another of the saddle stuffings, but they did not eat it with
any appetite, for their throats were parched up. I had tea
for the last time, and made a thorough good meal off moist
tinned provisions.

April 29th. We started at daybreak with the five camels
which still survived. Just as we were starting, Islam Bai
came and with a heavy heart told me he had found one of
the iron pitchers empty, and that he and the other men suspected Yollchi of having drunk the water, for they had heard
him moving stealthily about and fumbling in the dark. However, we had no proof that he was guilty; but our suspicions
against him were strengthened when he came creeping to my
feet, complaining of pains in the breast and stomach. We
believed it was all pretence. Nevertheless it was my duty
to set an example to the rest, and keep up the other men's
courage, so I gave him half of my allotted portion to drink.
After that we lost sight of him; nor did he show himself
again until the following morning.

We vainly scanned the horizon for "land." There was
not a sign of a living creature to be seen. The desert ocean
extended before us and around us to an infinite distance.
The country decreased a little in elevation, but the relative
dryness of the atmosphere remained unaltered. The ridges
now stretched from north to south, their steep sides being
again turned towards the west, which of course greatly added
to the difficulties of our advance. Looking eastward from
the top of a high crest we had before us an unending succession of steep banks of sand, which, by an optical illusion,

looked like a series of easy steps. Westward the eye glided across the long, sloping, windward faces of the dunes, so that towards that quarter the surface appeared almost level. The effect of this was to reduce us to despair. We fancied the dunes were growing higher and higher, and consequently the road more and more difficult with every step we took. Here, too, the sheltered sides of the dunes frequently showed a sprinkling of minute fragments of micaceous schist of a steel-gray color.

This day our hopes were spurred by the discovery of the skeleton of a vole (gen. *Arvicola*), as well as of a hoary, withered poplar. And yet it was building upon an extremely slender foundation, for the vole's skeleton may have been carried to the spot where we found it by a bird, and the poplar was without a root. If only it had been rooted in the ground! That alone, for as little a thing as it was, would have kindled our hopes anew.

We travelled through that awful sand the whole day; consequently our pace was painfully slow. The camels' bells echoed at longer intervals apart, for the poor creatures were half dead with fatigue. All the same they still marched on with the same calm dignity and majestic gait which always distinguish them. Their excrement contained next to no straw, for they were living almost entirely upon their own flesh, and were growing fearfully thin. They presented a wretched appearance, every rib they had plainly showing through their hair. The three camels we had abandoned were no doubt by this time dead; in any case, it was too late to do anything to save them, even though we should come across water immediately.

It was a still, calm day, although the atmosphere was still saturated with dust. The men said, and with truth, that it was God's blessing the past few days had been cool, and we had not had the burning sun to contend against. Otherwise every camel we had would have given in, and we ourselves should be on our last legs.

I walked for twelve and a half hours without stopping; we covered altogether nearly seventeen miles before we encamped for the night. Eastward there was not the slightest sign of an improvement in the surface of the country. The same billowy sea of sand stretched right away to the horizon; there was not a single object except sand upon which the eye could rest.

April 30th. The thermometer fell to a minimum of 41.2° Fahr. (5.1° C.), and even when morning came it was decidedly cold. Clouds of fine dust still floated about in the atmosphere; but it cleared sufficiently to let us see the position of the sun—*i.e.*, a faint brightening that loomed through the haze. We gave the camels another saddle stuffing and all the bread we had, and so considered they would be able to last out another day. There were two tumblerfuls of water left in one of the pitchers. While the men were engaged in loading up for the start, Islam Bai caught Yollchi with his back to his comrades and the pitcher at his mouth. There ensued an unpleasant and painful scene. Islam Bai and Kasim, boiling with rage, flung themselves upon Yollchi, hurled him to the ground, struck him in the face, kicked him, and would assuredly have killed him had I not intervened with my authority, and compelled them to let him get up. He had drunk half of what there was, leaving about one-third of a pint. At noon I proposed moistening each man's lips, and in the evening intended to divide what was left into five equal portions. I wondered how many days we should hold out after that. Mohammed Shah said that once in Tibet, many years before, he had struggled on for thirteen days without water.

Again the funeral bells began their mournful ding-dong, ding-dong: the caravan got into motion for the east. At first the dunes were only 25 feet high; but we had not advanced far before we were once more struggling through the mazes of *chong-kum* (big sand). A little wagtail circled round the caravan, twittering, and once more caused our rapidly expiring hopes to flicker up. Islam Bai was so encouraged by the incident that he proposed to go on in advance with the iron pitchers and fetch water for us all. But I said "No." I needed him now more than ever; and we went on all together.

From the very start almost Yollchi was missing. The other men believed that he was unable to keep up with us any longer, but would die on our track. They were all embittered against the man. At the last lake we passed, he swore that we only needed to carry water sufficient for four days, and undertook within that space to bring us to a region where we could get water by digging for it. But the men believed that, from the very beginning, he had entertained a treacherous design against us, that he had of deliberate purpose led us into a part of the desert where we must inevitably perish of thirst, that he had stolen some of the water for his own secret use while he hastened, after the wreck of our caravan, to inhabited parts to fetch some other "gold seekers" of the same stamp as himself to come and plunder my goods. It was not easy to determine how much of truth there was in this theory, and the matter was never cleared up.

Every evening up to this point I had kept a fully detailed account of each day's incidents in my journal; and those accounts constitute the foundation of my description of that awful journey. The last lines I wrote in my book, which might have been the last I ever was to write at all, were penned on the afternoon of April 30th, and ran as follows:

" Rested on a high dune, where the camels gave up. We scanned the eastern horizon with a field-glass—nothing but mountains of sand in every direction, not a blade of vegetation, not a sign of life. Nothing heard of Yollchi, either in the evening or during the night. My men maintained he had gone back to the stores we left behind, intending to keep himself alive on the tinned provisions, while he fetched help to carry off the rest. Islam believed he was dead. There were still a few drops of water left for the morning, about a tumblerful in all. Half of this was used in moistening the men's lips. The little that remained was to be divided equally between us all in the evening. But when evening came we discovered that Kasim and Mohammed Shah, who led the caravan, had stolen every drop! We were all terribly weak, men as well as camels. God help us all!"

My account of what happened during the immediately succeeding days rests upon pencil notes scribbled on a sheet of
folded paper.   But besides recording the course of events, I
never under any circumstances omitted to note the bearings
of the compass, and to count the number of paces I took in
each direction.   When at last I found leisure to rest on the
banks of the Khotan-daria, it was my first and principal concern to write out my notes with complete fulness of detail, so
long as the particulars were fresh in my memory.

CHAPTER XLV

THE CAMP OF DEATH

May 1st. The night was cold; the thermometer fell to 35.9° Fahr. (2.2° C.), the lowest reading we had during the twenty-six days we were crossing the desert. But the atmosphere was pure, and the stars glittered with incomparable brilliancy. The morning dawned calm and gloriously bright —not a speck of cloud in the sky, not a breath of wind on the tops of the dunes. No sooner had the sun risen than it began to be warm.

The 1st of May! The day which in the Northern land of my birth marks the beginning of spring. What a crowd of happy recollections, of joy, of pleasure, of cheerful gayety; and, above all, what pleasant memories of the social cup and its pearly contents are there not associated with those poetic words — the 1st of May! I tried to persuade myself that even in the barren deserts of the Far East the same day would also be a day of rejoicing. On the 1st of May a year ago I arrived at Kashgar, where I found both rest and comfort after the severe inflammation which attacked my eyes, and I hoped that this 1st of May would again mark a turning-point in our destinies—and it did!

Early in the morning Yollchi, whom we all looked upon as dead, once more put in an appearance in camp. He had recovered, and was so bold as to prophesy that we should certainly discover water before the day was over. The other men refused to speak to him, but sat silent and downcast, drinking the last few drops that remained of the camels' rancid oil, which they had warmed, and eating some fragments of stale bread. All the previous day I had not tasted a drop of water. But suffering the extreme tortures of thirst, I ventured to swallow about a tumblerful of the horrible and abominable concoction which the Chinese call brandy, stuff that we carried to burn in our Primus cooking-stove. It burned my throat like oil of vitriol. Yet what of that? It was at any rate liquid, and so calculated to maintain the moisture of my body. When Yoll-dash saw me drinking he came running up, wagging his tail. But when I showed him it was not water, he slunk away downcast and whining. Fortunately the men refused to touch the liquor. Afterwards I hurled the bottle with loathing into the side of a dune.

However, in the mean time my strength left me, and as the caravan slowly struggled on, ever towards the east, my legs failed and refused to carry me farther. In the still atmosphere the funereal camels' bells rang out clearer than ever before. We had left three graves behind us. How many more were we destined to leave by the side of our track? The funeral procession was rapidly approaching the churchyard.

Islam Bai went on first, compass in hand. The five camels were led by Mohammed Shah and Kasim. Yollchi followed close behind the last camel and urged on the string. Dead tired, and tortured by a consuming thirst, I staggered on a long way behind in the rear of the caravan. Down they went out of sight behind each sand-hill in turn; then up they mounted again to the crest of the next after it. The echo of the camels' bells sounded fainter and fainter, and at longer and longer intervals, until at last they died away in the distance.

I dragged myself on a few steps farther; then I fell again. I scrambled up, reeled on a short distance, and once more fell. This was repeated time after time. I could no longer hear the sound of the camels' bells.

A dead silence reigned all round me. But the caravan had left its trail behind. This I stuck to like grim death, all the time steadily counting my heavy, dragging footsteps. At length, from the summit of a dune, I once more caught a glimpse of the caravan. It had halted. The five camels were dead beat, and had thrown themselves down. Old

Mohammed Shah lay flat on his face on the sand, mumbling prayers and crying to Allah for help. Kasim sat in such shade as he could find behind one of the camels, and gasped for breath. He told me the old man was completely done up, and unable to go another step. All the way, ever since they started, he had been delirious, raving about water the whole time.

Islam Bai was a long way on ahead. We shouted to him to come back. He was now far the strongest of us all, and again proposed to hurry on on foot with the iron pitchers. He thought he could do thirty-five miles during the night. But when he saw the pitiable condition to which I was reduced he abandoned the idea. After we had rested awhile, Islam had another plan. He suggested we should seek a piece of firm ground, and use such strength as remained to us in digging a well. Meanwhile he undertook to lead the caravan. The white camel was freed of his load, consisting of the two ammunition-chests, two European saddles, and a carpet. These things we intended to leave behind. Then with great difficulty, Islam helping me, I scrambled on the white camel's back. But the animal refused to get up. It now became clear to us all that it was impossible to go on any longer groping our way in this fashion in the burning heat; especially as Mohammed Shah was perfectly delirious, laughing to himself, weeping, babbling, playing with the sand, and letting it run between his fingers. He was absolutely unable to go any farther, and we could not, of course, abandon him.

We resolved, therefore, to remain where we were until the hottest part of the day was past, and then continue our journey in the cool of the evening and during the night. We let the camels remain where they had thrown themselves down, but took off their loads. Islam and Kasim once more put up the tent, so that we might get a little shade in the inside of it. They spread our last carpet and a couple of felts on the ground, and rolled up a sack to serve as a pillow. I then crept in —literally crept in on my hands and knees—took off all my clothes, and lay down on the bed. Islam and Kasim followed my example, and so did Yolldash and the sheep—that is to say, they too came inside the tent. Yollchi remained outside, keeping in the shade. Mohammed Shah still lay where he first fell. The poultry were the only creatures in the caravan which kept up their spirits. They sauntered about in the blazing sunshine, picking at the camels' pack-saddles and the provision bags. As yet it was only half past nine. We had not covered more than three miles, and had an interminably long day before us. Nobody ever longed for sunset so earnestly as we did that 1st of May in the year 1895.

I was completely overcome by weariness, and scarce had strength to turn myself over in bed. At this time despair took possession of me—though never before, and never afterwards. All my past life flitted before my mind as in a dream. I thought I saw the earth, and all the noisy world of men and their doings; and they seemed to me to be at an immense distance from me, absolutely unattainable. I thought all this disappeared, and the gates of eternity stood ajar, and I felt as if in a few hours I should be standing on their threshold. I thought of my home in the Far North; and my soul was harrowed when I pictured the uneasiness, the anxiety which would seize upon those who were near and dear to me when we never came back and nothing was heard of us. They would wait expectantly year after year, and they would wait in vain; no information would ever reach them. There would be nobody to tell the tidings of our fate. Mr. Petrovsky would, of course, send out messengers to inquire about us. They would go to Merket, and would there learn that we left that place on April 10th, intending to steer our course due east. But by then our trail would be long obliterated in the sand; and it would be absolutely impossible to know in which direction we had gone. By the time a systematic and thoroughly exhaustive search could be set on foot, our bodies would probably have been buried several months under the unresting, devouring billows of sand.

After that an endless panorama of pictures from my former travels passed in succession before my mind's eye. I had travelled through all the Mohammedan countries of Asia for

a whole year like a dervish, and now I had reached my last
camping-ground. Fate said to me, " Thus far shalt thou go,
but no farther." Here the strong pulses of my
cease. It was ten years ago when I first
travels. I had admired the Palace of the
Ispahan. I had listened to the waves of
beating against the pillars of Shah Abbas's
and enjoyed the cool shades of Cyrus's
temple halls of Xerxes and of Darius, and
arcades of Persepolis, I had learned to under
of the poet's words—

> "Det härliga på jorden, förgänglig är de
> (To perish is the lot of all things here

How beautiful it was to rest under the sha
palms of Basrah! Would that the Tigris co
few drops of its muddy water! What would
the water-carrier of Bagdad for his skinful
fluid, which he hawked about through her na
lanes, getting a few copper coins for an ass's lo
of my adventures in the land where the incidents of the
Thousand and One Nights are everyday occurrences. Nine
years previously I had left Bagdad with a caravan of Arabian
merchants and Mecca pilgrims with fifty francs in my pocket,
which I relied upon to take me to Teheran. But the slow
rate of travel and the monotonous mode of life were too much
for my patience. One dark night I ran away from the caravan, in company with an Arab to whom I gave the little
money I had left.

Our horses were almost done up when we came within
sight of Kermanshahan. I went to a rich Arab merchant
living there, named Aga Mohammed Hassan. I remember
how his eyes sparkled when I told him I was a son of Charles
XII.'s country. He wanted to keep me as his guest for half
the year. I could only stay with him a few days; but during
those few days I lived the life of Nur-ed-Din Ali in the
Thousand and One Nights. Over against the house in which
I lived there was an enchanting garden, full of sweet-scented

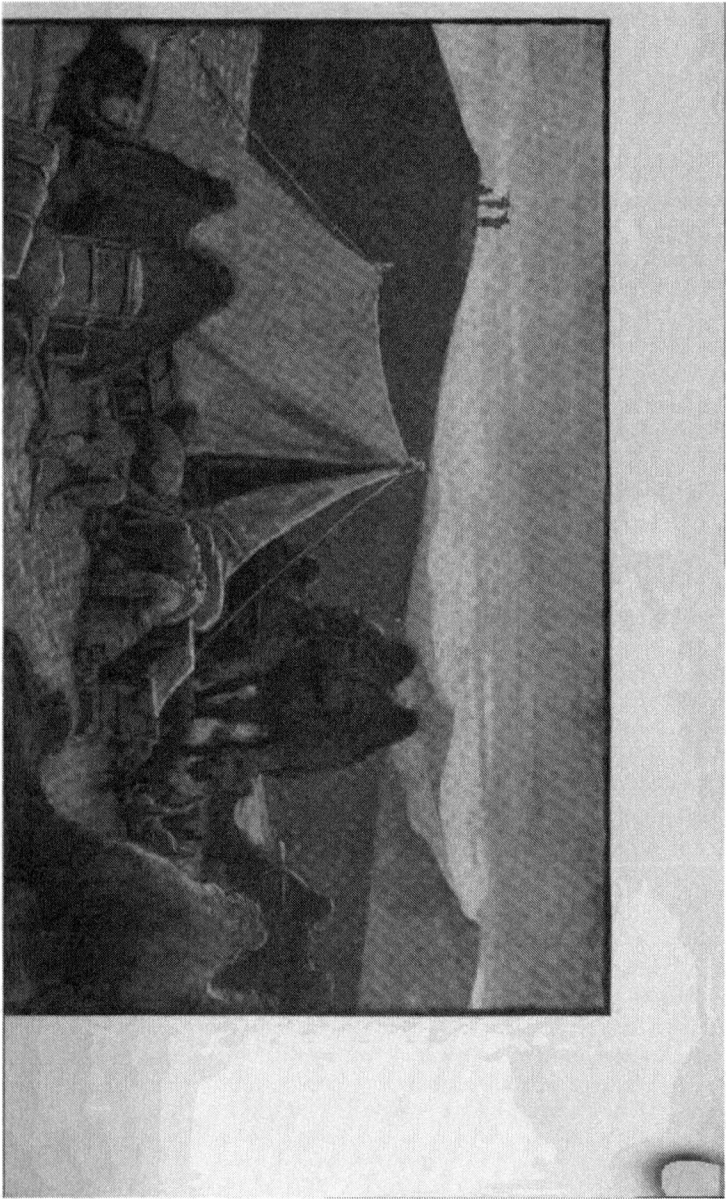

s and lilacs in full bloom. The paths were strewn with
s of marble, and in the middle of the garden there was a
: white marble basin filled with crystal water. From the
re of the basin a fountain shot up a delicate rod of water,
ch broke at the top and fell back in a thousand drops,
kling like a silver cobweb in the sunshine. And when
ist I tore myself away from these fascinating delights, my
erous host pressed into my hand a purse overflowing with
r coins.

saw before me, every feature distinct, the noble and wise
ntenance of the unhappy Shah, Nasr-ed-Din, as he was
n, his uniform blazing with jewels, he received King Os-
s embassy in the Imperial Palace at Teheran; and that
ied my thoughts back to the Emaret Sepa Salar, where
odged, and where of an evening we strolled underneath
spreading planes and cypresses.

ll these scenes of the past flitted through my mind like
eam; but those adventures were as nothing in compari-
with what we had just gone through.

hus I lay all day long, wide awake, with my eyes open,
ing at the white covering of the tent, without fixing my
: upon any one definite object, but seeing everything in
urred, confused chaos. Once or twice only did my vision
v dim and faint, and my thoughts muddled; that was
n I dropped off in a half-slumber. In these few odd
nents I imagined myself resting again on the green
dow-grass under the shade of the silver poplars. How
er was the awakening to reality! When I came to my-
I fancied I was lying in my coffin. The funeral proces-
had reached the churchyard; the funeral bells had
sed their lugubrious tolling; the graves were almost
ly; the next sand-storm would shovel them up level with
l. Who among us would be the first to die? Who
ild be the unhappy wretch that should die last — whose
s would be filled with the pestilential stench from the
ses of his comrades? God grant the end may come
kly—that I may not be overlong tortured with this fear-
bodily torment—this fearful mental anguish!

The hours followed one after another as slowly as dying camels in a desert-wrecked caravan. I kept looking at my watch; every interval between looking seemed like an eternity. But stay—what was that? My body was bathed in a sudden coolness, so refreshing, so comforting! The tent-flap was rolled up. It was noon. Yes, a faint breeze was flitting across the overheated sand-dunes. But faint though it was, it was strong enough for my sensitive skin to feel it. It continued to grow stronger and stronger, until, about three o'clock, it became so fresh that I was obliged to draw a felt covering over me.

Shortly afterwards something happened which I can only look upon as a miracle. As the sun drew nearer and nearer to the horizon, so did my strength gradually return; and by the time he rested like a glowing cannon-ball on the tops of the dunes in the west, I was completely recovered. My body had regained all its former elasticity. I felt as if I could walk for days and days. I burned with impatience to be up and doing. I *would* not die. The thought of how the dear ones at home would miss me; the thought of how they would mourn for me; and how it would grieve them if they were unable to send a wreath to be placed on my unknown grave—these were the thoughts that tormented me most. I resolved, therefore, during the immediate following days to strive my uttermost to keep going — going — going, to drag myself on, creep on all fours if I could not get on in any other way, but at all costs to keep struggling — struggling on towards the east, even though all my men—all my caravan—should long have given up and died. The temptation to just lie there and wait—for oh, how delicious it is to rest when you are dead tired! You quickly slumber off, and forget all your pains and anxieties in a long, heavy sleep, out of which you never wake again — this temptation I now put from me finally once and for all.

At sunset Islam Bai and Kasim both revived. I told them my resolve. They were both of the same mind as I was. Mohammed Shah still lay where he had fallen. Yollchi lay on his back in the shade of the tent. Both were delirious.

neither answered when we spoke to them, but kept on muttering incoherently and confusedly to themselves. After twilight set in, Yollchi moved; and as his senses returned the wild animal in him awoke. He crept up to where I was lying, shook his fist at me, and in a discordant, hollow, threatening voice, cried, " Water! water! Give us water, sir !" Then he began to weep, fell on his knees before me, and in a whining tone of entreaty begged me to give him a little water—just a few drops. What could I say to him? I reminded him that he had stolen half of our last supply, that he had had more than the rest of us, and had been the last to get a good drink; consequently he ought to hold out the longest. Half choking with ill-suppressed sobs, he crept away.

Was there *no* means of imparting moisture to our bodies before we left this hateful spot—even though it were only a moistening of the lips and throat? We were all suffering incredible agonies of thirst, the men more than I. My eyes chanced to fall upon the cock that still remained alive. He was walking about among the camels with all the gravity of his kind. Why not tap and drink his blood? One of the men made an incision in the animal's neck. The blood trickled out slowly and in small quantity. It was not enough; we wanted more. Yet another innocent life must be sacrificed. But the men hesitated a long time before they could bring themselves to slaughter our docile travelling-companion, the sheep, which had followed us through every danger with the fidelity of a dog. But I told them it was to save our own lives, which might be prolonged a little if we drank the sheep's blood.

At length Islam, with an aching heart, led the poor creature a little to one side, turned its head towards Mecca, and, while Kasim tied a rope round its legs, drew his knife, and with one sweeping cut severed the arteries of the neck. The blood poured out in a thick reddish-brown stream, and was caught in a pail, where it almost immediately coagulated. It was still warm when we fell upon it with spoons and knife-blades. We tasted cautiously at first; it was repulsive. A sickening odor rose from the pail. I managed to get down a teaspoonful of the blood; but could not persuade myself to touch another drop. Even the men found it disagreeable, and offered it to Yolldash. Yolldash licked it, then went his way. We were sorry afterwards that we had killed our faithful friend to such little purpose; but it was then too late.

I understood now how thirst can make a man half insane. Islam and the other men gathered a saucepanful of the camels' urine. They poured it into an iron cup, and added vinegar and sugar; then, holding their noses, swallowed the abominable concoction. They offered the cup to me; but the mere smell nauseated me. All the others drank it except Kasim. And he was wise to abstain; for after a while the other three men were seized with violent and painful vomiting, which completely prostrated them.

Gaunt and wild-eyed, with the stamp of insanity upon him, Yollchi sat beside the tent, gnawing at the dripping sheep's lungs. His hands were bloody; his face was bloody; he was a horrible sight to look upon. I and Kasim were the only two who were fit for anything. Islam Bai pulled himself together a little, after getting rid of his nauseous draught. He and I, once more, for the last time, went through our baggage. We decided to abandon the greater part of it. I put together in a little heap such things as I considered were indispensably necessary, such as my drawings and some route-plottings, specimens of rocks and of sand, maps, scientific instruments, pens, paper, the Bible and Swedish psalm-book, together with a number of other small articles. Islam Bai likewise picked out what he thought indispensable, such as provisions for three days (flour, tea, sugar, bread, and a couple of cases of preserved food). I proposed to leave behind all our Chinese silver money, half a camel-load of it, amounting to nearly £280 in value. I hoped we should soon discover water; then we should be able to return and fetch what we were now putting aside. But Islam Bai would not hear of the money being left behind; and events proved that he was right. In addition to the things already mentioned, Islam found room for a couple of boxes of cigars and cigarettes, some cooking utensils, which we had brought on with us from camp No. XVII., all our weapons, and a small supply of cartridges, candles, a lantern, bucket, spade, rope, and a number of similar objects.

Among the things left behind I may mention—two heavy ammunition-chests, the tent, some felts, together with our last carpet, several cases filled with miscellaneous articles, cloth, caps, and khalats, which I had intended as presents for the native chiefs, several useful books of reference, both my photographic cameras, with over a thousand plates, of which a hundred or more had been used during our journey across the desert; further, some saddles, the medicine-chest, drawing materials, unused sketch-books, all my clothes, winter boots, winter caps, gloves, etc.

We packed up the things we were not taking with us in some eight packing-cases inside the tent, the tent-canvas being turned in underneath them, so that they might help to hold up the tent in stormy weather. We counted upon the white tent - canvas, which was visible a long way off, more especially as we pitched it on the top of a sand-hill, serving as a sign-post if we should come back in quest of the goods. I dressed myself entirely in white, from top to toe. If I was doomed to die in the sand, I wanted to be properly attired: I wanted my burial clothes to be both white and clean.

The things we deemed it indispensable to take with us were packed in five Sart *kurchins*, or double wallets made of sail-cloth. We stripped the camels of their pack-saddles, and put these on their backs instead. One camel carried the heavy things, such as the rifles, spades, and so forth, all wrapped up together in a *kighiz* or felt carpet.

Before starting, we opened a couple of boxes of preserved food; but although the contents were moist, we experienced the utmost difficulty in getting them down, our throats were so parched.

The camels had lain all day in precisely the same places where they fell in the morning. Their labored breathing was the only sound that broke the deathly silence. The unhappy creatures were dying, but wore an air of indifference and resignation. Their big baggy throats were shrivelled up and of a whitish-blue color. We had great difficulty in persuading them to get up.

CHAPTER XLVI

THE CRISIS COMES

AT seven o'clock that evening the death-bells rang for the last time. In order to husband my strength, I rode the white camel, it being the freshest. Islam Bai, who had squandered his strength over the abominable draught he had swallowed, led the caravan at a miserably slow pace. Kasim followed in the rear, and kept urging the camels on. Thus we crawled away from the Camp of Death, steering east, ever east to where the Khotan-daria rolled on through its fresh green woods.

As we left the unhallowed spot, Yollchi crept inside the tent and took possession of my bed, still gnawing away at the sheep's lungs, greedily, voraciously draining them of every drop of moisture. Old Mohammed Shah still lay in the same place where he fell. Before we left I went to him, called him by his name, and placed my hand on his forehead. He glared at me, his eyes ashy-gray and wide open, and with a confused look in them; but an expression of unshaken calmness, of quiet rapture spread over his face, as though he expected the next moment to enter the pleasure-gardens of Paradise, and partake of its innumerable joys. Possibly for several days past he had seen floating before his dazed vision glimpses of Bihesht, about whose voluptuous delights he had read so many times in the Koran; and no doubt the thought of the joys to come comforted his spirit in the bitter agonies of shaking itself free from his body. No doubt he imagined his heavy life's work was done and he had lain down to rest, and would never more toil and drudge in attending upon camels, never more wear out his old age in tramping with caravans from one city to another through the sand-wastes of

East Turkestan. He looked terribly shrivelled up and wasted away, shrunk to a mummy-like old man. His copper-brown face was the only part of him that still wore any look of fresh-ness. His breathing came very slowly and irregularly, and every now and again sighs mingled with the death - ruckle which broke over his lips. Again I stroked his dry, wizened brow, placed his head in a more comfortable position, and said, in as calm a tone as my emotion would allow me, that we were going to hurry on ahead and should soon find water. We would fill the pitchers and hasten back to him. I bade him lie where he was till his strength returned ; then he might come along our trail to meet us, so as to shorten the distance we should have to travel back. He tried to lift one hand, mumbling something of which the only word I caught was " Allah." I understood only too well—and so, perhaps, did he —that we should never meet again. He had not many hours left to live. His eyes were dim and glazed ; his slumber would pass gradually over into the deep sleep of death. He was en-tering upon his eternal rest, environed by the mighty silence, and by the ever-shifting sand-dunes moving on towards their mysterious goal.

With my heart bleeding and lacerated by self-reproaches at having this life upon my conscience, I dragged myself away from the dying man.

I also took farewell of Yollchi, and exhorted him to follow on along the trail of the caravan. That was the only way he could save his life. I did not upbraid him for leading us astray ; nor did I reproach him with having deceived us when he said he was well acquainted with the desert, and within four days would bring us to a place where we could get water by digging for it. What good would it have done if I had rebuked him for putting only a four days' supply of water in the tanks instead of a ten days' supply ? It would only have embittered the man's last moments ; and I could not do that. I was so terribly sorry for him.

The last six hens made a tragic-comic picture as, cackling contentedly to themselves, they feasted with every mark of satisfaction upon the carcass of the dead sheep. No doubt they had not yet missed the cock, but they would miss him afterwards.

Why did we not kill the poor things? Well, why did we not, with more reason, kill the two unhappy dying men, and so release them out of their misery? These are questions which cannot be answered at a distance. When death stands open-mouthed waiting for you, you grow less sensitive to other people's sufferings. We were all doomed. It was only a question of hours with us all, and it seemed the most natural thing in the world that the oldest and weakest should die first. And as each fresh member of the caravan collapsed and sank to the ground, it did not in the least surprise us. We merely asked ourselves, "Whose turn is it next?" To kill a human being, even though he is struggling in the agonies of death, is murder, and always must be. We did not abandon the camels without some slight hope of being able to return to them with water and save them. But the men could not possibly live so long. They were, in fact, virtually dead already. Otherwise, so long as there was the smallest chance of saving them, I should not, I could not, have left them behind. To have stayed beside them until the end came would have entailed the needless sacrifice of our own lives. We could do nothing to assuage their sufferings, for of water—the one thing they needed—the one thing that might possibly have saved their lives—we had none—absolutely not one drop. Nor could we have given them any comfort in the last dread moments. They were delirious—completely unconscious; their minds were dead already. But why did we not take them on with us? For the sufficient reason that it was physically impossible. They were much too far gone to walk, and the camels were much too weak to have carried them. Besides, even supposing the camels had been strong enough to carry them, to have taken dead men with us would, under the circumstances in which we were then situated, have been tantamount to an act of suicidal folly—an outrageous madness. Our own strength was seriously undermined. Our own lives depended upon a successful race against fast-ebbing energy and fast-running time, and we did not know how far we might have to go before we reached water—the precious life-restorer. We were stripping ourselves of everything except the barest indispensable necessaries in order to husband our strength, to facilitate our progress, to economize time. To have burdened ourselves, therefore, with two helpless, hopeless sufferers, for whom we were utterly incapable of doing the least thing further, would only have been to imperil our own lives for absolutely no purpose. All the same it wrung my heart to have to leave the unhappy men behind in the desert. My conscience was loud in its reproaches. I suffered intense agony of mind. Yet what could I do? The bitterness of that hour—it was more than I can describe. It is known to God alone!

As for the hens, I had a presentiment that they *ought* not to be killed, since they might be useful, if we did come back to fetch the tent; besides, with the carcass of the sheep to feed upon they would be able to preserve their lives for a long time. In this I was not wrong, as was proved in the end of May, 1896, more than a year later. But I must not anticipate the natural course of events.

Meanwhile we marched on slowly, Yolldash still faithfully following us, although as lean as a skeleton. The camel-bells tolled a mournful peal for the dying veterans of the caravan. From the top of the first dune we surmounted I turned and sent back a sigh over the Camp of Death, where my two attendants were breathing their last. The tent stood out like a sharply cut black triangle against the lighter-tinted western sky. Then I went down the dune, and it vanished from my sight. I experienced a feeling of relief when it was no longer visible. I never looked back again.

Before us were the black night and the treacherous ocean of sand. But I was buoyed up by an abounding energy and the joy of life. I *would not* die in the desert. I was too young. I had too much to lose. Life had still much to give me. Never before had I valued it as I did now. My travels in Asia should not end in that place. I must traverse the continent from side to side. There were numerous problems I wanted to solve before I reached my far-distant goal—

Peking. Never before had I been so full of overflowing gladness, never before had my vital spirits been so buoyant with energy. I was determined I would get through, even though I should crawl it like a worm through the sand.

Our pace was slow, desperately slow. Nevertheless we kept scrambling over one high dune after another. At length another of the camels fell. He at once stretched out his legs and neck, prepared to die. We transferred his load to the back of Ak-tuya, the white camel, which seemed to be the strongest. We released the dying animal from the rope that bound him to the camel immediately in front of him, let him keep his ill-omened bell, and left him to his fate in the darkness of the night. With the other four camels we steered our way as well as we could see towards the next sand-dune.

The night was pitch-dark. The stars twinkled brightly through the pure atmosphere, but their light was too faint to enable us to judge of the inequalities of the ground. We were stopped by every sand-dune we came to. For a few minutes we had a level slope, which we got down easily enough; then all of a sudden a wall of sand would rise up immediately in front of us. The camels' strength was exhausted. Even the cool night air was incapable of revivifying them. They kept stopping incessantly. First one hung back, then another. Somehow the rope that bound them together would get loose, and one or two of the camels would lag behind, and we would go on some distance before we became aware of our loss. When we did perceive it we had to halt and turn back and fetch them.

Islam Bai was completely done up. He writhed in continual pain, and was seized with repeated vomitings of an extremely violent and convulsive character; and, as his stomach was empty, they rapidly drained away what little strength he had left. Poor fellow! he suffered fearfully, writhed on the ground, and retched to such an extent that I thought he would bring up his very intestines.

Thus like worms we crawled along through the darkness. But I saw clearly we could not go on in that way, stumbling

blindly over the dunes in that happy-go-lucky fashion. I got
down off my camel, lighted a lantern, and went on to
find out the easiest passages between the gigantic
the sandy ocean. I carried my compass in my
steered due east. The lantern cast a faint
the steep dune-sides. But again and again I
stop and wait for the rest of the caravan.
o'clock I no longer heard the distant tinkle
bell—there was but one left now. The dense
the night and a deathly silence environed me
I put the lantern on the top of a dune, and
the sand, tried to sleep. But not a wink could
up and listened, holding my breath, hoping
some faint, far-off sound. I looked eagerly
east to see if I could not catch a glimpse of
fire, marking the forest beside the Khotan
there was no such beacon of hope. All
as the grave. Nothing—nothing at all bet
semblance of life. It was so still I could
own heart beating.

At length I caught the sound of the last of the camels' bells.
It sounded at longer and longer intervals; but it approached
gradually nearer. When they reached the top of the dune
on which I sat, Islam Bai staggered up to the lantern, fell
heavily to the ground, and gasped out that he could not take
another step. His strength was totally exhausted.

Seeing that the last act of our tragic desert journey was
now about to be played, and that all would soon be over, I
determined to give up *everything* and hasten on eastward as
far as my strength would carry me. In a scarcely audible
voice Islam whispered that he could not go with me. He
begged to be allowed to remain with the camels, and said he
would die where he lay. I encouraged him, telling him I was
sure his strength would return after he had rested an hour or
two in the cool night-air; and when it did I solemnly *commanded* him to leave the camels and their loads—everything—
and follow on in my footsteps. To this he made no answer,
but lay on his back, with his mouth and eyes wide open.

ABANDONING THE WRECK OF OUR CARAVAN

ıen I bade him farewell and left him, fully believing that
had· but a short time to live.

Kasim was still fairly brisk. Like me, he had had the good
ıse to abstain from the abominable draught at the Camp of
؟ath. The only things I took with me were the two chro-
·meters, a bell, the compass, a penknife, a pencil and a piece
paper, a box of matches, a pocket-handkerchief, a box of
ıned lobsters, a round tin box full of chocolate, and, more
accident than by design, half a score of cigarettes. Kasim
rried the spade, bucket, and rope, in case we should have
dig a well. Inside the bucket he put the sheep's fat tail,
o or three pieces of bread, and a lump of coagulated sheep's
ɔod. But in the hurry he forgot to take his cap, and, when
ɔrning came, had to borrow my handkerchief, which he
ɔund round his head to protect himself against sunstroke.
But we were unable to derive much advantage from our
·etched provisions, because our throats and their mucous
؟mbranes were parched up, as dry as the skin on our hands
d faces, so that it was impossible to swallow. If we tried
get anything down, it stuck fast in our throats. We felt
.if we were being suffocated and made haste to put it out.
ıt a man who is tormented by the agonies of thirst gradu-
y loses all sense of hunger. For the first few days the
rtures of thirst are so poignant that you are on the brink
losing your senses. But when your skin ceases to per-
ire, or when your perspiration becomes imperceptible in
ɔsequence of the blood flowing continually thicker and
ɔwer through your veins, a rapidly increasing weakness
kes possession of you and quickly brings matters to a
isis.

It was exactly midnight when we abandoned the wreckage
our caravan, which only a few days before had made such
brave show. We were literally shipwrecked, and had to
ave behind us our "ships of the desert" a prey to the mer-
less ocean of sand. We set out to seek the "coast"; but
ıew not how far we should have to travel over those rolling
ıllows of sand before we reached it.

The four camels that now remained lay silent, resigned,

patient as sacrificial lambs. They breathed heavily and with difficulty, and their long necks were stretched out flat on the surface of the dune. Islam Bai did not glance up when we left him; but Yolldash sent a wondering look after us. No doubt he believed that we should soon come back again, perhaps with water; for the caravan was staying behind, and we never left it very far. I never saw the faithful creature again, and I missed him greatly.

I placed the lighted lantern close behind Islam, and left it there. For a little while it served us as a sort of light-house, telling us how far we were advancing away from it, and also guiding us in our course towards the east. But its pale rays speedily became lost behind the sand - dunes, and we were swallowed up in the night.

CHAPTER XLVII

A DESPERATE MARCH

MAY 2D. After leaving the death-doomed caravan behind, I felt I was freer to choose my own course. My only concern now was to keep pushing on, and to steer as straight a line as possible to the east, so as to shorten the road all I could. We marched on at a brisk pace for a good two hours without stopping; the sand continuing all the time every bit as high and heavy as it had been before. At the end of the two hours we both became so sleepy that we were forced to lie down for a while. But we were only lightly dressed. Kasim wore nothing except a simple jacket, his baggy trousers, and boots. I had on woollen underclothing, a thin suit of white cotton, a white Russian cap with a peak to it, and stiff leather top-boots. It was not long, therefore, before the chilly night air woke us up. We walked on smartly till we got warm. Then the desire to sleep once more seized us, and this time with such overpowering force that we did sleep. At four o'clock the nipping air woke us up again, for it was just about dawn, and I felt chilled to the bone. We got up and walked on for five hours without stopping—that is, till nine o'clock. Then, being tired, we gave ourselves an hour's rest.

While we were resting a crisp westerly breeze sprang up and cooled the air, so that we were able to go on a little way farther. But by half-past eleven the heat grew so oppressive that everything turned black before our eyes, and we sank down on a dune utterly spent. There, on a steep slope facing north, where the sand was not yet heated by the sun, we rested the remainder of the day. Kasim dug out a hole immediately under the crest of the dune, going down till he came to the layers of sand that were still cool from the night air. We took off every stitch of clothing and buried ourselves up to the neck in the sand. Then, putting up the spade and hanging our clothes over it, we made a sort of screen to shelter our heads from the sun. And so we lay all day long, cool and comfortable; sometimes, indeed, we were actually cold. But the sand gradually grew warm from the heat of our bodies and from the sun-saturated atmosphere. Then we crept out of our hole, and Kasim dug a fresh one, heaping the cool sand all over me. How delicious it was! like a cold douche in the burning sunshine. We left nothing but our heads sticking out, and these we protected to some extent against sunstroke. One midge and two flies kept us company. But then they might have been blown by the wind from a great distance!

Thus we lay buried alive in the eternal sand, uttering never a word, and yet not being able to sleep. We did not move until six o'clock in the evening; then we got out of our sand-bath, dressed, and continued our journey at a slow and heavy pace, for in all probability the dry sand-bath had weakened us. Nevertheless we stuck to it doggedly, although we had innumerable stoppages, pushing on eastward, ever eastward, until one o'clock next morning. Then, thoroughly wearied out, we lay down and went to sleep on the top of a dune.

May 3d. After a refreshing sleep we woke up at half-past four in the morning. We always travelled best just before sunrise, because, the air being then fresh, we were able to go long distances without stopping. That day our dying hopes once more revived, and our courage was rekindled. All of a sudden Kasim stopped short, gripped me by the shoulder, and with wildly staring eyes pointed towards the east, without uttering a word. I looked and looked in the direction towards which he pointed, but could see nothing unusual. But Kasim's eagle eye had discovered on the verge of the horizon the green foliage of a tamarisk—the beacon upon which all our hopes of safety were now concentrated. We steered our course straight for the solitary tree, taking the

utmost precautions not to lose its bearings. Every time we dipped into the hollow between two sand-dunes we, of course, lost sight of it; but, immediately we climbed the next dune, there it was still before us, and we were approaching nearer and nearer to it! At length we reached it. Our first act was to thank God for bringing us so far safe.

We revelled in the fresh greenness of the tree, and, like animals, chewed away at its sappy leaves. It was really alive. Its roots evidently went down to the water stratum; we were now within reasonable distance of open water. The tamarisk shot up from the top of a sand-dune, and there was not a yard of flat, hard ground to be seen anywhere near it. A strange existence these tamarisks (*Tamarix elongata*) lead. Their branches and tough, elastic stems, seldom exceeding seven feet in height, are bathed in burning sunshine; while their roots penetrate to an almost incredible depth, and, like siphons, suck up nourishment from the subterranean supplies of moisture. In fact, that solitary tree reminded me of a water-lily swimming, as it were, on the billowy surface of the desert ocean. Merely to look at the tamarisk was a pleasure, and to stretch our parched and weary limbs beneath its sparse shade for a little was rapture indeed. It was the olive-branch, telling us that there was an end to the sandy ocean, after all—the outermost islet of the Skärgård,* or skerry fence, proclaiming to the shipwrecked mariners the near proximity of the coast. I gathered a handful of leaves, which were not unlike the needles of the pine, and thoroughly enjoyed the sweet, fresh scent they gave off. My hopes now rose higher than they were before, and with our courage renewed we again pushed on towards the east.

By this the dunes had decreased in height, reaching not much above thirty feet. In one of the hollows we came across two small, scanty patches of kamish, or reeds (*Lasiagrostes splendens*); we plucked the wiry stalks and chewed them. At half-past nine we came to another tamarisk, and saw several more farther on. But our energy was paralyzed

---

* The belt of islands which fringes the eastern coast of Sweden.

by the intense heat, and we dropped exhausted in the shade of the bush, and, as we had done the day before, dug a hole in the sand and buried ourselves in it naked.

For nine mortal hours we lay as if dead. Kasim hardly had strength enough to cover me with fresh sand. At seven o'clock we started again in the twilight, at first with tottering limbs. After walking for three hours Kasim stopped short again, exclaiming "Tograk!" (poplar). I saw something dark looming up two or three dunes ahead; and, sure enough, he was right. It was three fine poplar-trees, with their leaves full of sap. But the leaves were so bitter that we could not chew them; we rubbed our skin instead until it became moist.

We were so completely spent that we lay for a couple of hours utterly incapable of making a closer examination of the locality. We began to dig a well close to the tree-roots. But we had to stop. We literally had not strength enough to do it; the spade kept turning in our hands and falling out of them. The sand was scarcely damp at all; the water was clearly a long way down. Nevertheless, we hung about the place a little while, and tried to scratch the sand away with our hands; but we soon found we could not do much that way, and gave up the idea of digging a well.

Our next plan was to gather together in a heap all the dry branches we could find round about the poplars and set fire to them, making a huge flaming bonfire, which flung its ruddy glare a long way across the dunes. Their tops, catching the murky gleam, looked like ghosts stalking out of the darkness. Our object in making the bonfire was partly to give a signal to Islam Bai, supposing he was still alive, which, however, I very seriously doubted, and partly to give the alarm to anybody who might chance to be travelling from Khotan to Ak-su, by the road that runs down the left side of the Khotan-daria.

Our purpose being a good one, we kept up the fire with feverish energy for fully two hours. Then we left it to die out of its own accord. Kasim fried a slice of the sheep's tail, and after very great exertions managed to swallow it.

I had but little better fortune with the lobsters. The rest of our "provisions" we left behind us, not wishing to burden ourselves unnecessarily. But I took the empty chocolate tin with me. I was going to drink the water of the Khotan-daria out of it! After that we had a good sleep beside the fire, which prevented us from feeling the chilliness of the night.

May 4th. We began to move at three o'clock in the morning, and at four o'clock made a start. Then, with our strength drooping at every step and our legs tottering under us, and with innumerable halts, we stumbled on till nine o'clock. Then the desert ocean once more opened its raven-ous jaws before us, and appeared to be waiting with mali-cious joy the fatal moment when it should devour us. After the three poplars we saw no more, and the tamarisks were so few and far between that we could scarcely see from one to the other. Our courage began to sink; we began to be afraid it was merely a depression we had passed, and that we should soon be engulfed again in the everlasting sea of sand. At nine o'clock we fell helpless at the foot of a tamarisk, and there we lay, exposed to the blazing sun, for ten mortal hours.

Kasim was sinking fast. He was incapable of digging a hole in the sand to lie in; and as he was also unable to cover me with cool sand, I suffered terribly from the heat. All day long we never spoke a word. Indeed, what was there we could talk about? Our thoughts were the same, our ap-prehensions the same. The fact is, we really could not talk; we could only whisper or hiss out our words.

Where now were the sand-storms which a week ago inter-posed such a perfect screen between us and the sun? We looked in vain for the black cloud which alone could shield us from the coppery glow. Sun and desert had conspired together for our destruction.

But even that long, weary day had an end; the sun once more dipped down towards the west. By a desperate effort I roused myself, shook the sand off my body, which looked as if it were encased in tight-fitting parchment of a reddish-brown color. I dressed myself, and called upon Kasim to come with me. He gasped, in reply, that he was unable to go any farther, and with a gesture of despair gave me to understand that he considered all was lost.

I went on alone, alone with the night and the everlasting sand. It was still as the grave, and the shadows seemed to me to be darker than usual. Occasionally I rested on the dunes. Then it was I realized how lonely I was, alone with my conscience and the stars of heaven, which shone as brilliantly as electric lamps. They alone kept me company; they were the only things I saw and knew; and they inspired in me the conviction that it was not the valley of the shadow of death I was walking through. The air was perfectly still and cold; I could have heard the faintest sound a long way off. I placed my ear close down upon the sand and listened; but I heard nothing except the ticking of the chronometers and the faint and sluggish beating of my own heart. There was not a sound to indicate there was any other living creature throughout all the wide universe of space.

I lit my last cigarette. The others we had smoked the day before, and so long as they lasted they had to some extent stilled the tortures of thirst. I generally smoked the first half, and gave the rest to Kasim. He puffed and sucked away at the paper mouthpiece for a long time, and declared it did him a world of good. But that last cigarette I finished myself, for I was absolutely alone.

May 5th. I dragged myself on and on until half past twelve, when I sank down under a tamarisk. After trying in vain to kindle a fire, I dozed off.

But what was that? There was a rustling in the sand. I heard footsteps. I saw a human figure gliding past in the darkness. "Is that you, Kasim?" I asked. "Yes, sir," he answered. The coolness of the night had revived him, and he had followed in my footsteps. The meeting cheered us both, and we continued our way for a time in the pitch-dark night.

But our strength was rapidly deserting us, our legs tottered under us; we struggled hard against weariness, against the desire for sleep. The steep faces of the dunes now looked almost exclusively towards the east. I slid down them. I crept long distances on my hands and knees. We were growing indifferent; our spirits were flagging. Still we toiled on for life—bare life. Then imagine our surprise, our amazement, when on the long, sloping surface of a dune we perceived human footsteps imprinted in the sand! Down we went on our knees and examined them. There was no doubt of it. They were the footprints of human beings. Somebody had travelled that way. Surely we could not be very far from the river now; for what could bring people out into the sandy waste! In an instant we were wide awake. But Kasim thought that the trail looked wonderfully fresh. "Just so," I rejoined; "that is not at all strange. There has been no wind for several days. Perhaps our signal-fire of the night before last has been seen by some shepherd in the forest beside the river, and he has come a little way into the desert to ascertain what was the cause of it."

We followed up the trail till we came to the top of a dune, where the sand was driven together in a hard, compact mass, and the footprints could be more distinctly made out.

Kasim dropped on his knees; then cried, in a scarcely audible voice, "They are our own footsteps!"

I stooped down and convinced myself that he was right. The footprints in the sand were plainly enough caused by our own boots, and at regular intervals beside them were the marks of the spade; for Kasim had used it as a staff to support himself by. It was a discouraging discovery. How long had we been going round and round in a circle? We comforted ourselves with the assurance that it could not possibly have been very long. It was only during the last hour that I had been so overcome with sleep that I forgot to look at the compass. But we had at any rate had enough of tramping for a while, and at half-past two in the morning lay down and slept beside the track.

We awoke at daybreak and pushed on again. It was then ten minutes past four. Kasim was a fearful object to look at. His tongue was white, dry, and swollen, his lips bluish, his cheeks sunken, his eyes dull and glassy. He suffered from a convulsive hiccough, which shook him from top to toe; it was like the singultus, or hiccough of death. He had hard work to stand up; but he did, and managed somehow to follow me.

Our throats were on fire with the hot dryness. We fancied we could hear our joints grating, and thought they would catch fire from the friction of walking. Our eyes were so dried up that we were scarcely able to open and shut them.

When the sun rose we turned our eager eyes towards the east. The horizon was sharp and distinct, and had a different outline from what we were accustomed to see. It was no longer denticulated as if formed of innumerable series of ridges of sand; it was a horizontal line, showing scarce perceptible inequalities. After going a little farther we perceived that the horizon was edged with a black border. What joy! What blessed fortune! It *was* the forest that lined the bank of the Khotan-daria. We *were* approaching it at last.

Shortly before five o'clock we came to a *darah* (strictly speaking, valley) or depression in the sand, and I soon arrived at the conclusion that it was a former bed of the river. Numerous poplars grew in its lowest part. There must be water not very far below them. Once more we seized the spade; but we had not strength enough to dig. We were forced to struggle on again towards the east. We travelled at first across a belt of low, barren sand. But at half-past five we entered the thick, continuous forest. The trees were in full foliage, and their leafy crowns filled the forest beneath with gloomy shadows. After all, we were not to lose our spring, the season dedicated to hope!

With my hand to my brow, I stood riveted to the spot by the marvellous sight. It cost me an effort to collect my senses. I was still half giddy, as if newly awakened from a hideous dream or distressing nightmare. For weeks we had been dragging ourselves, slowly dying by inches, through the valley of the shadow of death—and now! All around us, in whichever direction we turned our eyes, life and spring-time.

; of birds, the scent of the woods, green leaves in
ty of tint, refreshing shade, and over there, among
patriarchs of the forest, innumerable spoor of wild
igers, wolves, deer, foxes, antelopes, gazelles, hares.
s alive with flies and midges; beetles went whizzing
wift as arrows, their wings humming like the notes
1; and the morning songs of the birds trilled from
:h.

d grew denser and denser. At intervals the stems
ars were entwined with creepers; and our progress
iterrupted by impenetrable labyrinths of dead trees,
nd brushwood, or equally often by dense thickets
ushes.

minutes past seven the forest grew thinner. We
n the trees indistinct traces of both men and horses.
impossible to determine how old they were, for the
ected them against the obliterating effects of the
s. What joy! what bliss! I felt—I was sure we
now.

ted that we should go straight through the forest,
ie east, for in that direction the river could not be
'ay. But Kasim thought that the trail, which un-
marked a road of some kind, would gradually lead
iver banks. And as the trail was easy to follow,
ll the time in the shade, I adopted Kasim's sug-

nd struggling, we followed the trail towards the
by nine o'clock we were completely done up by
l heat, and dropped on the ground in the shade of
e poplars. With my naked hands I scratched out
veen the roots, and lay there, tossing and turning
g from the heat, without being able to sleep a wink.
s stretched out on his back, muttering deliriously
ng to himself; nor did he answer when I spoke to
even when I shook him.

seemed as if it would never end. My patience was
e uttermost; for I felt certain the river must be in
iate vicinity, and I was dying to get to it.

It was seven o'clock before I was able to dr.....
I called upon Kasim to come with me to the ...
he was beaten at last. He shook his head ...
gesture of despair signed to me to go on alon..
bring back water to him; otherwise he would ...
he lay.

I took off the blade of the spade and hung ...
which stretched across the path, so that I mig...
find again the point where we entered the for...
had hopes of being able to recover the bagga...
behind—we had only to go due west from the...
we struck the forest and we should come to it...
that Islam and the other men were already dea...
shaft I took with me. It would be a staff to he...
and would also serve as a weapon if I wanted ...

I cut right across the forest, still directing m...
east. It was anything but easy work. Two o...
very nearly got stuck fast in the thorny bush...
clothes and scratched my hands. I rested up...
roots and fallen tree-trunks; I was fearfully tired ...
came on. It grew dark. It cost me almost inconceivable
efforts to keep awake. Then all at once the forest came to
an end, as abruptly as though it had been smitten by fire,
and to the east stretched a dead level plain of hard, consoli-
dated clay and sand. It lay five or six feet below the level of
the forest, and showed not a single trace of a sand-dune. I
recognized it at once; it could not possibly be anything but
the bed of the Khotan-daria. And I soon had my inference
confirmed. I came across the trunks and branches of poplar-
trees, half buried in the ground; I noticed furrows and sharply
broken edges a foot high or more, all evidently due to the
action of a running stream. But the sand was as dry as the
sand in the desert dunes. The river-bed was empty, waiting
for the summer floods to come down from the mountains.

It was inconceivable that I should perish in the very bed
of the river I had been so long and so desperately seeking,
that I could not believe. I called to mind the tendency of
the Yarkand-daria to shift its channel to the east, and recol-

CRAWLING THROUGH THE FOREST IN SEARCH OF WATER

lected the ancient river-bed we had crossed in the forest.
Very likely the Khotan-daria obeyed the same tendency.
Very likely *its* current clung by preference to the eastern
bank; I must therefore find it, if I would find the deepest
places in the river channel. I resolved to cross over to the
other side before I gave up all hope.

I now changed my course to due southeast. Why so?
Why did I not keep on towards the east, as I had always
done hitherto? I do not know. Perhaps the moon be-
witched me; for she showed her silver crescent in that
quarter of the heavens and shed down a dim, pale-blue illu-
mination over the silent scene. Leaning on the spade-shaft,
I plodded away at a steady pace in a straight line towards
the southeast, as though I were being led by an unseen but
irresistible hand. At intervals I was seized by a traitorous
desire to sleep, and was obliged to stop and rest. My pulse
was excessively weak; I could scarcely discern its beats. I
had to steel myself by the strongest effort of will to prevent
myself from dropping off to sleep. I was afraid that if I did
go off I should never waken again. I walked with my eyes
riveted upon the moon, and kept expecting to see its silver
belt glittering on the dark waters of the stream. But no such
sight met my eyes. The whole of the east quarter was enshrouded in the cold night mist.

After going about a mile and a half, I was at length able
to distinguish the dark line of the forest on the right bank
of the river. It gradually became more distinct as I advanced. There was a thicket of bushes and reeds; a poplar
blown down by the wind lay across a deep hole in the river-
bed. I was only a few yards from the bank when a wild
duck, alarmed by my approach, flew up and away as swift as
an arrow. I heard a splash, and in the next moment I stood
on the brink of a little pool filled with fresh, cool *water—*
beautiful water!

CHAPTER XLVIII

HUMAN BEINGS AT LAST

It would be vain for me to try to describe the feelings which now overpowered me. They may be imagined; they cannot be described. Before drinking I counted my pulse: it was forty-nine. Then I took the tin box out of my pocket, filled it, and drank. How sweet that water tasted! Nobody can conceive it who has not been within an ace of dying of thirst. I lifted the tin to my lips, calmly, slowly, deliberately, and drank, drank, drank, time after time. How delicious! what exquisite pleasure! The noblest wine pressed out of the grape, the divinest nectar ever made, was never half so sweet. My hopes had not deceived me. The star of my fortunes shone as brightly as ever it did.

I do not think I at all exaggerate if I say that during the first ten minutes I drank between five and six pints. The tin box held not quite an ordinary tumblerful, and I emptied it quite a score of times. At that moment it never entered my head that, after such a long fast, it might be dangerous to drink in such quantity. But I experienced not the slightest ill effects from it. On the contrary, I felt how that cold, clear, delicious water infused new energy into me. Every blood-vessel and tissue of my body sucked up the life-giving liquid like a sponge. My pulse, which had been so feeble, now beat strong again. At the end of a few minutes it was already fifty-six. My blood, which had lately been so sluggish and so slow that it was scarce able to creep through the capillaries, now coursed easily through every blood-vessel. My hands, which had been dry, parched, and as hard as wood, swelled out again. My skin, which had been like parchment, turned moist and elastic. And soon afterwards an active per-

)iration broke out upon my brow. In a word, I felt my
hole body was imbibing fresh life and fresh strength.   It
'as a solemn, an awe-inspiring moment.

Never did life seem to me richer, more beautiful, more val-
able than it did that night in the bed of the Khotan-daria.
'he future smiled upon me from the midst of a magic sea of
ght.   Life was worth living.   The talk about life being a
ale of misery seemed to me utter nonsense.   An angel's
and had guided me through the darkness of the night to
ie little pool in the river-bed.   I imagined I saw a heavenly
eing floating by my side, and thought I could hear the rus-
e of his wings.   Never before, and never since, have I so
ividly realized the sublime influence of the Eternal.

After drinking my fill, and making sure of my wonderful
scape from a miserable death, and after the ecstasy had sub-
ided which came upon me when I felt new life streaming
hrough my veins, and as soon as my entire physical being
ad entered upon a more normal course, I drank several
iore tins of water.   After that my thoughts began to flow
iack in ordinary channels, and I awoke to the realities of the
noment, and became attentive to my immediate surround-
ngs.

The pool was situated in the deepest part of the river-bed,
iear the eastern bank, and had been left behind by the pre-
eding summer's flood.   It lay, therefore, below the general
evel of the river-bed, so that I had been unable to observe it
intil I almost stumbled into it.   Had I gone fifty paces
arther to the right or fifty paces farther to the left, I should
iave missed it; and, as I learned afterwards, it was a long
istance to the next pool both up and down the river.   The
ierchants who are accustomed to travel every spring with
ieir caravans between Khotan and Ak-su know where all
hese pools are, and always make them their camping-places
ir the night.   Perhaps I should have lost my way if I had
ot found the pool; perhaps my strength would not have
eld out until I reached the next.

The eastern bank of the river was fringed with the dry, yel-
w reeds of the previous year, and the young, green spring

sprouts were pushing themselves up between the tall, close-set stalks of the old.   Behind the reed-beds towered the forest, sombre and threatening, with the silver crescent of the hanging in the crown of a tall poplar.   I sat beside and noticed that its bright surface, seen under the shadows of the forest, was black as ink.   The pool twenty yards long.

Then I heard a rustling in the thicket close beside sound of stealthy footsteps, and the crackling of the as they were pushed aside.   It might have been a anyway I felt not a quiver of fear.   I had just been renewal of life.   The mere thought of seeing a tiger with its glittering eyes, peeping out of the reeds, had of fascination for me.   I would look into them fearle ask the beast how he durst think of taking my dear life.   But the intruder, whatever he was, withdrew. O steps died away in the reeds.   Whether it was a tiger other wild animal of the forest, which had come do pool to drink, it had at any rate deemed it prudent at a distance so long as the place was haunted by being.

Then my thoughts flew back to Kasim, whom I left lying alone in the forest, fighting against death, unable to move a yard, still less drag himself a distance of three hours to the pool of water.   He was in urgent need of immediate help. The chocolate tin was too small to carry water in: it would merely have wetted his lips.   What was to be done?   How was I to carry him a sufficient quantity of the life-giving elixir?

My boots!   Of course; my Swedish water-proof boots. They were quite as good, quite as safe, as any other utensil. Plump they went into the pool.   Then I threaded the spade-shaft through the straps, and carrying it like a yoke over my right shoulder, hastened back with a buoyant step along the track by which I came.

The boots were filled to the brim with the precious liquid that was going to give fresh life to Kasim.   Some of it was spilled owing to the haste I was in; but not a drop came

hrough the leather. Master Stjernström in Stockholm
.ever made a pair of boots before which not only saved a
ɪan's life but also travelled right across Asia and back
gain. In consequence of this my boots afterwards became
ɪ their way famous.

The moon still poured her soft mellow light along the
iver-bed, so that I had no difficulty in following my own
ɔotmarks through the sand. Besides, it was no longer heavy
ʳalking, my weariness had disappeared, and I almost flew
ɔwards the forest that lined the left bank. In the forest it
ʳas not so easy to get along. My socks were thin, and my
ɛet were continually getting pricked by thorns and splinters.
Jut a worse evil was a thick veil of cloud, caused, no doubt,
y the rising mist, which came between the moon and me, so
ɪat the forest became pitch-dark, and I lost the trail. I
ghted matches, and vainly tried to rediscover it. I had re-
ɔurse to my compass. I shouted " Kasim "; but my voice
ied away among the thousands of poplars without eliciting
ɪ answer. For a while I went on at haphazard, constantly
ɪouting my attendant's name with all the strength of my
ɪngs. But at last I grew tired of that aimless wandering;
was only getting lost deeper and deeper in the silent forest.
resolved, therefore, to stop and wait for daylight. I chose
ut an impenetrable thicket in which lumber, dead branches,
ɪd shrivelled tree-trunks lay heaped together in wild con-
ɪsion, and set fire to them. In a trice the flames were leap-
ɪg up fiercely; the dry branches crackled, spluttered, ex-
loded. The draught from the bottom was so strong that it
ʳhistled and sizzled, and a tall column of fire licked the
ʳunks of the poplars standing near. It was as light as noon-
ɪde: the forest, lately so black, was lit up with a reddish yel-
ow glare. Kasim could hardly help seeing such a fire as
that, or hearing its loud crackling, for he could not be any
ɡreat distance away. Again I shouted out his name, and,
ʋith the light of the fire to help me, again looked for my trail;
ut I did not find it. I lay down flat on the sand, and watched
he furious burning of the fire; and so watching fell asleep.
'or a couple of hours I slept calmly and well; having first

taken the precaution to lie down in a spot where the fire could not reach me, yet near enough to be safe from tigers and other wild animals.

Day was breaking when I awoke. The fire had dwindled a good deal, since its progress was checked by a fresh belt of live poplars, which it had only been able to blacken and scorch; and a heavy column of smoke hung over the forest. My boots, which were leaning against a tree-root, had not lost one drop of their precious contents; the earth underneath them was not even damp. I swallowed a mouthful of water and set about looking for my trail of the night before, and now I quickly found it. When I came to Kasim, he was lying in the same position in which I left him. He glared at me with the wild, startled eyes of a faun; but upon recognizing me, made an effort, and crept a yard or two nearer, gasping out, " I am dying."

" Would you like some water?" I asked, quite calmly. He merely shook his head, and collapsed again. He had no conception of what was in the boots. I placed one of the boots near him, and shook it so that he might hear the splashing of the water. He started, uttered an inarticulate cry; and when I put the boot to his lips, he emptied it at one draught without once stopping; and the next moment he emptied the second.

May 6th. Kasim went through the same series of changes that I had gone through the evening before. As soon as he recovered his reason we took counsel together, and as the outcome of our deliberations decided that our best plan was to go back to the pool and take a good rest somewhere near it, and wash ourselves, a luxury we had not enjoyed for more than a week. But Kasim was still so weak that he was unable to keep up with me. He reeled about like a drunken man, and I kept constantly sitting down. Seeing that he was on the right track for the pool, and that I could not do more for him than I had done already, I hurried on ahead. When I came to the pool I drank and bathed, and then waited full an hour. But Kasim did not come.

Hunger began to be importunate. It was of the first im-

ortance that I should find human beings as soon as I possi-
ly could, both for the sake of food and also to enlist their help
ɔ return into the desert to the assistance of Islam, and to
tch such of our goods as might be saved. In the mean time,
ɪerefore, I left Kasim to his fate, and hastened on at a rapid
ace up the right bank—that is, due south. My boots were
ill so wet that I was unable to get them on, and so went
arefoot.

At nine o'clock there sprang up an extremely violent storm
·om the west, which drove clouds of sand and dust before it
cross the bed of the river, and darkened the sun so that I had
ot the smallest occasion to complain of excessive heat. But
ɪe thick haze completely shut out every view of the surround-
ɪgs, so that I could see neither the forest on my right nor
ɪat on my left. After going a stretch of about three hours
 was again tormented by thirst, for my mouth and throat
·ere parched by the hot drift-sand and the buran (storm), and
etween them they nearly choked me. I turned aside into
ɪe forest and sought shelter in the undergrowth. I sat there
 while, full of anxious thought. All at once it flashed across
ɪy mind that it might be days to the next water-pool, and
ɪat it would be unwise to leave the one which I had in such
 wonderful manner discovered. Moreover, I thought it would
e an excellent thing to see Kasim again. I therefore turned
ack towards the north. But I had barely gone half an hour
·hen I stumbled by chance upon a tiny pool, scarcely a yard
cross, and containing a little muddy water with a faintly
ɪltish taste. I drank an enormous quantity of it. I was
vercome with weariness; but did not know what was the
isest thing to do. There was water here, and I had no im-
ɪediate use of Kasim. On the other hand, I found I was un-
ɔle to travel far towards the south. Perhaps it would be best
ɔ wait, and as soon as the storm ceased, by means of signal-
res warn any persons who might chance to be travelling the
ɪrest road that ran along the river-bank.

I therefore cast about for a dense thicket close to the pool,
ɪd well protected from the storm. Placing my boots and
ɪp under my head for a pillow, I slept deeply and heavily—

the first good sound sleep I had had since May 1st. When I
awoke it was already dark, and the storm still roared through
the forest. It was eight o'clock in the evening. After
other good drink out of the pool I made a big bonfire,
sat down beside it and stared into the flames for a while.
But I was tormented by the pangs of hunger. With the hope
of cheating my stomach a little, I gathered some young
shoots of reed, and a bunch of young frogs out of the pool.
The frogs were refractory; so I gave them a nip at the back
of the head and swallowed them whole. After that I
scraped together a big pile of dry branches to feed the fire
with during the night.

If only I had had Yolldash with me to keep me company.
Perhaps he was still alive, and had followed our trail to the
river. I whistled as loudly as I could, whistled again and
again. But no Yolldash came scampering up. At length I
dropped off again.

May 7th. The storm had ceased, although the atmosphere
was still heavily charged with dust. This "black storm"
suggested a gloomy and depressing idea. It was the first
since the caravan collapsed. It had come to cast the first
shovelfuls of earth over my dead attendants and the camels,
and it would blot out every trace of our trail through the
sand; so that Islam Bai, supposing he still lived, would perhaps never be able to find us. But then, again, he had a
compass. And even supposing we did come across men,
and supposing they were willing to go with us into the desert
as far as the tent, we should now experience the utmost difficulty in finding it, seeing that we could no longer retrace our
footsteps through the sand.

Then I thought of another thing. There was not a single
trace of human beings in that immediate locality, not a sign
of anybody having passed that way at all recently. Perhaps
nobody travelled that way during the hot season? If I
waited there for help, I might perchance die of hunger before
help came. My last examination of Przhevalsky's map seemed
to show that we should strike the river in the district called
Buksem, about 25 Swedish or 150 English miles from the

town of Khotan. If I went well, I ought to travel that distance in six days.

To decide was to act. At half-past four off I started. I
followed the middle of the river-bed in as straight a line as I
could; and as a consequence of the almost dead level, the
channel was pretty nearly straight, and varied from half a
mile to two miles in width. I took the precaution to fill my
boots with water; but at the end of some hours my feet were
so sore and blistered that I was obliged to try and protect
them by doubling my socks over them, and by bandaging
them in strips of my shirt.

After a while I came upon another small pool, containing
fresh water. I emptied my boots of the brackish water I was
carrying and filled them with the sweet. After that I followed the left bank of the stream, and there, to my great joy,
discovered a sheepfold constructed of branches of trees. But
upon examining it I saw it was a long time since it had been
used. In the river-bed close beside it I perceived signs of a
well having been dug.

Weariness and the heat of the day combined drove me,
about half-past eleven, into the shelter of the forest. There
I halted, gathered young reed-shoots and grass, cut them up
fine, and mixed them with water in the chocolate tin. That
was my breakfast.

After noon I went on again hour after hour, until I really
could go no longer. It was eight o'clock when I stopped,
and made my fire, and "camped."

May 8th. I started before daybreak, still keeping to the
left bank, which ran towards the south-southwest. Strange I
did not meet anybody! Perhaps the caravan-road lay deeper
in the forest, so that I might easily pass people without seeing them. I thought I had better go and look; so I crossed
through the forest, going due west. It was only about half
a mile wide, and on the other side of it I came upon that
terrible ocean of yellow sand, which I knew so well, and now
fled from with horror. Another hour later, the sand-dunes,
which stretched from north-northwest to south-southeast,
came down in several places close to the brink of the river.

Along the edge of the desert there were poplars growing singly and at wide intervals apart. Overcome by the heat, I threw myself down under the shade of one of them to rest. On my way to that point I had passed no less than eight small pools; in most of them, however, the water had a faint saltish taste.

After resting a couple of hours, I continued my solitary journey towards the south. If there was a caravan road alongside the river, it was manifest it did not follow the left bank, for nobody would travel through the sand-dunes unless they were compelled to do so. I must cross over and see what promise there was in the forest on the right bank. At this place the river-bed was about a mile and a quarter wide. But I found no caravan-track in the forest on the right bank either. I therefore went back to the river-bed, and travelled close beside the bank and the edge of the forest. About 350 yards farther on there were two small islands in the river, covered with bushes and poplars; and between the southern island and the river-bank I perceived, shortly before sunset, the fresh footmarks of two barefooted men who had gone that way, but in the opposite direction—that is, towards the north—driving four donkeys before them.

Footprints of human beings! A remarkable, an encouraging sight! I was not absolutely alone, then, in that inhospitable region. The footprints were so fresh that every detail of the men's feet was plainly marked in the sand. At the most they could not be more than a day old. Strange I had not met them, seeing that we were travelling in opposite directions. But perhaps they rested during the day and only travelled at night? Where had they come from? Where were they going to? Where was their last camp? Was it in a dwelling-place of men, or was it merely by the side of a pool in the river? To follow them up would have served no purpose, for they had too long a start of me; I should never be able to catch them up. I had no alternative, therefore, but to follow the trail in the opposite direction. I observed the impressions of these human feet with the greatest interest and attention; and led on by them, I hurried along southward, keeping close to the right bank of the Khotan-daria.

CHAPTER XLIX

WITH THE SHEPHERDS OF THE KHOTAN-DARIA

TWILIGHT was beginning to spread its dusky wings over the silent scene when, as I was passing a projecting headland, I thought I heard a wonderful sound. I stood stock-still; I held my breath and listened. But all was silent as before. I concluded it must have been a thrush or some other bird which had several times startled me already, and made me stop and listen. But no; there it was again, an unmistakable shout; and it was immediately followed by the lowing of a cow, a voice which in my ears was welcomer than the singing of a prima donna.

I hurriedly pulled on my wet boots, so as not to look like a madman, and with my heart in my mouth hurried in the direction from which the sounds proceeded. I pushed my way through thorny thickets; I jumped over fallen tree-trunks; I stumbled; I tripped again and again; I forced myself through dense beds of kamish, through heaps of crackling branches. The farther I went the more distinctly I heard the voices of men talking and the bleating of sheep, and through an opening in the forest I caught a glimpse of a flock of sheep grazing. A shepherd with a long staff in his hand was keeping watch over them, and when he perceived me, in my tattered clothes and blue spectacles, breaking out of the tangled thickets, he was not a little startled and amazed. Probably he took me for a goblin of the forest, or an evil spirit from the desert, who had lost his way and wandered thither by mistake. He stood as though rooted to the spot with terror, and could do nothing but stare at me open-mouthed. I greeted him with the usual " *Salaam aleikum !*" (Peace be with you!), and began to tell him in a few words how I came thither. But he turned abruptly on his heel and disappeared into the nearest thicket, leaving his sheep to their fate.

After a while he came back in company with an older shepherd, who was more amenable to reason. I greeted him in the same way as I had done the first man, with "*Salaam aleikum!*" Then I told him the whole story of my journey across the desert. When I said that I had eaten nothing for a week and asked them for a piece of bread, they led me to a hut close by constructed of branches, and scarcely five feet high. I sat down on a ragged felt carpet, and the younger shepherd brought out a wooden platter, with some freshly-baked maize bread. I thanked them, then broke off a piece and began to eat; but I had not eaten above half a dozen mouthfuls when I turned suddenly faint. The shepherds gave me a pan of sheep's-milk, which tasted excellent. After that they went away and left me for a little while alone, except that two big dogs stayed behind and barked at me unceasingly.

Soon after dark the two men returned to the hut, accompanied by a third shepherd. Meanwhile the sheep had been driven into the sheepfold, to protect them from tigers and wolves during the night. I and the three shepherds slept under the open sky beside a big fire.

May 9th. At daybreak the shepherds went off with their flocks. Their hut stood on a little hill on the edge of the forest, and through the trees commanded a view of the Khotan-daria. A small creek came close up to the hut, and in it was a pool of fresh water. But in addition to that the shepherds had digged a well in the bed of the river, so that they had a plentiful supply of good, clear water.

At noon the three men brought back their flocks, so that they might rest around the well during the hottest part of the day. This gave me an opportunity to become better acquainted with my hosts. Their names were Yussuf Bai, Togda Bai, and Pasi Akhun, and they were pasturing 170 sheep and goats, besides 60 cattle, belonging to a bai (rich man) in Khotan. Winter and summer alike they lay out in

e woods with their flocks, and for their monotonous work
ere paid collectively only 20 tengeh* (or 9 shillings) a
.onth, together with maize meal and bread. After their
ocks had eaten up all the grass in one pasture-ground they
noved on to another, and in each fresh place they came to
hey built a hut, unless there was one there already, left
.tanding from the previous year. They had been only five
lays in the spot where I found them, and they were shortly
;oing to a better place. The district as a whole was called
3uksem (Close Tangled Wood).

The life these shepherds lead must be exceedingly lonely
nd devoid of pleasure, and one day remarkably like another;
:t they looked both cheerful and contented. Togda Bai was
arried, but his wife lived in Khotan. When I asked him
hy she did not accompany him into the forest he told me
at the Chinese, who sometimes travelled that way, would
:rsist in molesting the native women, so that for this reason
: preferred to be alone. Once or twice a year, however, he
t leave to go into the town to see his wife. My arrival at
eir camp was clearly an important event in their monotonous
e. All the same, they looked askance at me; it was evident
ey regarded me as a suspicious character. But their suspi-
ɔn was to some extent disarmed by the fact that I was able
speak their own language, and readily conversed with them.
They lived almost exclusively upon maize bread, water,
ıd tea, this last strongly flavored with pepper. Twice a
ıy they baked a large loaf and divided it between them.
hey mixed the maize flour with water and salt, kneaded
e dough, and shaped it in a circular wooden vessel or dish;
en spread it out in the form of a flat cake upon the glow-
g embers and covered it up with hot ashes. In three-
ıarters of an hour it was cooked, and tasted exquisitely.
fairly revelled in it, and the shepherds were generous,
əspite the fact that they knew perfectly well I had not a
.ngle tengeh to give them in return.

* A tengeh of Khotan is equivalent to two tengeh of Kashgar; and a
tengeh of Kashgar is worth about 2¾*d.*

Their personal belongings were not many. They consisted, in the first place, of the clothes they wore—namely,
a *chapan*, or outer coat; a *telpek*, or sheepskin cap, with the
wool on the outside; a *belbagh*, or girdle, in which they carried
their utensils for making tea. Their lower extremities were
swathed in long bandages, and their feet encased in pieces of
sheepskin fastened on with cord. Besides their clothes they
possessed a large wooden platter (*kazang*), another of medium
size (*ayag*), and a small one (*jam*), a gourd (*kapak*) for holding
water, a large ladle or spoon (*chumuch*) roughly shaped out
of the root of a poplar, a felt carpet (*kighiz*), and a three-
stringed guitar (*jävab*). But by far the most important of
their belongings was the axe (*balta*), a most useful implement,
whether they wanted to make a hut, or cut firewood, or clear
a path for their flocks through the thickets, or in the spring
lop off the young shoots and branches of the trees to feed
their sheep and goats on. Another indispensable instrument
was the steel (*chakmak*) for striking fire; but once they have
got a fire lighted they take care not to let it go out until they
move on to another place. Before driving their flocks into
the forest to graze they covered up the fire with ashes, and
when they came back again in the evening they opened out
the ashes, placed a few dry sticks on the embers, and quickly
fanned them into a flame. But they also used dried dung for
fuel. They kept their maize meal in a sack, and placed it
and all their other belongings on the roof of the hut, to keep
them safe from the dogs.

There was first-rate pasturage, they told me, on both banks
of the river all the way to the town of Khotan, and it grew
more plentiful as the town was approached, except that in the
immediate environs there were no pastures; so that the bais
who owned sheep kept them all the year round in the forests
that fringe both banks of the Khotan-daria. In the seasons
during which the river was dry people always travelled along
the bed of the stream, which was as hard and dry as a street,
and only travelled by the forest paths when driven out of the
river-bed by the water.

After the noontide heat was passed, the shepherds again

went off into the woods with their sheep and goats and cattle, and I was left alone, though not for long.   For a caravan
of about a hundred donkeys, carrying rice from Khotan to
Ak-su, went past the hut.   The caravan leaders rode straight
on without observing me ; but Pasi Akhun had seen them,
and told them of my adventures.   As soon as they were gone
by I went into the hut to rest ; but almost immediately hearing the rattle of stirrups and the echo of voices, I hurried
out again.   It was three well-to-do merchants, each riding a
capital horse, on their way from Ak-su to Khotan.   They
had left the former place eleven days before, and hoped to
reach the latter in six days more.

They came riding through the forest at a smart trot, and
bore straight down upon the shepherds' hut.   They hastily
dismounted, and advancing towards me, without hesitation,
as though they knew I was there and had come to seek me,
they politely greeted me.   I invited them to sit down.   Then
one of them, a well-dressed man with a black beard, told me
some news which beyond measure delighted me.   The day
before, while riding along the left bank of the river, some
twelve hours north of Buksem, they saw a man, more dead
than alive, lying by the side of a white camel, which was
grazing on the border of the forest.   Like the good Samari-
tan, they stopped and asked him what was the matter.   All he
could answer was to gasp out " Su ! su !" (Water ! water !).
One of the merchants immediately rode off to the nearest
pool and brought the man a *kungan* (iron pitcher) full of
water.   The sufferer, who, I soon understood, could be nobody but Islam Bai, drained the pitcher at a single draught.
They gave him bread, and raisins, and nuts to eat.   He revived, and told them how he came to be there in the pitiable
condition in which they found him.

Islam then begged the three merchants to look for me ;
although, he said, he did not know whether I was alive or
dead, for he had lost my trail two days before.   If they found
me, he earnestly besought them to lend me one of their
horses, so that I might ride to Khotan, and rest and recover
from the journey.   Thereupon they looked for me all along

the road, until at length they found me in the hut; and they now offered me the use of one of their horses, that I might accompany them to Khotan. But I never hesitated a moment as to the course I ought to pursue. I decided to stay where I was until Islam Bai rejoined me. Seeing that he had succeeded in bringing one of the camels out to the river, probably he had saved a portion of my belongings. Possibly my diaries and maps relating to our desert journey were not lost. Possibly we might even be able to reorganize the remnants of my shattered caravan.

My hopes as to the future began to revive and shine out in rosy colors. During the morning I had been considering the effects of the shipwreck of my caravan, and what plans I should adopt for the future, so that my journey might yield the best results possible under the circumstances. I had almost made up my mind to accompany the first best merchant that went past to Khotan, and thence go on to Kashgar, whence I could send jighits to the first Russian telegraph station with despatches for Europe for a fresh stock of instruments and a fresh equipment, and with them, and what I could effect with the rest of the capital I had left behind in Kashgar, I might travel to Lop-nor, and thence return home through Siberia. But now that Islam Bai was alive, and had brought out one of the camels, I felt certain we might make an attempt to recover the tent and the stores we had left in it; so that, instead of curtailing my plans for the future, I began to extend them.

I therefore let the three merchants go on their way, after they had given me a good supply of wheat bread, and lent me eighteen silver tengeh (about 8*s*.). We arranged to meet again in Khotan, and settle the accounts outstanding between us. The shepherds were now thoroughly satisfied of the truth of my story, and I dropped hints that their generous services to me should not go unrewarded.

May 10th. A strong northeasterly gale loaded the atmosphere with dust. I lay and slept inside the hut all day long. The tremendous physical exertions I had undergone during the last few days of that terrible desert journey now took

ieir revenge upon me. I felt tired to death, like an invalid
ho is convalescent after a year's illness.

At sunset I was awakened by the screaming of a camel,
id hurried out. There came Pasi Akhun, leading Ak-tuya,
ie white camel, with Islam Bai and Kasim following behind
im. My excellent Islam flung himself with sobs of joy on
ie ground before me, and clasped my feet with his hands. I
: once lifted him up and bade him calm his emotion. In
is own mind he had as little expected to see me as I had
xpected to see him.

The white camel was laden with two *kurchins* (double wal-
:ts of canvas). One of them contained all my instruments
:xcept those for measuring altitudes), my drawings and itin-
rary notes, paper, pens, and such like; the other the Chinese
ilver money, the lantern, teapot, cigarettes, and several other
hings. Moreover, Islam had saved the two Husqvarna rifles,
.nd brought them wrapped up in a felt.

Islam ate a piece of bread, and rallied a bit, and then told
ne his story. For several hours after **we** left him on the
iight of May 2d, he lay where he fell; but finally he managed
o get up and follow our trail, though very slowly, for the
our camels, which he brought along with him, resisted being
irged along. Later on, in the evening of May 3d, he saw
he big signal-fire, which we made beside the three poplars;
iut it was a great way off. However, it gave him fresh cour-
ge, for by it he knew, not only that we were alive, but that
ie had reached the outskirts of the forest, perhaps discovered
'ater. He reached the three poplars on the morning of
fay 4th, and observed the marks of our abortive attempt to
ig a well. But as the day was oppressively hot, he stayed
:veral hours in the shade of the poplars. With his axe he
azed the bark of one of the trees, and sucked out of the
ound fully a cupful of sap, which both quenched his thirst
id strengthened him. There he left one camel-load of goods.
'n May 5th he continued to press on in our footsteps, and
n the following day arrived at the first dry river-bed, where
e again observed our unsuccessful attempt at a well. There
.e lost one of the camels, the one which had been freed from

I.—39

its load. The animal broke loose, and of its own acc
went off towards the east. Up to that point Yolldash d
though dying, had dragged himself along after the carava
but from that time Islam never saw him again, and there
concluded he must be dead. On May 7th my riding-came
Boghra, fell, and about an hour later Nähr also. The latt
carried all the instruments for measuring altitudes, cigars, te
sugar, candles, and some macaroni. At last Islam succeed
in reaching the river with the white camel ; but when he s
it was dry, he gave way to despair, and deliberately lay dow
to die, calmly and in peace. That was on the morning
May 8th ; and as if by a miraculous interposition, at noon
that same day the three merchants came that way, saw him
and gave him bread and water, and he was saved. Short
after that he fell in with Kasim, who told him that I had g
on splendidly, but that he had not the slightest idea where
had gone to. Kasim was stupid enough to say he believ
I had gone to the north, towards Ak-su ; but Islam was for
unately sharper witted, and decided to look for me towar
the south, in the direction of Khotan. Then he met Pa
Akhun, whom I had sent in quest of him, and now -there he
was.

Thus, as will be seen, Islam Bai had acted like a hero ; for
while I and Kasim thought only of ourselves, he had done
his utmost to save that portion of my belongings to which he
knew I attached the greatest value. He had therefore gradually transferred them all to the back of the white camel,
which still continued to be the strongest. Thanks to Islam,
I was now in a position to carry out my journey as it was
originally planned. Two and a half years later, after Islam
Bai reached his native town of Osh in Fergana, King Oscar
rewarded him with a gold medal.

That evening, round a big fire near the shepherd's hut, we
celebrated our escape from the clutches of the desert in a
"sumptuous" feast. After many "ifs" and "buts" Pasi Akhun allowed himself to be persuaded to sell us a sheep for
thirty-two tengeh (about 15s.). It was at once slaughtered
I had a *chisslik* (steak) of kidneys, grilled over the glowing

ile the men boiled some of the choicer parts in a pot.
my pulse had risen to sixty. But it was only three
:er, when I had properly rested and recovered, that it
to eighty-two.

11th. The grass in that locality being all finished,
pherds proposed to move to " other pastures green,"
ix miles down the river, and on the right bank. We
our belongings on Ak-tuya and went with them. We
our camp on a little mound which stood beside the river,
s surrounded by thickets and kamish, and overhung
e ancient poplars. Between two of the poplars my at-
s made me a forest hut, its frame consisting of branch-
e the walls and roof were formed of boughs twisted
ed together. It afforded splendid protection against
, and was further sheltered by the adjacent trees. The
inside was levelled and spread with felt carpets. The
h knapsacks, which contained the pieces of Chinese
1oney, were my pillow; a small wooden cigarette-box
ne for table. My instruments, map portfolios, drawing-
ind writing-materials lay in convenient disorder at the
one of the poplars. Considering our circumstances, I
iot have wished things better. I was perfectly com-
and cosey in my forest hut, quite as comfortable as if
een in my own study in Stockholm.

i and Kasim made themselves at home beside the
re underneath a third poplar. The shepherds quar-
hemselves with their flocks in the reeds close by.
a day Pasi Akhun brought me a bowl of rich milk
iece of maize bread, and I had sufficient tobacco to
couple of weeks. The most consummate epicure
ot richer enjoyment out of life than I did during the
at followed; and yet my lonely life in the forest bore
ittle resemblance to the existence which Robinson
led on his island.

12th. Shortly after one o'clock we perceived a small
approaching our camp from the north. They were
ng along the bed of the river, but were still a long
; and we impatiently awaited their arrival. Islam and

Kasim hastened down to the riverside, so as to call to
and guide them to the hut. They turned out to be a
of four merchants, belonging to Khotan, who left the to
Kucha thirteen days earlier. They had gone thither
time before with a supply of grapes, which they sold, anc
the money the grapes fetched they had bought ten h
some donkeys, and a cow, and were now taking the an
to Khotan, where they expected to make a good pr
them.

They told me that at Sil, the place where the Yar
daria was joined by the Khotan-daria, the former rive
tained so much water that it reached up to the waist of a
on horseback. All the way up there were small pools
bed of the Khotan-daria, and failing them, it was alway:
to get water by digging a well. The summer flood w
pected in the beginning or middle of June; but it woul
attain its maximum volume for from one to two months
that.

We pounced upon these four merchants like hawk:
in half an hour bought from them three first-rate hors
750 tengeh (about £17 5s.), although they had only give
tengeh (about £13 15s.) for them in Kucha. Besides
we also bought three pack-saddles and bridles, a sack of
for the horses, a bag of wheat flour for ourselves, a pair of
for Islam, who had gone barefoot ever since we left the
of Death, a pinch of tea, a *kungan* (iron pitcher), and t
three porcelain cups—all for sixty-five tengeh (less than
This made us independent of help from Khotan; wit
horses and the white camel we might now try to sav
loads of the two camels which were the last to give up.

In the evening we had a visit from two young hui
They were armed with long guns, which they supported
rest when they fired them. They had only just come t
forests of Buksem in pursuit of deer; they wanted the ar
to sell to the Chinese, who gave a good price for ther
medicinal purposes. As the young men were intimatel
quainted with all that region, I instantly engaged them t
company Islam and Kasim in quest of the Camp of Dea

CHAPTER L

A RESCUE PARTY

MAY 13TH. The four merchants continued their journey
rards Khotan. The two young hunters went off among the
lerwoods; but after the lapse of an hour returned with a
:r (*boghe* or *maral*) which they had shot the evening before.
was flayed and quartered, and Islam very soon had an ex-
ent soup ready. The deer's flesh was both delicate and
ty.

Jne of the hunters, Kasim Akhun, told me that the sand
the desert, which stretched between the Khotan-daria and
Keriya-daria, was very high; but in crossing it you could
water by digging wells during the first few days.

The season was, however, already too far advanced, and I
refore gave up my original plan of crossing that portion of
desert as well.

During the course of the day the father of the two young
iters arrived. Ahmed Merghen (" Merghen " means " hunt-
) was a splendid type of the Central Asiatic, tall, slim, broad-
ouldered, with a big nose and a pointed imperial. He was
y friendly, and took a great interest in our adventures;
l gave us valuable advice in our consultations for organiz-
a rescue party. Nobody could have been more willing
n he was to make a trip into the desert. He was a god-
d to us. He remembered having once lost his way while
iting, and then passed near the three poplars where I and
sim had made our signal-fire.

The morning was spent in arranging the details of the res-
: expedition, and at one o'clock the men set out from our
np in the forest. The expedition consisted of Islam Bai,
sim, Ahmed Merghen, and one of his sons. They took with

them the three horses and one camel, and, by way of pro
sions, bread, flour, mutton, and three *kapaks* (gourds) and a s
(goat-skin) filled with water. Just as they were on the p
of starting, Ahmed advised me to move out to a little isl
in the bed of the river, for the place where my hut st
abounded in scorpions. He was right; for I afterwards
several of these unpleasant creatures. Their trail in the s
bore a striking resemblance to a lace pattern. But I l
my forest hut so well, and was so coseyly at home in it, and
sides it would have been so much trouble to flit, that I
ferred to stay where I was and defy the scorpions.

The rescue party left the camp at an hour which woul
low them to reach that same evening the spot where I
hung up the spade for a sign - post. Ahmed went on
with his gun over his shoulder; the other three men rode
horseback. It was a pleasure to see how easily my t
friend, the hunter, like a mighty Nimrod or man of the woo
made his way through the thick undergrowth, sweeping
bushes aside and moving among them with such a light s
that he almost seemed to fly.

After they had gone, I was again alone with the th
shepherds, and put on the armor of patience for perhaps
full week. The shepherds' camp lay a few hundred pac
from my hut; but Pasi Akhun agreed to sleep near me,
as to keep up the fire during the night. He brought t
bread and milk three times a day, and I could get plenty
water from a well in the bed of the river.

May 14th. When I awoke at five o'clock, the sky w
dark with clouds and there was a thick mist and a fine d
zling rain. Although the rain only lasted a very short sp
and scarcely wetted the ground, it freshened the air—a
and unexpected phenomenon! At seven I got up.
during the long, solitary days I spent in that forest hut I
by no means idle. I elaborated the rough notes I had ta
during the later stages of my desert journey, and plo
some of my maps of the dunes. Betweenwhiles I lay a
on my " bed " and read the Bible and the Swedish psalm-l
in which I discovered many a masterpiece of Swedish po

A big yellow scorpion came walking over my sleeping-carpet, and when I molested him to kill him, fought like a mad thing. It now struck me as little short of wonderful that, while wandering about the forest by myself, and sleeping and resting as I did at all hours among the undergrowth, I had never disturbed any of these venomous animals. Considering the feeble state I was in, a sting might have proved serious, for the scorpion's sting is not to be despised.

Half a score of merchants, with a caravan of forty donkeys, carrying raisins and *kishmish* (currants) to Ak-su, passed my hut, and stopped a moment to greet me. I bought a bag of raisins from them, and the shepherds got a treat.

These merchants told me that Masar-tagh consisted of two parallel ridges running towards the northwest, but that neither extended very far into the desert. The desert in the vicinity of the ridges was said to be extremely desolate and barren; high sand-dunes preponderated, and there were but few patches of bare, hard ground. The name was derived from a masar or saint's tomb, the position of which was indicated by *tughs*, or sticks with pieces of rag attached to them, stuck in the ground on a conspicuous spur of the dunes. The custodian of the shrine was a sheikh, who generally lived in Khotan, but spent a small part of the winter in the desert. He was rewarded for his services by the contributions, amounting to 200 tengeh (about £4 10s.) a year, of the owners of the sheep which grazed in that region.

The following days slipped past peacefully and quietly, and I gradually recovered from the almost superhuman exertions I had undergone in the desert. All the same, I had to summon up my patience; for it did get monotonous, sitting there alone day after day and night after night in my lonely hut in the midst of the forest. Yet I had everything I wanted. I enjoyed the best of health, drank in the forest air, and listened with pleasure to the lisping murmurs of the northeasterly wind, as it dallied with the leaves of the poplars. The heat was never oppressive; for the atmosphere was generally impregnated with dust, and the thick forest shade kept it cool. It was as silent and peaceful around me as on an

uninhabited island. The only break in the uniformity of
the day was when Pasi Akhun brought me ... ...
came to make up the fire. I used to get ...
but at that hour the flocks were already ...
and I found the bread and the milk ...
side.

It was very strange that for three days ...
the river-bed without seeing a soul; ...
going between Khotan and Ak-su passed ...
rule each band of merchants came up out ...
hut, and gave me a friendly greeting. ...
they never had any other wares except ...
wool, cotton, and domestic animals. How ...
a pleasure to me to talk to them; and ...
valuable information about the trading ...
Turkestan, and about the river Khotan; ...
the region generally.

The news of our journey and wonderful ...
wild-fire both up the river to Khotan and ...
A merchant from the former place told me ...
talk of the bazaars, and that our arrival was being awaited
with great impatience. I was growing very anxious to reach
Khotan, as I intended staying there some days to reorganize
my caravan, so that I might make a start for Northern Tibet.

May 15th. Two or three merchants coming from the
north reported to me that they had met Islam's party. That
was at the end of the second day after they started; and they
intended resting one day, so as to replenish their supplies of
water.

The next day brought the bai who owned the flocks which
my friends the shepherds had charge of. He came to super-
intend the shearing of the sheep, a task which is done twice
in the year, in spring and autumn. The wool sold in Khotan
at five tengeh (2s. 3d.) for a chäreck (about 18 pounds avoirdupois). When there is a good clip of wool, it takes ten to
twelve sheep to give a chäreck; but at that season of the
year the wool was thin, a good deal having been torn off by
the thorny bushes of the underwoods, so that it would take

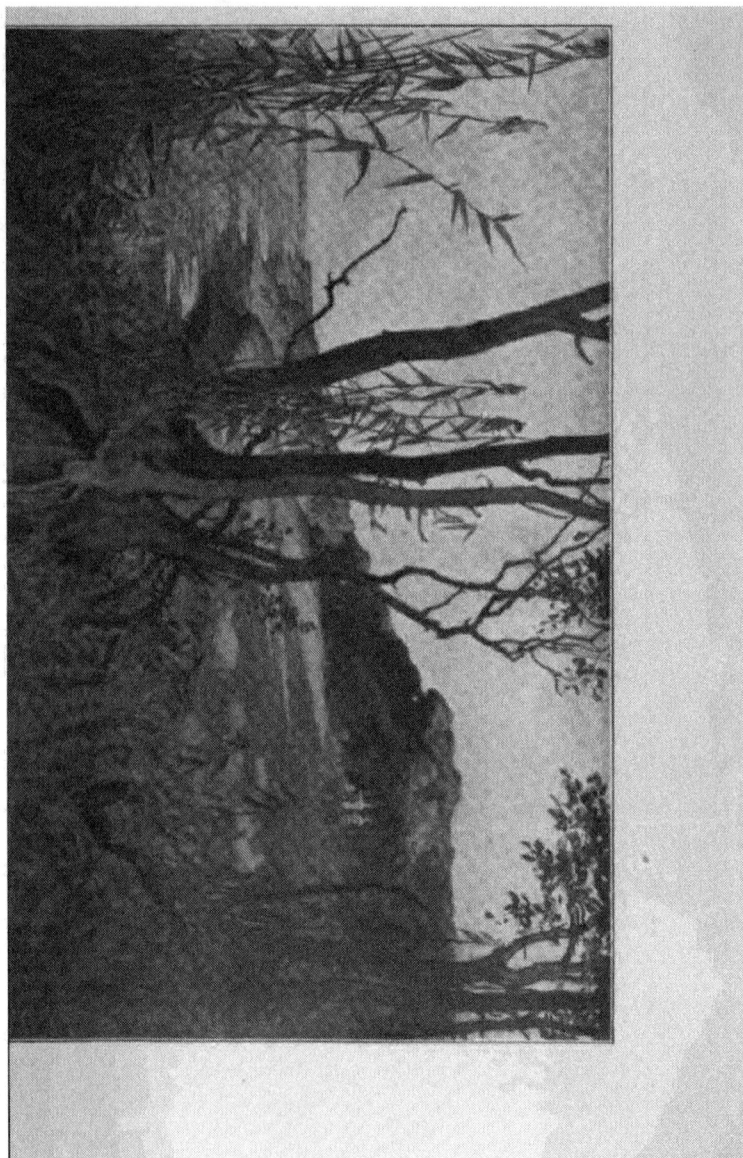

fifteen to twenty sheep to yield a chäreck. The bai hoped
to shear about thirty chäreck altogether, for he had another
flock of 500 sheep some distance higher up the river.

At dusk on May 21st Islam and the other men returned.
The report they brought was not very satisfactory. They
had travelled due west from the edge of the forest; but
had not ventured to go as far as the place where we left the
tent, because the days were getting hotter. The only things
they brought back with them were those which we left behind under the three poplars, and which were of relatively
little value. They had been guided thither by the dead body
of the camel Boghra, for its pestilential stench was perceptible a long way off. But the most remarkable thing of all
was that they did not find the camel Nähr, who carried the
three aneroids, the boiling-point thermometer, the field-glass,
two revolvers—one of them a weapon of the pattern that is
used by the officers of the Swedish army—fifty cartridges, 200
cigars, besides several other things. They easily discovered
the place where Islam had left the animal, because he had
tied his girdle to a tamarisk close by to serve as a sort of
guide-post. The tamarisk was still there on the top of a
sand-dune; but the girdle was gone. Instead of it the
branches of the tree were tied together with a piece of white
felt. Round about there were footprints of a man's boots,
whereas Islam had been barefooted. The camel and his
valuable load were gone. And not only could they not find
the animal, they could not even find a trace of him.

The question was, who was this man who had taken away
Islam's girdle and left the felt rag in its place? I asked Islam whether he thought it could be Yollchi, who might have
revived after we left the tent; but Islam pronounced that to
be impossible, because he had never seen a glimpse of the
man since he left the Camp of Death. Was it possible it
was either of the three merchants who had fetched Islam
some water, and lent me eighteen tengeh? No, for they had
travelled straight from Islam to Buksem, to look for me.
Besides, how would they have been able to find the camel?
We were completely at a loss; but were unable to do any-

thing. If somebody had found Nähr alive, and had led him to the river, where he could get water and food, the finder, whoever he was, if he was an honest man, would have brought the animal to us. But if he had stolen the camel, together with his load, he must surely have left a trail of some kind behind him, and there were only two routes to choose between: either he must have gone northward to Ak-su, or southward to Khotan. But my shepherd friends always kept a sharp lookout upon the latter road, and they had seen no camel answering to our description of Nähr. There only remained, therefore, the route to Ak-su; and we gradually became convinced that the camel had been stolen, and his trail deliberately obliterated.

Ahmed Merghen then said he had seen the trail of a camel in the forest, and had followed it. But it brought him to the young camel, which had broken loose at the three poplars and run away into the woods by himself without his load. He had evidently found water somewhere, and after his ten or twelve days' free grazing in the forest was in excellent condition. But he had become so shy that he fled as though he had never seen a man before, and Ahmed had the greatest difficulty in catching him. I shall return to this point again later on, when I speak about the wild camel of Central Asia.

It may possibly occasion surprise that I relate all this at such length and in such detail; but I do it for two reasons. In the first place, in consequence of my loss my plans were entirely upset and altered; and in the second place, these events were followed a year later by a highly dramatic sequel.

My original plan of travelling into Northern Tibet was completely knocked on the head. I had lost my instruments for measuring altitudes, and my equipment was sadly crippled. The only course now open to me was to return to Kashgar, and re-equip and repair my losses. Although it was a longer road, I chose the route *via* Ak-su. And yet within less than a twelvemonth I could not resist travelling in Marco Polo's footsteps from Kashgar to Khotan. But before I give a brief account of our return to Kashgar, I should like to say a few words about those portions of the courses of the Yarkand-daria and the Khotan-daria which came under my own observation.

A comparison of these two rivers, which flow pretty nearly parallel to one another, and seek the same goal, shows that they are in more than one respect dissimilar. The Yarkand-daria is the most important river in East Turkestan. Its channel is plainly marked and deeply eroded, and it contains water all the year round; indeed, in the month of June its flood rises to portentous dimensions. Except when it is ice-bound in winter, the river can only be crossed by means of ferries. The Khotan-daria, on the other hand, remains dry during the greater part of the year; it is only in the height of the summer that its channel holds any quantity of water. But it is so broad and shallow that the only place where a ferry can be used is at Khotan. The river flows through the worst section of the Takla-makan Desert, and has a far harder fight of it with the drift-sand than its sister stream to the west. Indeed, the sand is seriously threatening to choke it up and cut it off from the main river, the Yarkand-daria or Tarim, which it flows into—a fate which, as we shall see later on, has already overtaken the Keriya-daria.

Again, the belt of forest which accompanies the Yarkand-daria is frequently interrupted by steppes and marshes; whereas the Khotan-daria is accompanied by its forest-belts all the way to the confluence of the two streams, and the forest is thicker and altogether wilder than the forest of the Yarkand-daria. The sand-dunes nowhere approach near to the banks of the Yarkand-daria; but in the case of the Khotan-daria they stretch quite close up to the western forest-belt.

In one respect, however, the two streams agree. Both have shifted their channels towards the east, as is proved by the existence, in both cases alike, of former river-beds lying west of and parallel to their present courses, whereas there are no such disused channels to the east of them. It is also worthy of remark that the caravan-roads which

run alongside both rivers keep to the left bank; no doubt
that is the safer side when the rivers are in flood. Moreover, almost all the towns along the middle course of the
Yarkand-daria are situated on the left bank, and generally
at some little distance from it. There are no towns along
that part of the Khotan-daria which flows through the forest,
the only inhabitants in those tracts being the nomad shepherds. The caravan-road down the Khotan-daria possesses
only a local importance; but between Maral-bashi and Yarkand—that is, along the middle portion of the Yarkand-daria
—runs one of the chief commercial highways in the centre of
Asia.

May 23d. I was awakened at half-past three in the morning by a terrific buran (hurricane)—a perfect fury of a wind
—from the west. It completely ruined my poor hut, and
even threatened to tear up the trees by their roots. It roared
and whistled through the tops of the poplars, which, being
full of leaf, were bent over parallel with the earth, threatening
every moment to snap in half. The branches, being dry,
cracked and broke, and were flung to the ground. The
reeds bowed in humiliation before the fierce tyranny of the
storm. The entire forest roared and thundered, as though
it were filled with the noise of many water-falls. It was, moreover, choked with dense clouds of drift-sand, which was blown
in almost solid masses across the level bed of the Khotan-
daria. The hurricane only lasted half an hour, and was succeeded by the same perfect calm which had preceded it.

At half-past seven we were all ready to start from the camp
where I had spent such a long time, although a time rich in
pleasant memories. Indeed, my thoughts often fly back, and
with both gratitude and sadness commingled, to the happy
days I spent beside the Khotan-daria. It was there I got a
new lease of life; it was there I shook off my feet the sand of
that awful desert; it was there I once more saw human beings
like-fashioned unto myself, men who received me with kindness, fed me, tended me. Finally, it was there I enjoyed a
beneficial and much-needed rest in the delightfully cool air of
the forest. I gave each of my shepherd friends thirty tengeh

ı 3*s.* 9*d.*), and they were overjoyed. Then we went on our
ʳay, with the two camels and the three horses; and the last
f the camels' bells once more echoed clear and sonorous, no
ɔnger sounding for a funeral, but ringing in a new life, with
ew hopes.

CHAPTER LI

DOWN THE KHOTAN-DARIA

WE did not travel in one party, but divided. Islam Bai and the two hunters travelled by the caravan-road that traversed the forest on the left bank of the stream, in order to keep a lookout for the trail of the missing camel. Ahmed Merghen and I rode down the bed of the river, and Kasim followed us in charge of the two camels. But as we rode hard, we soon lost sight of him. In the afternoon we came to the little pool which had saved my life. There stood the reed thicket as before, and the poplars leaned over the water, which had dropped nearly five inches since May 6th. It retained the same shape, however. There I rested a good hour, partly to wait for Kasim to come up, but more particularly that I might drink again of that splendid, that glorious life-giving water. Ahmed Merghen called the pool Khoda-verdi-köll, or the "God-given lake."

After a ride of ten hours we all met again in the part of the forest called Kuyundehlik (the Place of Hares). Several shepherds were encamped there looking after their flocks. Islam had not seen any signs of the camel in the forest. Even though there had been any trail, it would have been destroyed by the hurricane.

May 24th. We decided to rest a day, chiefly in order that some of the men might scour the forest, in that part from four to eight miles wide, with their dogs. Five shepherds, in charge of five hundred sheep and sixty cattle, had been four days at Kuyundehlik. It was only a short two hours' journey to the pool of God's gift. Had I gone north on May 6th, instead of going south, I should scarcely have fallen in with these men, for at that time they were encamped in another place; and it was several days from Kuyundehlik to the next shepherds' camp, near the confluence of the Khotan-daria with the Yarkand-daria.

A short distance below the camp of Kuyundehlik the Khotan-daria divided into two arms. The arm on the west was narrow and winding, and hence was called the Inchicke-daria, as well as hidden in a thick wood; while the right-hand branch was broad, and entirely destitute of forest on its eastern bank. In the height of the summer both branches are filled with water. The latter washes the foot of a series of large sand-dunes known as Ak-kum (the White Sand). The shepherds asserted that the Inchicke-daria was only formed about eight years previously. But the thick woods proved conclusively that it was the older channel, and that the river was gradually abandoning it for its more easterly neighbor. The absence of forest on the right bank of the eastern branch proved also that vegetation had not yet suc-ceeded in maintaining its ground on that side against the persistent assaults of the drift-sand. When the Khotan-daria is in flood, caravans for Ak-su travel along the delta or island between the two branches, and consequently have to cross them by the fords. The distance between the fords is about two days' journey. During the dry portions of the year the pools in both the main branch and the Inchicke-daria occur near the right bank.

The district had a bad reputation for thieves and robbers, who make a practice of plundering small and weak caravans. But the new amban (Chinese governor) of Khotan had started a systematic war of extermination against the evil-doers; all whom he caught were summarily beheaded.

May 25th. My excellent friend Ahmed Merghen returned home to Tavek-kel, near Khotan, but left his son Kasim with us. We rode down the winding bed of the Inchicke-daria, the banks of which were covered with young forest. Farther back from the stream the trees were much older, and in many places stood so close together that it was not easy to pass between them. The tendency of the forests on both banks is to unite and form one continuous forest, and this will no

I.—40

doubt happen as soon as the summer floods entirely desert this channel for the right-hand branch. In fact, the Inchicke-daria was only forty or forty-five yards wide as it was. After a long day's ride we stopped for the night beside a pool in the bed of the river, at a place called Bedelik-utak (the Clover-Field Lot).

May 26th. Kasim, Ahmed's son, refused to go with us farther than one day's journey from Kuyundehlik; it was dangerous, both on account of robbers and of tigers, to spend the night alone in the forest. I and my two men, Islam and Kasim, continued our journey therefore without a guide. As the river became more and more sinuous in its course, we resolved to strike farther into the island, which consisted of prairies, interrupted by low dunes and small groves of forest trees. But as the river-bed made the more convenient road to travel by, we soon went back to it. Both banks were planted with luxuriant woods, so that we often seemed to be journeying through a park, or rather a tunnel of foliage.

At length we reached the point where the Inchicke-daria rejoins the Khotan-daria. The forest opened out like a door, and before us was the level bed of the Khotan-daria, lying, in consequence of the more powerful erosive force of its larger volume of water, some five feet lower than the bed of the Inchicke-daria. We encamped a short distance below the confluence, in a tract called Bora-tyshkyn (Beaten down by the Storm). There was a little island in the river; but so infested with ticks and scorpions that we preferred to make our fire for the night in the bed of the river, at some distance from the bank.

May 27th. As is generally the case in that part of the world after a clear night and a west wind, followed by a calm day, it was pretty warm on the morrow, and the heat began to make itself felt early in the day. For instance, at seven o'clock in the morning the thermometer registered 76.8° Fahr. (24.9 C.). The hard, level river-bed ran almost directly due north, at the same time gradually narrowing to a general breadth of about half a mile, and winding in and out round projecting "buttresses" of forest. It will, of course, be readily

understood that the high-summer flood, being spread over
the wide, shallow channel, is subject to active evaporation, so
that the current necessarily diminishes in volume the farther
it advances towards the north.

Again the river divided into two branches—the Yanghi-
daria (New River) on the left and the Kovneh-daria (Old
River) on the right. We travelled down the former, and met
a large donkey-caravan laden with groceries from Ak-su, from
which place they started eight days before. The Kovneh-
daria was shut in on both sides by sand-dunes exclusively.
Despite its name, it is probably the newer channel, seeing
that the forest trees have not succeeded in establishing themselves along its banks. The result of my observations upon
the tendency of the Khotan-daria to shift its channel towards
the east goes to show that it does not do this regularly and
conformably throughout the whole of its course, but does it
piecemeal, a portion at a time. The river-bed gets choked
up here and there with the alluvial detritus brought down by
the current. In every place where this happens the stream
gradually rises above the general level of the adjacent land,
and seeks a new passage towards the east.

In the evening we came upon a large pool, some 500
square yards in area, the largest I had hitherto seen. We
made our fire on a hill overhanging the river, and from our
camp obtained an extensive view of the surrounding country.
In this place the current had delved a deep trench close
under the right bank of the river, in which in the course of
the next day's journey we found a string of small pools.
Upon bathing in the large pool I discovered that it was
deep, for I was unable to reach the bottom.

May 28th. During the course of this day's march the
river-bed gradually became wider. As a general rule, where
the channel is broad and level, there are no pools, and the
trenches made by the last season's floods are scarcely discernible; but where it is narrow there exist numerous pools,
and the trenches made by the current are plainly marked in
serpentine curves. I also observed that the forest was appre-
ciably thinner on the right bank than on the left; in fact, in

many parts it ceased altogether, its place being taken by
bare sand-dunes. Close under the western bank the river-
bed itself was occasionally overgrown with grass; but that
was never the case along the right-hand side of the river.
Everything tended to show that the current flows stronger
on the right or eastern side than it does on the left or western. But in any case the movement of the current towards
the east takes place at such a slow rate that the afforestation
of its banks is enabled to keep pace with it. A few isolated
poplars, like those near which we made our signal-fire on
May 3d, still maintained a precarious existence on the west
side of the stream; but they are doomed to perish.

At six o'clock we were still riding along the river-bed;
Islam Bai had gone on in advance to seek out a convenient
spot for camping on, when all at once the whole of the west
became enshrouded in a dark, yellowish-gray cloud. At first
it looked like a low wall; then it rapidly mounted higher,
till it reached half way to the zenith; and then the next moment it was directly over our heads. The sun faded to a
pale lemon disk; then totally vanished. A distant murmur
arose along the border of the forest. It approached rapidly
nearer. We heard the twigs and branches snapping off with
a louder and louder echo. Towards the northwest the forest
was enveloped in haze. Columns of sand and dust came
spinning across the river-bed like theatrical wing-scenes moving on invisible rollers, alternately shooting on in advance of
each other; and in a moment the forest was entirely blotted
out. The first outfliers of the storm burst upon us; the black
buran followed close at their heels, striking us with terrific
violence, swallowing us up in its impenetrable clouds of dust.
The sand was swept along in eddying sheets which trailed
along the ground, putting me in mind of comets' tails.
Track, trenches, storm-driven boughs — nothing was to be
seen. In such a storm as that your head goes round; you
imagine the earth, the atmosphere, everything is in commotion; you are oppressed by a feeling of anxiety lest the next
moment you yourself should be caught up in the frenzied embrace of the wind. It turned as dark as midnight, and for

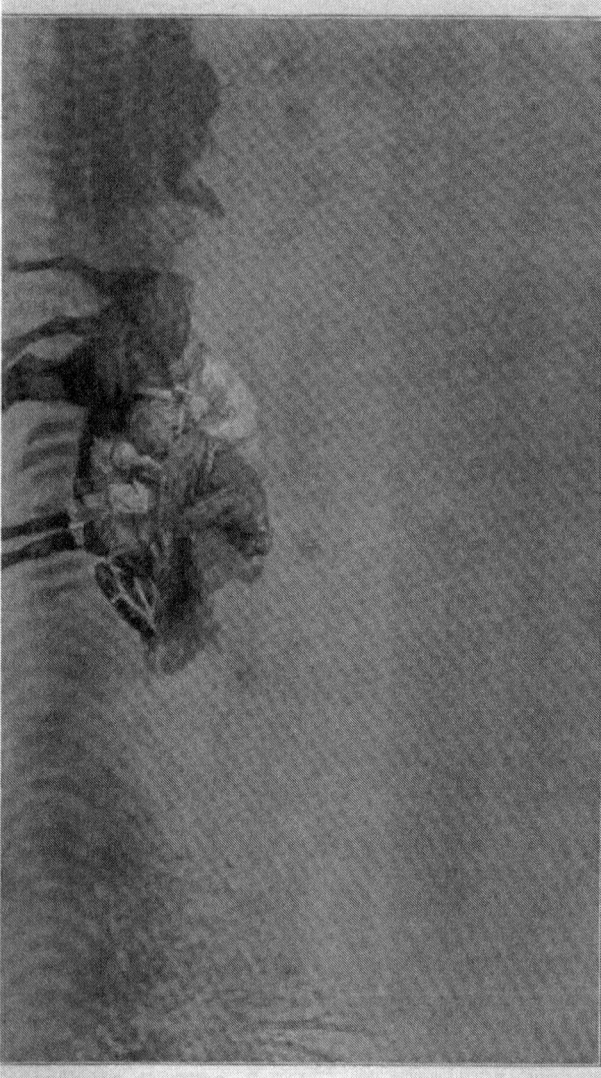

ie time we dare not move a step from the spot where we
)d.   The instant the storm burst Islam was lost to sight;
it was only by the merest chance that we came together
in.   He just saw the dim outline of the caravan, like some
;e monster, slowly crawling through the haze.

ieeing that the storm—one of the worst we had experienced
howed signs of lasting some time, we cautiously piloted
 way to the river-bank, and sought shelter behind the
:k brushwood in the heart of the forest.   There we de-
:d to encamp for the night.   We afterwards dug a well in
:pression of the river, and reached water after a few spades'
ths.   As soon as it grew dark (night), the men set fire to
 undergrowth on the lee side of our camp.   The flames,
ned by the gale, spread with portentous rapidity, giving
 to a magnificent, but wild, spectacle.

Iay 29th.   The storm still continued.   The air was so
sely charged with dust that we saw but little of our sur-
ndings.   Fortunately we were able to get along by keep-
close to the left side of the river-bed, and in that way
nced to stumble on a sign-post, consisting of a pole with
orse's skull on the top, fixed in a poplar tree.   Upon go-
up to examine it more closely I discovered a path lead-
into the forest, a path which I took for granted went to
- su.   We decided to follow it.   It led us towards the
thwest, along a plainly marked river-bed, now dry and in
t sanded up, and shut in by sand-dunes, poplar holts, and
hes.   In all probability it was a former arm of the delta
he Khotan-daria.   At intervals, as the road crossed sev-
 belts of barren sand, the caravan-leaders had erected poles
 gallows-like arrangements to serve as sign-posts.

'hat afternoon we encamped near some shepherds from
·su, who were comfortably installed in the forest in huts
le of stakes and reeds.   At first they regarded us with
ie suspicion; but soon gained confidence, and offered us
ad, milk, and eggs.   They lived with their flocks in the
)ds all the year round.

'he Yarkand-daria, which we now saw a short distance
ad of us, is generally ice-bound for about four months in

the year. The shepherds said they expected the summer floods in about three weeks, and would then be driven by the overflowing of the river higher up into the forests. Just at that time, however, the river was at its lowest level. The next day we crossed the stream at a well-known ford. Its breadth was eighty-five yards, its greatest depth 1½ feet, and its volume 265 cubic feet in the second.

On the other side of the river we continued on towards the north by a path which led to the town of Avvat (Abad), meaning "populous," through a district that was in very ill repute on account of highway-robbers and stealers of live-stock. The road lay sometimes through tangled underwoods and thorny bushes, sometimes through kamish (reed) beds and open steppes, sometimes past shepherds' camps and small villages, now close alongside the right bank of the Ak-su-daria, now at some distance from it.

May 31st. Towards evening we approached the bazaars of Avvat, a place of about a thousand houses, with a beg, a Chinese tax collector, and a Hindu trader, Parman, who hospitably placed a comfortable serai (guest-house) at my disposal. All the same he was an arrant rogue. He loaned money to the peasantry at usurious rates of interest, and whenever they were unable to pay what they owed him took from them their wheat and maize and wool. The wool he sold in Ili (Kulja), the corn in the neighboring towns and villages. He confessed to me that he laid by 15,000 (Kashgar) tengeh (about £170) every year. The principal products of the district are rice, wheat, maize, and cotton. The little town stands on a branch of the Ak-su-daria, called the Kovneh-daria; it is crossed by a bridge which leads straight into the main street of the town.

June 1st. We rode the whole of the day through one continuous street, with canals on both sides of it, and shaded by avenues of trees, among which mulberries and willows predominated. The next day, at a place called Besh-arik-ustang (the Channel of the Five Branches), we came out upon the great highway which runs to Kashgar, and also crosses the Ak-su-daria to Yanghi-shahr (the New Town), a place enclosed within the walls of a Chinese fortress. Immediately we arrived I sent a man with my passport and Chinese calling-card to the Dao Tai, or chief officer of the district; but received back an indefinite sort of answer. Accordingly I did not take the trouble to call upon "His Excellency," a man who was notorious for his arrogance and drunken habits.

June 3d. We were now only a short distance from the Mohammedan town of Ak-su. Upon arriving there I was received with marked friendliness by Mohammed Emin, the aksakal (white-beard), or head of the West Turkestan merchants. He lodged me in his own good and comfortable house, sending the camels and horses to a neighboring caravanserai.

June 4th. During the past three days the white camel had pined away, refusing to eat grass or anything except a few broken fragments of wheat bread. On June 3d he had walked the short distance from the New to the Old Town without stopping; but every time anybody went near him he screamed out in a tone of suffering, as though he were afraid he was going to be hurt. At night he ate nothing; and next morning Kasim came with a concerned countenance to tell me that Ak-tuya was very ill. I hastened to the court-yard and found him lying on his side, with his legs doubled under him and his neck stretched out along the ground. He was breathing heavily; and, after one or two long-drawn breaths, he died.

This was the camel on which Islam had saved my diaries, maps, instruments, and other things which I set the greatest store by. Naturally, therefore, I felt sorry to lose the poor beast, which had rendered me such a signal service. All the way down the Khotan-daria I went to him at every place where we encamped and clapped him; but he always turned away his head and screamed, as though I were going to pull at his nose-rope. It seemed as though he knew I was the cause of the suffering he had endured. On the morning he died— the morning of the Feast of Mairam—it was still and quiet in the caravanserai court-yard. On that day no caravan came in, no caravan went out; ordinary work of every sort and kind was entirely suspended. Everybody was out-of-doors. The streets, the bazaars were gay with new khalats (coats) in the brightest and most variegated hues, new caps (calottes) in glowing colors, and snow-white turbans. Every person looked happy and contented. On this day the meanest servant is greeted with a "*Aid mubarek!*" (A happy holiday to you!) by his master, and from the windows of the minarets the muezzin's voice, uplifted in prayer and praise of the Almighty, sounds clearer and more musical than usual. What a contrast between the silent court-yard, where my dead camel lay, and this richly varied picture of life and happiness, every face beaming with delight on this the greatest Mohammedan holiday of the year! As it happened, in the year of our visit to Ak-su, the Feast of Mairam fell on Whit-Tuesday. Mohammed Emin was going to sell the two camels for me on the following day. The money value of the dead animal was a mere trifle; besides, by this I had become accustomed to losing camels! But this poor beast had been the means of saving my sketches and diaries, and my purse for defraying the expenses of the summer; and I felt as if I had lost a faithful friend, a friend in whose fidelity I could trust implicitly, who had sacrificed his strength and finally his life to help me out of an awkward predicament.

His travelling companion, the young camel Chong-sarik, a giant of his kind, which Ahmed the Hunter had caught in the forest, left his manger and walked across to the white camel, and regarded him attentively with a look of wonderment. Then he quietly walked back to his manger, and with an unimpaired appetite went on munching the green, sappy grass with which it was filled. He was the last of the eight. I had not the heart to sell him without knowing into whose hands he would fall. The custodian of the serai was of opinion that he, too, would soon succumb to the hardships and privations he had undergone. Finally I gave him as a present to Mohammed Emin, on condition that he should be allowed to graze all summer on the fat meadows at the foot of the Tengri-khan.

CHAPTER LII

FROM AK-SU TO KASHGAR

WE stayed three days in Ak-su in order to organize a
temporary caravan for the return journey to Kashgar, the
centre and base of my exploring journeys in Central Asia.
Thus I had an opportunity, though it must be confessed a
brief one, of seeing something of the town of the White
Water (Ak-su), so called because of the abundance of clear,
fresh water which pours through it from the eternal snow-
fields and glaciers. The town occupies a favorable position
on the left bank of the Ak-su-daria. In summer enormous
quantities of water roll down the river. In winter there is
but a fraction of it left, and the little there is freezes. A
short distance below the town the river divides into two
branches, the Yanghi-daria and the Kovneh-daria; but they
reunite before they join the main stream, the Yarkand-daria,
or Tarim. Immediately on the east the town is overlooked
by a terrace of conglomerate and loess strata, which rises to
a perpendicular height of 150 or 160 feet, and has been
carved out and shaped by the river floods. On all other
sides the town is surrounded by numerous villages, fertile
fields and meadows, splendid orchards, and brimming irrigation canals. Rice, wheat, maize, barley, cotton, opium, and
a vast quantity of garden produce are grown with signal success. Ak-su, with its 15,000 inhabitants, is only half as big
as Kashgar; nevertheless, in respect of its agricultural products it ranks considerably higher. The keeping of sheep,
which graze, as I have said, along the banks of the two large
rivers, is likewise a flourishing industry.

Ak-su possesses a mixed population of divers races. Among
others I noticed a great number of Chinese, a hundred or so

of Andijanliks (people of Andijan), or merchants from Russian Turkestan, besides three Afghans, who have paid periodical visits to Ak-su for a space of over twenty years. Mohammed Emin, the aksakal, or head of the Russian subjects trading to the town, was a Tashkendlik—*i.e.*, a man of Tashkend—and had been domiciled in Ak-su for a dozen years. The Andijan merchants trade principally in wool, cotton, and hides. Of the last-named commodity some 30,000 are sent every year to Tashkend on the backs of camels, *via* the pass of Bedel, Kara-kol (Przhevalsk), Pishpek,

MOSQUE AT AK-SU

and Auliehata. The caravans only travel during the winter. All the hot months of the year the camels run at pasture on the grassy slopes of the mountains near the town. Moreover, all communications are greatly hampered during the summer by the high state of the water in the swollen rivers.

Of "lions" that would repay a visit there were scarce any. The chief mosque, which, as usual, was called the Mesjid-i-Juma, or Friday Mosque, was not particularly remarkable, except that it occupied a picturesque situation on one side of a small open square, which communicated with the principal bazaar through a side lane. The square, called Righistan, is the centre of the life of Ak-su. On market days it is packed with people, and all sorts of commodities are offered

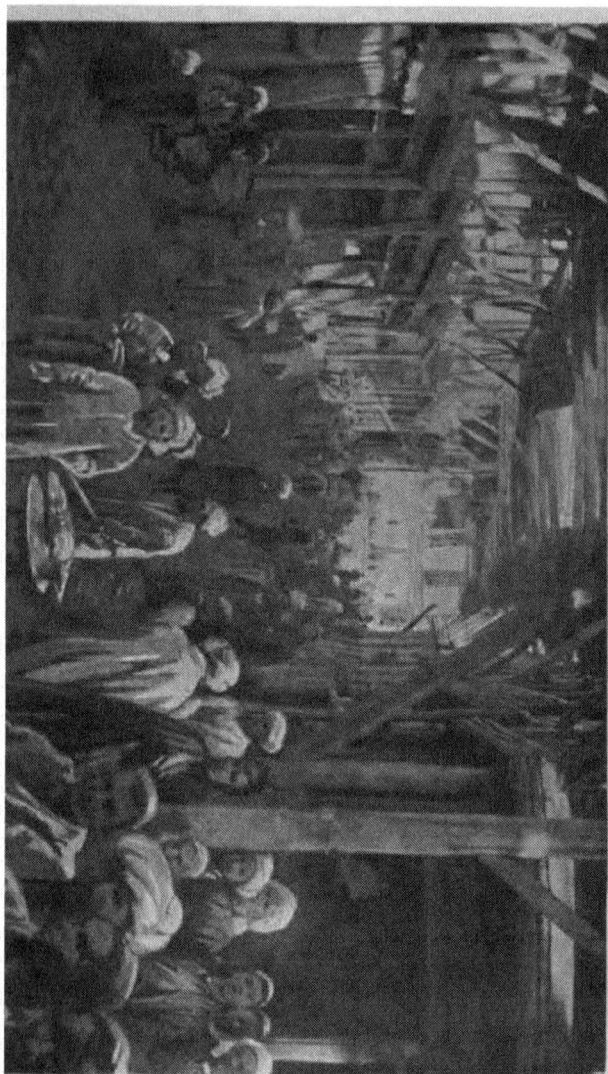

r sale on a multitude of little stalls.   Lumps of ice, col-
cted in winter and preserved in subterranean cellars, are
ι important commodity during the hot season, and one that
personally enjoyed in liberal measure.   In the principal
ιzaar there are two theological colleges, the Kok-madrasa
ιe Blue College) and the Ak-madrasa (the White College).
heir façades are plain, with poor earthen-ware decorations,
ιr can their balconies or cloisters boast of any architectural
erit.   The mollahs, or theological students, live in cells
ιening out upon the court-yard.   Some of the students had
eviously studied five, and even ten, years at the theological
llege of Mir-arab, in Bokhara.   The Chinese have two
nzas (a lanza consists of not quite one hundred men) at
anghi-shahr.   They maintain a larger garrison at Utch-
rfan, which commands the Bedal pass over the Tianshan
ountains into Russian Turkestan.

All over the Mohammedan world it is customary to cele-
ate the first few days of the Feast of Mairam by a great
ιmber of gala dinners, at which incredible quantities of *ash*
illau or rice pudding) and *shorpa* (soup made of green vege-
bles and macaroni) are consumed.   Some of these feasts I
ιared in company with the aksakal, Mohammed Emin.   But
e best entertainment of all was that to which the aksakal
vited me, and at which I was the only guest.   We rode
ιt to his garden, Sokha-bashi, situated about two miles from
e bazaar.   There a couple of gardeners live all the year
ιund, and occupy themselves with the cultivation of grapes,
ιricots, melons, plums, cherries, and vegetables.   We took
ιr places underneath a leafy mulberry-tree, beside a canal
led with clear crystal water.   A sheep was killed, and with
s own hands the aksakal prepared an ash or pillau accord-
g to the most approved recipe of the culinary art.   You
ke the best pieces of the meat, especially the breast and
e kidneys, cut them up fine, fry them in butter in a pan
ʼer the fire, thereafter fill the pan with well-washed, pure
hite rice, and add onions to flavor.   This dish, when prop-
ly prepared, is excellent.

An aksakal is a sort of consular agent.   The subjects of

the Russian empire have their aksakal in each of the larger
towns of East Turkestan. All these officers were subordi-
nate to Consul-General Petrovsky in Kashgar. My friend,
Mohammed Emin, the aksakal in Ak-su, was one of the best
Mohammedans I have met, a cheerful and worthy man
of about sixty, with a white beard; he had an intimate

SHOP IN A BAZAAR

knowledge of East Turkestan, and was able to give me much
valuable information. Even before I reached the town he
had done me a service. He made inquiries on all the roads
leading into Ak-su from the south after the thief who had, as
we suspected, stolen the camel we lost; though without any
result. Now he did me an even greater service. He declared his willingness to accompany me to Kashgar, a road
he had travelled scores of times. I was very glad of this, for
I knew he would be excellent company. He was quitting
his post without permission, but for that I took it upon myself to answer to Mr. Petrovsky for him.

We had a journey of 270 miles before us to Kashgar; but

we were in no hurry, and resolved to take things easy. By June 7th all was ready for a start. Mohammed Emin procured me some Sart *yakhtans* (boxes), and provided the needful provisions, such as sugar, tea, rice, vegetables, honey, and so forth. Mutton we should be able to buy everywhere along the road. I gave Islam Bai and Kasim a gratuity each for their faithful services, as well as dressed them out from top to toe in good new clothes. I had lost all my clothes, and bought myself a costume which was half Chinese, half Sart.

STREET IN A TOWN OF CENTRAL ASIA

This was the only occasion during my travels that I deprived myself of the prestige and respect which the European dress always inspires.

We hired four horses from a karakesh (owner of caravan animals), paying fifty-five tengeh (12s. 6d.) for each horse all the way to Kashgar. We left Ak-su at five o'clock in the afternoon; but that day we only rode a couple of hours. Our first stop was at the caravanserai of Langar. We travelled that short stretch down a continuous avenue bordered with rice-fields under water, cultivated fields, gardens, and houses, and encamped on a piece of meadow in a fine grove of poplars. Ten years before that Mohammed Emin had rested in the same spot with Przhevalsky, who was then on his way

I.—41

home from his fourth journey. Afar off in the north through the light dust-haze we caught a glimpse of the glittering white peak of Tengri-khan, towering up to 24,000 feet; but it was soon enveloped in the shades of night, and so disappeared from our view.

On June 8th we crossed the Kum-daria (Sand River), the name generally given to the Ak-su in that part of its course. The river was split into a number of branches, and the crossing was beset with no particular difficulties. A few days after that the ferry would come into use; but five weeks later, when the river would be in full flood, even the ferry would be useless, and for some time all communication between the opposite banks would be interrupted. Every year an average of half a dozen men lose their lives through attempting to ride across the river when the current is too powerful.

On the other side of the river we met a caravan of some two hundred horses and oxen; each animal was dragging after it on the ground two long beams of poplar wood (*terek*). The aksakal told me that a large dam or jetty was being built fifteen miles above the town, along the left bank of the Ak-su-daria, and that no less than three thousand men were engaged upon the work. The object of the dam, which is reconstructed every year, was to prevent the flood from doing injury to the terrace of conglomerate, and so eventually sweeping away both the Old and the New Town, and to force it over to the opposite or right bank. Thus the Ak-su-daria, which at that point flows south, also tends towards a more easterly course.

Four and a half hours later we rode across the Taushkan-daria (Hare River), the sister stream of the Ak-su-daria. It was much more difficult to cross, on account of the water flowing in a confined channel. We accordingly hired two *suchis* (water-men), who, being naked, carefully led the horses across the stony river-bed.

June 9th. We reached the little town of Utch-turfan, which owes such importance as it possesses solely to its position as a sort of half-way house between Ak-su and the frontier of Asiatic Russia, and on the road by which the wool, cotton, felts, carpets, hides, etc., of East Turkestan are exported. There were some eighty prosperous Andijan (*i.e.,* West Turkestan) traders established there, likewise under the authority of my friend Mohammed Emin. The town stands in the midst of fertile, well-cultivated fields, irrigated from the Taushkan - daria.

In the far distance we saw the snow-white bastions of the great Tian-shan mountains, and nearer at hand some ranges of low hills. The Chinese amban (governor) of Utch-turfan, Tso Daloi, received me with great politeness and invited me to dine with him. He was formerly stationed in Tarbagatai, in Dzungaria, where he had come a good deal into contact with the Russians.

After resting a day, we left Utch-turfan on June 11th, escorted by the entire colony of Andijan merchants wearing their best

MOHAMMED EMIN

khalats (coats). Our gayly dressed cavalcade excited not a little attention in every place we passed through. But at Sughetlik (Willow Village), where we were again offered tea and refreshments, our friends turned back. We went on to Ott-bashi (the Beginning of the Pasture Grounds) and encamped there in a park.

The next day we reached the kishlak, or winter village, of Bash-akhma (the River Source). and made our camp in a large Kirghiz aul consisting of nineteen uy (tents). The Kirghiz generally spend their summer there as well, for they are half-agriculturists, growing wheat, barley, and opium, although they continue to live in their kara-uy (black tents). A few of them, however, have taken to clay cabins. They only sow the ground every other year, letting it rest and recover during the intervening years; hence it would be more strictly correct to call them agriculturists-every-second-year. They possess also flocks of sheep and goats. The Kirghiz, who devote themselves entirely to the keeping of live-stock, spend the summer in the mountains, and only come down into the val-

CROWD AT THE ENTRANCE OF A BAZAAR

ley of the Taushkan-daria for the winter. There are seven septs, or families, represented in the district; but all obey one *bi*, or chieftain.

But I will curtail my account of this journey by hurrying over the next eight days. We travelled up the valley of the Taushkan-daria, crossed the ranges of low hills which shut in the valley on the south, and then continued in a southwesterly direction over the steppes and desert, until, on the afternoon of June 21st, we reached Kashgar—the westernmost town of China. The people we came in contact with were Kirghiz and Jagatai Turks. After the scorching heat of the desert of Takla-makan, I thoroughly enjoyed the fresh mountain air. As it was the rainy period, it was still further cooled by the rains, which often fell in copious quantities, and by storms, which drove up and down the valley from the east and from the west as though they were being discharged through a rifle-barrel. We passed the towns and auls of Utch-musduk (the Three Glaciers), Sum-tash, Kizil-eshmeh (the Red Springs),

PART OF KUM-DÄRVASEH, ONE OF THE GATES OF KASHGAR

Kustcheh (the Autumn Place), Jai-teve (the Grave Hill), So-gun-karaol, Kalta-yeylak (the Little Summer Pasture-Ground), and Besh-kerem (the Five Fortresses).

In Kashgar I stayed barely three weeks, and busy weeks they were, as I worked hard at equipping and fitting out an-other caravan. My old friend Mr. Petrovsky, who during my absence had been advanced to the dignity of consul-general, and, in addition, shortly after that was, for his invaluable ser-vices to me, honored by King Oscar with the star of a knight-commander of the Vasa order, welcomed me with much glad-ness and emotion, and did all in his power to help me with

COURT-YARD OF A MOSQUE IN CENTRAL ASIA

A GROUP OF KIRGHIZ AND A CHINAMAN

CPSIA information can be obtained
at www.ICGtesting.com
Printed in the USA
BVHW051029120421
604734BV00003B/472